The Siege of Sevastopol
1854 – 1855

The Siege of Sevastopol
1854 – 1855

Anthony Dawson

Frontline Books

THE SIEGE OF SEVASTOPOL 1854 – 1855
The War in the Crimea Told Through Newspaper Reports, Official
Documents and the Accounts of Those Who Were There

First published in 2017 by Frontline Books,
an imprint of Pen & Sword Books Ltd,
47 Church Street, Barnsley, S. Yorkshire, S70 2AS.

ISBN: 978-1-84832-957-7

For more information on our books, please visit
www.frontline-books.com
email info@frontline-books.com
or write to us at the above address.

Printed and bound by Gutenberg Press, Malta.
Typeset in 10.5/12.5 point Palatino

Contents

Introduction

The Crimea War

The Crimean War was a conflict forty years in the making. Britain had long been wary of Russia; as early as 1817 there were concerns amongst British politicians over Russia's European intentions. Many Radicals and romantics in Britain sided with the Greeks during the Greek revolt (1821-1827), putting them at odds with Russia and Turkey, and the Russo-Turkish War of 1827-1828, which led to Turkey granting major concessions to the Tsar (Nicholas I) producing the spectre of Russian control of Constantinople and the Black Sea. One of the leading Russophobes was George De Lacy Evans, a veteran of the Napoleonic Wars and later to command a Division in the Crimea. At the height of the Russo-Turkish War he published a diatribe *On the Designs of Russia*: he feared Russian expansion and the dismemberment of the Turkish Empire, causing disruption of European trade (particularly of France and Britain) and ultimately threatening British possessions in India. Evans argued that Britain and France were the only countries strong enough to halt the Russian menace.[1] In 1829 the Russians had established a pro-Russian Shah on the Persian throne, which caused considerable alarm in Calcutta, leading to the establishment of a pro-British ruler in Afghanistan in 1839 (supported by British bayonets), which became a buffer to perceived Russian expansionism. The pro-British regime was deeply unpopular and lead to the ignominious retreat from Kabul in 1842.

Russia's condemnation of the Liberal revolution in Spain (1825) and it's brutal suppression of the Polish Revolution (1830-31) put even more distance between Britain and Russia: British opinion was firmly with the Poles. *The Times* newspaper was particularly belligerent, even suggesting military intervention.[2] The Tory, Anglican *Manchester Examiner & Times* thundered that the fight for Polish independence was 'our own fight ... All the distresses of England and the continent might be traced to the first division of Poland.' The Tsar was a 'monster' and 'Justice demands redress at the hands of the civilised world.'[3]

France, which shook off the last of the Bourbon monarchy in the same year, 1830, also took Polish nationalism to heart.[4] British newspapers described French enthusiasm for the Polish cause exceeding 'everything that was seen in 1794, 1806, and 1812.'[5] The exiled Prince Czartoryski 'Poland's uncrowned king' lived for a time in Paris, and developed a strong community of Polish exiles there, including Frédéric Chopin. Russophobia in France, as in Britain, had been long-standing; Francois-Marie de Fromont published the Russophobic *Observations sur la Russie* in 1817 whilst the politician Dominique-Georges-Frédéric de Pradt interpreted Russia as the 'enemy of Liberty in Europe.'[6] French Catholics also expressed concern that their co-religionists in Poland were being forcibly converted to the Orthodox Church. French – later European anger – reached boiling point in 1846 with the reporting of the brutal treatment of Catholic Nuns in Minsk. A convent of Catholic Nuns in Minsk had been ordered to submit to the Orthodox Church but they refused and were bound and beaten; others were forced to perform heavy manual labour and some were tortured. In spring 1845 four of the sisters, including the Abbess, managed to escape, making their way to Paris via Poland. Florence Nightingale wrote 'The True Story of the Nuns of Minsk' in the magazine *Household Words*, edited by fellow Unitarian, Charles Dickens.[7]

When revolution broke out again in Europe during 1848, Polish and Hungarian nationalism became the *cause célèbre* amongst British and other European Radicals. Louis Kossuth, the leader of the Hungarian revolutionaries, became a celebrity in Europe, and promoted the Hungarian cause internationally as a public speaker. The cause of Hungarian nationalism took on a religious edge, too: Hungary had been one of the cradles of European Unitarianism with Francis David I (1510-1579) being Europe's first, and only, Unitarian King. Kossuth visited Manchester in 1851; the novelist Elizabeth Gaskell – wife of Rev. William Gaskell, minister of Cross Street Unitarian Chapel, Manchester – thought him 'wonderful' and 'eloquent' with a 'noble cause.'[8] Unusually for a pacifist church, a Unitarian Minister, Rev John Goodwyn Barmby, actually took to the French barricades in 1848, fighting alongside the French *Mouvement Communiste* against the Royalists.[9] Barmby was also friends with Italian nationalists Giuseppi Mazzini and Garibaldi.

The Russian suppression of nationalist movements in Poland and Hungary served to increase Russophobia, with Russia becoming the embodiment to many Liberals and Radicals of reactionary conservatism.[10] Louis-Napoléon (1808-1873) – the future Napoléon III – became the liberal icon for many in Europe and the United States, combining the heady mix of socialism and Bonapartism.[11] Unitarian theologian and essayist Ralph Waldo Emerson referred to Napoléon I as a prophet, '*the* man of the nineteenth century,' the figurehead of all those who sought 'liberty:' Napoléon III, however, was the 'Napoléon of peace.'[12] Thus, it is not surprising that Britain and France found common cause against Russia. Both countries had a long-standing distrust of Russia and taking an anti-Russian stance helped Napoléon III to overturn the anti-French Vienna settlement of 1815.[13]

It was against this pan-European mistrust of Russia that the issue of the 'Holy Places' in Jerusalem appeared in 1852. Napoléon III appealed to the Catholic Church in France to support the traditional French claim of guardianship. The new French ambassador in Constantinople, La Valette, was part of a powerful Catholic lobby that pushed an aggressive policy in the Near East backed up by French Warships. The Sublime Porte in November 1852 granted the French the right to hold the keys to the Holy Places, a policy that was supported by the anti-Russian British ambassador, Stratford Canning. The Tsar was furious and immediately ordered the mobilisation of his army, revealing to the British ambassador in St Petersburg that he planned to partition Turkey ('the sick man of Europe') and had a 'sacred duty' to defend all those who professed the Orthodox faith.[14]

In February 1853, the Tsar dispatched his own envoy to Turkey – Prince Alexander Menshikov. Backed-up by Britain, the Porte rejected Menshikov's demands for a new treaty which would assert the rights of the Tsar over the Orthodox citizens of the Turkish Empire. The failure of Menshikov prompted the Tsar to resort to military means but he did not necessarily want war, fearing the intervention of the Western Powers. In late June 1853, the Tsar's troops entered the Danubian Principalities of Moldavia and Wallachia (modern day Romania). The response in Britain was mixed: Prime Minister, Lord Aberdeen, who headed a weak coalition government, was in favour of peace whilst Home Secretary, Lord Palmerston, was the most belligerent, considering the Russian occupation an 'hostile act.' In Turkey, the mood was rapidly swinging toward war, led by radical Imams and theological schools (Madrasas) calling for 'Jihad' or Holy War. The religious leaders pressed the Sultan for war, and on 12 September 1853 issued an ultimatum: either declare war or abdicate. The Sultan chose war. The Western Powers were content to observe what was still a small, localised, war but when the Russians sank a Turkish fleet at Sinope in the Black Sea (30

November 1853), public mood – already suspicious of Russia – swung toward war with Russia. The newspapers worked themselves up in an orgy of anti-Russian sentiment. Finally, on 27 February 1854, Britain and France declared war on Russia.[15]

The war when it came, however, was not universally popular. The Religious Society of Friends (Quakers) had sent a Peace Mission to the Tsar to avert the war 1853-1854. They were led by Joseph Sturge – founder of the 'British and Foreign Anti Slavery Society' and 'The Peace Society' – but were not successful. Quakers also opposed the raising of income tax to pay for the war whilst John Bright, the Quaker MP for Manchester, was a strong voice in Parliament for peace; he eventually lost his seat because of his pacifism. British Yearly Meeting passed the following Minute:

> We feel bound explicitly to avow our continued unshaken persuasion that all war is utterly incompatible with the plain precepts of our Divine Lord and Lawgiver, and with the whole spirit and tenor of His Gospel; and that no plea of necessity or of policy, however urgent or peculiar, can avail to release either individuals or nations from the paramount allegiance which they owe unto Him who hath said 'Love your enemies.'

Allied with the Quakers were the Unitarians, who condemned war as immoral and 'un-Christian.' Rev. William Gaskell of Manchester thought that the war 'had no real cause' and had been 'got up by the war party' and 'rife militarism'. Rev. James Martineau of Liverpool described war as 'inflam[ing] the grosser passions, and tempts men what they may have begun with the noblest of intentions to carry on something with the thirst for vengeance or for gain.' Rev. Edward Higginson of Wakefield described war as being 'abhorrent' to 'all right-thinking persons.' Other denominations were less united in how they interpreted the war. In West Yorkshire, the Vicar of Wakefield described war as,

> a scourge on nations, visited by God for their sins…War is an unspeakable evil when between two nations professing to be to be subjects of the Prince of Peace. The Son of God was born to bring Peace on Earth, goodwill to all men.

Rev. William Bowditch of the working-class parish of St Andrew's, Wakefield, agreed, and thought that war was 'evil' and that whilst the upper and middle classes urged war, it was the working class and urban poor who would suffer the most. The Vicar of Thornes, Rev. Henry Smyth, thought 'war was abhorrent to a God who is revealed as a God of love.' Conversely, Rev. Wyndham Manson Madden, at the middle-class, evangelical, Holy Trinity, thought war was neither unchristian, unlawful, nor immoral. Rev. Robert Wilcox, minister of West Parade Wesleyan Chapel – the leading Methodist place of worship in the town – thought war was only 'justifiable in self defence', whilst his colleague in Leeds at Brunswick Chapel, described the war as 'a Godly war to drive back the hordes of the modern Attila, who threatens [the] Liberty and Christianity … of the Civilised World.'

Over the Pennines in Lancashire, the Dean of Manchester thought that, 'It is a just and necessary war, and one that cannot be avoided without national dishonour; the honour of nations must be maintained', whilst the Rev. John Meredyth at St Peter's, Stockport, parodied Isaiah 2:4, urging his congregation into action by declaring, 'Our ploughshares must be beaten into swords; and our pruning-hooks into spears.' For some, however, the Crimean War was the *wrong* war: many Evangelicals thought that Britain and France should have been allied with Russia against Turkey and regretted that 'we are leagued with Infidels, I mean the French and Turks. The French are but perverted Christians, and the Turk knows no better.' Perhaps the most extreme view was that of the revivalist Michael Paget Baxter who described Napoléon III as the 'beast' from the book of revelation, the Pope as the 'anti-Christ' and that Napoléon III would herald the 'end of times' and bring about the end of the world 'about or soon after 1873.'[16]

War had been declared whilst the cotton mills of Lancashire were on strike: the operatives demanded a pay rise of ten per cent (to meet the increase in the cost of living), which the mill owners refused. It was true that the declaration of war had resulted in an increase in the cost of living as well as a disruption of international trade, especially that in cotton. The *Stockport Advertiser* opined that:

> The rise in price of all the necessaries of life, and the stagnation of the export trade articles of home manufacture, are forcibly exhibiting themselves on the declaration of war, and altho' we have been looking for that event for the last eight months, a general panic seems to have seized everybody and everything at the moment.[17]

Upon declaration of war, the London Stock Exchange fell by one per cent; railway shares by ten per cent and shares in cotton and calico by twelve per cent 'without any sign of ultimate reaction.' The *Manchester Courier* was of the opinion in April 1854 that, 'There is no doubt that, with peace, cotton would advance materially; but, with war and dear money, the present prices cannot be sustained.'[18] A month later there was little improvement: 'There is so little fair cotton offering, and so little inquiry for this class [of cotton], that there is no alteration in prices for the better.'[19] In Stockport, of the fifty-six spinning mills, twenty-three were closed due to lack of work and four would declare bankruptcy by the end of the year.

In Yorkshire, many corn merchants were opposed to war with Russia due to disruption of trade with the Baltic States. The industrialists of Wakefield estimated that the war would lose them £200,000 of trade with Russia. A series of 'Orders in Council' declared trade with Russia illegal, even via a neutral port (when such goods would be declared contraband).[20] All Russian ships had to leave British (or Allied) ports or be considered impounded, along with their cargo, for the duration.[21] The Tory *Leeds Times* opined that the blockade of Russian ports was in fact causing more distress to the British economy than Russia's.[22]

The blockade of Russian ports prevented the importation of cheap flour, and as a result the cost of flour and wheat rose to 12s per quarter, putting bread out of the reach of many; 'anything fresh and choice … [is] very scarce.'[23] There were flour thefts across West Yorkshire and bread riots in Liverpool, Nottingham, Devon and the east end of London.[24] The situation in France was far worse, however: the harvest of 1853 had been poor, which led to a dramatic increase in the cost of flour and bread, leading to widespread rural starvation and depopulation.[25] This led, in turn, to bread riots;[26] so scarce were bread and meat that fruit and vegetables became the staple. Even worse, cholera was raging in the major cities, including Paris.[27]

Also affected by the war was the linen and paper trade, which was largely dependent on the importation of flax and hemp from Russia and Baltic; the paper trade also suffered because of the duty on paper produced in Britain but not on paper imported from the United States.[28] Hardest hit was the Scottish linen industry.[29] The French linen industry was also badly affected.[30] But war could also be profitable. The Royal Scots Greys purchased 3,000 tons of forage from merchants in Leeds in March 1854 and the cost of horses jumped from £35 for a 'good' horse to £80 or more. The shipping magnates of Liverpool found that their revenue sky-rocketed due to the bulk of men, horses and materiel passing through their port: receipts for the first quarter of 1854 were £344,006 19s 9d which represented a profit, compared to 1853 as a whole, of £28,365. Tonnage through the port for 1853 stood at 3,889,981 tons whilst for the first quarter of 1854 alone it was a staggering 4,316,583 tons![31]

Why Sevastopol?

The Russian naval base at Sevastopol had been built in 1783 when Russia annexed the Crimean Peninsula. It was systematically strengthened several times, first in 1805 (the works not being completed until 1818) and again in 1834 as the base of the Black Sea Fleet. The decision to invade the Crimea and to capture Sevastopol – and thereby neutralise Russian naval presence in the Black Sea and remove the potential threat of Russian warships in the Mediterranean – had been suggested by Napoléon III in February 1854.[32] But this idea was not taken seriously in Britain until May 1854. The war against Russia was envisaged as one of limited scope and aims: curbing Russian naval power – both in the Baltic and Black Sea – and maintaining the status quo in Turkey. Sevastopol and Bormasund were to be invested and captured in the manner of a 'grand raid.'[33] Britain would use her traditional naval superiority to blockade Russia in an economic war of attrition whilst an ally – in this case the French – would fight the war on land. This was a mode of warfare Britain had adopted, and with success, for over a century.[34] As a consequence, Anglo-French fleets were despatched to both the Baltic and the Black Sea.

The British Government, however, was divided over its war aims. Lord Aberdeen, wished to maintain the status quo, if needs be via a limited war in Turkey; Lord Palmerston, however, clamoured for a 'popular' European war, hoping to drag Austria along with Britain and France. Sir James Graham (First Lord of the Admiralty), Sidney Herbert (Secretary at War) and the Duke of Newcastle (Secretary of State for War and the Colonies) agreed with Napoléon III, and wanted to crush Russian sea power, and aim a decisive blow at Sevastopol.[35] Graham identified Sevastopol as 'the key of the Black Sea ... the Centre of all Naval Operations' the destruction of which would give Britain (and her ally) naval superiority in the Mediterranean and Black Sea.[36] The Cabinet, however, had little in the way of consensus, even the belligerent Palmerston thinking the raid on Sevastopol as 'too large an undertaking.'

With the Allied Fleet in the Black Sea, and protecting Constantinople and the Dardanelles, the Cabinet still hoped to bring Russia to terms over the principalities of Wallachia and Moldovia. In June 1854, Allied troops were landed in Turkey, massed at the port of Varna and there they remained, falling prey to cholera and heat-stroke whilst at home the newspapers clamoured for action.[37] Indeed, *The Times*, via its editorial of 15 June 1854 urging for an assault on Sevastopol, probably led to Aberdeen making such an attack the centre-piece of his war aims.[38]

Despite some misgivings over the state of his army, Napoléon III had quickly established his war aims. The Alliance with Britain was formally sealed on 10 April 1854 and two days later Napoléon issued his instructions to *Maréchal* Leroy de Saint-Arnaud (1801-1854) commander-in-chief of the French expeditionary force: he was to bring the Russians to battle in the Principalities (Moldavia; Wallachia) but was not to cross the Danube as that would cause Austria to enter the war. If he could not achieve his first objective, he was to attack Sevastopol and finally, if unable to proceed with either, to attack Odessa 'or another point' in the Black Sea. Napoléon urged caution to the *Maréchal*: he was only to attack Sevastopol if he had sufficient men and materiel for such a 'gigantic enterprise.'[39] Saint-Arnaud has often been dismissed as a 'political puppet' due to his support for Napoléon's *coup d'etat*, but as his recent biographer Ronald Zins has demonstrated, he was a charismatic leader of men and showed considerable strategic sense.[40] Alain Gouttman argues that whilst he was the best qualified for the role of commander-in-chief (usefully he was fluent in four foreign languages, including English), he was 'sacrificed' by the politicians in keeping the alliance with Britain afloat. Saint-Arnaud was fully aware of the weakness of the French army in terms of supply and transport but had no option other than to acquiesce to the invasion of the Crimea.[41]

There was a considerable degree of mistrust between the Allied powers. Sir James Graham always thought the alliance one of 'necessity' and mistrusted the French throughout the war, whilst the British establishment were still wary of the 'parvenu' French Emperor.[42] Saint-Arnaud, like most of the French generals, thought that they had been 'shackled to a corpse' and that the alliance with Britain, whilst politically expedient, left them hamstrung. He did little to hide his frustration with, as he saw it, the slowness of the British army and its lack of effective preparation. Indeed, he had felt pressured by his political superiors in Paris to 'adopt the English plan' to attack Sevastopol despite his own very grave misgivings.[43]

As late as 20 August 1854 Saint-Arnaud wrote to Paris expressing his doubts over landing in the Crimea: there was no suitable landing site to affect a landing and no port with which to shelter the fleet. He saw that the lack of a suitable port and 'difficulties of navigation in the Black Sea' would make it hard to transport and supply the army. Furthermore, without a port or landing site, any check or reverse on land resulting in an evacuation of the army 'under enemy fire,' would be a 'disaster.' There was a crucial lack of information about either

Sevastopol or the Crimea and, finally, it was too late in the year to contemplate a full-scale assault.[44]

Fitzroy James Henry Somerset, 1st Baron Raglan, the British commander-in-chief, expressed similar misgivings as his French counterpart:

> The descent on the Crimea is decided upon, more in deference to the views of the British government than to any information in possession of the naval and military authorities, either as to the extent of the enemy's forces, or to their state of preparations.[45]

General Sir John Burgoyne – destined to be Raglan's chief engineer – also had doubts, calling the expedition 'a most desperate undertaking' and warning Graham that the army was weakened by cholera, and crucially lacked any land transport: 'the available manpower was insufficient and intelligence … inadequate.'[46]

There was no proper plan of campaign for land warfare in the Crimea. Raglan and General Sir George Brown, who commanded the Light Division, also agreed that the commissariat 'was unfit to take the field.'[47] Of Raglan's five divisional commanders we know three (Brown, Sir George Cathcart and HRH the Duke of Cambridge) were opposed to the plan, so too Raglan's chief engineer, Brigadier-General Tylden.[48] As Sir Hew Strachan has argued, the invasion of the Crimea was a plan conceived by the navy, and largely enacted by the army, to maintain naval hegemony but due to weak leadership and lack of clear channels of communication, the army found itself unable to express its own inadequacies and doubts over strategic and logistical planning.[49] It was despite misgivings equally shared by the French and British commanders, that the Allied fleet set sail on from Varna on 8 September 1854, five days later than originally planned and ravaged by sickness, to invade the Crimea.[50]

PUBLISHER'S NOTE: Readers will note that whilst the title of the book includes the modern spelling of Sevastopol, the author has retained the previously common spelling of Sebastopol. The earlier spelling of Sebastopol is still occasionally used and the two are both regarded as technically correct.

Because of the large number of translations from different sources, there are many variations in the style and form of French ranks and military units. These have largely been retained as presented.

NOTES

1   E. M. Spiers, *Radical General: Sir George de Lacy Evans 1787-1870* (Manchester: Manchester University Press, 1983), pp.18-20.
2   Spiers, *Radical General*, pp.29-32.
3   'Editorial, Saturday January 23 1836', *Manchester Examiner & Times* (23 January 1836), p.2.
4   T. E. B. Howarth, *Citizen King. The Life of Louis-Philippe* (London: Eyre & Spottiswoode Ltd., 1969), pp.198-169*ff* and pp.202-203.
5   'The French Papers', *The London Standard* (29 December 1830).
6   O. Figes, *Crimea: The Last Crusade* (London: Allen Lane, 2010), pp.83-84ff.
7   L. McDonald, ed., *Florence Nightingale on Society and Politics, Philosophy, Science, Education and Literature* (Ontario: Wilfrid Laurier University Press, 2003), pp. 768-769; 'Religious Persecution in Russia', *The London Standard* (2 October 1845), p.7.
8   J. A. C. Chapple & A. Pollard, *The Letters of Mrs Gaskell* (Manchester: Mandolin, 1997), p.172.
9   P. L. Dawson, *Secret Wakefield* (Stroud: Amberley, 2015), p.55.
10 'The Polish Refugees', *Reynolds's Newspaper* (1 December 1850); 'Polish Independence', *The Northern Star and National Trades' Journal* (7 December 1850); 'Sympathy with Hungary and Poland', *The Northern Star and National Trades' Journal* (15 February 1851).
11 'A Memoir of Louis-Napoleon', *Nottinghamshire Guardian* (1 January 1852), p.3; 'Religious Liberty in Europe', *Quarterly Journal of the American Unitarian Association*, vol. 1 (1854), pp.187-188.
12 R. W. Emerson, *Representative Men* (New York: Thomas Y. Crowell & Co., nd) Chapter 6.
13 A. D. Lambert, *The Crimean War: British Grand Strategy Against Russia 1853-1856* (Farnham: Ashgate, 2011), 2nd edition, p.70, pp.252-253 and 247-352. See also H. F. A. Strachan, 'Soldiers, Strategy, and Sebastopol', *The Historical Journal*, vol. XXI, part 2 (1978), pp.303-325.
14 Figes, *Crimea*, pp.102-105.
15 ibid, pp.105-129.
16 A. L. Dawson, *Wakefield and the Crimean War*. Paper presented to Wakefield Historical Society, Westgate Chapel, Wakefield, 27-6-2012. See also A. L. Dawson, *William Gaskell, Manchester Unitarians and the Crimean War*. Paper presented to the Gaskell Society, Cross Street Chapel, Manchester, 5-11-2013.
17 'Home Prospects' *Stockport Advertiser* (17 April 1854), p.2.
18 'Manchester', *The Manchester Courier & Lancashire General Advertiser* (15 April 1854), p.6
19 'Manchester', *The Manchester Courier & Lancashire General Advertiser* (6 May 1854), p.7.
20 'Trade with Russia', *The London Standard* (17 March 1854), p.3.
21 'Further Orders in Council', *Leeds Times* (22 April 1854), p.8.
22 'Russian Trade and Its Effect on the War', *Leeds Times* (21 October 1854), p.4.
23 'Wakefield Corn Market', *Wakefield Journal & Examiner* (20 October 1854), p.5.
24 'The Bread Riots', *Liverpool Mercury* (13 January 1854), p.14; 'The Bread Riots in Liverpool', *Dublin Evening Post* (22 February 1855), p.1; 'Bread Riots in Devonshire', *Manchester Courier* (14 January 1854), p.5; 'The Nottingham Bread Riots', *Cheshire Observer* (30 September 1854), p.5; 'Bread Riots', *Leeds Mercury* (16 September 1854), p.4.
25 Dr. F. R. de Trehonnais, 'On the past and present state of French agriculture', *Journal of the Royal Society of the Arts*, vol. VI (November 1857-November 1858), pp.279-281.
26 'Bread Riots in France', *Leeds Times* (6 October 1855); 'Bread Disturbances in France', *York Herald* (6 October 1854), p.7.
27 'Letters from Paris. From our own Correspondent', *Belfast Mercury* (24 August 1854), p.2.
28 'Flax and Paper', *Leeds Intelligencer* (9 September 1854), p.10.
29 'Blockade in the Baltic', *Caledonian Mercury* (26 June 1854), p.3.
30 'The Flax and Linen Trade in France', *Dundee, Perth and Cupar Advertiser* (1 December 1854), p.3.
31 'Shipping', *Leeds Intelligencer* (12 August 1854), p.9.

[32] Sir V. Wellesley & R. Sencourt, *Conversations with Napoleon III* (London: Ernest Benn Ltd., 1934), p.54.

[33] Lambert, *The Crimean War*, p.153*ff*.

[34] Strachan, 'Sebastopol', p.307.

[35] Lambert, *The Crimean War*, pp.118-121.

[36] Strachan, 'Sebastopol', pp.311-312.

[37] ibid, pp.313-314.

[38] Lambert, *The Crimean War*, p.120.

[39] A. Goutmann, 'Objectif: Sebastopol', *Napoléon III*, no. 1 (Janvier – Mars 2008), pp.24-26.

[40] R. Zins, 'Saint-Arnaud: l'homme providentiel', *Napoléon III*, no. 2 (Avril – Juin 2008), pp. 62-67; see also R. Zins, *Les Maréchaux de Napoléon III* (Lyon: Hovarth, 1996), passim.

[41] Goutmann, *La Guerre*, pp.163-166.

[42] A. L. Dawson, *British Army Perception of French Army Support Services during the Crimean War* Unpublished M. Res Thesis, University of Leeds, 2012, pp.9-10.

[43] A. Gouttman, *La Guerre de Crimée* (Paris: Editions Perrin, 2003), pp.124-125; Goutman, 'Cap sur la Crimée', *Napoléon III*, vol. 1, no. 1 (Janvier – Mars 2008), pp.32-34

[44] Gouttmann, *La Guerre*, pp.185-186

[45] Strachan, 'Sebastopol', p.315

[46] ibid, p.317.

[47] ibid, p.321.

[48] ibid, pp.318-321.

[49] ibid, pp.324-325.

[50] The date of 2 September had originally been proposed, but to Saint-Arnaud's annoyance, the date was pushed back by Raglan to allow the British more time to prepare. Goutmann, *Guerre de Crimée*, pp.197-199.

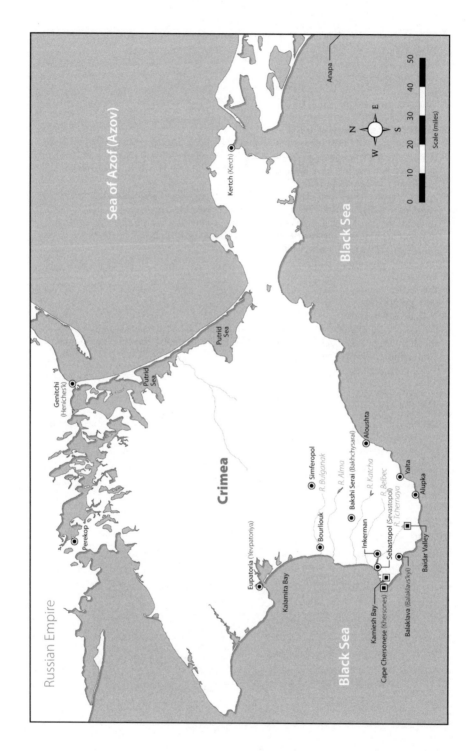

The Crimea, 1854 – 1855

Chapter 1

Invasion of the Crimea

The Allied fleets hove into view of the Crimean coast around dawn on Thursday 14 September 1854. From onboard the *Euphrates*, *lieutenant* Marie-Octave Cullet of the *20e Légère* watched as the coastline drew larger:

> The land is seen; through the sea-fog we see the serrations of the enemy coast … before us, the beach extended off to the horizon; flat, barren and deserted.[1]

Maréchal de Saint-Arnaud was mindful of his orders from Paris: to capture Sebastopol quickly before winter set in. A speedy landing and march on Sebastopol was of the essence.[2] By 07.00 hours the Allied fleet was formed in three parallel lines; the first line was composed of warships with their guns run out to protect the landings. With them were the transports of the French *1e Division*, in the second line the *2e Division* and in the third line the *3e Division*. The *4e Division*, accompanied by Allied warships commanded by Admiral Dundas was to land further south, at the River Katcha where they would 'simulate a landing' with much firing of artillery and rockets, to keep the Russians guessing as to the Allies' intent. At 07.10 hours a rocket fired from the French flagship, *Ville de Paris* was the order to commence landing.[3]

Within minutes the first French troops were making their way ashore in the aptly-named Kalamita Bay: 'In an instant', wrote *lieutenant* Cullet, 'the sea was covered with rowboats, canoes, landing-craft of all dimensions' conveying the troops ashore.[4] There was a race to see which regiment could plant their Eagle on the beach first. *Capitaine* Charles Nicholas Lacretelle, of the *Légion Étrangère* (Foreign Legion), remarked:

1

The Division Canrobert (1e), of which my battalion was a part, disembarked first, and advanced toward the beach in a line of landing-craft, their flags flying, the band playing the national hymn. The spectacle was imposing; a calm sea favoured us. To our great astonishment, the Russians did not stop us, and did nothing to oppose our movement.[5]

Colonel Jean-Joseph Gustave Cler, commanding *2e Régiment des Zouaves*, however, claimed the glory of landing on the beach for his regiment:

Three of my companies were the first to land on the beach, having at no point met any resistance, and all the army disembarked without a single Russian to soldier to fight. The inhabitants have all left in fear at our approach.[6]

French historian César Louis de Bazancourt, who accompanied the expeditionary force, watched as:

The *1e Division* was the first to land on the beach. Its 1e Brigade was directed to the right, towards the hills... the 2e Brigade directed to the left, where to its left was the 2e Division ... Conducted by General Bosquet to their camping site, they soon established their bivouac. The 3e Division, which was commanded by the Prince Napoleon, here took its place on the left of the French line, and not far from the right of the English; and, in almost a twinkling of an eye, the Zouaves had formed their bivouac, and thrown out their pickets.[7]

Capitaine J. F. J. Herbé of the *20e Légère* noted that:

At a signal from the flagship, the landing craft moored to the sides of the warships, boats of all kinds, were put to sea, and filled with soldiers; the small steam ships taking in tow several of the boats and took them as close as possible to the shore.

To disembark, the soldiers jumped into the water, and gained the terra firma, getting wet just up to the knees. The generals of division set the example, [and went first] followed by their troops. At 2pm all of the infantry was landed; at 5pm, 60 pieces of artillery, their caissons, horses, even our mules and bât horses.

The cavalrymen, directed by the officers of the staff, and without wasting any time, marked the line of battle on which we must place our small tents, and at 6pm, we occupied our locations; the camp was established. The line described a semi-circle, with each end resting on the sea; the French on the right, the English on the left; the division of the Prince [Napoleon, i.e. *3e Division*] occupying the middle of the half-circle; the Turks were in the centre, backing on to the sea. The disembarkation continued into the night, but the wind came up, so the operation had to be suspended.[8]

By 15.00 hours the French had completed landing the infantry of the *1e*, *2e* and *3e* Divisions:

> The *maréchal* [de Saint-Arnaud] disembarked and all the army paraded in front of him whilst marching from the beach to occupy its position. All the men saluted him with cries of 'Vive l'Empereur,' our general in chief, of which almost everyone knows the sufferings and agonies. The disembarkation continued after dark with the unloading of artillery and horses. Our men carried their knapsacks containing eight days' rations of rice, sugar, coffee, bacon and biscuit. In front of our brigade, the first battalion of the *20e* is detached, and sent forward a kilometre to form the advanced posts.[9]

The officers had landed without their baggage or their bât ponies; *colonel* Le Breton (commanding *74e de Ligne*) complained that 'we are without baggage, only carrying cartridges for four days and biscuit and salted lard.'[10] He wrote home asking for a parcel of 'several geese, meat paté, chocolate, four bottles of good old wine.'[11] Staff officer Henri de Bouillé complained that the French staff had not eaten any soup or had any coffee to drink for thirty-six hours due to a lack of water.[12] *Capitaine* Herbé related that before the officers had landed they had each taken two loaves of bread (each weighing 1kg) but neither officers nor men had their soup or ate a meal the first night ashore.[13]

Amongst the French troops that landed in the Crimea were the three Minart brothers: Charles (aged 30) who was serving as a *capitaine* in the *27e Régiment de Ligne*; Alfred (aged 26) who was a *sergent-major* in the *27e* and Édouard (aged 20) who was a *caporal* in the *1e Régiment des Zouaves*. Charles wrote to their mother before the French fleet left Varna informing her that all three sons were in good health.[14] He wrote again on 29 September:

> The 14th, the fleet continued its movement to the chosen point of disembarkation. The disembarkation commenced at ten o'clock in the morning, and the operation took place with no resistance ... the terrain represented a vast plain, without cultivation, lightly

undulating. Our first camp in the Crimea is established at the Old Fort. In the afternoon, there were several razzias [raids], and we captured a wagonload of plums, and one was given to each man. The sojourn in the camp is disagreeable, the water is brackish and wood scarce. I interrupt my letter, to communicate the promotions … Alfred is promoted to sergeant-major of the *voltigeur* company in my battalion.

The 16th. Our sojourn in the camp of Old Fort continues; the previous day we had seen for the first time Russian uniforms. A post of ten men with a sergeant were taken prisoner [by us].[15]

The newly-promoted *sergent-major* Alfred Minart was also eager to inform his mother of his promotion and that all three were well:

Charles is constantly at Division, for the Council of War, for which he is the *rapporteur*. Édouard is ten minutes away from me. I do not see him [Charles] often because he is on such a high perch.[16]

The landings were not without incident: as *colonel* Le Breton (*74e de ligne*) relates:

16 September 1854. I disembarked around two o'clock. My horse is thrown into the sea at the nightfall and I arrive swimming with a few light bruises The sea swept with such violence that the boats and barges could not quite get to the beach … several horses are wounded; some of them have drowned. A vigorous sailor grabbed me by the shoulders to drag me to land, and I was able to land on foot.[17]

Despite being terminally ill with congenital heart disease, *maréchal* de Saint Arnaud presented 'indomitably energy' and was to be seen in all quarters of the French camp:

We were amazed see him gallop on a superb horse, when a daybed would be certainly more suitable to the state of his health. Every day since the landing, he was in the saddle; and there, returning for a moment his vital forces he visited all the bivouacs, stopped in front of each battalion, addressed a few words to the soldiers in their familiar language; he had the gift, reminding them of memories of Africa, the glorious episodes for their regiments. Nothing can give the idea of the enthusiasm this wonderful soldier inspired in his troops, he looked so proud, the absolute confidence which he has communicated to his army.[18]

Pushing Inland

The French immediately began pushing inland to find clean water and fuel as both were scarce. *Capitaine* Herbé described the men of the *20e Légère* returning to camp encumbered with liberated foodstuffs:

> Each one carried two large mess kettles, one filled with water, the other with wine; several were carrying geese, ducks, fowls, all products of the marauder; for myself, I headed to the village which had been indicated to me 4km distant, hoping to persuade them not to commit such an act of indiscipline.
>
> I arrived at a sort of winery in the middle of a large vineyard; I found several soldiers grumbling against their comrades who had preceded them; in fact, to fill their kettles, they had ripped open with their bayonets sixty or eighty barrels of wine, and could not gain entry to the cellar without wading knee-deep through the wine.
>
> I perceived on my way, crossing paths with a number of *Zouaves*, *Turcos* [nick-name for the *Tirailleurs Indigenes*], soldiers of the Line, all carrying victuals ... What a sad spectacle! I was upset! ... and I felt helpless.[19]

But it just wasn't the French who were pillaging, 'The English captured a convoy of sixty arabas carrying flour; and the French had the good fortune to bring to camp another fifty arabas carrying flour, as well as a herd of cows.'[20]

The French had landed their small cavalry force (one squadron of *Spahis* and one squadron of *Chasseurs d'Afrique*, around 300 sabres in total). The *Spahis* were French cavalry raised from native horsemen in Algeria in 1830; one squadron of them accompanied the French expeditionary force as the 'Service Squadron' to *maréchal* de Saint-Arnaud, acting as his personal escort, as couriers and orderlies. The *Spahis* were dressed in an oriental type costume, with a large flowing white robe called a *burnous* – worn to this day – covering man and horse. They drew many adverse comments from British observers. Lieutenant George Shuldham Peard thought them 'strange-looking fellows':

> They accompany the French army, and are principally used by them for escort and foraging duties. They go by the name of 'Old Women' in our army; and certainly they strongly resemble them the hoods

affixed to their cloaks being generally drawn over their heads. They ride very small horses, which are excessively active, and answer most admirably their sharp bits. When they passed our camp, they were generally received with a shout of laughter.[21]

On the morning of 15 September French 'scouts ... confirmed the presence of a Russian general in a village and its environs. But even if the general cannot be taken it might be possible to capture several Russian officers, non-commissioned officers and to obtain information.' Therefore the *Spahis* were ordered to scout out the village, and take prisoner as many Russian officers and functionaries as possible.[22] The *Spahis* were commanded by *capitaine* Paul de Molènes:

> 15 September. ... The *Maréchal* ordered immediately the Spahis, to the number of sixty or thereabouts, ... To take post and capture the villages, to make a *razzia*. Therefore, at their head, [went] M. de Molène, accompanied by M. Ladislas Chandwitz – nowadays Inspector of the Station Saint-Lazarre – as interpreter, a former officer in the Polish service.[23]

De Molènes recalled that *colonel* Trochu 'ordered me to take my detachment to a Russian village to find the Russian functionaries and an infantry position which I was to capture.' A Tatar wearing the flowing *burnous* of the *Spahis* was to act as their guide. They returned in the evening having requisitioned all the farm carts and animals (mostly sheep and goats) as well as a 'chaise de poste' (and its contents) used by the Russian postal service.[24]

Accompanying the *Spahis* were the *Zouaves* commanded by *colonel* Cler who, approaching the village, 'attacked immediately.'[25] *Colonel* Cler wrote:

> The men ... whilst seeking with those of other regiments for wood and water, came across a large Russian village, which lay about a league in advance of their outposts. The inhabitants had fled; and with the exception of the manor-house – occupied by a few companies of English Rifles – the village was entirely deserted.[26]

The 'Manor House' had been owned by a 'colonel in the Russian Imperial Guards' who with his family had abandoned it, leaving only his stewards in charge. When Prince Napoléon (commanding the *3e Division*) arrived, the steward 'hastened to place the house, and all that it contained, at his, and the disposition of the other French officers.'

Upon entering the 'manor house', *colonel* Cler found everything in utter disorder which:

> Showed plainly, how precipitate had been the flight of the master. Just opposite, a glass door, which opened out onto one of the terraces, a handsome piano stood open, its stop strewed over with pieces of French and German music; – upon a stand in the middle of the parlour, lay scattered a heap of those innumerable little trifles, with which women of elegant tastes so love to surround themselves; – portraits of the colonel and his lady hung suspended from the walls; while, upon a work-table ... lay open a collection of Lamartine's poetry.[27]

As he left, Prince Napoléon handed the steward 'a few gold pieces for distribution among the servants', leaving the 'major domo quite overcome with astonishment, at the discovery that he had been receiving in his master's house, a French Prince, of the far-famed name of Napoléon.'[28] This was probably the same villa which newly-commissioned Ensign Clutterbuck and men of the 63rd Foot encountered a few days later:

> The night was fine, but cold, and the next morning we went into the village and there saw the first sign of war. There was a gentleman's house there deserted by the inhabitants, with the piano and books and everything just as they were left. Part of the house was burnt out and 3 labourers were lying shot dead. An old man told us that the Tatar Cossacks had done it.[29]

The British Disembark

Raglan commenced landing his infantry half an hour after the French; the first ashore were men of the Light Division commanded by General Sir George Brown. Colonel George Bell of the 1st Royals described the 'race of boats' between the French and British troops to see who would be the first to plant their standard on hostile ground:

> The French had the inside of the course, and had the advantage, and even if they had not the first landing, they would have claimed it. The landing was accomplished most admirably and with great success, thank to the great Russian army who declined to be inhospitable to England's first visit to their soil. Had they marched down in hostility, there must have been a frightful smashing of our boats coming ashore, from their guns and mortars, however well we

may have been covered by our own ships of war…. The sea was calm, the sandy beach favoured approached, and every boat landed its cargo in safety. The different divisions quickly formed and marched onward a mile or two to bivouac. It was dusk when I got all my regiment ashore and ready to move off. The men left their knapsacks on board by order, taking three days' cooked provisions in their haversacks; a blanket, greatcoat, shirt, pairs of shoes and socks, all strapped up in their greatcoat. The officers had nothing but what they carried on their backs, little or much, as they pleased. We were all in full dress uniform![30]

Unlike the French who landed with their full kit – which could weigh 65kg (ten stones) – the British had landed with a few essentials rolled into their greatcoat: a blanket, a shirt, a pair of socks and a pair of boots. Even the officers had to reduce their campaign impedimenta; Clutterbuck of the 63rd wrote that 'I have now experienced real campaigning.' He and his brother officers carried on their backs:

3 days' provisions and a keg of water, 3 pints … one pound pork, 10 biscuits, a little tea & sugar, which we boil how we can, and if we can carry, cloak and macintosh [sic].[31]

He later added:

We suffered intensely from the wet and cold, for the nights are bitterly cold and this sort of campaigning is no joke. We have been taught by experience to make a sort of tent with 3 blankets and a macintosh which covers two persons with much comfort.[32]

Hospital Sergeant Henry Simpson of the 33rd Foot (Duke of Wellington's) described his experiences of landing in his journal:

We landed below Eupatoria the next morning … and our light division (when I mention the Light Division you may be sure our regiment, the 33rd was there), and the Rifles leading, marched about five miles into the country to a village that was there, and when they got to the place … they observed the Russian commissariat going towards Sebastopol guarded by Cossacks. The Rifles gave chase, and they captured 98 arabas, drawn by bullocks or camels, loaded with beautiful flour. That was out first prize, and a welcome one it was, for at that time we had no prospect of getting our rations up for the want of conveyance. I was down on the beach at the time waiting for my pannier pony to come on shore to take up our medicine to the regiment; and a severe night it was. The wind blew, and it rained in torrents; we had nothing to lie on, and no covering but our blanket, and the wet ground for our bed. That was on the 14th of September. That was my first night's bivouack.

15th. I could not get my pony ashore, for the surf ran so high they could not land the horses, so I had to make application to the commissariat for one of the prize arabas, for the flour was sent on board ship, and I got one with two very large dromedaries in it. I thought if had been in Cawood then, what a fortune I would have made, for I was in possession of such a pair of huge beasts as never appeared in your part of the country. But … I got up all safe about five o'clock in the afternoon, and I got a good glass of grog, and made myself as comfortable as I could, with only the sky for my covering, and my wet blanket again. I had five orderlies, and they mustred some wood out of the village, so we got our feet as close to the fire as we could with safety and slept as comfortable as on a feather bed.[33]

Unlike the French who had their handy little 'tente d'abris' (two man pup tents), Sergeant Charles Usherwood of the Green Howards described in his service journal the miseries endured by the British army during their first night on the beaches without any shelter:

During the night the rain came down pretty smartly, and as myself, John Thompson and Nicholas Hopkins had made what we thought a comfortable shelter from quantities of dried grass which he had gathered, we ensconced ourselves thereunder placing over the top my blanket for a roof. Tho' of course we had better shelter than the others from our timely exertions in procuring the stubble nevertheless like the remainder were saturated to the skin although not so dirty as they who both men and officers had to sleep on the mud that had been created by the tramp of many feet assisted by the deluge of rain. Poor sorry creatures they did look when daylight broke upon them and many were the long faces that greeted the rising sun.[34]

Usherwood was luckier than his colleagues because he had 'provided myself prior to disembarkation' 3lbs of tea, and '4 or 5 lbs of sugar' which he had obtained from the steward on the transport ship he had sailed on:

Having been joined by J. Thompson and N. Hopkins as companions in my mess who between them brought about 14lbs of rice in a bag, we fared sumptuously every day in comparison to other who had on the 2nd day finished their whole stock of the 3 days cooked provisions. We of course kept our own counsel and managed our affairs admirably and invariably could have tea in a morning so long as our stock lasted.[35]

The tents were landed on 16 September 'having been brought from off board temporarily in the evening.' The tents had been unloaded after dark when many of the men already made rough shelters. The tents had to be put up in the dark.[36] Suddenly, when 'many of the men had quietly ensconced themselves'

> The cry of 'Stand to Arms' ran through the various camps with the quietness of electricity proceeding as it did from the outlying picquet of the 19th Foot, all of a moment everything was in confusion for from the darkness of the night added to the uncertainty of the position where the arms were piled owing to the tents having just been pitched which confused the men and the condition in which they were, members having divested themselves not only of accoutrements but coats, trousers and boots rendered the scene not only ludicrous but dangerous, supposing the enemy were approaching but which happily was not the case as shortly afterwards it was ascertain that the alarm was false.[37]

Despite 'Strict Instructions' from Lord Raglan forbidding foraging, many British soldiers ignored them. Sergeant William Morris Jnr. (63rd Foot) confided to his journal that on 16 September 'our foraging parties penetrated further into country,' and when they returned,

> were laden with all things, all, more or less, serviceable. Amongst the rest were a few sheep, and some horses and ponies; the latter, viz. the horses and ponies, were readily disposed of to our officers …
>
> On the 17th, being Sunday, we all fell in, clean and smart, and the troops listened, with more than ordinary attention, to an excellent sermon from our respected chaplain.
>
> On the 18th we got a fresh supply of rations. The French foraging parties were particularly successful in obtaining supplies, as some of our advanced pickets had reported that they had seen whole droves of bullocks and sheep being driven toward the French camp by

'Spahis,' curious-looking fellows employed by our allies for foraging and escort duties.[38]

Landing the Cavalry

The British cavalry was landed over the next few days. Cornet Wykeham Martin of the 17th Lancers did so with a sense of foreboding:

> The Infantry effected a landing without opposition, having dodged the Russian camp that was waiting for us; however, I suppose we shall have them down on us tomorrow… The unfortunate infantry were out all last night in a pouring rain, and as we do not take our tents with us they must have got awfully wet, killing more of them than the bullets of the Russians. The French manage this better, as they all had their tents … The Light Cavalry will have fearfully hard work, there are so few of them … that we shall be out every night on picket duty, and as there are swarms of Cossacks here whose tactics are never to charge but to harass the enemy… we stand a poor chance … I land to-morrow, morning and shall be sent forward in out-post, nasty work after having had regular meals and a good bed, to be six weeks on shore with no bed, and only salt pork, biscuit and water.[39]

Lieutenant-Colonel Lord George Paget (4th Light Dragoons) described some of the difficulties of landing horses on the flat-bottomed barges in rough surf:

> Sept. 16. We are at last landing now horses. Lucan and staff just landed. Surge rather increasing. Herds of cattle being driven in by those picturesque-looking fellows, the Spahis, with their white flowing robes and veils. It is distressing to see the poor horses, as they are upset out of the boats, swimming about in all directions among the ships. They swim so peacefully, but look rather unhappy with their heads in the air and the surf driving into their poor mouths. Only one has drowned as yet, to our knowledge.[40]

As soon as the British cavalry was landed it was sent inland to scour the countryside for means of transport, fuel and water. On 15 September Captain Louis Nolan, ADC to General Richard Airey (the Quartermaster General) accompanied a patrol of the 13th Light Dragoons, commanded by Captain Goad and led by Captain Wetherall (Deputy Assistant Quartermaster General) 'to the front.' Whilst there, the party was attacked and, according to Nolan, 'surrounded by Cossacks who however did not attack. We captured some Cossacks and I caught my friend Schneider [a German prisoner that Nolan had captured], who attempted to escape.'[41]

The Light Brigade spent 15 and 16 September on patrols of the surrounding country to procure 'carriages of all sorts' to transport the tents and wounded, but only 'sufficient … for the sick & for some of the [tents of] Officers of higher ranks.' Nolan led a reconnaissance by the 4th Light Dragoons on 17 September to ostensibly to find supplies to feed the army.[42] A trooper in the 8th Hussars described how one of these cavalry patrols led by the Earl of Cardigan got hopelessly lost:

> Immediately after landing we saddled, and Lord Cardigan took us and the 17th Lancers about 15 miles up the country. Such a mad-brained trick I should was never played before. We started at ten o'clock in the morning, at length we stopped at a Russian village about 15 miles from the place we started from; here we fed our horses and remained an hour – in fact, it was getting quite dark before we thought of going back. We came over gigantic mountains, and as we were to go back the same way it struck us all how easily we could be attacked and the whole of us cut to pieces by men who knew the country; and, to mend the matter, his Lordship forgot the road.
>
> When we came up in the afternoon we had an immense sheet of salt water to ford, but it was only a foot and a half deep; on returning, when we came to the water, we found that instead of a foot and a half deep it was about five feet deep. We made a detour to the right, and found that the tide had, in our absence, come in, and the place we had forded in the morning was four feet deep. We were obliged then to make another detour to our extreme left, and at length got to a place where the water was only three feet deep, but it was nearly a quarter of a mile across. I thought how easily we could have been cut off when we were wandering about in search of a ford. When we got back to the beach it was twelve o'clock and the night very dark; our horses were picketed, and for the first time, I slept without a covering over me, but I slept as soundly as if I was in a decent bed, and the dashing of the waters on the beach served to make me sleep sounder.
>
> We had to get up at three in the morning, after about two hours' sleep; we saddled in the dark, and then learnt that we should not march until eight o'clock, which was afterwards changed to twelve. We took the road to Sebastopol, and stopped at a deserted village which had recently undergone pillage by the French, encamped near it (that is the 8th and 11th Hussars, the 4th and 13th Light Dragoons, the 17th Lancers and two Troops of the Horse Artillery), under the

command of the Earl of Cardigan, but, to the satisfaction of all of us, the Earl of Lucan came up the same evening and assumed the command. We had on that evening an outlying picket of 60 men, who were stationed about a mile from the camp, and they threw forward some videttes. About one in the morning some of the videttes were driven in by a body of Cossacks, the officer of the picket reported the same to Lord Lucan, and the trumpet then sounded 'Turn Out'. I was comfortably asleep in my cloak by the side of a small wood fire, when I was awoke by the firing, and then roused by the trumpet. I ran to my horse – saddled and bridled her up, returned to where I left my horse, and found her gone – I looked around the stable, or out-house, where she had stood, asked my comrades about her, but she was clean gone. Seeing a horse lying down I made it get up, saddled it and mounted, and had the pleasure of finding the animal dead lame. In spite of myself I could not help laughing to think, if a Cossack should attack me, how I was to contrive a circle around him according to our rules, and beat him. Luckily they retired when they had got us all out of our beds, and we turned in and got two hours' sleep.

The next morning we marched on the road to Sebastopol again, and I on my dear old mare, the chance of whose loss made me more sensible of her value. The whole of this day we fasted for want of food, and all we had the day before was a small bit of salt pork and a handful of small biscuit. I assure you, sir, the days' march was long and fatiguing.[43]

Fraternisation
Colonel Le Breton wrote to his wife that he had made friends with 'un colonel Anglais, M. Bel' – presumably Lieutenant-Colonel Sir George Bell (1st Royals) – who made him a gift of,

a magnificent big fat sheep, which I shared liberally with my superior officers and entourage. I have been hunting with Saïd, galloping over a course for over an hour, with a troop of 12 fine, beautiful horses from the hunting stables of a Russian noble ... Everyone admires the frantic gallop of Saïd.[44]

According to Sir George Bell, the gift of this 'magnificent sheep' came about as follows:

17th. During Divine service this morning an immense flock of sheep game galloping into our camp, from across the steppe, having, unfortunately for their individual safety, mistaken their way. The men not engaged at church parade thought all this providential meeting with fresh rations, and, without leave or licence, made a rush amongst the flock, killing and slaying them off-hand in a very coarse and uncouth manner.[45]

Despite Sir George Brown ordering them to desist and to 'confine every man caught in the act', 'the culprits vanished amongst the forest of tents' leaving 'very fine, fat Russian mutton ... on the grass' but 'in some way or another a joint got into my tent' admitted Lieutenant Colonel Bell, 'I suppose the fairies put it there.'[46] He continued:

> A French officer sent his servant over from his camp with a polite note to me requesting a bit of mutton, if there was any to spare ... At the moment a fine sheep lay on the sod at my feet. I said, 'Take that bit of mutton to your master with my compliments.' Away it went, on the back of his nimble rifleman, double quick, a valuable prize, for I had such a bundle of thanks the next day.[47]

Capitaine Herbé (*20e Légère*) noted that many British officers were 'embarrassed' because their 'kitchen establishments' had not been landed; groups of them would nonchalantly enter the French camp and attempt to scrounge food. Herbé observed a 'group of three or four outside my tent',

> carrying in their hand the head of a cow, from our abattoir, and stripped of all its fleshy parts; after this group, came two other officers, who had not had the same good fortune as their comrades. Before my tent were gathered the six officers of my mess; we were just about to go to table; a quick look at our menu: potage with bread, broiled beef, duck ... and salad of haricot beans. I expressed to my comrades a desire to exercise common fellowship, by inviting the two English officers to partake of our meal and as gracefully as possible, I made our invitation, which was accepted immediately with undisguised satisfaction. But what was our surprise at seeing these two gentlemen, without any discretion, taking the majority of each dish! ... the next day, on two occasions, both of them walked past my tent without even a salutation.[48]

Waiting for the British
By 16 September the French had finished disembarking their troops and materiel and were ready to march. It took the British until 18 September to finally get ashore. Saint-Arnaud, conscious of his orders

from an enthusiastic Napoléon III, expressed his frustration with the slowness and apparent lack of urgency displayed by the British in a letter his wife:

> 17 September 1854.
> Two notes, very quick, my sweet love. The English are not ready, they keep me here, I am furious. Their disembarkation will finish this evening; mine is finished since yesterday evening. Tomorrow I will march on the Bulganeck, and on the 19th hopefully beat the Russians; I will push forward as quickly as possible. When you read this letter I'll be in Sebastopol, well established.[49]

It was not just Saint-Arnaud who was frustrated by the slowness of the British. *Général* Canrobert thought 'it was considered urgent to march'[50] whilst *capitaine* Charles Alexandre Fay, *aide de camp* to *général* Bosquet, thought the next few days were spent inactive, passing slowly: 'the most pitiable, for water and wood, the two elements essential for the bivouac, are very rare.'[51] *Lieutenant* Cullet acidly remarked:

> The 16th, 17th and 18th of September were passed in a state of inactivity. It was not difficult for us to see that the English were the cause of the delay. This might be disastrous as it allowed Prince Mentschikoff time to strengthen his position.[52]

Finally, an exasperated Saint-Arnaud wrote to Lord Raglan on 18 September, informing him that:

> I have waited long enough, and have issued my orders to march tomorrow, at nine o'clock … nothing will stop me.[53]

The march on Sebastopol finally began the following morning; despite his warning, *maréchal* de Saint-Arnaud was left waiting from 06.00 hours until Lord Raglan declared he was able to move after 09.00.[54] Saint-Arnaud's urgent suggestion two days earlier that the Allied armies needed to move further inland, to locate a source of clean water, find fuel, and to secure a better landing place, had been ignored by Raglan.[55] Saint-Arnaud joked to his personal physician, Dr. Cabrol, that 'either these Allies or this Campaign will kill me.'

March on Sebastopol

The Allies finally moved on Sebastopol on 19 September; the French had sounded reveille around 06.00 hours and were on the march at

07.00, the *1e Division*, which formed the advanced-guard moving first. Charles Usherwood admired the 'whole of the British and French army formed up in order of battle, ready at any moment to move,' but yet no order came:

> So we were ordered to pile arms and cook ... breakfasts. It will be well to mention, that that the word of breakfast was often uttered after the daylight parade, yet as the rations of the men consisted of only 1lb of salt meat and 1lb of biscuit breakfast was certainly out of the question, in the sense conveyed to the old and fat homestead epicures of England, who while munching hot toast and muffins overloaded with butter, delighted themselves with following the movements of the Army as described by the non-scrupled self-designated correspondents of the newspapers attached to the Army.
>
> However, breakfast or no breakfast I had mine, after nearly burning all the hair off my head together with half frizzling my face even as was always the case at these bivouacks of the absence of fuel and the non appearance of a hedge or tree, or bush or stick, nothing in fact save the long dry grass which I took up by handfuls placing a heap together and the camp kettle on the top half filled with mud and the remainder half with water I blew away at the fire with my mouth causing every now and then the fire to flare up spontaneously and which almost as soon died away.
>
> However, after the great exertion and much patience I got the kettle boiled and with Thompson and Hopkins sat down to our morning repast on which a sorrying eye cast its reflecting glance and so mournfully depictures. 8 o'clock having arrived, the two Armies began to move ... the Light Brigade leading the British advance, covered by the 2nd Bn. Rifle Brigade, the French having the right and the British the left of the Allies.[56]

Leeds-born Colour-Sergeant George Spence (33rd Foot) reminded his wife that 15 September was his thirty-second birthday and that,

> on the 19th of the month, at four o'clock in the morning, we got under arms, and remained so until day-light. We then broke off and got our bits of things together, and about seven o'clock in the morning we fell in and marched for about a mile. We then halted until the whole of the army got formed up; and at about ten o'clock in the morning we got away, and marched and halted until about four or five in the afternoon, as near as I can tell.[57]

Bringing up the Rear

One troop of the 4th Light Dragoons and General Torrens' brigade (63rd Foot; and two companies of the 46th Foot) of General Sir George Cathcart's 4th Division remained on the beachhead,

> to clear the beach and put everything in boats that was left there, and we did not leave till late in the evening, after working all day without anything to eat. And then we at last marched away, the men dead beat from hard work.[58]

Lieutenant Newenham (63rd Foot) relates that General Torrens, despite having a map, managed to get his brigade lost, and they had to retrace their steps:

> On we went till after dark till at last we got to a deserted village thro' which we padded and bivouacked on the other side of it. We were up again at daylight and then our Brigadier found that he had lost his way, tho' he had had a map and had only to follow the coast along. Well, there was no help for it, he did not know which way to go. So there we waited and got something to eat and then he had a man flogged, by way of amusement.
>
> At last, about eleven o'clock, he made up his mind which way to go, we nearly retraced our steps. The village where we stopped about five or six miles at right angles to the correct road. After marching some time we met a Staff Officer, who had come to direct us, so we plodded our way along within sight of the sea. What a terrible holiday.
>
> The Staff Officer had told us that there was a general action to be fought that day, which enlivened the men. They gave three cheers and again put their best foot forward. At last, near evening, we came to a sort of little village, where some of the transports were, and we were told to pull out all the weakly men and make a forced march. We could for the latter part of the day see the smoke of the Battle in the distance.[59]

Newenham's colleague, Clutterbuck, reported that the 63rd, after a 'forced march' of 17 miles were 'dreadfully knocked up;' 'We marched all day long and I was never so beat in all my life. Directly as we arrived at the place the men dropped as if shot and we could hardly get them up again.'[60]

Lord George Paget thought it had been: 'A fearfully hot day without a drop of water.' Advancing as he was in the rear-guard, Paget came across 'stragglers ... lying thick on the ground ... Men and accoutrements of all sorts lying in such numbers, that it was difficult for the regiments to thread their way through them.' He thought the entire scene 'resembled a battle-field.'[61] Up with the advance guard, Albert Mitchell relates how they begged, borrowed or stole carts from the local villagers to transport the 'young men (mere boys) of the Rifles, many of whom had never marched a days' march before ... many of them, laid down by the wayside ... some would not move, or attempt it.'[62]

Rear guard on the Bulganek

Around noon the French advance guard from Canrobert's *1e Division* stumbled across Menschikov's rear guard, blocking the route to Sebastopol, in a position commanding the River Bulganek. *Sergent* Édouard Minart (*1e Zouaves*) informed his mother that,

> on the 19th, after a long and very fatiguing march in grass and scrub that was waist-high, we saw Russian sharpshooters. Immediately we dropped our knapsacks and went forward in cover ahead of the main guard ... the enemy Cavalry wanted to attack, but the cannon began to shoot and they were dispersed.[63]

The scouts of Canrobert's *1e Division* reported to French HQ that the way ahead was blocked by the Russians. Saint Arnaud and his staff arrived on the 'summit of the hill' at the gallop and ascended a rise from where he saw a major Russian force 'batteries established half a score, troops reached the top of the heights and taking defensive positions; before the [River] Alma, in the plain, the enemy cavalry was advancing.'[64] A French naval officer attached to the Staff wrote:

> At midday, our advance guard crowned the hills of Zembrouck ... separated by a vast plain two kilometres wide which extended from Zembrouck to the [River] Alma ... the Maréchal was halted for a time at Zembrouck, but he went to the heads of the column to attack a party of the Russians in the plain, on the right bank of the Alma. Canrobert descended to the east ... and in a moment fell on the right of the Russians engaged in the plain. Until two o'clock in the afternoon, Menschikoff remained immobile, entrenched behind the village of the Alma, on their inaccessible plateau on the left bank.
> At two o'clock, or thereabouts, during our immobility ... for a hesitation to allow us to consult the formidable position, there debouched into the plain a strong column of cavalry (Dragoons of

the Guard), supported by a column of infantry marching in close column.

The Russian cavalry then deployed, and executed a beautiful manoeuvre, [and] we admired their speed and precision. They attacked our advance posts and we fired several volleys of artillery, and they replied, the infantry forming square and marching resolutely forward. Our line remained immobile. [65]

During this 'hesitation', Saint-Arnaud remarked to an ADC that he did not wish to,

jeopardize my benefits by too much precipitation, we must not be forced to the attack, we must battle with the troops rested and with the advantages of time. It is too late tonight I'll wait until morning. I will prepare my plan, and bring together all generals.[66]

Obviously, Saint-Arnaud thought it too late in the day to bring the Russians to battle. As a result, the *maréchal*'s tent was set up to allow him to rest – he had been in the saddle since 05.00 hours – upon the advice of his physician, Dr Cabrol. Canrobert's division was deployed in line, supported by artillery. Dr Cabrol remembered, 'A regiment of Russian cavalry was seen to approach our *grand gardes*, [and] several shells were fired [at them].'

At the first cannon shot, Saint-Arnaud 'sprang up' and left his tent crying '*À Cheval!*' His favourite horse, Isabelle, was made ready and in several moments he and his staff were galloping off, sabre in hand, toward the scene of action.[67]

The commanding officer of *2e Zouaves* recalled that:

Prince Mentschikoff … sent a few squadrons of cavalry, with a battery or two of horse artillery, to reconnoitre the allied armies, and these troops even exchanged a few cannon-shot with the English … without endeavouring to bring on an engagement with them – yet the *grand gardes* were so close to the Russians, that for some time the Zouaves fancied, that it was the English who were thus in front of them.[68]

Down in the plain, the advanced forward positions of the French army had been found by the *20e Légère*, 'the *grand garde* posted a thousand or twelve-hundred metres from the army. The colonel Labadie [*sic*, Lagondie] chose the emplacement of the two companies of the *20e*, which he drew from the ranks of the brigade of [general] Thomas.'[69] The two companies were posted,

On a small hill, the second further in advance, towards a valley; a post of thirty men from the same company was further forward, as lone sentinels, forty or fifty metres beyond. In the middle of the valley, in the bottom, were burned farms where we caught several parties of Cossacks; facing us, on the opposite slope, a body of cavalry, whose arms glinted in the sun.[70]

Capitaine Lacretelle recalled seeing an 'officer of hussars' galloping across the plain:

> At 2 pm we halted on the banks of the Boulganag … Around 4 pm, a Russian officer, in a brilliant Hussar's uniform, on a horse richly caparisoned, came out from the gardens that border the river. I was sitting at a position ahead in the process of talking with some friends. The Russian officer advanced with confidence, we are preparing to fire. At 200 meters he halts, and greets us; and making his horse prance, about-turns, and re-enters the gardens … Certainly this was not [an act of] bravado, he had wanted to do it, an act we interpreted as courtesy, an exchange between enemies who feel that between one another there is no sentiment of hatred. On the contrary, a mutual sympathy exists.[71]

By all accounts, the leading elements of the British army – cavalry and the Light Division – did not arrive until late afternoon. Colour-Sergeant Spence (33rd Foot) wrote to his mother in Leeds that,

> we then came to a muddy river, and marched through it; and we then came to a halt for the night. We took off our things, and away ran our men to get a drink of water, for we had not been able to get any the whole day, which had been very hot. In a few minutes after the Cossacks came in sight, so we had to spur up, on with our traps, and to take the road for about another mile. We then came to a halt; the Light Division formed in line, and our Artillery got their guns into play.[72]

Another Yorkshireman, Private John Burgoyne of the Royal Welch Fusiliers, informed his father in Wakefield that,

> on the 19th our Regiment marched in front of the army with Sir George Brown at our head. At 12 o'clock we met the enemy but our appearance put them to flight, and they were pursued by our artillery, which gave them what they did not like.[73]

Colour-Sergeant Thomas Bairstow of the 33rd wrote to his family in Halifax that,

> after marching eight miles we saw the enemy on the hills in front of us. We crossed a river, which took us up to the knees in fording. We advanced and the Russians retired to another hill. As soon as we got to the top of that hill, the Russians commenced firing cannon at us, and our artillery commenced firing at them. It lasted for an hour, when the Russians retired again. We had only one artilleryman wounded, the Russians thirteen killed. No more fighting that day.[74]

An anonymous sergeant in the 47th Regiment, writing to his brother at home in Ayrshire informed him:

> We came to a halt about four o'clock in the evening, we were surprised by hearing a 12-pounder shell tear the air over the heads of our division. However, it did no harm, any more than making our lads salute it as it passed by kneeling as low as they could. Our division was then ordered to advance up the hill, to see what was going on, covered by a battery of artillery, and the 11th Hussars. The artillery fired on them [the Russians], and they retreated. The 11th Hussars charged them, but did not do them much hurt, as they were covered by artillery. We then formed line, and rested our arms all night.[75]

Watching from the heights, one British observer saw how:

> Heavy masses of cavalry advanced from the Russian right over the broad plain. They came on slowly, cautiously, and as they approached the French position, our Allies, who at first were gazing idly at this demonstration of the enemy suddenly ran to arms and form up on the crest, while some guns were advanced and opened fire.[76]

Not long after the British arrived, down in the valley, the situation for the French advanced guard had 'become critical':

> A regiment of *Uhlans* descended rapidly into the plain, passing to the left of the burned farms and marched right on our advanced-posts. The situation is critical; our thirty men grabbed their weapons and prepared to defend themselves one against twenty; the enemy which was not more than three hundred metres when suddenly the scene changed. From behind a small hill, which covered the left of

the English outposts, debouched at the gallop a squad of 25 English hussars, who fired their carbines at the enemy and then withdrew. The Russians were astonished at their audacity. At the same time an English battery, which had followed the intrepid horsemen, opened fire on the Russian cavalry; on our right, several guns from Canrobert's division arrived at the gallop, and fired some balls into the middle of the *Uhlans* who stopped, and turning abruptly, galloped off to the foot of the heights.[77]

Capitaine Lacretelle had also observed 'the Russian troops mounting the heights, the battalions descending' towards an 'an inexplicable goal.' The Russian troops,

> offering us, as we discovered, big targets, yet out of reach of the rifles of our *Chasseurs a Pied* , but not our howitzer projectiles; skirmishers were deployed at the same time among the trees of the gardens. Is there going to be a battle today? ... At this moment, we hear behind us the gallop of horses, the rumble of guns and their caissons; the artillery arrives. They deploy in front of us, forming a battery at the gallop, and an instant later, the first cannon shots of this great war are fired. Several shells were fired in the plain on the battalions below the crest and make wide gaps [in their ranks]; several rounds of canister shot are fired into the gardens: [the] battalions and skirmishers disperse in several instants.[78]

Four British squadrons (11th Hussars, 13th Light Dragoons) were sent forward under the command of Captain Nolan into the valley in skirmish order, but as soon as they got within '200 yards of them [the Russians] ... they retired.'[79]

The British squadrons advanced cautiously over the plain; Nolan thought that the Russians were trying to draw the British cavalry into a trap, endeavouring to induce the British to follow them.[80] Lord Raglan then ordered forward four more squadrons (8th Hussars, 17th Lancers) and the troop of horse artillery commanded by Captain Maude. Skirmishers were thrown out and the 'Enemy's light horsemen came down to meet them.' About at one hundred yards, the two skirmish lines began a lively fire-fight. The Russian horse artillery opened fire and Raglan ordered his own to reply. Bombardier John Weeks (Royal Artillery) wrote:

> We came across some Cossacks and artillery, into which we gave a surprise; they opened fire on us; upon which two of our batteries

and one troop of horse artillery, along with our light cavalry, charged them, and three of our division were wounded.[81]

For gunner John Horn of Applbey, serving in Captain Maude's troop, it was his first time under fire:

> Lord Cardigan with two troops of Light Cavalry and our Horse Artillery, received orders to reconnoitre. We started up the hill at full gallop; they were on the other side of the hill, ready to receive us, so a few of our Light Cavalry were sent out as Skirmishers. The enemy also sent out a party of skirmishers, and they fired at each other for about fifteen minutes, when the enemy brought ten guns to bear on our Cavalry. Our troop galloped up, the bullets whistling past our ears, which had a strange effect on me till we were brought into action, then I had something else to think about and something to do. The very first shot I fired sent one of the enemy's gun barrels out of its bed. By this time C Troop came to our assistance with a few of the battery's guns, and in a short time we went them all flying; but it was a very severe skirmish.[82]

A private from the 8th Hussars confirms Horn's assertion that one of the Russian guns was dismounted:

> We got the exciting words '8th Hussars, 17th Lancers, and Captain Maud's [sic] Troop Royal Horse Artillery, draw swords! Gallop.' Upon our advance we found the enemy with his artillery drawn up on a commanding height, so we halted, our artillery formed for action; then enemy commenced first by sending shots of well-directed 9-pounder guns among our men, one very narrowly missed hitting the colonel, but killed two horses; then our artillery opened upon the Russians, and Lord Lucan, who was close to us, said their firing was beautiful. The very first shot dismounted one of the Russian guns, and then the Russians, who were pretty strong, both in cavalry and artillery, thought to outflank us. As soon as this was seen, another division of our artillery was sent to meet these would-be outflankers, and send round, grape, canister and shells amongst then so hotly that they judged it expedient to retire.[83]

William Pearson of 4th Light Dragoons informed a friend that:

> On the 19th we commenced our march – had about 15 hours of it, and an affair of outposts in the evening. And here I may remark that

the first man who fell was an intimate friend – Sergeant Priestly, 13th Dragoons – the life of our quadrille party in Newport last winter. A round shot took off his leg.[84]

The Russian cavalry attacked *général* Canrobert's *1e Division* which,

formed three squares, flanked by their supporting artillery. My God! How the heart in me beat! They would be destroyed by that mass of 3,000 horsemen launched at the gallop. But no! A terrible cannonade of musketry and artillery fire; the horses fell to the ground, a great number running around without riders in all directions, and the mass of cavalry fell into disorder and quickly reformed behind their infantry. Bravo! Bravo![85]

Despite the initial French success, the Russian cavalry reformed out of artillery range and prepared for a second charge, which was similarly met with a 'furious' fire of artillery and musketry. Once again the Russians were stopped in their tracks, forcing them to 'turn their backs.'[86]

It was at this point that the Earl of Cardigan and his superior, the Earl of Lucan, 'had an animated controversy': Cardigan wished to charge the Russian cavalry whilst Lucan wished the cavalry to retire.

The debate was cut short by Lord Raglan ordering the cavalry to retire, a movement covered by the fire of the Horse Artillery, much to the chagrin of the Light Brigade who had to forgo the 'yells & hootings' of the Russian cavalry as well as of the British infantry. W. H. Russell of *The Times*, however, had seen,

our Lancers and Light Dragoons were preparing to charge when the Russian cavalry practiced a *ruse*, of which our Generals should have been aware … They very coolly opened their ranks, and disclosed a battery of ten or twelve field pieces, which instantly opened a heavy fire on our cavalry.[87]

With the action over, Saint-Arnaud and his staff rode amongst men of the *1e Division* to congratulate them and their commander, *général* Canrobert. Édouard Minart relates how:

The *Maréchal* Saint-Arnaud came to see the artillery, then my battalion that supported [it]. We started to shout '*Vive le Maréchal*' but the brave man told us: 'Go and rest my children, because tomorrow we will have to fight a grand battle, and shout "*Vive les Zouaves*", instead of "*Vive le Maréchal!*"'[88]

Saint-Arnaud also offered the following advice to his men:

> Well! my children, I promised that you would see the enemy; I have kept my word: the Russians are ahead of you, they will experience you tomorrow ... If, if, my children, you are willing to wait, they will fight well, but we do not fear them. I recommend especially do not shoot much or waste your powder, aim carefully, slowly, coldly, and do not draw your blows; remember that [in the] battle, there are not French and English, but there are only braves![89]

NOTES

[1] L'Abbé S. Roche, *Un Regiment de Ligne Pendant la Guerre d'Orient. Notes et souvenirs d'un officier d'infanterie* (Lyon: Librairie Generale Catholique et Classique, 1894), p.67.

[2] 'The Emperor Napoleon's Instructions to Marshal St. Arnaud', *The United Service Magazine for 1855*, part II (1855), pp. 258-261.

[3] C. L. de Bazancourt, *L'éxpedition de crimée, jusqu'a la prise de Sebastopol* (Paris: Librairie d'Amyot, 1857), édition spéciale pour l'armée, vol. I., pp.179-182.

[4] Roche, *Un Regiment de Ligne*, p.67.

[5] J. de la Fay, *Souvenirs du General Lacretelle* (Paris: Emile-Paul, 1907), pp.71-72.

[6] Anon, *Campagnes de Crimee, d'Italie, D'Afrique, de Chine et de Syrie 1849-1862* (Paris: E. Plon, Nourrit et Cie., 1898), p.97. Letter 62: Colonel Cler to Marechal de Castellane. 15 September 1854.

[7] Bazancourt, *L'Expedition de Crimee*, vol. 1, p.184.

[8] J. F. J. Herbé, *Francais et Russe en Crimee. Lettres d'un officier francais a sa famille pendant la guerre d'Orient* (Paris: Calman-Levy, 1892), pp.73-74.

[9] Roche, *Un regiment de ligne*, p.68.

[10] Devanlay, 'Lettres de Crimée du General le Breton', 1e Partie', p.751.

[11] Devanlay, 'Lettres de Crimée du General Breton', 2e partie, *Carnet de la Sabretache*, vol. 18 (1909), pp.17-18.

[12] F. de Marcy. 'Lettres de Campagne du General de division Henri de Bouillé, *Carnet de la Sabretache*, vol. 11 (1912), p.87.

[13] Herbé, *Francais et Russes*, p.74.

[14] Capitaine Minart, 'Lettres écrites pendant la campagne de crimée par les frères charles, alfred et édouard minart', *Carnet de la Sabretache*, vol. 8 (1909), p.8.

[15] ibid, pp.9-10.

[16] ibid, p.232.

[17] Devanlay, 'General Breton, 2e partie', p.19.

[18] De la Fay, *General Lacretelle*, p.72.

[19] Herbé, *Francais et Russes*, pp.74-75.

[20] ibid, p.75.

[21] G. S. Peard, *Narrative of a Campaign in the Crimea* (London: Richard Bentley, 1855), pp.40-41.

[22] G. Bapst, *Le Maréchal Canrobert, souvenirs d'un siecle* (Paris: Librairie Plon, 1912), 7e edition, vol. 2, pp.238-239.

[23] Dr. Cabrol, *Le Maréchal Saint-Arnaud en Crimée* (Paris: Tresse & Stock, 1895), pp.264-265.

[24] P. de Molènes, *Commentaires d'un Soldat* (Paris: Librairie des Bibliophiles, 1886), p.62.

[25] Cabrol, *Saint-Arnaud en Crimée*, p.264.

[26] G. B. McClellan, trans., *Reminiscences of an Officer of Zouaves* (New York: D. Appleton & Co, 1860), p.167.

[27] McClellan, *Zouave Officer*, p.167.

28 ibid, pp.167-168.
29 MRA, Clutterbuck Letters, Clutterbuck to Father, 1 October 1854.
30 B. Stuart, ed., *Soldier's Glory. Being 'Rough notes of an old soldier'* (Tunbridge Wells: Spellmount, 1991) p.210.
31 Manchester Regiment Archives, Ashton-under-Lyne, Clutterbuck Letters, MSS, Clutterbuck to father, 18 September 1854.
32 ibid, Cluttberbuck to Father, 1 October 1854.
33 'Letter from a Serjeant in the 33rd Regiment', *Leeds Intelligencer* (30 December 1854), p.11.
34 Sergeant Charles Usherwood, *Service Journal*. Courtesy Regimental Museum of the Green Howards.
35 ibid.
36 ibid.
37 ibid.
38 T. Morris, W. Morris, & W. Morris Jnr, *The Three Serjeants or phases of the soldier's life* (London: Effingham Wilson, 1858), pp.195-196.
39 Mrs. Wykeham Martin, ed, *Letters written from the Crimea to several members of his family by the late Major Fiennes Cornwallis* (Privately Published, 1868), pp.14-15.
40 C. S. Paget, ed., *The Light Cavalry Brigade in the Crimea. Extracts from the Letters and Journal of the Late Gen. Lord George Paget, KCB, During the Crimean War* (London: John Murray, 1881), p.15.
41 A. J. Guy & A. Massie, eds., *Captain L. E. Nolan, 15th Hussars. Expedition to the Crimea* (London: National Army Museum, 2010) p.48.
42 ibid, p.49.
43 'The Crimea', *The Bristol Mercury* (11 November 1854). The same letter also appeared as: 'Private letters from the Seat of War. Letters from Soldiers', *Daily News* (14 November 1854).
44 Devenlay, 'General Breton, 2e partie', p.21.
45 Stuart, *Soldiers Glory*, p.213.
46 ibid, p.214.
47 ibid.
48 Herbé, *Francais et Russes*, pp.76-77.
49 Cabrol, *Saint-Arnaud en Crimee*, pp.272-273.
50 Bapst, *Canrobert*, vol 2, p.214.
51 General Fay, *Souvenirs de la Guerre de Crimée* (Paris: Berger-Levrault et Cie., 1889), 2e edition, pp.42-43.
52 Roche, *Un Regiment de Ligne*, p.69.
53 Fay, *Souvenirs*, p.43.
54 Cabrol, *Saint-Arnaud en Crimée*, pp. 275-276; M. Adrien Pascal, M. Brahaut, and Capitaine Sicard , *Histoire de l'Armée et de Tous le Régiments* (Paris: Dutertre, 1864), Tome 5, pp.202-207; C. L. de Bazancourt, *L'Éxpedition du Crimée* (Paris: Amyot, 1857), Edition Special pour l'Armée, Tome 1, pp.184-196.
55 Cabrol, *Saint-Arnaud en Crimée*, p. 272. See also: M. Lévy, ed., *Lettres du Maréchal de Saint-Arnaud* (Paris: Michel Lévy Frères, 1855), Tome 2, pp. 572-574.
56 Usherwood, *Service Journal*.
57 'The Battle of the Alma: Letter from a Leeds Soldier', *Leeds Mercury* (21 October 1854).
58 Manchester Regiment Archives, Acc. MR/16/2 Lieutenant Newenham, Mss, Newenham to family, 24 November 1854.
59 ibid.
60 MRA, Cluttberbuck MSS, Clutterbuck to father, 1 October 1854.
61 Paget, *The Light Cavalry Brigade*, p.18.
62 L. W. Crider & G. Fisher, *Recollections of one of the Light Brigade by Albert Mitchell* (Crimean War Research Society 2009), pp.29-30.
63 Minart, 'Charles, Alfred et Édouard Minart', 2e Partie, *Carnet de la Sabretache*, vol. 9 (1910), pp.418-419.

[64] Cabrol, *Saint-Arnaud en Crimée*, pp.276-277.
[65] 'Une lettre écrite au *Moniteur de la Flotte*', *Le Moniteur de l'Armée* (11 Octobre 1854), p.3.
[66] Dr. Cabrol, *Saint-Arnaud en Crimée*, p. 277.
[67] ibid.
[68] McClellan, *Zouave Officer*, p.124.
[69] Roche, *Un Regiment de Ligne*, p.70.
[70] ibid, p.71.
[71] De la Faye, *General Lacretelle*, p.75.
[72] 'The Battle of the Alma: Letter from a Leeds Soldier', *Leeds Mercury* (21 October 1854).
[73] 'Letters from the Crimea to Wakefield', *Wakefield Journal & Examiner* (29 December 1854).
[74] 'The Battle of the Alma', *Leeds Mercury* (14 October 1854).
[75] 'Letters from the Field of Alma. An Ayrshire Soldier', *Paisley Herald and Renfrewshire Advertiser* (21 October 1854), p.6.
[76] Sir E. Colebrook, Bart., *Journal of two visits to the Crimea in 1854 and 1855* (London: T & W Boone, 1856), p.17.
[77] Roche, *Un Regiment de Ligne*, p.71.
[78] De la Faye, *General Lacretelle*, pp.75-76.
[79] Crider & Fisher, *Recollections of one of the Light Brigade*, pp.33-35.
[80] Guy & Massie, *Nolan*, p.52.
[81] 'Letter from a Leeds Soldier', *Leeds Mercury* (16 December 1854).
[82] 'Letter from the Crimea', *Kendal Mercury* (28 October 1854), p.8.
[83] 'The Crimea', *Bristol Mercury* (11 November 1854), np.
[84] 'Letter from the Seat of War', *Kendal Mercury* (28 October 1854), p.8.
[85] 'Une lettre écrite au *Moniteur de la Flotte*', *Le Moniteur de l'Armée* (11 Octobre 1854), p.3.
[86] ibid.
[87] 'The Skirmish on the 19th', *The Sheffield & Rotherham Independent* (14 October 1854), p.11.
[88] Minart, 'Charles, Alfred et Edouard Minart', pp.418-419.
[89] Cabrol, *Le Maréchal de Saint- Arnaud*, p. 279.

Chapter 2

Battle of the Alma

After having driven off the Russian rear-guard on the Bulganek, the Allied armies settled down into their bivouacs, remaining on alert as a night attack was expected. During the evening, *Maréchal* de Saint Arnaud held a conference with Lord Raglan. It was attended by all of Saint-Arnaud's Generals of Division and *L'Amiral* Hamelin (Commander of the French Fleet) and his staff – this was a combined force action, the fleet shadowing the Allied movement onshore and providing a mobile artillery reserve. Saint-Arnaud wrote in his journal:

> The fleet should protect ... the right; General Bosquet (*2e Division*) will attack the enemy to turn his flank, who is far from expecting a surprise such as this. The three other divisions will attack the centre, whilst the English, on the extreme left, will make a flanking movement to turn the enemy and converge, to fully envelope the enemy, who will be engaged in the centre on a cross-fire ... The arc of the circle which is to be executed by the English is very long but so too is that of the Division of Bosquet ... the Cavalry will be provided by the English.[1]

Général Francois Canrobert, commander of the French *1e Division* wrote a similar description:

> The plan of the battle for the following day was well conceived. Relying on our superiority of numbers, we would profit from this and turn the enemy.
>
> The Division of General Bosquet (2e), along with the Turkish Division, were to cross the Alma by the sea, scale the cliffs which dominate the river and debouche onto the plateau, attacking and putting into disorder the Russian left flank. At the same time

28

Bosquet arrives on the heights, the Division of Prince Napoleon (3e) and the rest of the army will cross the river and attack in front ... The *Maréchal* proposed to Lord Raglan that the English would make the same movement but by inversion. The Division of Bosquet was to leave camp at 5 o'clock in the morning, the other troops at 7 o'clock. No one raised any objections to this plan, which seemed rational.[2]

An anonymous French Staff Officer (but probably *colonel* Trochu) wrote that at,

> seven o'clock in the evening, *Maréchal* Saint-Arnaud communicated to his Generals of Division his plans for the battle on the morrow. The English army was to occupy the left, and would march, at daybreak, crossing the Alma behind the strong position and redoubts defended by the Russians, and, once established on the plateau, attack their right flank and their means of resistance that they have accumulated there. At the same time, général Bosquet, who also had under his command the Turkish Division, commanded by général Yusuf, should leave their camp, and, along the sea coast, climb the plateau by the escarpments which end by the coast. Overwhelmed by the Allies in this double manoeuvre, the Russians would only be able to show a feeble resistance to the frontal attack to which the remainder of the French army was committed.[3]

Général Bosquet's Aide-de-Camp, *capitaine* Fay, goes into more detail over the exact role to be played by the British:

> The 19th, in the evening, General Bosquet received from the *État Major General* a plan for the battle, which was to be executed based on a field of manoeuvre, which concerned our *2e Division*. With a reserve formed from Turks, we received the order to depart at 5am, directed toward the village of Almatamak, and passing this, half resting on this point and half at the barrier. The squadron of *Chasseurs d'Afrique* was to join our column. On the extreme left, the English were ordered forward at the same time, to make an effort on the enemy's right and to march in the following order, covered by the Riflemen and one battery of artillery: the division of Sir De Lacy Evans (second) and of Sir G. Brown (fifth) at the left of Prince Napoléon (3e), having behind them, in the second line, the division R. England (third) and than that of the Duke of Cambridge (first). The division of Cathcart (fourth) and the Cavalry to take place on the extreme left, and rear, ready to face the enemy, in case they

attempted to turn our flank. The probable moment when these two movements would combine is at 7am.[4]

Contre-Amiral Bouët-Willaumez, chief of staff to *Amiral* Hamelin, reported he received orders from *général* le Comte Édouard de Martimprey (Saint-Arnaud's chief of staff) on 19 September in the evening. He received verbal and written instructions as well as a map showing the disposition of the Allied and Russian forces, lines of march, timing etc.: 'the *1e* and *3e divisions* of the French army deployed in the first line... *4e division* in reserve... *2e division* ... To cross the Alma ... and gain the heights in the rear of the Russian left. English Army... to turn the right of the Russian army.'[5] Bosquet's attack was to be supported by guns from the French steamers *Mégère* and *La Cacique*.[6]

After the evening conference with Saint-Arnaud was concluded, Trochu went over to the British to confirm with them, in writing and verbally, the plan. In the presence of Colonel Rose, British liaison officer at French HQ, 'Lord Raglan approved everything, and it was agreed that the Prince Napoléon and Général Canrobert ... with the Allied generals, to operate simultaneously.'[7] Due to the length of the interview, Trochu did not return until 'very late in the evening' towards 23.00 hours. He reported that Lord Raglan had listened very carefully to everything he [Trochu] had said, 'gave every indication of agreeing with the written and verbal instructions' and that the plan was to go ahead.[8]

Why wasn't the plan put into action?

Our anonymous Staff Officer suggests that the plan failed to work because of 'the inability of the English divisions to manoeuvre, which was relatively simple in our plan of the battle.' Furthermore, Saint-Arnaud had mistakenly under-estimated the strength of the Russians.[9] *Colonel* Trochu in a very frank letter to the state-newspaper *Le Moniteur* states how at 06.00 he repeatedly sent Staff riders to British lines to enquire why they were not moving. The consistent reply from them was that 'we are not ready.' Finally, in a fit of pique, around 07.00 hours, Trochu himself galloped over to Lord Raglan, who informed the *colonel* that the British would not be ready to move for a further two hours.[10] A similar story is relayed by other French officers: 'The English were not ready.'[11] No one appears to have told the French fleet that the plan of attack had been altered, nor were any orders passed on to the British fleet, which Bouët-Willaumez assumed was the role of Raglan's staff.[12]

Canrobert wrote:

At five o'clock in the morning Bosquet commenced his movement: the columns of manoeuvre, the bayonets flashing in the sun, snaking along the sea coast. At seven o'clock the other divisions formed in line of closed columns by battalion; the artillery deployed in the intervals between each brigade, with the general reserve in the second line, The Maréchal passed in front of his troops, to direct the left, where the English army should have been deploying. Annoyed by the constant inaction, he sent Colonel Renson to General Bosquet to halt his movement. Colonel Trochu was sent to Lord Raglan to find out the reason for the delay.[13]

Neither *général* Canrobert nor Prince Napoléon could understand the 'inconceivable' delay.[14] Prince Napoléon went to find General Sir De Lacy Evans. He found him 'in his tent, the only one in the division.' Prince Napoléon announced to Evans 'Why have you not attended to your orders? Our troops are ready, and you have had notice to take arms: you and your troops should be ready.'[15] Canrobert and the Prince explained to Evans the plan for the British to turn the Russian right flank.[16] When *colonel* Trochu found Lord Raglan, he inquired as 'to the cause of the inaction, causing the plan to be halted':

> Milord, the *Maréchal* thought that, conforming with the plan to which you agreed yesterday evening, your troops would form the left wing and line of battle, and you were to commence your movement at 6 a.m.[17]

Lord Raglan Replied 'Some of my troops were late arriving last night in the bivouac, this has caused some delay, but I have given my orders.' Trochu responded:

> Milord! Le *Maréchal* begs you to move. The delay has disorganized and upsets the attack; every minute lost, is lost a chance of success.[18]

Trochu galloped off, swearing at the 'damned, perfidious English.'[19] An order was sent to halt Bosquet.[20] Staff Officer *capitaine* Claudius-Amédée Perrotin estimated that Trochu had galloped 'more than two leagues' [about fifty miles] between the Allied headquarters during that morning.[21]

Sir Edward Colebrooke interviewed Lord Raglan after the battle; Raglan was of the opinion 'to attack both flanks of the enemy, unless the assailing force was greatly superior, would have been a very hazardous movement.'[22] He further adds that because of the Allied

31

command of the coast, the principal attack against the Russians should have been on the Russian left, and any flanking attack would have taken considerable time to develop. Crucially, he was of the same opinion as Trochu: the failure of Saint-Arnaud's plan was due 'to the difficulties of a divided command.'[23]

Saint-Arnaud held an emergency meeting with Raglan where a revised plan was enacted.[24] It was impossible at such a late stage to re-work the entire French battle plan as the French army and fleet was currently in motion, but the British flank march was called off. Instead of marching around the Russian flank, the British would take the Russian position head-on, attacking the batteries and redoubts that Saint-Arnaud had been eager to avoid tackling in front.[25]

En Avant Bosquet!

Général Pierre Bosquet's *2e Division* had been selected to lead the attack. Bosquet was forty-four-years-old at the Alma, having served in the Army for over twenty years, becoming *général de brigade* in 1848:

> Around six o'clock [remembered capitaine Fay], after our soup is eaten, the right wing is put in movement, the remainder of the French army was under arms, is preparing to leave its bivouac, but the *Maréchal* halted this because the English were not able to leave at the hour convened … I carried the order to suspend his march to *général* Bosquet; it was eight o'clock … The *général* expressed his great displeasure towards our allies… Around ten o'clock, the halt having become more prolonged, some soldiers ran down to the sea whilst others found clean water and made their coffee.[26]

Lieutenant Cullet (*20e Légère*) had watched Bosquet's division depart:

> Over on our extreme right, *général* Bosquet skirted the sea; his brigade seemed to bury itself in the crevices of the cliffs; its artillery followed the columns. On our side, Canrobert's division (*1e*) went straight ahead to the river, and like ours (*3e*) the head of its column was hit by fire from riflemen posted in the vineyards and in the undergrowth, which bordered the course of the Alma.[27]

Finally, around 11.00 hours, as *capitaine* Fay relates, the order to renew the attack was given:

> The men joyfully put their knapsacks to the rear; drums and bugles and music were heard all along the line, and we finally marched on

the enemy. The Second Division, ahead of the main body by about 1,500 metres, advanced in two columns: Bouat's brigade [*6e de Ligne; 7e Légère; 3e Chasseurs*] towards the bar, the brigade of d'Autemarre [*3e Zouaves; 50e de ligne*] towards Almatamack. Each one of these columns was accompanied by its own artillery battery; but the first ford being found impractical for the caissons, the battery that followed the first brigade also came through the village, which brought it quicker to the crest.

The Russians, placed on the heights on the left bank of the River Alma as on the steps of an amphitheatre, had, since dawn, been able to see all our movements. A captured Russian officer taken prisoner told us he believed the move was only a diversion to weaken them in the centre.[28]

The attack against Almatamack was led by the *3e Régiment des Zouaves*. Thirty-one-year-old *capitaine* Henri Brincourt was a company commander:

The river, with steep banks along its course, served as a line of entrenchments and fixed batteries that extended for about two leagues distant. They were some twenty thousand, perfectly formed field artillery and cavalry. We have only one thousand men of English cavalry and one gun per thousand soldiers. Their position was formidable. The English had to make a great circuit to turn their right. A center column composed of three divisions should attack their center, and finally our 2nd Division, supported as needed by the Turks, was to attack their left.

The action began at 5 am. The newspapers will undoubtedly tell you what happens, I can only speak of my division, and even of my regiment. Our mission seemed most difficult. We had to cross the river near its mouth and climb the steepest slope. We crossed the river at 10 minutes past 12. Naturally the *Zouaves* were in the lead. Climbing up like cats the steepest heights, they were scatterred at first, but were soon on the plateau. The few hundred Russian infantrymen were so surprised at the speed of their [the *Zouaves*] arrival in the ravine they discharged their weapons and ran away in disorder; but after a moment they rallied, but without the presence of our Colonel [Tabouriech] (who had his horse wounded under him) one of our companies attacked so quickly they could not touch their bayonets, and would have been surrounded. [They] were vigorously received, the Russian soldier not turning his back as briskly as the Bedouin.[29]

Général Bosquet and his staff rode forward with his men to the river. A party of French engineers, lead by *commandant* Dumas, cleared the way for the batteries of *capitaines* Marcy and Fiévet. *Capitaine* Roulet had his *sapeurs* build a ramp to enable the guns and caissons to cross the river; *chef d'escadron* Barral managed to get his guns across the river but the battery attached to d'Autemarre's brigade, despite the best efforts of the engineers, could not ascend the cliffs. *Chef d'Escadron* Barral, commanding Bosquet's artillery, ordered all the artillery to cross at the position prepared by the *sapeurs*. Covered by the *Tirailleurs Algérien* the guns were rapidly brought up the heights.[30]

It was not a moment too soon; both of Bosquet's brigades had mounted the heights and came under fierce Russian artillery fire as described by *captiaine* Brincourt:

> No sooner have we had the time to deploy on the plateau than three Russian artillery batteries arrived at a gallop to the rescue of the Russian infantry. They maneuvered well and were placed so as to overwhelm the troops debouching by the way we had come. The *Tirailleurs Algérien*, who came after us ended the column. They [the Russian guns] swept away a few files, men literally cut in half, and very nearly did our men run down the cliff as quickly than they had scaled it!
>
> Our first battalion and three companies were deployed as skirmishers whilst the remainder were deployed in line. The rest of the second battalion was behind a low hill, but one of the Russian batteries took us in the flank. My company was outside the fold of the hill. I was at the extreme right and a little in a hollow, the cannon balls coming from all sides and crossing over my head, with a little unharmonius whistling! I gave myself three minutes to live, when I was ordered to put my company in movement, to find shelter from the fire of the two batteries … and gave us some time to breathe.
>
> Finally, our artillery arrived on the plateau. During several minutes, we had only two guns that were firing and those much too small a calibre to compete with the Russian batteries. Our guns were behind our position. Naturally the two artilleries endeavoured to dismount each other, in order to make it easier to fire on the infantry. During an hour and a half, we found ourselves between the two, sheltered, it is true, but stunned by the whistling of cannon balls and shells: one might believe in the midst of fireworks, rockets and not bombs.[31]

Capitaine Fay described how 'our batteries had joined the infantry, but not without much effort, and had the honour to fire the first shot of the battle':

During this struggle, which lasted more than one hour and a half, our twelve pieces of artillery, 12-pounders (gun-howitzers, *canon de l'Empereur*), commanded by *commandant* Barral, successfully fought the forty pieces of ordnance which were used against them ... Their [Russian] infantry remained motionless; their cavalry tried to turn us by the ravine of Ulukul; shells fired by the steamers *Megere*, *Le Cacique* and the *Canada*... and some shots, fired at a thousand metres by our *chasseurs à pied*, obliged them to turn and disengage our right flank.[32]

Capitaine Henri-Victor-Alpin Adrien, 2nd battalion, *6e Regiment de Ligne* wrote to *capitaine* Joppé:

The 1st Brigade of the 2nd Division had a serious struggle in support on the heights. A very lively cannonade was heard. The strengh of fire from our frigates caused the Russian cavalry to abandon the plain. The turning movement was completed, and the left wing of the Russians was forced to fall back. During this movement, the 1st and the 3rd Division attacked the enemy's centre.[33]

Seeing the danger Bosquet was in up on the heights, *général* Canrobert ordered forward two of the reserve batteries, which opened fire on the Russians. *Capitaine* Brincourt watched as:

From time to time, some of the shot and shells from our artillery fell short and landed amongst us, but fortunately did not cause much harm. Suddenly the Russian artillery, which had started to dismount, but did not diminish its fire even when the Russians were retreating, turned to provide support to their centre which was being vigorously attacked, although protected by a fixed battery and a redoubt built in stone. We marched forward, and we saw from afar the capture of the Redoubt, on which was planted the tricolor to the cry of *Vive L'Empereur!*[34]

Capitaine Fay remembered seeing Bosquet 'gallop from one battery to another, with this small group of officers and staff, encouraging everyone' when suddenly,

opposite us, French skirmishers appeared on the crest before the Telegraph Tower; those of the first division at the White-House; those of the third at the village of Bourliouk, had resolutely approached the out-posts of the enemy; a battery drawn from the cavalry division, the two from the division of the Prince [Napoléon] and two from the reserve, posted on the right bank to effectively protect this movement.[35]

General Canrobert's attack goes in.

With the Russian left pinned down by Bosquet, Saint-Arnaud ordered forward the *1e* (Canrobert) and *3e* (Prince Napoléon) Divisions, to attack the Russian centre. As soon as Canrobert had observed Bosquet scale the heights, he ordered forward his Division; protected by artillery fire, the *1e Zouaves*, *1e* and *9e bataillons des Chasseurs à Pied* leading in skirmish order (*en-tirailleur*). The *1e chasseurs* were under the temporary orders of *commandant* Montaudon of *3e Zouaves* who had been seconded to them following the return to France of their commanding officer, *commandant* Tristan Legros, who was ill with cholera.[36]

The two batteries commanded by *chef d'escadrons* Huegenet (*capitaines* Hugon and Creuzet) and two more commanded by *chef d'escadron* Bertrand (*capitaines* Lainsecq and Claudet) pushed forwards to within 200 metres of the Russians.[37] Artillery officer *capitaine* Joseph Paul Alfred Rebillot, watched the attack go in:

> Our skirmishers engaged with them [the Russians], and shots were exchanged between the Russian guns on the crest, and ours on the plain. The first enemy shot was received by the battery under the orders of commandant L[ainsecq], it burst a bag of oats ... but it did no harm; it was accompanied by general laughter, and we did not take our adversaries seriously, that is to say, because of the inaccuracy of their fire.[38]

The *1e Zouaves* and *1e Chasseurs à Pied* led the attack of *général* Espinasse. *Commandant* Montaudon recalled later in life:

> Half-past twelve ... the order is given. All the columns of the centre boldly advance; they were ordered to advance straight ahead, without worrying about protecting the flanks.
>
> As soon as my skirmish line started to advance, it came under Russian fire from skirmishers in the bushes and the vines on the banks of the Alma ... we experienced a few losses. But our men, were far from being stopped by this feeble fire, or by the artillery placed on the heights, they did not hesitate to fall on the enemy, and pursued them with the bayonet in the kidneys, and forced them to the other bank, leaving a lot of dead and wounded on the field.[39]

Sergent Édouard Minart (*1e Zouaves*) wrote to his mother after that battle:

We were greeted by bullets: our skirmishers advanced to drive back the Russians. In this case, a wretch who was next to me was shot in the mouth, which broke his jaw. Another was struck in the chest and died.

We dropped our knapsacks and we were told to lie down on our bellies behind a low rise. Bullets whistled above our heads, but I stooped not, something told me that I would not be hit. Finally, after fifteen or twenty minutes, we stood up and we were given orders to clear the enemy position.[40]

Général Vinoy's brigade was ordered forward in support of Espinasse. Serving under Vinoy were Charles and Alfred Minart of *27e de Ligne*; Charles wrote:

At two o'clock the action began with the skirmishers fighting in the vineyards along the banks of the Alma. When we heard the cannon of the English and the 2nd Division, we dropped our knapsacks and we went running up to the river. There, we each crossed the river: we climbed the slope and we found ourselves on the plateau, in the middle of the Russians.[41]

Sergent-Major Alfred was by his brother's side throughout the battle, under heavy Russian artillery fire:

A cannon ball landed at my feet. Another one struck a corporal standing at the side of Charles.

We dropped our knapsacks, and we set off at the run through the vines and the gardens, a spent cannon ball came down twenty paces from me. On arriving at the river, we had to jump over a bank ten feet high, I left myself slide to the bottom. The water was up to our knese. Once on the other side, we were ordered to support the *Zouaves* and *Chasseurs à Pied* who were in front of us.[42]

Prince Napoléon advances
Simultaneous with the attack of *général* Canrobert, Prince Napléon's *3e Division* moved forward to attack the Russian centre. Leading the way were the *2e Zouaves*, led by *Colonel* Cler:

At half past twelve, the skrmishers of the regiment entered the village and in the gardens bordering the right bank of the Alma. In that time, the enemy started the fight with their riflemen, firing with precision, and the artillery opened fire; several cannon balls fell on the first line without hurting a single man.

The *Colonel* [Cler] has ordered one of his companies forward as skirmishers to reinforce the two already strongly committed near the river. The two battalions dropped their knapsacks and lay in wait, the *2e Régiment* behind the dry stone walls which border the gardens, whilst the *1e Régiment* left their knapsacks behind the river bank. The river was in flood, and deep in the wooded part of its course where we had to cross. The only ford practicable to wagons, cuts through the middle the battalion. The men had water up to their waists …

The three companies deployed as sharpshooters were strongly engaged on the banks of the river, but they had become very compromised; the Russian batteries redoubled their fire and the *Colonel* had to take immediate, prompt and determined action.

The *Colonel* of the *2e Zouaves* recognized on the range of hills, a vulnerable position occupied by the enemy. On a detached hillock in front, on a spur on an oblique eminance in the valley, three Russian battalions were placed. The left side of this position was defended by the enemy artillery; the right of the position was ploughed by the fire of the French line. The 1st Division was preparing to attack; on the slopes to our left, the artillery of the division had taken position. *Colonel* Cler urged his Brigadier General to move quickly with his first battalion to the head of the enemy's position. And he set in motion the 2nd battalion of the Regiment to bring support.[43]

At this 'critical moment' Cler took the initiative, and ordered his regiment to charge:

Under a hail of lead and iron, he crossed the river Alma mounted on his charger, whose waters were up to his midriff. He crossed and re-crossed the tortuous river three times. He fell and remounted his horse, but climbed up under the fire of the Russian battalions onto the ridge of hills, and reached the first position. Together, the *Zouaves* and the *1e Bataillon Chasseurs à Pied* had attacked the left flank of the position. The three battalions of Russians, taken by surprise by this daring attack, gave way and abandoned their knapsacks and threw away their muskets.

Master of the first slopes of the plateau, the 1st Battalion was soon joined by the 2nd Battalion, which formed extended line. The *Colonel* formed his regiment to the left of the 1st Battalion of the *1e Zouaves*, forming a square to resist a Russian cavalry charge which was made by a regiment of lancers across a short distance. The position occupied now by the *2e Zouaves* could provide no shelter from the two enemy batteries and two Russian regiments; in minutes, thirty men fell by the bullet or by shrapnel.[44]

Struggling up the heights came *général* Thomas' Brigade of the *3e Division*. *Lieutenant* Cullet (*20e Légère*) described the advance of his brigade:

> In front of our battalions of the *20e* and *22e Légère*, were Russian infantry in a profound mass ... formed in columns, we deployed for combat: we traversed the old Russian camp formed from huts made from straw, where we escaped some of the enemy fire. Our elite companies deployed as skirmishers and commenced a violent fire; on our right twelve pieces of artillery of *commandant* Bertrand, protected by the *19e chasseurs*, fired on the Russian infantry masses with shells and rockets. The ground was covered with Russian dead. We advanced slowly; the undulations of the ground caused many cannon balls to richochet over our heads; our losses were almost none.[45]

Fight for the Telegraph Tower

Three French infantry divisions were now engaged on the heights; dominating the position was the half-finished stone telegraph tower. The French began to sense that the battle was turning their way; the Russians were giving away and pinned their line on the telegraph. It became the focus of the French attacks, regiments scrambling to plant their eagles on it's scaffolding. *Colonel* Cler led the *1e* and *2e Zouaves* in a charge against its defenders:

> Taking advantage of the astonishment and terror the first attack had made in the Russian camp, Cler hesitated a moment between a bayonet attack on the main square of Russians opposite, or to attack an octagonal tower under construction up on a mound in the very centre of the Russian line, dominating their position. He decided on the latter project, and, within the angle formed by the two regiments, he rushed at the gallop in crying 'To me, my Zouaves! At the Tower!' He attacked with the *2e* and the *1e Regiment de Zouaves*, and planted his standard on the Tower with the cry of '*Vive l'Empereur!*'[46]

Capitaine Fay saw how the 'struggle concentrated around the telegraph, the principle point of Russian resistance':

We regarded with attention this little eminence, covered with resolute enemies and ready to receive the assualt of our soldiers. At the same time, we saw a large mass of Russian infantry, which wanted to fall on the division of Canrobert which, having just arrived, was not yet formed, and didn't yet have its artillery. At the request of general Canrobert, one of our batteries rapidly deployed, and opened a violent short-range fire with case shot which soon put the ranks of the enemy column into considerable disorder.[47]

Advancing in support of Canrobert was *général* d'Aurelle's brigade of the *4e Division* (*Général* Forey). The commanding officer of the *74e de Ligne* described how,

we [*74e Ligne*] crossed the river last, therefore without loss, although bursts of shells and many cannon balls, aimed at our *Chasseurs à Pied*, fell in large numbers around my battalions. *Maréchal* Saint-Arnaud sent me orders to march to the rescue of the English who had captured the position: the fire stops, I halted and to my right I deployed my men. The *39e Régiment* had just engaged and occupied a blockhouse which the *Zouaves* had first attacked. I arrived beside it [the blockhouse], and placed myself in the first line on its left. A battery fired on our two regiments, stubbornly out of reach of musket-shot. They never ceased their fire for half an hour, a hail of cannon balls and shells passing over our heads, thanks to an undulation in the terrain that made them ricochet.

Well the *39e* was well placed, with about forty killed and wounded; its standard-bearer was killed. I had a very close call, a bullet brushed past me. [*Colonel*] Beuret [*39e de Ligne*] had his horse injured by a shell-splinter. The *lieutenant-colonel* O'Rianne, had his horse killed while close to me.[48]

Led by *colonel* Cler, the French rushed at the telegraph tower:

Colonel Cler, who had been the first to reach the foot of the tower, seized the Eagle of his regiment and planted it upon the scaffolding, amid the cries of '*Vive l'Empereur!*' Sergeant-Major Fleury, of the *1e Zouaves*, who managed to get on top of the upper range of scaffolding, sustained the flag in this position for a moment or two, but soon fell a lifeless corpse, struck down by a grape shot in the head. The colours of the *1e Zouaves* were quickly seen floating side by side with those of the *2e*; and had hardly been raised there, before the colour-staff was cut in two by a shell …

Lieutenant Poidevin, colour-bearer of the *39e de Ligne*, seeing the glorious place occupied by the colours of the *1e* and *2 Zouaves*, rushed forward in advance of his battalion, and planted those of his own regiment on the tower – and as he pressed the colour-staff close to his heart to hold it up, he had his breast torn open with a round shot, and payed, with his life, for the performance of this act of generous daring.[49]

The British enter the fray

As the French under Saint-Arnaud faught their way onto the plateau, Raglan's British infantry remained motionless. At around 13.00 hours, as the fight on the plateau raged, Raglan had ordered his infantry forward, close to the line of villages and farms straggling along the Alma. The Light Division of Sir George Brown formed the left of the line; De Lacy Evan's 2nd Division was on the right. In the second line, behind the 2nd Division was Sir Richard England's 3rd Division and behind the Lights came the Duke of Cambrdige and the 1st Division. Hospital-Sergeant Henry Simpson (33rd Foot) was part of Codrington's brigade of the Light Division:

> 20th. A beautiful morning; got up as soon as daylight and got a good blow out of rough stuff and ready for the road. We got in the order of march about six o'clock, the French on our right, leading. The English were in the centre. We halted for about two or three hours before we came in sight of the Alma, to allow the French to get in front. Well, when they got to the front we got the order to march to our right, and soon the heights of Alma appeared in sight with thousands of Russians on the top. Onward we went, and when we got about one mile from them they set fire to a village, which completely covered them from our sight with smoke. Our Rifles were in front. We then formed line, and by this time our Rifles and the Russian sharp shooters had opened a very brisk fire, while we marched onward in line, and soon the bullets came rolling to where we were. Then came the tug of war, our brave fellows advancing as coolly as though nothing was the matter, till they came to the river Alma.[50]

Colour-Sergeant Thomas Bairstow of the 33rd wrote to his family in Queenshead, near Halifax:

> On the 20th under arms an hour before daylight, all formed for action. We marched eight miles, until we came to a village named

41

Alma, then we formed in four lines, light division in front, first next, second next, and third next – seven regiments in each line. Then we advanced until our line was within gunshot of the village. The Russians set fire to it and retired along a bridge over a river, then commenced to cannonade us. All the infantry then laid down on their bellies. Our artillery advanced and commenced firing on them; we laid in this position for an hour. I must here thank God again for His mercy to me, a wicked sinner, for the cannon balls went buzzing over our heads, and rolling through our ranks, and many of our comrades were launched into eternity. At last we were ordered to stand and advanced. I had to step out to the front, Mason on my right and Serjeant Spence in my left, six paces in front of the lines, directing the advance, when bullets when whistling past us as nearly as thick as hail.[51]

Bairstow's colleague, Colour-Sergeant George Spence narrated that:

When we got to within about two miles of them, the Russians set fire to the stacks and villages, so that the smoke would baffle our view. In the rear of these villages there runs a river, and across this we must pass; but, as I said, when we got to within about two miles of the hills, the enemy commenced firing at us. We then deployed into line – the Light Division and the 2nd heavy Division – the light to the left, the heavy to the right. The heavy advanced about 100 yards; then we advanced 200 yards, and so on, until we came to the within about 500 yards of the river.[52]

Sergeant Usherwood wrote in his journal that no sooner had the Light Division deoployed and began its advance than the Russian artillery opened fire with,

round shot at long range and which as we still advanced ploughed through its ranks one shot smashing the leg of a Grenadier named Keogh and the leg of Lieut. Wardlam of the 19th Foot. Advancing still further covred by the 2nd Battn Rifle Brigade who had now opened fire upon the enemy skirmishers in their front leaving every noe and then behind them a fallen comrade or two, orders came that we were to lie down so that the shots from the enemy might not do as much damage …

Just prior to receiving this order to make haste for cover under the wall, several round shots passed through the ranks of the 19th Foot, two of these striking my own company, one of which grazed my [cartridge] pouch as I turned to avoid it and striking the hind leg of Carden's horse immediately in rear of myself wounded it severely, the other shot alluded to striking the front part and at the top of Pte. Patrick Budgen's chaco, which coming so suddenly not a little astonished him, tho' it did him no bodily harm at this time and while the round shots were plunging through our ranks the men of the 2nd Battalion Rifle Brigade had reached near to the wall and as we were still further advancing in line the enemy's sharpshooters who it appeared were concealed behind the wall, poured into us a volley of musketry coming upon us suddenly and unperceived startled us very much tho'… not a shot took effect, the whole flying over our heads with a rushing noise similar yet still more powerful to a large flight of small birds …

While as we lay thus inactive awating orders to advance and which was understood to be when the French had somewhat established themselves, our other Divisions especially the first approached nearer also in line and became targets for the enemy's cannons.[53]

Moving up in support of the infantry came the guns of the Royal Artillery. Bombardier John Weekes wrote to his family at home in Leeds:

Just as we were getting within their range they set fire to a village, and then opened fire upon us with their big guns of position, which made everybody look about. Our battery was ordered to [the] front, and was very soon followed by the other batteries, both English and French; and before we got fairly into action we lost two men one with his leg broke, and the other killed; both men belonged to my gun. Immediately after the infantry was formed into line, and the artillery ceased firing, when the whole body advanced, leaving us in the rear; and then, soon after, for the first time I beheld such a sight as I never shall forget: some with legs off, some without arms, and others blown quite to pieces.

We commenced about one o'clock, and were on the heights of Alma about four. When our battery arrived on the hill, we saw a large body in front, some said they were Russians, some said French, but we soon found out what they were. Our battery advanced amid the cheers or our infantry to the front, and opened fire upon the columns of the enemy, and made a road through them that the whole battery could have marched through. I must let you know that the B battery, which is my battery, fired the first and last shot at the Battle of Alma; our loss being one captain and three men killed, and six wounded, besides twelve horses. We lost more than any other battery in the field, as we were exposed to the hottest of the fire.[54]

Sergeant Usherwood was not entirely grateful for the timely arrival of the guns:

> As a small rising piece of our ground on the left o fthe 19th Foot appeared protected by the walls of a burning house, the officer brought up a gun and while we set to and pulled down a portion of the house so as to make a gap, but just as the Artillerymen were engaged in loading their piece, Sir Geo. Brown espied them and galloping up to the officer in charge expostulated with him in undignified terms on the unreasonablness of the attempt peremptorily ordering him to limber up and take his gun away as he had not only drawn the enemy's fire upon himself but upon the Division also.[55]

The Great Redoubt

As the red-coated battalions reached the river, they came under increasing Russian artillery fire and became tangled in the vineyards that flanked the river. Pushing through the vines and blinding smoke from the burning village, the now disorganised infantry waded across the river to assail their opponents. Private John Bourgoyne of the Royal Welch Fusiliers wrote to his father in Wakefield:

> At 12 o'clock we halted, and got orders to prepare for the enemy; General Saint Arnand [sic, Marshal Saint-Arnaud] came with the news. We all rose and gave three cheers. At half-past one we met our foe mounted on the heights miles above our heads, their cannons pouring upon us, but we advanced coolly with General Brown at our head. He said – 'Now Royal Welsh, let them see what you can do!'[56]

Colour-Sergeant Bairstow continues his narrative:

> We came to the river, which we had to ford, and in doing so it took us up to the middle in water. After we had got through the river we were out of the fire of the Russians, and it caused the 7th, 23rd, 33rd, 77th 88th and 19th Regiments to be a little out of order, all being so eager to get at the Russians. We never waited to form line properly, but up the embankment we went, in great disorder, when a regular

volley of musketry and grape commenced to be poured into us from the Russians, and then we commenced firing too, and a regular engagement took place, which lasted for an hour.

After being engaged half an hour, Mason was shot through the thigh; one ball had hit the peak of his cap, and slightly grazed his forehead; another ball went through the leg of his trousers, and another ball cut the string of his water barrel, so he had a narrow escape. He was carried on a stretcher to the rear by Sandy and Dr. Marison… I was wounded about two minutes after Mason. I went to the rear, out of shot reach, and remained there till the fighting was over, which, lasted three hours and a half; then I went and joined my regiment, and went among the sick the following morning.[57]

According to Colour-Sergeant Bairstow, the colour parties came under the particular attention of Russian sharpshooters:

I am wounded through the small of the arm, just below the shoulder joint, clear of the bone – shot with a musket ball. Mason[58] is shot through the thick of the thigh, not touching the bone. I, Mason, Serjeants Spence,[59] William Sirea [sic, Siree][60] Sugden,[61] and Mr Greenwood,[62] were all with the colours, and all were wounded.[63]

Hospital-Sergeant Simpson watched as the Light Division attacked the Great Redoubt:

They dashed onward, and the Russians retired as they advanced. Our brigade, that was composed of the 7th, 23rd and 33rd Regiments, and the left and right regiments of the adjoining brigade, got into the fire of three Russian batteries, and poor fellows they did suffer severely, for the grape and canister shot was firing as thick as possible, and our ranks got terribly thinned. But onward they went in spite of all the grape and canister; nothing could stop t hem. A captain of ours took possession of one of the guns and wrote his name on it with his sword.

The Russians were retiring in large columns, when all at once a fresh body of the Russians appeared on the top of the hill and by mistake they took them to be the French that had got round the flank of the Russians, and for a few moments they stopped firing. The Russians got heart at this; the retiring columns turned round nad fired a most tremendous volley into our poor fellows and made a great slaughter, but when out men found out their mistake they set to work again and soon had them scampering off in all directions.[64]

Corporal William Hargreaves (7th Royal Fusiliers) of Leeds wrote to his mother two days after the battle:

> The light division formed brigade lines and advanced. They gave us round shot, shell, grape and canister from the hills, which made us suffer rather severely. In about and hour and a half our line was ordered to advance. We entered the village. It was dreadful. The shot falling like hailstones, and the men kept dropping all along. I lost my place and got into No. 1 Company, and there were others of other regiments in the same place. We rushed through the river on the right and opened fire on the enemy's flank; the regiment crossed further up the river, and in about half and hour we drove them from their post. They did not show fight after. The engagement lasted three hours and twenty minutes. I fired twenty-three rounds and made them tell well, but I never got touched by a single shot. Poor J. McDonald[65] of Ripon, got shot while advancing up the hill.[66]

Whilst leading on the Royal Welch Fusiliers, Lieutenant Colonel Chester and eight other officers were killed:

> The 23rd was awfully cut up, having eight officers killed and five wounded in the space of about five minutes. The Russians were in a very strong position upon the hills above the Alma, where they had one hundred guns entrenched, and our guns could not reach them. They light division went up succeeded in driving back the troops opposed to them, especially the 23rd, who behaved most gallantly. After they had driven back their adversaries a large column of the Imperial Guard came down on their right flank, whom they mistook for the French. It was a fatal error, for when the 23rd ceased firing the Russians poured in such a terrible fire that the men turned and retreated. The officers sprang to the front, to bring them on once more, and were instantly shot down. The colonel (Chester), two captains, and five subalterns (among them poor [Sir] William [Young]) were killed on the spot.[67]

Private William Hamlet Floyd of the 23rd was wounded in three places, and in a letter to his mother conveys some of the chaos of the fighting:

> I have been severely wounded in three places, which is as follows:-
> A musket-shot through the right arm which I received about an hour after we commenced the action, but being determined to pay them for making a hole through my jacket and the flesh part of my arm

above the elbow, I would not fall to the rear, but made my comrade tie a handkerchief round it, and fought through the action, which lasted three hours after; but just as we thought the action was over, for the Imperial Russian army was routed, and we had gained the entrenchments and forts, they halted and wheeled around and made another stand, which did not last long for General Sir G. Brown, or Lord Raglan (I do not know which of them), ordered us, the Royal Welch Fusiliers, Scots Fusiliers Guards, Grenadier Guards, and the 33rd Regiment of the Line to form up for the charge, which we did directly; and now came a grand charge, and away they went after a few moments, wounding with the bayonets, but not before they had left me with a bayonet wound in the left thigh and a rifle ball through the left breast which passed through the breast bone and left lung, and going out under the shoulder blade.

My other wounds are trifling to compare with the latter, for they are nearly healed up. The wound through the breast is closing up quite fast outside, but it will be months, the docters [sic, doctors] tell me, before it will be healed up inside, and that I will always have to take great care of myself, for any convulsive or quick movements will be dangerous to me.

They seem to think it quite a miracle that I should live for they have agreed that the ball passed between the leading strings of the heart and about half an inch from the heart. Yet I am better, and live in hopes to live better a long time, although I shall never have much power in my left arm, nor shall I ever be upright; at least I can hardly expect it – but it must be for the best. I never did despair, and nor shall I. I have served my Queen in the best manner I could through an arduous campaign until I became mutilated with wounds; it is now her turn to serve me during the remainder of my days.[68]

Sergeant Usherwood had also seen the brooding Russian column:

The Russians not expecting such determination from the British immediately betook themselves to flight who when in the act of extricating their cannons out of the battery alluded to lost two pieces together with some of their horses attached as they were to the guns. In this affair within the battery several men made themselves conspicuous Pte. Pat Bulger of the 19th Regiment being one and Troughton of No. 3 Company another. Bulger during the rush made for the guns killing his man while standing on the horse's back. Both beaten however tho' the trench and battery were in our hands.

The Russians reattacked [sic] us by bringing up fresh masses and who as I observed myself did not deploy into line but opened fire as they stood in column ... The suddenness of the approach of this column together with a report being circulated that we were firing on the French threw us into disorder, it at this time being out of the question for any Regiment to keep its formation owing greatly to the losses each had sustained in Officers and men ... we ... gradually retired toward the bank of the river in order to gain formation and to allow the Brigade of Guards to engage who at this moment were marching up from the River.[69]

Forward, the Guards!

With the Light Division falling back in confusion, the 1st Division, including the Guards and Highland brigades renewed the attack. Lieutenant Hugh Annesley of the Scots Fusilier Guards described their advance:

The light division advanced to the attack, supported by the first division (Guards and Highlanders). They got across the river, and then advanced against the entrenchments. The 23rd [Royal Welch Fusiliers] was in column when the brigade of Guards charged in line. My company (4th) was next to the colours, and in the very centre of the line. We got up to within fifty yards of the ditch, when the regiment before us (which had the three senior officers killed) turned right about, and came down in our face, thus breaking our line.

We were about thirty paces then from the ditch, and the fire was so hot that you could hardly conceive it possible for anything the size of a rabbit not to be killed. I kept on shouting, 'Forward, Guards!' to the few men that were not swept away by the [redacted], when a ball came and stopped my mouth most unceremoniously. It entered the left cheek, and whent out at the mouth, taking away the front teeth. I instantly turned to the rear, feeling it was about 100 to 1 against my ever getting hit there, as the bullets were whizzing round me like hail. I tripped, and thought it was all over with me. However, I got up again with the loss of my sword and bearskin, and at last got into the river and out of fire.[70]

Colour-Sergeant P. F. Davis, 3rd Battalion Grenadier Guards, described how his,

battalion ... bravely advanced in line, amidst showers of shot of all sizes, right up to the enemy in their trenches before firing a shot; and then we opened, to a good tune. This was the sort of cool British bravery that stagnated and then set our foes to flight; and in that flight they were actually moved down by hundreds.[71]

Lieutenant John Astley (Scots Fusilier Guards) recalled later in life:

Shot and shell kept whizzing and whistling over our heads, and the dirt sent flying every now and again as the shot struck, and some poor fellow to the right or left would be carried to the rear....

Immediately in front of us was one of those infernal earthworks armed with eight or nine big guns, well served with grape and canister, also a regiment of Russian riflemen ... one and all taking pot shots as us as we came up the hill, and they must have been bitter bad marksmen, or else our line of two deep ought to have been annihilated. We had fixed bayonets, and I verily believe we should have driven the Ruskies out of their battery, but just at the critical moment the 23rd Welsh Fusiliers – who had been terribly cut up, and had gathered round their colours at the corner of the battery – got the order to retire, and they came down the hill in a body, right through the centre of our line, and carried a lot of our men witih them.

This caused our line to waver and retire, leaving the officers in front, and just as I was yelling to our company to come back, I got a feaful 'whack' and felt as if some one had hit me hard with a bludgeon on the neck. Fortunately did not fall, but turned and went down the hill, feeling awfully queer and dizzy.[72]

The check suffered by the Guards was only momentary; coming up on the left of the Scots Fusiliers Guards were the Coldstreams and beyond them, the Highland Brigade under Sir Colin Campbell, 42nd (Black Watch) leading, with the 93rd (Sutherland Highlanders) and 79th (Cameron Highlanders) in echelon. Sergeant Frazer (42nd) wrote to his wife in Paisley two days after the battle:

My dear wife, I thanked the Almighty for His kindness to myself, for allowing me to pass through all that day's dangers, for it was awful. There were three or four regiments had to retire, and then the Highland Brigade came up under all the enemy's fire. The general can't see yet how we escaped being cut to pieces, for we went right in their faces, and forced them to retire, and if we did not pitch into then, then, it's strange to me. They ran like a lot of wild sheep. Some of the prisoners that we took say that they call use the devils, for we would not turn back. It was on of the best positions the had that we

49

(the Highlanders) took from them. The 77th did not go forward – they stood and let us pass them, and by their standing took the enemy's attention off us altogether.[73]

Writing on the same date, Sergeant William Stathearn of the 42nd informed his wife in Glasgow that:

I was on the colour with Sergeants McNair, Johnstone, and Torrance, four of us, and we all escaped unhurt. We formed in line, and advanced under a heavy fire from the enemy's guns, mounted the hills in our front in gallant style, driving the Russians in disorder down the other side. We cheered and hurraed [sic, hurrahed] and poured volley after volley into the crowd in front of us, until the threw off their packs, cut their accoutrements, cast away their arms, and away they went. By this time, our artillery had come up and commenced pitching shot and shell into the confused mass.[74]

An anonymous sergeant from the 93rd wrote to his family in Inverness:

Shot and shell were playing amongst us, but we had to advance, first through a vineyard, and then through the river Alma. When we reached the side of the river, they opened an awful fire upon us; however, we crossed, and rushed up the banks on the other side, where we were for a moent under cover. But that would not do, so we started and stormed the heights in the face of the most terrible fire that was witnessed by any of the men engaged. The regiment was the first that gained the heights on the left: the carnage was fearful. They had about 50,000 men in an entrenched position, yet these we completely routed in three hours and twenty minutes.[75]

On to Victory

It was now probably about 15.30 hours and the battle was drawing to a close; the French had scaled the cliffs on the Russian left and threatening the Russian centre, focused on the unfinishsed telegraph tower. The British had crossed the river, scaled the Kourgane hills, and were attacking the Great Redan. George Higginson of the Grenadier Guards recalled in his memoirs that he came across Sir George Brown 'absolutely indifferent to the hail of musketry' as the Guards advanced, and drove on to victory, remarking to him,

'Go on! Press on! The day is yours!' Halting for a moment by his side, I noticed a heavy column of the enemy moving rapidly down to reinforce the hesitating troops defending the breast-work, and pointed out our danger to the general … the general replied 'Don't you get excited, young man, I tell you the day is yours; press on!' Sir George, being short of sight, had not seen the approaching column. Our apprehension, however, was speedily relieved, for Turner's Troop of Horse Artillery galloped up on our right, wheeled half-left, and, with their customery speed and accuracy, threw shot and shell into the advancing columns …

Meanwhile our line advanced with firm and impressive regularity until it came within fifty yards of the breast-work. The word 'Charge!' rang out; the line broke into a run, bounding over the parapet, our Grenadiers flung themselves on the few Russians remaining inside. The guns had already been removed by the Russians; only one was left for a trophy… it was evident that our enemy had had enough; the army which Prince Menshikov had led the Emperor to believe held an impregnable position was in full retreat.[76]

Corporal George Senior of the 13th Light Dragoons recounted to his family in Huddersfield how,

just as the Infantry captured the last fortification and drove the Russians back in great disorder, we (the Cavalry brigade) were ordered to advance. We had to come down a very narrow lane, and could only ride in single file. We were obliged to halt, on account of some guns being in the way, something like a quarter of an hour. Had we or could we have charged up the heights when ordered to do so, we might have had an opportunity of charging the retreating Russians; but this delay gave them an opportunity of retreating. We came up to the top of the heights just in time to see them gain another of the heights, something in appearance to those we had then taken.

When we came in sight they opened fire with some heavy guns, and several shells burst but a few yards away from where I was mounted. Our artillery opened fire at them, which must have done great execution, for their shells dropped right amongst them. I had a slight accident, when charging up the heights, by coming in contact with a large bush of underwood. I had no other alternative but to leap my horse at it, when, I suppose, the horse was not strong enough to clear it, caught it with his fore legs, which pitched him on his head. I also came on my head or shako (head dress), and the horse rolled on the top of me, but, thank God, did me no injury, any further than shaking me a little. When I got again on my horse I

51

found it had shook the saddle nearly off, and knocked the bit out of its mouth, which hurt it very much, but that was all. I put things right again, and proceeded up the remainder of the hill, and joined my troop again.

On gaining the top the Infantry were cheering in a most excited way, throwing up their caps and head-dress, and each successive regiment, as they gained the heights, which had cost so many lives and much blood in taking, was echoing from a thousand voices, which must have spread terror amongst the retreating Russians. [77]

After the battle, with night coming on, George walked over his first battlefield:

The Russians were laying [sic, lying] in heaps, some dead and some living, and others had laid down and nothing the matter, but shamming. In one or two instances they got up, when some of the Infantry were going past, and shot them. The English behaved in the kindest manner to them. Two days were employed in burying the dead and carrying the wounded off the field to the hospitals. I went down to one hospital the second day after the engagement, and the most horrible sight met my view – men laying dead who had died under some operation, and others, in all directions, were undergoing amputation of either arm or leg, and heaps of legs and arms of all lengths were scattered in confusion over the place.[78]

A steady stream of wounded picked their way from the heights to the dressing stations set up behind the line as one surgeon relates:

There was besides myself Surgeon [redacted] and we had the entire charge of over 200 wounded comrades. The poor fellows were brought in one after the other, and there they laid waiting for their turn to have balls extracted and limbs amputated. You know what is called 'field day' at the hospitals in town. Perhaps an amputation or two, with half a dozen surgeons to assist if necessary, and a hundred surgical eyes looking on. Can you imagine our field day on the banks of the little river Alma? If God spares me again to see Old England, I shall probably never witness as much practice in my whole lifetime as I saw there in two hours!

The pluck of the soldier no one has yet truly described. They laugh at pain and will scarcely submit to die. It is perfectly marvellous, this triumph of mind over body. If a limb were torn off or crushed at home, you would have them brought in fainting, and in a state of dreadful collapse. Here they come with a dangling arm or riddled elbow, and it's 'now, doctor, be quick if you please – I'm not done for so bad but I can get away back and see!' And many of these brave fellows, with a lump of tow wrung out of cold water wrapped around their stumps, crawled to the rear of the fight, and, with shells bursting round then and balls tearing up sods at their feet, watched the progress of the battle.

I tell you as a solemn truth that I took off the foot oof an officer, captain [redacted], who insisted on being helpd on his horse again, and declared that he could fight now that his 'foot was dressed.' Surgeon [redacted] told him that if he mounted he would burst the ligatures and die on the spot, but for all that he would have returned to the hill if he could have prevailed on anyone body to help him mount.'[79]

Unlike the French who had efficient teams of ambulance mules and *Infirmiers* to collect and tend to the wounded, the British relied on their bandsmen and boys. One bandsman from the 55th Foot wrote to his wife the day after the battle:

Emma, I was knocked down by the shock of a Russian cannon ball; it passed between me and Bainbridge as we were carrying the stretchers for the wounded; it was the awfulest [*sic*] day I ever experienced in my life … We have great numbers of the 55th Regiment seriously wounded. I was busy with the remainder of the band carrying the wounded to the rear, and had to run up under a heavy fire of shells from the Russian batteries. I helped to carry Major Rose and Lieutenant Bisset, or our regiment, to the rear.

Captain Shaw and Major Rose are dead. Major Whimper is wounded in the leg, and Lieutenant Armstrong, of our company, is wounded; and Colonel Warren had one epaulette blown off and slightly grazed on the shoulder, and the adjutant a Bayonet wound. Serjeant Kershall, one arm blown off, and Whitehead, the married man, his fingers blown off. Jack Ross had his water-barrel shot from him by a cannon-ball – a narrow escape. McGarty, that was formerly a drummer, had his left hip blown away … Lake and several of our men have their legs blown off.[80]

Hospital Sergeant Simpson of the 33rd Foot described how:

The Medical Staff halted about half a mile in the rear, and everything was prepared for the reception of the wounded men, and as soon as they came in, poor fellows, the doctor, and his assistants dressed their wounds that night – by 12 o'clock 110 wounded soldiers of the 33rd Regiment were attended to; and you may be sure I was not idle all that time, but gave my assistance to my wounded comrades. I did my best to relieve their wants, for that wa smy charge, and may be sure I did not spare it … I tried to steal about one hour's sleep on the cold ground amongst the wounded and those dying of cholera, for that disease had not left us, so you may guess the rest I had.

21st. Well, as soon as daylight, we got arabas, and got them all removed on board ship by eight o'clock in the morning; then we packed up for further work. We then went to another part of the field and picked up the remainder of our poor fellows, and dressed them, and got them removed by the crews of the men of war ships, who were busy removing the men as fast as they could to the General Hospital, and from thence on board ship. It was nine o'clock at night when we finished, and a sorry task it was, but I did it and was thankful that I was spared to assisst my comrades.

I paced the field of battle in search of those that were missing, and many of my poor mates and dear friends I found to rise no more. My dear brother, to see the wounded Russians! It would have surprised you to see how such a little army could destroy such a number of men; but the English fought like lions, or they neer would have gained such a position as they did. The Russian army was greatly disorganised, and if we had had cavalry to have followed them up, scarcely a man would have escaped us.[81]

Sergeant Simpson was not alone in this conclusion. *Maréchal* de Saint-Arnaud mused, 'If I had several thousand cavalry, the Russian army would have been destroyed or taken prisoner.'*Colonel* Le Breton agreed: 'lack of cavalry' meant the Allies were 'unable to complete our victory.' As it was, the Russians withdrew 'on a strong position, behind another small river, the Loukou, 7 or 8 kilometres from us'.[82]

NOTES
[1] Dr. Cabrol, *Le Maréchal de Saint-Arnaud en Crimée* (Paris: Stock et Tresse et Co., 1895), p.280.
[2] G. Bapst, *Le Maréchal Canrobert, Souvenirs d'un Siecle* (Paris: Librairie Plon, 1912), 7 Édition, Tome 2, pp.242-243.
[3] 'La Bataille d'Alma', *La Presse* (22 Octobre 1854), pp.1-2.
[4] Le General Fay, *Souvenirs de la Guerre de Crimée 1854-1856* (Paris: Berger-Levrault et Cie., 1889), 2e edition, p.49.
[5] L. Guérin, *Histoire de la Derniere Guerre de Russie, 1853-1856* (Paris: Dufour, Mulat et Boulanger, 1858), Tome 1, p.230.
[6] ibid.

[7] C. L De Bazancourt, *L'Éxpedition de Crimée jusqu'a la prise de Sebastopol*, (Paris: Librairie d'Amyot, 1857), Édition special pour l'armée, Tome I, p.200; A. Pascal, M. Brahaut, et Capitaine Sicard, *Histoire de l'Armée et de tous Régiments* (Paris: Dutertre, Librairie-Editeur, 1864), p.210.

[8] Bapst, *Canrobert*, pp.246-247.

[9] 'La Bataille d'Alma', *La Presse* (22 Octobre 1854), pp.1-2.

[10] 'La Bataille d'Alma', *Le Moniteur* (11 Octobre 1854).

[11] 'La Bataille d'Alma', *Le Moniteur de l'Armée* (11 Octobre 1854), p.3; Jacques de la Faye, ed., *Souvenirs du General Lacretelle* (Paris: Emile-Paul, 1907), p.76.

[12] Guérin, *Derniere Guerre de Russie*, Tome 1, p.230.

[13] Bapst, *Canrobert*, p.246.

[14] ibid; Pascal *et al*, *Histoire de l'Armée*, p.210.

[15] ibid.

[16] ibid.

[17] Pascal *et al*, *Histoire de l'Armée*, p.211.

[18] ibid.

[19] 'La Bataille d'Alma', *Le Moniteur* (11 Octobre 1854).

[20] Pascal *et al*, *Histoire de l'Armée*, p.210.

[21] E. Févelat, 'Vieux papiers et Souvenirs d'un Combattant de Crimée', *Societe Archeologique, Historique, et Artistique 'Les Vieux Papiers': Conference 24 Mai 1910*, p.7.

[22] Colebrooke, *Journal*, p. 161; see also Guérin, *Dernier Guerre*, p.231.

[23] Colebrooke, *Journal*, p.164.

[24] Cabrol, *Saint-Arnaud*, p.284.

[25] ibid, pp.282-284; Bapst, *Canrobert*, pp.248-249.

[26] Fay, *Souvenirs*, pp.50-51.

[27] L' Abbe S. Roche, *Un Regiment de Ligne pendant la Guerre d'Orient. Notes et souvenirs d'un officier d'infanterie 1854-1855-1856* (Lyon: Librairie Generale, Catholique et Classique, 1894), p.115.

[28] Fay, *Souvenirs*, p.51.

[29] Commandant Charles Brincourt, 'Lettres du General Brincourt', *Carnet de la Sabretache anee 1923* (1923), pp.77-78.

[30] L. Guérin, *Histoire dernier guerre de Russie, 1853-1856* (Paris: Dufour, Moulat et Boulanger, 1858), vol. 1, pp.237-238.

[31] Brincourt, 'Lettres du General Brincourt', pp.78-79.

[32] Fay, *Souvenirs*, pp.54-55.

[33] E. Joppé, 'La Campagne de Crimée d'apres les letters du Commandant Adrien au Capitaine Ed. Joppé', *Carnet de la Sabretache*, vol. 16 (1907), p.14.

[34] Brincourt, 'Lettres du General Brincout', p.79.

[35] Fay, *Souvenirs*, p.56.

[36] Général Montaudon, *Souvenirs Militiare. Afrique – Crimée – Italie* (Paris: Librairie Charles Delagrave, 1898), p.249; see also Guerin, *Derniere Guerre*, p.241.

[37] Anon, *Guerre d'Orient. Siege de Sebastopol. Historique de service de l'artillerie 1854-1856* (Paris: Berger-Levrault et Fils, 1859), p.63.

[38] Général Rébillot, 'Souvenirs de Crimee', *Revue de Cavalerie, année 1912* (1912), p.259.

[39] Montaudon, *Souvenirs Militires*, p.264.

[40] Capitaine Minart, 'Charles, Alfred, Edouart Minart', p.419.

[41] ibid, p.11.

[42] ibid, p.231.

[43] Anon, *Campagnes de Crimée, d'Italie, d'Afrique, de Chine et de Syrie 1848-1852. Lettres Addressees au Maréchal de Castellane* (Paris: E. Plon, Nourrit et Cie., 1898), pp.103-104. Letter 66: Colonel Cler to Maréchal de Castellane.

[44] ibid, pp.105-106.

[45] Roche, *Un Regiment de Ligne*, p.77.

[46] Anon, Campagne de Crimée …, pp.105-106.

[47] Fay, *Souvenirs*, p.57.

[48] Commandant Devanlay, 'Lettres de Crimée du Général Breton, 2e partie', *Carnet de la Sabretache*, vol. 18 (1909), p.22.

[49] G. B. McClellan, *Reminiscences of an Officer of Zouaves* (New York: D. Appleton & Co, 1860), pp.180-181.

[50] 'Letter from a Serjeant in the 33rd Regiment', *Leeds Intelligencer* (30 December 1854), p.11.

[51] 'The Battle of the Alma', *Leeds Mercury* (14 October 1854).

[52] 'The Battle of the Alma: Letter from a Leeds Soldier', *Leeds Mercury* (21 October 1854).

[53] Charles Usherwood, *Service Journal*.

[54] 'Letter from a Leeds Soldier', *Leeds Mercury* (16 December 1854).

[55] Usherwood, *Service Journal*.

[56] 'Letters from the Crimea to Wakefield', *Wakefield Journal & Examiner* (29 December 1854).

[57] 'The Battle of the Alma', *Leeds Mercury* (14 October 1854).

[58] Probably Colour Sergeant William Mason, who is listed as being wounded at the Alma.

[59] Probably Colour Sergeant George Spence, who is listed as being wounded at the Alma; his account of the Alma was published in the *Leeds Mercury* 21 October 1854 and is reproduced later.

[60] Probably Lieutenant C M Sirree 'wounded severely' at the Alma: according to Colour Sergeant George Spence, he was wounded three times 'in the belly' and died from his wounds.

[61] Probably Colour Sergeant William Sugden, who is listed as being wounded at the Alma.

[62] Probably Ensign J. J. Greenwood, wounded in the stomach at the Alma.

[63] 'The Battle of the Alma', *Leeds Mercury* (14 October 1854).

[64] 'Letter from a Serjeant in the 33rd Regiment', *Leeds Intelligencer* (30 December 1854), p.11.

[65] Probably Private James McDonald who is recorded as being killed at the Alma.

[66] 'The Battle of the Alma', *Leeds Mercury* (14 October 1854).

[67] 'Incidents of the War. Death of Sir W. Young', *Norfolk News* (4 November 1854), p.3.

[68] 'Private letters from the camp before Sebastopol', *Wakefield Journal & Examiner* (10 November 1854). W. H. Floyd died from his wounds, aged twenty-nine, on 26 May 1856 in Bristol.

[69] Usherwood, *Service Journal*.

[70] 'A Young Guardsman at Alma', *Staffordshire Sentinel* (21 October 1854), p.2.

[71] 'A Sergeant's Letter from the Camp Near Sebastopol', *Daily News* (26 October 1854).

[72] Sir J. D. Astley, *Fifty years of my Life, in the World of Sport, at Home and Abroad* (London: Hurst & Blackett Ltd., 1894), vol. I, pp.213-216.

[73] 'Letters from the Field of Alma. A Highlander's Letter' *Paisley Herald and Renfrewshire Advertiser* (21 October 1854), p.6.

[74] 'The Gallant Forty-Second', *Paisley Herald and Renfrewshire Advertiser* (21 October 1854), p.6.

[75] 'Private Letters from Alma', *John O'Groats Journal* (20 October 1854), p.2.

[76] General Sir. G Higginson, *Seventy-One years of a Guardsman's Life* (London: Smith, Elder & Co., 1916), pp.152-153.

[77] 'Letter from a Huddersfield man in the Cavalry Brigade in the Crimea', *The Huddersfield Chronicle* (28 October 1854), np.

[78] ibid.

[79] 'A surgeon's letters from Alma Hills', *Daily News* (27 OCtober 1854), p.7.

[80] 'Letters from the Field of Alma. 55th Regiment', *Paisley Herald and Renfrewshire Advertiser* (21 October 1854), p.6.

[81] 'Letter from a Serjeant in the 33rd Regiment', *Leeds Intelligencer* (30 December 1854), p.11.

[82] Devanlay, 'General Breton, 2e partie', p.25.

Chapter 3

March on Sebastopol

After success on the Alma, the Allies spent three days on the battlefield collecting their wounded and burying the dead, a process the French had completed by 22 September. Once again, the French were left waiting for their Allies, and the clock was ticking on Sebastopol. *Capitaine* Fay reported the 'English are again not ready... just as at Old Fort' whilst Saint-Arnaud wrote in his journal for 22 September 'How slow our movements are! One cannot make war by being nice.'[1] *Lieutenant* Cullet (*20e Légère*) caustically wrote that:

> The army was impatient to continue on its way. Everyone understood that if we gave the enemy time they would strengthen their new position and we would lose all the advantages we had gained from the first victory. Alas! we must get used to the slowness of our allies. God forbid if we do not do justice to the eminent qualities of the British army, as to their solidity and cold bravery; but it is impossible not to see that we lost, by their fault at Old Fort, two days when the success of the campaign could depend on the rapidity of our movements. At the Alma, their four-hour delay made the execution of the *Maréchal's* plan impossible.
>
> The days of the 21st and 22nd, lost on Alma battlefield, allowed them [the Russians] time to recuperate and to select a new position; happy if, later, these unfortunate delays our allies had caused, had not ended in far more dire consequences.[2]

Lord Raglan, however, was having reservations about the 'grand raid' as conceived by Sir James Graham and the Duke of Newcastle. He also lacked confidence in his chief engineer, Tylden. As a result, Sir John Burgoyne was called upon. Burgoyne had been 'horrified' at the idea of the landing close to Sebastopol and it was he who had urged finding a landing site further away from the city. In fact, Burgoyne was opposed to the whole operation against Sebastopol: 'the plan struck him to as 'impracticable.'[3]

After the Alma, Raglan – like Saint-Arnaud – had wanted to quickly assault the forts to the north of the city, following the concept of the 'grand raid,' but Burgoyne advised a formal investment and siege, thus clashing with his political superiors in London and Paris.[4]

The French chief engineer, *général* Bizot, also had reservations about taking Sebastopol by *coup de main*, and he too advised a formal siege, an idea which was approved of by Raglan and he advised London as such.[5] *Général* Canrobert records that on the afternoon of 22 September 'Sir John Burgoyne came to Lord Raglan and proposed not to attack Sebastopol from the north side' and instead proposed attacking from the relatively undefended south.[6] *Général* Bizot, however, 'had already raised the same idea the day before the battle in a letter to *Maréchal* Vaillant [the Minister of War]'.[7] This plan, however, was opposed by the French commander and his generals. Lying ill on a couch *Maréchal* de Saint-Arnaud

> received the English general [Burgoyne] … naturally, general Bizot supported the proposal of his English colleague. The others were all formally opposed, particularly Prince Napoléon. 'The works on the north side had not existed before we landed' he said, 'they could therefore present little danger; the Russian army is demoralised after their defeat; it is absurd not to attack immediately.'[8]

General Sir George Cathcart was of a similar opinion as Prince Napoléon about the defences of Sebastopol, describing those around the south side as 'something like a low park wall, not in good repair.'[9] He later bragged 'I could walk into it with scarcely the loss of a man.'[10] Admiral Sir Edmund Lyons also urged an immediate assault, suggesting to do so would cost less than 500 men.[11] The decision was all the more controversial because the city was garrisoned by only 16,000 men, who in the opinion of the Russian commander, Admiral Kornilov, would have been unable to defend the city against the Allies if they had assaulted immediately.[12]

On 23 September, at the break of day, a French reconnaissance was directed along the coast towards the northern side of Sevastopol:

> It observed Fort Constantine and the works in the surrounding area, covering the mouth of the Belbec; [because of them] there would be an impossibility of establishing on this point the depots of the

trenches and the disembarkation of the materiel for the siege would be difficult and dangerous.[13]

In other words, the French were now concerned over the strength of the fortifications and that their presence would compromise their ability to invest the city. Admiral Sir Edmund Lyons thought that Saint-Arnaud was increasingly concerned about the Russians making a stand on the Belbec (including the defences which commanded the mouth of the river) and the strength of a large Star Fort to the north of the city which was supported by three earth redoubts and a chain of defences. Lyons believed that they could be taken by *coup de main*.[14] Therefore, the decision of the Allies, at the suggestion of John Burgoyne, to commit to a formal siege of the city – rather than by an immediate assault – was taken.[15]

The decision to invest the south side of the city, rather than the north side as originally proposed by Burgoyne and Bizot, was one which was therefore forced upon the Allies. A naval reconnaissance of Sebastopol also revealed that the harbour had been blocked rendering it useless as a landing-ground and forcing any naval attackers out to sea. Saint-Arnaud wrote on the morning of 24 September:

> The Russians have committed an act of desperation which shows how beaten and terrified they are. They have blocked the entrance to Sebastopol by sinking three of their large ships and two of their frigates; it is the beginning of La Moscowa [the Battle of Moscow in 1812]. This bothers me a lot, because it forces me to change my plans of attack, and take the attack to the south, the side of Balaklava.[16]

Saint-Arnaud was obliged to march around Sebastopol, to attack the south side of the city. In the evening he confided that: 'We march on Balaklava; I will bivouac on the Tchernaya.'[17] This, however, allowed the Russians time to reinforce their garrison and under the tutelage of the skilled Todleben, and build imposing defences on the south side of the city. The formal siege would open 17 October 1854.[18]

The Allies Advance
Cholera had once again broken out amongst the Allied armies; *capitaine* Adrien (*6e de Ligne*) notes that 'The Colonel Tabouriech, of the *3e Zouaves*, Monsieur Michel, surgeon-major of the *7e Leger* and three other officers of that regiment died from this terrible illness.'[19] The two armies had to move to find clean water; the French army renewed its march on 23 September, toward the River Katcha. Adrien continues:

The army left the heights of the Alma and bivouacked on the heights of the Katcha. This position is parallel to the Alma. We thought it would be defended as [at] the Alma, but the Russians have had enough ...

In passing the village on the Belbeck, we made a *razzia* for tomatoes, grapes and vegetables. I assure you they were needed; for ever since we have been here the commissariat feeds us very badly, and sometimes not at all.[20]

Colour Sergeant Davis agreed with *capitaine* Adrien, about the ability of the commissariat of both armies, even this early on in the campaign, to supply them with rations:

On the 23rd we continued our onward march to Sebastopol. This evening (Sept. 23) we covered nine miles, to just such another position as the Russians had held at the Alma, lofty hills, with a pretty considerable river and a village at their base. At this place we wrongly thought they would have made another effort to stay our progress. But not so. They burned down the village, and every place likely to give us shelter, and then made themselves very scarce indeed. At this place they must have halted and collected their scattered army, remaining all night and moving off in the morning. Here likewise, on the 23rd we halted for the night. Here I saw the greatest profusion of grapes I ever beheld; many acres of splendid vineyards.

Then were told before being dismissed to take as many as would do us good. The vineyards were beyond the river, and as soon as the men were dismissed, there followed one of the most determined charges ever performed by British soldiers. Down the hill, and right through the river they went, thousands trying for first place – in water up to their knees, and if it had been up to their chins it would have been all the same. They soon returned loaded with the finest grapes I ever saw.[21]

Whilst out foraging, French troops came across a 'fine villa, a spacious house, well laid-out, ornamented with all the furniture of our best and richest French houses.' It was apparently the summer residence of a Russian general but which soon fell to axe and bayonet as Allied soldiers merrily looted it, stripping pictures from the walls and hacking the furniture into fire wood.[22] One anonymous officer of the 20th Foot thought the house 'very pretty' and 'elegantly furnished' but by the time he arrived, pieces [of furniture] were strewn about in every direction. Being on Picket, I took a walk through the grounds and indulged cautiously in some delicious fruit, although it is hard to resist the tempting grapes, which are everywhere most abundant and excellent. I could not carry off the piano from the chateau, so contended myself with the second volume of a French novel, which sufficed to pass an hour of this idle day.[23]

The same officer left a graphic account of the march in a letter to friends:

Each man carries everything he possesses. We are allowed no tents and no baggage-waggons, so you may imagine the difficulty and delay of moving an army of this description. At the end of a march each man is glad to hunt for wood, fill his little water barrel (every officer and man carries one), cook his rations, and get to sleep till daylight, should he be fortunate enough not to be for picket or have night surprise from the Cossacks. We have had three; the first was rather exciting. We heard exchange of shot with our outposts, and immediately our division [the fourth] was silently ordered to stand to their arms and extinguish all fires. We were behind the main body of the army some distance, and thought our division was to have the glory of a fight all to ourselves, but unfortunately it all passed off quietly.[24]

On the morning of the march, the 63rd Foot, which had missed the battle of the Alma because of being in the rear guard, once again found itself bringing up the rear, as Lieutenant Newenham relates:

The 4th Division which did not leave till some hours after the rest. We then moved on in battle order to the Katcha River where we again joined the rest of the Army. When we were all settled I went and had a good bath in the River and got lots of grapes. They were very refreshing after a long dusty march.

The next morning the whole Army marched together. It was a magnificent sight. It was a hard hot march over such very deep and steep valleys. At last we crossed the Belbeck, and then the poor 63rd. came in for it again. The whole Regiment on Patrol and Outpost duty, back at the other side of the river.

We were then called in the next morning and just as we thought we were to have a little quiet we were sent across the River and up the hills again and spread out as rear guard. The rest of our Division remaining quietly where they were. The worst of it was Genl.

Torrens never gave us time to get anything to eat and our meal has been often left on the ground, without even having time to be cut up, by his bad management. The coffee was served out green so the poor men had to roast it the best way they could. I think the men lived on nothing but biscuits and water & their ration of rum and any grapes they could find.[25]

Menchikoff's Baggage

The British Heavy Brigade of cavalry landed at the Katcha on 24 September in a miserable state: the 1st Royals had lost 150 horses and the Inniskillings more than seventy during the sea crossing from Varna. The Scots Greys were incapacitated through sickness with 120 men (nearly half the effective strength) suffering from diarrhoea (which could and did prove fatal) as well as several fatal cases of cholera. To make matters worse, they were without their tents, and as it had rained overnight night they were 'soaked to the skin.'[26]

The following day the Heavy Brigade joined the army and the pursuit of the Russian rear guard. At around 11.30 hours they stumbled across the Russians at Mackenzie's Farm, and caught the Russians by surprise. Captain Nolan immediately wanted to attack and requested permission for Captain Maude's Troop RHA to come to the front, but Raglan declined the request 'for fear of exposing our artillery without sufficient support.' During this delay, the Russians had recovered from their surprise and 'advanced at the trot' against the single troop of the 8th Hussars commanded by Captain Chetwode and two of Captain Maude's guns. Luckily, the Earl of Lucan led the main cavalry force out into the open whilst the remainder of Maude's guns were galloped forward 'unlimbered and fired.'

The British cavalry prepared to attack the Russians, but at the last moment the latter veered off, unmasking an infantry battalion in square, which opened fire. Lucan ordered the cavalry to break off their attack and Maude's guns to open fire on the infantry; the Scots Greys were pushed forward in skirmish order with one troop dismounted, to drive off the Russian infantry. The Russians were pursued for over a mile by the 17th Lancers; by Nolan's estimation they captured 'twenty-two waggons and horses and well as Prince Menschikoff's fine carriage and all his baggage.'[27]

One private in the Scots Greys wrote:

We floundered (in the sense of the word) for about six hours through brushwood and dwarf oak, having to go for miles in single files. Our regiment was dismounted, when the advance guard came on the rear guard of a large force of Russians. *We* did not know what was the matter, but received the word to mount and get out of the wood as far as we could: off we went at a gallop, following each other for about three miles, when we came to a plain, and saw the remains of a very recent encampment, the fires still burning, and a few heavy carriages over turned on the side of the road. We very naturally supposed we were about to be engaged at once, but we got up and found the enemy had bolted, leaving only a few stragglers, and a quantity of baggage and ammunition which we captured. My troop was ordered to dismount, and sent into the wood on the road side to examine if any of them were hidden, and I never had such a job in my life-time; a part of us lost our way, and had to beat about through a dense wood of dwarf oak for nearly two hours, encumbered with our big caps, two days provisions, sword, spurs, and the scales of our coats, besides our carbines, no joke of a load for a rifleman; however, we managed to get to our horses again and then bivouacked in the valley of the Blackwater.[28]

One officer of the Guards remembered seeing,

the Scots Greys and some of our artillery in advance...where they intercepted a Russian army of some 15,000 men and a large convoy of provisions and ammunition. The party of Greys was only twenty strong, but so cowd were the Russians and taken by surprise, that half their army cut off … Every waggon [sic] was destroyed, the flour given up to the our men, powder scattered, cartridges destroyed, camp equipments thrown over the precipices.[29]

Instead having the foresight to keep the captured wagons and provisions, Colour-Sergeant Davis of the Grenadier Guards wrote that,

what we did not use we destroyed, waggons and all. We amused ourselves by rolling them headlong down from a high and rugged precipice, and their smash at the bottom was as like thunder.[30]

William Pearson of the 4th Light Dragoons suggests that 'about 5p.m. [we] came upon a Cossack barracks':

The surprise was complete. For our want of cavalry, the men generally escaped, but we took their ammunition and stores of every description. The buildings were sacked, and soon fires of mahogany chests of drawers, sofas, chairs and tables, blazed upon the plain.

The men doze in easy chairs till midnight, when, the order to move being give, they were pitched into the flames, the barracks fired, and off we went.[31]

Lieutenant Newenham of the 63rd continues his narrative:

Our Division marched the next morning thro' the wood … I was on Baggage Guard that day. How the poor men fell out and died by the road side. Some got buried and some did not. It was a dreadful march. We at last arrived at another river, I believe in English it is called the Black River, one march from Sevastopol. The French were encamped close to us.

There was rather an amusing scene took place, after the arms were piled and the men at work getting their dinners and water and foraging for what they could get. Both French and English. There was an alarm of Cossacks, such running and tumbling over each other, but all were under arms in a minute, it soon turned out to be a false alarm.

It was caused as follows: at a farmhouse a French and English soldier were running after the same hen, the Englishman got blown and the French was on the point of catching the hen, when the Englishman in despair shouted our 'Cossack! Cossack!!' Away ran the Francais giving the alarm and the Anglais got the chicken.[32]

The British camped on the banks of the River Tchernaya for the night and on the morning of 26 September two regiments from the Light Brigade were detached under the Earl of Cardigan to 'intercept a convoy making its way to Sebastopol.' Cardigan, however, was unable to intercept the Russians because of the 'totally unfit state [of] the English Troop Horse.' They were so weak that 'they can hardly raise a Canter' despite having done any actual real work; The horses 'soon dropped down' from exhaustion and the pursuit of the convoy called off.[33]

Death of Saint-Arnaud

Although more than decade younger than Lord Raglan, fifty-three year old *Maréchal* de Saint-Arnaud was becoming increasingly frail. He was suffering from rheumatic heart disease, which frequently left him exhausted, with chest pains, night sweats and variable energy levels. His personal physician, Dr Cabrol, reported that on 23 September 'the health of the *Maréchal* [which] was stable during the preceding days' had suddenly turned for the worse: 'very weak, very tired, and experiencing some disturbances in the bowels.'[34]

That night his condition deteriorated, but the following morning, he was able to mount his favourite horse, Isabelle, and lead his army on its march toward the Belbek.[35] By the evening of 24 September he had taken a turn for the worse again and was diagnosed as having contracted cholera. Despite knowing that the disease could prove fatal, Saint-Arnaud faced it with 'complete calm and strong courage.' The knowledge that the man who held the 'confidence and admiration of the whole army' was dying caused shock in the French army: 'the most profound sadness' coming after the triumph of the Alma.[36]

On 26 September, command of the French army was transferred to *général* François Certain Canrobert, who had held a dormant commission from Napoléon III to take command of the army in case of the death of Saint-Arnaud. One of the last officers to see him was *lieutenant* Coste (*3e Genie*):

> In front of his tent, Spahis of the Escort, had placed their long red cloaks on the ground. On this carpet, that was on the grass like a blood stain, the *Maréchal*, in grand uniform, was lying full length, immobile, eyes closed, his face as pale as the cadavers on the battlefield. Several more mounted a Guard of Honour around him.[37]

Saint-Arnaud embarked upon the *Berthollet*, with his personal staff, his physician and chaplain (*Abbé* Parabère) for France. He died at 15.00 hours on 29 September. Dr Cabrol had administered a sedative around 13.00 hours and the *Maréchal* died 'sweetly, without pain.' Before lapsing into unconsciousness, his final words were:

> Ah! My god, pardon me. You bid me come. I obey. I have nothing to say; I've seen my wife, poor Louise![38]

Opening the Trenches

The Allies set up camp on the heights surrounding Sebastopol, on the Chersonese Plateau. The French to the west, secured on their harbour at Kamiesch, the British on the east, bringing supplies up from Balaklava. The French were to attack the west side of the city, the British the east. The British attacks were divided into 'left' (i.e. west) and 'right' attack, separated by the Woronzoroff Road, which ran in deep defile leading to the inner (Man of War) harbour.

Whilst Lord Raglan had to send all four of his infantry divisions down to the trenches, *général* Canrobert elected to divide his force: *général* Forey was given command of the *3e* and *4e Divisions* charged with the duties of the siege whilst *général* Bosquet with *1e* and *2e*

Division was to form the 'Army of Observation', camped on the Inkerman Heights, to protect the Allies' rear.

The British Cavalry Division, the 93rd Highlanders, a battalion of Royal Marines and several batteries of heavy artillery were despatched to defend Balaklava. The French were able to bring up considerable reinforcements: The *5e Division* (*général* Lavaillant – *1e* and *2e Régiments Legion Étrangère; 5e Legere; 21e, 42e, 46e de Ligne*) together with the *4e Chasseurs d'Afrique* (and the remainder of the *1e Regiment*) and the *1e Hussards* which landed on 4 October. Lord Raglan established his Head Quarters in an abandoned farmhouse on the uplands, where he also ensconced his staff. *Général* Canrobert, in direct contrast, lived in a tent, pitched in the centre of his army sharing the lot of his men.

From the camp of the Brigade of Guards, Colour-Sergeant Davis described the uplands around Sebastopol as 'a perfect garden of Eden':

> We are bivouacked just out of harm's way, over a hill from Sebastopol, and where the Russians cannot see one jot of our operations, which must vex them sadly. They are upon a corner of the board, and have not a move left. We have them hemmed in on all sides. They keep shelling us and shotting us, not a shot of which we have returned.[39]

Colour-Sergeant Thomas Bairstow writing to his family at home in Queenshead, Halifax opined that,

> the encampment of the allies occupies more ground than I anticipated. You might imagine Halifax and Bradford, the two extremes of our boundaries, with several hills between, forming positions for besiegers or besieged of great strength, but I am happy to say that our army is in possession of the whole of the country above described, which reflects great credit and discretion on the choosers of the same.[40]

Lieutenant Newenham, of the 63rd had more misgivings:

> I don't advise a siege at all, one is continually in the trenches either as a guard or working party, and I don't see any pleasure in lying in a dirty ditch for 24 hours being fired at without having a chance to return it.[41]

Service in the trenches was arduous, nerve-wracking, hard work, providing both digging and covering parties. The troops silently defiled into the trenches at dusk each day and were relieved at 08.00 hours the following morning. *Sergent-major* Alfred Minart relates:

> All our trenches are made, and the batteries armed … Our service is very pitiable, you have to be awake both day and night, and take the guard in the trenches. For the man on watch, the Russians send quantities of shells, of 60 and even 80 pounds. The other day, one of these projectiles fell right on us, I was able to jump out of its way and warn my captain who was sheltering behind some rocks. The shell exploded before reaching us, but the fragments passed above our heads. To give you an idea of this inferno, I'll tell you, the Russians fired more than 2,000 cannon shots… There have been many killed and perhaps more wounded, because the soil is very rocky, and the stones wound more than the shell fragments.[42]

One anonymous British cavalry officer relates how even in early October the weather was beginning to turn and rations were already become scarce:

> I landed with what clothes I stood in (a hussar jacket and trousers, and Busby, full dress in fact), my horse was got ashore, and off I started for my regiment … The officers had a room in a deserted cottage, and it was funny to see an honourable subaltern and his captain, eating with gusto a piece of ration pork, and washing it done [*sic*, down] with some coffee water out of a broken pannikin, cautioning me at the same time that I was not to fancy that the fellows in camp lived nearly half so well, which I afterwards found to be true enough …
>
> We bivouac in the open air, and as for eating, I have plenty of biscuit, and occasionally am lucky enough to get a piece of meat, but, for the charity of my neighbours, however, I must eat it raw, as I have no cooking utensils, no drinking cup, no plate. I generally eat off a piece of deal, or the lid of a tin, if lucky; in fact I am pretty near starving. One thing we have in plenty, grapes; there are hundreds of vineyards, and we gorge all day long, in spite of cholera, which carried off some fort or fifty daily – in fact it is decimating us. My regiment is a prefect skeleton.
>
> They days are very hot; the nights are very, very cold, with the heaviest dews I ever saw. We lie down in boots and spurts, and dress jackets, covered with a cloak, not to sleep for it is too cold for that, but to rest. … The regiment is so weak that all our servants are put in the ranks; a lucky thing for me, as this morning my servant

brought back a hen, which he had plundered when on patrol. By the way, we have plundered the country awfully, and the French have in addition destroyed everything they could not carry off. Our patrols sweep the valleys and bring in everything eatable, but they are now quite bare.[43]

Over-work, sleeping in the open air and lack of food and decent clothing led to the men falling sick but already the medical supplies were proving insufficient:

The cholera is still raging, the last account I heard was that forty-five had died that day, but really the wonder is that any are left alive. We (that is the men and regimental officers) are either starved, or east food against which our stomachs turn, and in order to live we are obliged to eat loads of grapes from the vineyards close at hand. The days are very hot, the nights are very cold, and our clothing consists of one suit on our backs, the dew wets us through every night, just like rain.

When taken ill we have no medicines, no place to be nursed in, no one to care a straw about us, no place to mense mortality has made and invariably so, everyone more or less callous. In fact, people taken ill may recover, but by a sort of miracle. One officer of the 77th, Crofton, a man I knew, died in a ditch by the road-side, with as little ceremony as a dog. When the officers are so badly off, I leave you to guess how the men are. I am myself so weak from diarrhoea that I can hardly sit on horse-back, indeed, I am quite prepared to see it turn to cholera, as I cannot stop it. I feel low spirited… and I am in bad condition to resist disease. I went to the General Hospital yesterday, and the horrible sight of so many dying of cholera, and all suffering horribly, quite stunned me. The surgeons have all along done their duty well, and have died in heaps.[44]

The French were also beginning to suffer from exhaustion and erratic supplies:

The work and the trench guards becomes increasingly distressing, officers and soldiers on duty two or three consecutive nights. Even with reinforcements, our work is not reduced; the trenches have a large front to guard and the workers are very numerous. Our food does not improve, the lack of bread is cruelly felt; one can go into Kamiesch and find a poor wine at three francs per litre, but the prices are not affordable.[45]

Both the British and French armies formed volunteer units of 'sharp shooters' or 'Francs-Tireurs' in October 1854, to carry out trench raids and to pick-off Russian gunners in their batteries. The French formed two hand-picked companies of 'Francs-Tireurs' – who became known amongst the French army as 'Les Enfants Perdus' ('the lost children' or 'children of the lost/dammed') – commanded by one capitaine, one lieutenant, two sous-lieutenants, forty-eight NCOs and 150 corporals and privates drawn from the regiments of Zouaves and battalions of Chasseurs à Pied, armed with rifles and sword bayonets.[46]

A further three companies were formed from hand-picked regiments of the Line in December.[47] The British sharpshooters were formed from ten men chosen from each battalion, commanded by a lieutenant and captain, on rotation. Charles Usherwood notes in his journal:

> In order to assist the operations more fully the Commander in Chief adopted a voluntary measure consisting of sharpshooters of 10 men from each Regiment of the various Divisions, to be under charge of 1 Captain and 2 Subs and Non Comd. Officer from each corps, with directions that each man should select the spot that suits him best, and be guided only in that choice upon the cover it may give him of an effectual fire on the embrasures; Captain Bright of the 19th Foot having charge of the sharpshooters from the Light Division.[48]

One Zouave who volunteered as a 'Franc Tireur' informed his parents that:

> I am almost like a poacher! I go out every day to shoot Russians! This is the way we do it: As early as two in the morning, our toilette completed – and that of a Zouave is not long – we leave, carrying with us ammunition, and one or two biscuits. Arriving in the entrenchments we take a sandbag, a spade, and a pickaxe; then at a signal, we leap from the parapets with the rapidity of deer, and establish our homes close to the forts.
>
> There we dig a hole, a sort of warren to hid ourselves in. We place our [sand] bags to protect us, and our residence is then completed. We remain in these holes all the day, and it is not until night is rather advanced that we are permitted to leave them. This we often do amidst a shower of grape-shot. You will ask me, dear father, what we do in the holes all day? Very good work, I assure you.
>
> We fire almost as fast as we can load, and every discharge demolishes a Russian artilleryman. The other day two officers climbed up a large pole on the summit of a tower opposite my

lodgings, and they began to examine our works. With two shots I brought them both down. Then a storm of balls, shells and grapeshot was directed against us; but, happily, we were so near the forts that it passed over our heads without touching any of us.[49]

One British officer noted some of the 'Tricks of the Zouaves':

At night, we have had glorious salvos, caused, it is said, by witty and adventurous Zouaves. Two of them go out on an expedition, with five or six muskets strapped to their backs. As it is quite dark, they are enabled to creep round the Russian sentries and get close to the walls, when they, as rapidly as possible fire their weapons. Immediately the Russian artillerymen fly to their guns, a storming is expected and off goes every gun ... As soon as the Zouaves have alarmed one extremity, they rush to the other, and again rapid musketry is heard and again the artillery set to work ... whereas the two Zouaves have quietly retreated ... and have a hearty laugh with their comrades.[50]

The Siege Opens

By the first week of October, the Allies had established their siege batteries: the French had fifty-three guns and the British seventy-three in their batteries. The main French battery was established on 'Mont Rudolph' armed with forty-nine guns directed towards the 'Bastion Central'. The British established two principal batteries; one 'Chapman's Battery' on the 'Green Hill' (forty-one guns) directed towards the Redan whilst twenty-six guns were mounted in 'Gordon's Attack'. In addition were two batteries mounting the experimental Lancaster Guns.[51]

At dawn on 17 October, the first bombardment of Sebastopol commenced, from land and sea as Gunner Edwin Peat of Barnsley told his sister:

We commenced the Siege of Sebastopol at 6a.m. on the 17th ult. Our company fired the first shot, and I was one of the number, and, believe me, dear sister, there was never a fire opened on an enemy as that they opened on us! They fired thirty guns to our one, and sent out works to the very devil. They at home may take about the Russians as they like, but they can do their work well. Shot and shell came in all directions. I will leave you to guess if I was not glad when my twelve hours were up (that is the time we are relieved), for I thought they would have slaughtered every one of us before that

70

time, but I am happy to say that our company did not lose a single man, nor even had one hurt. Were we not fortunate? We are the luckiest company, as yet, as there is not a company of artillery here but what has got some men killed or wounded. There is not half sufficient artillerymen here, as we have all the fighting to do. At present we have nothing to do but mind our guns, and that is one great advantage. The infantry are supplying us with what we require, such as shot, shell, &c., so that we can manage to keep close under cover, as I assure you it is very dangerous being exposed to shot and shells larger than your head. I have seen several poor fellows blown to pieces while in the act of bringing us what we require to the guns.

They will never take Sebastopol with artillery. It is the strongest fortress in the world. It is my opinion that they have got guns mounted in every window, for the constant fire they keep up is terrific. We have tried every means with artillery. We have set it on fire several times, but they put it out, and the only way it can be taken is by storming it, - that is by cold steel, the bayonet, and it is expected that will be done in the course of a week.[52]

Colonel Le Breton (*74e de Ligne*) was the field officer in command of the French trenches on 17 October. He wrote to his wife that:

It is painful to admit, but our artillery, though great, was not enough. After an hour and a half of rolling fire, two of our small powder stores were blown up by the effect of Russian bombs and our batteries were reduced to silence.

The English alone, whose attack is on the other front from ours, continued to fire until nightfall, with minimal superiority, but still appreciable … All this infernal fracas of cannon balls, of shells, of bombs, perfectly respects me. I have not yet been wounded. It is our first duty, with these preliminaries of the siege, to protect our troops from the effects of artillery, but even then, we would have lost nothing but the insignificant losses in the double explosion of our magazines.

Our losses are around a hundred men killed our wounded and twenty-five in the attack on the right, where I am charged with commanding a battalion of *Zouaves*, half a battalion of chasseurs, and a battalion each of the *7e*, the *19e* and *26e Légère*. The Russians saw we had ceased-fire, and attempted a sortie, which was vigorously repulsed. Then the Navy bombarded two forts for around two hours, enormously noisy, but doing little damage.[53]

From onboard the *Montebello*, Henri-Marie-Dieudonné Garreau described the bombardment by the Allied fleets:

> Today there commenced the fire of the batteries of the siege and, to make a useful diversion, the squadron went to bombard the forts at the entrance to Sebastopol and cannonaded them for around five hours. We were at a distance of more than 2,000 metres, and in consequence, our shots did no more harm than those of the enemy ... We had not begun against these immense stone batteries, however when two magazines exploded. On our side, we have had insignificant damage. The *Montebello* and the *Charlemagne* arrived first and during a half hour we alone received the fire of the enemy. However, we have lost 5 men killed and 21 wounded. It is hoped we have hurt them more. There were around 26 ships engaged: 14 French, 10 English and 2 Turkish. The fire commenced at one o'clock and did not cease until night.[54]

Staff officer Henri de Bouillé was far more upbeat as to the results of the first bombardment:

> The Russians have a formidable artillery, against which we will have a great difficulty in resisting; the fleet made a grand demonstration, but with little success. However we have achieved some success; two Russian batteries, in part, have been destroyed. Every day we construct new batteries and sap closer to the city. The Russians attempt every night sorties against our works and batteries ... Today [22 October] at three o'clock in the morning, a Russian officer, with 120 volunteers, marching on foot, so as not to be heard, is spotted near a mortar battery, and fell upon the gunners, who were working there to repair the battery. The Russians hoped to spike the guns, but the gunners, to the number of 30, saluted them with their carbines, charged the Russians and, aided by a company of the *74e de Ligne*, routed them, after killing ten men and wounded 5 or 6 others, who were retrieved the following day. The Russian officer was wounded by a gun shot to the head, a ball in the leg and had his stomach opened by a sword-bayonet. He died in the morning ...
>
> With us, since the commencement of the siege, have had lost 680 men killed or wounded: not many of them officers. However, on the 19th, when I was on trench duty, general d'Aurelles had two captains killed: one had his head taken off by a cannon ball and the other was cut in half.[55]

Russian Sorties

In order to disrupt the Allied siege operations, the Russians continually probed their defences, especially the weak-spot around the British base at Balaklava. Captain Louis Edward Nolan's journal reveals just how tiring – and frequent – these duties were:

> 3d October Tuesday. A Patrole [*sic*] of the Scots Greys report the advance of a Russian Army into the Valley of the Tshnaya [*sic*, Tchernaya][.] No notice whatever taken of them or their movements[.]
> 4th Wednesday
> Rode out to the extreme right on a Reconnaissance with Genl. Airey & Sir De Lacy Evans.[56]

Général Canrobert reported on 6 October that: 'At the point of day, an enemy reconnaissance, of around 3,000 men and 1,600 or 1,800 cavalry, supported by two batteries of horse artillery' approached the British positions; the British artillery 'fired several shells' into the Russians, which caused them to retire.[57]

The 4th Dragoon Guards and the Scots Greys were surprised by a Russian reconnaissance in force early in the morning of 7 October. Two regiments of Hussars, a regiment of infantry and 'an untold number of Cossacks' crossed the Tracktir Brigade and attacked the British pickets, taking three members of the 4th Dragoon Guards prisoner.

The alarm was raised and 'large detachments of … Greys and Dragoons were sent out, accompanied by two troops of Horse Artillery. Among them was Captain Maude's Troop of horse artillery,' which opened fire on the Russian Hussars, forcing them to make a 'sudden retreat.' For 'some unknown reason' the British cavalry did not pursue. A second 'light skirmish' took place in the evening when Cossacks again probed the pickets of the Greys and 4th Dragoon Guards.[58] Nolan records:

> Saturday the 7th Octr
> I was awoke at 6 o'clock AM by a report by Mr Woomwell [*sic*, Wombwell] 17th Lancers that the Russian Army had forced our Picquets in the [Tchernaya] Valley & were marching in great force on Balaklava.[59]

This was a reconnaissance in force, which had surprised a patrol of the 4th Dragoon Guards under Cornet Edward Fisher Rowe, and drove them in killing two men and taking a third prisoner. They were thus able to cross the Tchernaya and advance toward Balaklava. Captain Nolan received orders that 'should the attack be pushed home' for the 93rd Highlanders under Sir Colin Campbell, to retire from the village of Kadikoi to 'the conical hill in the gorge' [Canrobert's Hill]. The Cavalry Division was ordered to,

> oppose the Advance of the Enemy but if driven back by superior force to retire[,] throwing back its right so as to fall back towards our own position.[60]

From the Balaklava Heights, the Russians could be clearly 'seen with the Telescope on the further side of the River.' According to Nolan, Lucan was content to simply observe the Russians rather than deploy his brigades in the valley to check the Russian advance. Lucan allowed Nolan to detach one squadron from the 17th Lancers to 'go forward to see what they [the Russians] were doing' and in so doing counted '8 Batt[alio]ns Inf[antr]y and five Reg[i]m[e]nts of Cavalry.'[61]

Général Canrobert also records that later on the same day, there was a Russian sortie directed towards the French: 'At 11 o'clock at night, a column of the enemy, of two battalions of infantry, two pieces of artillery, and a squad [*peloton*] of cavalry' probed the French left near the 'burned house'[*Maison brulée*]. They were repulsed with much loss; the French suffered just two men wounded.[62]

On 13-14 October 3,000 Turkish troops landed at Balaklava from Constantinople to reinforce the garrison. They were immediately set to work building five redoubts on the Causeway Heights, which were armed with twelve iron 12-pounder guns. At the same time, the French built a redoubt on a conical hill christened 'Canrobert's Hill' after the French Commander-in-Chief. One officer estimated the garrison of Balaklava to be 500 Royal Marines with six field guns; the 93rd Highlanders; Maude's Troop RHA and, of course, the cavalry. The usefulness of the cavalry in the plain before Balaklava was open to question, however, due to the rocky broken ground. The cavalry was also thought to be of even less use during a night attack.[63] Opinion was divided as to whether the Russians would attack or not: one officer believed the Russians would – and in force[64] – whilst a second believed that the Russians would be foolish to attack because of the presence of HMS *Agamemnon* in Balaklava Harbour whose guns 'will sweep them [the Russians] away by fifties.'[65]

At dawn on 18 October one officer reported 'about 12,000 Russians – half of whom are Cossacks' advancing into the Balaclava plain. They came under fire from the Turks in the redoubts on the Causeway Heights.[66] An officer of the Royal Marines related that:

> I had scarcely… taken my *al fresco* ablution, and was preparing for breakfast… when our drums beat to arms – the Highland pipes brayed – and all was accoutre and arm. The Russians, in force, were on the plain below – artillery, cavalry, and infantry – in all about 10,000. Their cavalry appeared to be their largest arm. Our cavalry and horse-artillery, with some Turkish battalions … advanced … the Russians retired without coming to an action. Our field-guns opened on them; but they retired, out of range.[67]

It was thought that this had been a reconnaissance in force, rather than a 'strong attack.' It was considered that the Russians would *not* attack the redoubts protecting Balaclava due to the presence of 'The Devils in Red' and 'had we [the Royal Marines] not been here they might have seriously inconvenienced the army before Sebastopol, by taking them in the rear'.[68]

French had spotted the Russians about noon; an officer reported to *général* Canrobert that the Russians were 'making a general attack on … Balaklava.' *Général* Bosquet was advised to 'make dispositions for battle' and Canrobert set off for Balaklava whilst French staff officers sought in vain to find Lord Raglan – Canrobert met him on the way. On the left, on the heights, was the brigade of *général* Vinoy, and in the plain the 93rd Highlanders and the cavalry under Lucan. Canrobert remembered how it was 'the Turks alone engaged; the Russians did not want to seem to push the matter. They were content just to observe.'

Unlike British observers, Canrobert realistically estimated the Russians to have been 'only about two or three thousand men.'[69] The garrison remained on the alert for the remainder of the day; 'many officers returning retired to their tents, and slept uncommonly well after being under arms all day.'[70] That evening Canrobert and Raglan held a meeting to discuss the defences of Balaklava.[71] Following this meeting, Canrobert wrote to Lord Raglan:

> My Dear General,
> The cavalry of the enemy, who are very numerous, and are growing in strength every day, is composed of Dragoons who are good troops; their infantry is also numerous: these considerations have caused me to examine this evening your defensive position and I have suggested the following disposition:

I would create at the Pass of Balaklava a barrier, which would be a sufficient obstacle to the cavalry. It is the matter of a few pickaxes to make. If, at some point, the totality of the Russian infantry marched against the left and against the English right, this would certainly give serious problems … and if at the same time the enemy launched on the pass of Balaklava with six thousand cavalry, they might go galloping on, three squadrons wide. It would be more than a few guns or gunshots that would stop this avalanche. Your right would be turned and the besieged at your back.

Always give strength to your enemy, and in this order of ideas, we must predict as I indicate. Make therefore tomorrow your ditch and bank. It must be a sufficient obstacle to stop the momentum of a large body of cavalry.[72]

The Russians made another feint two days later. The 'Special Correspondent' from the *Illustrated London News* reported on the afternoon of 20 October:

> The Russians attempted a diversion, by marching several battalions of infantry, and a quantity of cavalry and guns to the front of Balaclava. The Turks fired several rounds at them from their new redoubts [on the Causeway Heights], and Sir Colin Campbell thought it necessary to send for reinforcements. General Goldie's brigade moved out at three in the morning to the front of Balaclava. Lord Lucan's brigade of Cavalry struck tents, but the Russians retired without having molested us.[73]

An officer of the Royal Marines reports that the Russians had appeared 'in great force, and Sir Colin Campbell ordered the whole of the division to be on the alert.' Two companies of the Marines were sent down into the plain where they remained until evening but not before being startled by the 'Turkish advanced sentries firing at – perhaps Russians' and then 'by our own people firing with rockets and great guns on – I think, brushwood (it was a very dark night).'[74] Four days later, having found the British defences woefully unprepared, the Russians would press home their attack in earnest, in their first attempt to raise the siege of Sebastopol.

NOTES
[1] Fay, *Souvenirs*, p.60.
[2] Roche, *Un Regiment de Ligne*, pp.79-80.
[3] Lambert, *The Crimean War*, p.145.

[4] ibid, p.151.

[5] ibid, pp.146-151.

[6] Bapst, *Canrobert*, p.260.

[7] ibid.

[8] Bapst, pp.260-261.

[9] A. W. Kinglake, *The Invasion of the Crimea. Its origin and account of its progress down to the death of Lord Raglan* (London: William Blackwood & Sons, 1889), vol. 4, pp.174-177ff.

[10] Kinglake, *Invasion of the Crimea*, vol. 4, p.175.

[11] ibid, pp. 171-172 and pp.453-455.

[12] Lambert, *Crimean War*, pp.157-158ff.

[13] Dr Cabrol, *Saint-Arnaud en Crimee*, p.318.

[14] Lambert, *Crimean War*, p.151.

[15] Bapst, *Canrobert*, p.261

[16] Fay, *Souvenirs*, p.63.

[17] ibid.

[18] Lambert, *Crimean war*, p.160ff.

[19] E. Joppe, 'La Campagne de Crimée d'après les lettres du Commandant Adrien au Capitaine Joppe', *Carnet de la Sabretache*, vol. 16 (1907), p.211.

[20] Devanlay, 'General Breton', 2e partie, p.12.

[21] 'A Sergeant's Letter from the Camp near Sebastopol', *Daily News* (26 October 1854).

[22] Cabrol, *Saint Arnaud en Crimée*, p. 320.

[23] 'Campaigning in the Crimea', *Norfolk News* (28 October 1854), p.3.

[24] ibid.

[25] MRA, Acc. MR1/16/2, Newenham Mss., Newenham to family 24 November 1854.

[26] Dawson, *Light Brigade*, p.47.

[27] ibid, p.48.

[28] 'Private Letter', *Dorset County Chronicle* (10 May 1855), pp.18-19.

[29] 'The March on Balaklava', *Leeds Mercury* (14 October 1854).

[30] 'A Sergeant's Letter from the Camp Near Sebastopol', *Daily News* (26 October 1854).

[31] 'Letter from the Seat of War', *Kendal Mercury* (28 October 1854), p.8.

[32] MRA Acc. MR/1/15/2, Newenham Mss., Newenham to family, 24 November 1854.

[33] Guy & Massie, *Nolan*, pp.71-72.

[34] Carbol, *Saint-Arnaud en Crimée*, p.319.

[35] ibid.

[36] ibid, p.322.

[37] 'Souvenirs de la Guerre de Crimée par le General de Division Coste', *Revue de Midi*, Tome XXXXI (Decembre 1908), p.718.

[38] Cabrol, *Saint-Arnaud en Crimée*, pp.338-339.

[39] 'A Sergeant's Letter from the Camp Near Sebastopol', *Daily News* (26 October 1854).

[40] 'Letter from a Soldier in the Crimea', *Leeds Intelligencer* (30 December 1854), p.11.

[41] MR/1/16/2, Newenham MSS., Newenham to family, 24 November 1854.

[42] Capitaine Minart, 'Charles, Alfred et Edouard Minart', 2e partie, p.237.

[43] 'The Crimea', *Daily News* (27 October 1854), p.3.

[44] ibid.

[45] Roche, *Un Regiment de Ligne*, p. 99.

[46] V. L. J. F. Belhomme, *Histoire de l'Infanterie en France* (Paris: Henri Charles-Lavauzelle, 1894), tome 5, p.344.

[47] ibid, p.345.

[48] Usherwood, *Service Journal*.

[49] 'A Letter from a Zouave to his father', *Hampshire Telegraph* (18 November 1854), p.7.

[50] 'Tricks of the Zouaves', *Nairnshire Telegraph and General Advertiser* (11 January 1855), p.4.

[51] Kinglake, *Invasion of the Crimea*, vol. 4, p.489.

[52] 'Letter from a Barnsley Man at Sebastopol', *Wakefield Express* (2 November 1854), p.8.

[53] Devanlay, 'General Breton', p.82

[54] Commandant E. Martin, 'Souvenirs de la Guerre de Crimée. Lettres du Commissaire de Marine Garreau', *Carnet de la Sabretache*, vol. 21 (1912), p.175.

[55] F. de Marcy, 'Lettres de Campagne du General Henri de Bouille', *Carnet de la Sabretache*, vol. 11 (1912), pp.91-92.

[56] Guy & Massie, *Nolan*, pp.77-79.

[57] 'Journal des Operations de l'armée devant Sebastopol, du 1er au 22 Octobre', *Moniteur de l'Armee* (11 Novembre 1854), p.2.

[58] 'Skirmish at Balaclava', *The Daily News* (24 October 1854).

[59] Guy & Massie, *Nolan*, pp.77-79.

[60] ibid, p.79.

[61] ibid.

[62] 'Journal des Operations de l'armée devant Sebastopol, du 1er au 22 Octobre', *Moniteur de l'Armée* (11 Novembre 1854), p.2.

[63] 'Preparations against the attack: Letter from Balaclava, Oct. 16', *Supplement to the Illustrated London News* (11November 1854), p.494.

[64] ibid.

[65] 'Warning of the Russian Attack: Letter from Balaclava October 13', *Supplement to the Illustrated London News* (11 November 1854), p.491.

[66] 'Balaclava: Letter from an Officer, October 18', *Supplement to the Illustrated London News* (11 November 1854), p.491.

[67] 'Balaclava: Letter from an Officer of Royal Marines, Oct. 22', *Supplement to the Illustrated London News* (11 November 1854), p.491.

[68] ibid.

[69] G. Bapst, *Le Maréchal Canrobert. Tome Second: Napoléon III et sa cour, la Guerre de Crimée* (Paris: Plon-Nourrit et Cie., 1912), 7e Edition, pp.306-307.

[70] 'Balaclava: Letter from an Officer of Royal Marines, Oct. 22', *Supplement to the Illustrated London News* (11 November 1854), p.491.

[71] Bapst, *Canrobert*, p.307.

[72] ibid, pp.308-309.

[73] 'The Siege of Sebastopol', *Supplement to the Illustrated London News* (11 November 1854), p.496.

[74] 'Balaclava: Letter from an Officer of Royal Marines, Oct. 22', *Supplement to the Illustrated London News* (11 November 1854), p.491.

Chapter 4

Battle of Balaklava

The British Cavalry Division, commanded by Lieutenant General the Earl of Lucan was wracked, on the one hand, by the feuding between Lucan and his noble brother-in-law, the Earl of Cardigan, and on the other by the intrigue and 'turn ups' between Cardigan and his subordinates. The feuding between the two Earls was well-known: the French commander-in-chief, François Canrobert thought that they 'passed their time bickering, and annoyed Lord Raglan in their arguments, one against the other.'[1] Furthermore, Canrobert simply could not understand how two officers who had not seen recent active service had been appointed to command.

Lucan had served as an observer during the Russo-Turkish war of 1828-29 (his first and only time under fire) whilst Cardigan had been on active service in India, albeit briefly, and spent more time socialising in high society than with his men. Neither of them were held in high esteem by their officers, leading to a crucial lack of trust. Many of Cardigan's officers feared his violent temper and worried that a 'row with Cardigan was imminent.' One officer opined that Cardigan was 'one of the greatest old women in the army' and had 'as much brains as my boot.'[2] Lord George Paget (Cardigan's second in command) fell foul of him twice, as did his protégé, Colonel Douglas of the 11th Hussars.[3]

Lucan, by contrast, had been 'so long on the shelf that he has no idea of moving cavalry, does not even know the words of command.' As a result, he attempted to return to the 'old' cavalry regulations, which he remembered. Lord George Paget opined 'Instead of bending to the new order of things he sought to unteach his troops the drill which they had been taught.' Eventually, Paget managed to make Lucan see sense with regards to the drill manual.[4] Lieutenant Colonel Sir John Yorke (1st Royals) thought that Lucan was a 'hot-heated, nit-wit Irish man' who was apt to 'throw the blame' on anyone else for any mistake he made.

The whole Cavalry Division was 'fearing his want of temper' and felt that a disaster was imminent.[5]

Not only were there problems at the top, but also the cavalry troopers and their horses were suffering. The Heavy Brigade had lost several hundred horses on the voyage from Varna to the Crimea; the 1st Royals were reduced to a single squadron, having lost 150 horses and the Inniskillings seventy-one in a storm at sea. The surviving horses were 'much reduced' for 'want of proper nourishment,' and subsequently falling sick and dying.[6] The Royals received remounts from using the 'spare horses of other regiments' of the cavalry division, bringing them up to 'two weak squadrons' by the middle of October.[7] The men, too, were sickly, with nearly half of the Scots Greys being invalided with diarrhoea or dysentery. Officers too were struck down by sickness and exhaustion. Sir John Yorke, commanding officer of the Royals, found himself in temporary command of the Heavy Brigade during September 1854 due to the high rate of sickness. The 5th Dragoon Guards had been so affected by sickness whilst at Varna that 'what remained of the officers and men were incorporated into the 4th Dragoon Guards' leaving only the 4th Dragoon Guards and Scots Greys as 'effective.'[8]

Ever since landing in September, the men of the Light Brigade had had no change of clothes because their valises had been left on board ship; the Hussars had also left their warm, fur-trimmed pelisses on board ship, too. Their clothing was 'in rags': 'every man slept ready dressed.' Sergeant-Major George Loy Smith had, 'not had my overalls off since we landed, nor a change of any underclothing ... Water has generally been too precious ... to be used for washing.[9]

Thus, it was a divided and weakened cavalry division that was roused from their slumber an hour before dawn and mustered in the drizzle on 25 October.

Since early in the month, the cavalry had turned out an hour before dawn, posting 'In-lying' and 'Out-lying' pickets both to observe the Russians and to prevent the camp from being surprised. To bolster the defences of Balaklava, some 3,000 Turkish troops were landed 12-13 October, who built a series of six redoubts on the eponymous 'Causeway Heights' to defend Balaklava. Balaklava was commanded by Sir Colin Campbell, the garrison consisting of Lucan's cavalry, 500 Royal Marines, and the 93rd Highlanders; the French were well-established on the Sapoune Heights over-looking the plain of Balaklava.

Everything that morning had seemed 'normal' until, at daybreak, 25,000 men commanded by General Liprandi attacked the positions defending Balaklava in earnest. Writing from camp, George Winterburn of the 5th Dragoon Guards informed his parents that:

About daybreak the first shot was fired. I was on outlying picket at the time, and we were preceding to the spot on which to place our videttes to watch the surrounding country, when, having ascended a hill near the village of Camara, we suddenly came upon the vanguard of the enemy. We were only 18 men in all, therefore we retired as fast as our horses could gallop, pursued by about 200 of the Russian cavalry.

We, however, proved too swift for them, gained the plain on which our brigade by this time was formed, and rejoined our regiments. The enemy began to open a brisk fire upon the most advanced line of Turkish batteries which over-looked the neighbouring plain. After a heavy cannonade the infantry advanced, charged the Turks up the hill, who remained skirmishing too long, and, after a few minutes' struggle at the point of the bayonet, the Turks gave way, completely overpowered and fled down the hill towards our camp.[10]

The outlying picket of the Scots Greys was commanded by Lieutenant Hunter, who informed his wife that:

All was quiet at 3AM & afterwards, till day break (about 5 ½ AM) when an immense Column of the Enemy, & our fire opened from our field works, which unfortunately… were entirely manned with Turks. The Russians stormed, & took them, the Turks only making a stand at one work, and bolting as soon as the bayonets crossed.[11]

One French officer watching from the Heights saw how,

about a score of Russian battalions and a numerous body of cavalry were signalled at daybreak. Soon after the Russian artillery commenced its fire against the works in front of Balaklava. The Turks, who occupied them, withdrew before the mass of the enemy. The Russians rushed on the works, and at the same time sent forward their cavalry towards Balaklava.[12]

Often thought to have simply run away, one sergeant of the Scots Greys wrote to this mother that the Turks put up a stiff resistance:

Early in the morning of the 25th, we heard heavy firing up at the village [Kamara], mounted immediately, and went to see what was up. The Turks made a brave resistance at this point, being nearly all killed before they gave in, and we could give them no assistance.[13]

81

One French observer thought the Turks made a valiant, if futile, resistance against overwhelming odds:

> attacked with the bayonet, in vain they offered resistance; the Ottoman troops were tumbled into, but not without sustaining a lively and murderous fight ... they left 170 dead.[14]

The Earl of Lucan had ridden forward with his staff to inspect the redoubts on the Causeway Heights. With him were his Aide-de-Camp, Captain Walker; Lord George Paget; Lord William Paulet and Major Thomas McMahon. Paget remembered that no one knew what the two signal flags flying from Canrobert's Redoubt signified, until the guns started firing! Captain Walker wrote on the following day how:

> Early in the morning the Russians attacked our line of redoubts, which the Turks gave up without a struggle (the brutes), came into the plain ... When I arrived they had retired, but occupied a valley beyond our redoubts in force, holding two of them and the village of Kamara. Soon after they opened fire on us, and just at that time came the peremptory order from Lord Raglan to attack. [15]

The cavalry came under fierce artillery fire. A Mancunian trooper of the 1st Royals wrote to his family two days after the battle:

> In about one hour's time after they [the Turks] retreated, Lord Lucan collected all the two brigade of cavalry which consisted of five regiments of the light dragoons and five of heavy dragoons and two troops of horse artillery. We were ordered to advance, which we did, and showed fight ... which I am sorry to say played the very deuce with us, as we were in a very dangerous position ... exposed to the Russian batteries ... They peppered into use nicely, as our artillery could not act.[16]

An NCO of the Royals wrote on 26 October that:

> We advanced to the end of the plain and within range of the Russian guns, which began to play upon is in a very rapid manner. A large 32-pound shot passed through our squadrons, breaking the legs of two horses, and we soon began to think it was time to move off, as in another minute a ball struck a man right in the head, and of course, killed him instantly. Several other casualties took place in the Right squadrons ... our light field guns were no match for the

immense artillery which the enemy brought against us: besides, our artillery began to suffer severely in men and horses. As we were not supported by British infantry, of course we were obliged to retire.[17]

Captain Maude's troop of Royal Horse Artillery came into action 'to the right of redoubt [No.1], firing on the enemy's artillery in the plain below.' The right half-Troop soon changed position to the right and fired shrapnel on the enemy's advancing skirmishers. Severely out-gunned, Maude fell wounded within twenty minutes of opening fire. Barker's Battery (Royal Artillery) was ordered to the front to support what remained of Maude's troop, but they were rapidly running out of ammunition.

Captain Shakespear recounted that 'A.D.C.s came to me one after another, "Bring forward the guns to support the Scots Greys!" My answer was, "No ammunition."' The withdrawal of the artillery and Heavy Brigade led to the flight of the Turks.[18] Corporal Joseph Gough (5th Dragoon Guards) related to his family that:

> We could not see our enemies; but they kept firing at our artillery, and shell was flying over our heads and dropping all around us. Our artillery had to retire, as they had no more ammunition; so after a while, the Turks started, left the batteries, and ran down the hill as hard as they could.[19]

'In *this foolish manner*' fumed the commanding officer of the Royals, 'we lost 2 men and seven horses'.[20] A sergeant-major of the Inniskillings wrote:

> We had a serjeant who had one of his legs blown off with a cannon ball. He was in front of me, and how I escaped is a mystery. We could see the cannon balls hopping down the hill and go a long way on the ground, some striking horses and breaking their legs.[21]

One anonymous cavalry officer wrote from Kadikoi to family in Dublin:

> The way of it was this: we have the misfortune to have a contingent of Turks here, who were paced in strong redoubts covering the rear of our position, and about miles in front of Balaklava; fortunately we had a second line of defences behind these, about one mile from the time, which were held by Marines and Highlanders and so quite safe. Well, about seven o'clock a.m. ...
>
> The Russians advanced in force having about 8,000 infantry and 3,000 cavalry, with a heavy artillery which they served remarkably

well; their guns were principally 18 and 24 pounders. The troops of Royal Horse Artillery and cavalry soon advanced to the ridge, but after some time, retired on the line to Sebastopol, thus drawing on the Russians: but first the Turks had bolted, and got to the rear of our troops into the town and commenced pillaging everything, even the tents of our troops. The Russians then became exposed to a heavy fire from our batteries; their cavalry advanced into the plain …

Another body of them made a charge at the Highlanders, who did not even form square, but received them in line, gave them a volley and charged, whom they also cut off. In the meantime, the Russian infantry were busy removing the guns from the redoubts deserted so shamefully by the Turks, and got off seven guns – a great victory to them.[22]

Withdrawal of the Cavalry

The Allied commanders met on the Heights sometime around 07.30 – several hours after the attack had started and the Turks were on the point of breaking. Therefore, it is no surprise that most British observers thought – quite unfairly – that the Turks had simply 'run away.' Half an hour later, Raglan ordered his cavalry to retire out of range of the Russian artillery:

> Cavalry to take ground to the left of the second line of redoubts occupied by the Turks.

This is a very ambiguously worded order: there was only one line of redoubts – unless Raglan interpreted the Highlanders and Marines at Kadikoi as the *first* line – and Raglan should have been using points of the compass rather than 'left' and 'right' as 'to the left' whilst making sense to Raglan from his vantage point would make little sense to those who were expected to carry out his order.

The Earl of Lucan, however, correctly interpreted Raglan's intentions and withdrew from the valley, to the western end of the Causeway Heights. The heavy brigade made its way back along the South Valley, retiring in line by alternate squadron. As the heavies retired out of range of the Russian artillery, Lord Paget had 'the mortification of seeing all the redoubts occupied by the Turks … abandoned one by one.'[23]

Hunter of the Scots Greys remarked the Russians 'commenced at 6 o'clock to pepper us, with shot, shell & rifle balls. We had no infantry, & stood their fire for some time, loosing a few, but were obliged to retire as the fire got hot.'[24] According to Lord George Paget, this movement may have taken around an hour to complete.[25] The brigade had 'very difficult ground' to cross, including a vineyard surrounded by banks and ditches and their old camping ground.[26] The whole brigade had got into a state of disorder.[27]

Seeing, however, that this movement had precipitated their flight, Raglan sent his second order to the cavalry ordering them back into the Balaklava South Valley to support the Turks:

> Eight squadrons of Heavy Dragoons to be detached towards Balaklava to support the Turks who are wavering.

Four of the five regiments (Inniskillings, 4th and 5th Dragoon Guards, Scots Greys) of the Heavy Brigade, therefore, were ordered to advance into the South Valley towards the beleaguered Turks, although what use eight squadrons of heavy cavalry and their supporting horse artillery would have been in support of the Turks fighting for their lives in the redoubts is questionable.

The Thin Red Streak

As the Turks broke and fled, Russian cavalry swarmed over the heights – part of the 4th Light Cavalry Division commanded by Major-General Jabrokritsky: two regiments of hussars (Kievksi and Ingermanland), one regiment of Cossacks (Ural Regiment) and attached horse artillery. In total around 2,500 sabres.

Seeing the isolated position occupied by the 93rd Highlanders and Royal Marines, some of the Russian cavalry veered off to attack them believing them to be Turks from their long grey greatcoats.[28] It is not clear which Russian cavalry regiments attacked the 'thin red streak topped with steel' as Russian sources do not agree on this point.

One officer suggests that it was the Ural Cossacks alone who charged the 93rd, whilst General Todleben argues it was six squadrons from the Ingermanland Hussars and the Cossacks who attacked. Whereas, according to their regimental histories, both regiments of Hussars attacked the British heavy brigade with the Cossacks charging the Highlanders.[29] W. H. Russell scribbled in his journal:

> The Russians dash at the highlanders. The ground flies beneath their horses' feet; gathering speed at every stride, they dash toward the thin red streak topped with steel.

Captain Shakespear RHA thought that the 'whole plain swarmed with cavalry':

The left column charged the 93rd, who, under Sir Colin [Campbell] stood on some rising ground with Turkish infantry on both flanks, the whole flanked by Pippons entrenched battery of position guns on the right and Barker's battery on the left. The Highlanders ruined the charge in line, the guns worked on them with grape and case; the enemy fled in great confusion.[30]

The British infantry had been ordered to lie down, as some protection from the Russian artillery. Hector McPherson of the 93rd wrote:

We declared that we would die to a man rather than not maintain the position assigned to us, and, wheeling in line to our right so as to front the enemy, and with our brave general at our head determined to give them battle, numerous although they were, if they advanced upon us. By this time the Enemy had occupied a rising ground to the left of our line, and with their guns began to play fiercely upon us. Here we remained for an hour, when the Enemy's cavalry, to the number of 4,000, were discovered making their appearance on a rising ground about 1,000 yards in front of us.

When they had wheeled in column and actually fronted us, they halted, and, after viewing us for a minute or so, they began to advance at a walking pace, we still lying on the ground and in line, never moved. After they had advanced a few paces they began to trot, then at full speed came rushing down upon us, when we sprung to our feet, and waited with the utmost coolness and determination until they came within about 200 yards of us, when we opened a well-sustained and well-directed fire upon them.

Still they continued to advance, until within 50 yards of our line, when, finding that instead of flinching we became more bold and determined, they wheeled to their left, evidently with the intention of attacking us on the right flank; but instantly perceiving their design, we charged first upon our right, and bounding after them with the quickness of fury, were fronting them again, before they were able, although at the gallop, to complete their movement, and at the same time we still sustained our destructive fire, which soon forced them to their heels.[31]

From the French position, *commandant* Lacretelle watched as:

At half past nine, the Russian cavalry was launched in the direction of Kadikoi, onto the emplacement of the English camp. Maintaining their composure, the Scots let the Russians approach: they were stopped by fire at almost point blank range. The Brigade of General Scarlett, in their turn, penetrates like a wedge into the mass of Russian cavalry, puts them into disorder, and forces them to beat retreat. This cavalry reforms beyond the redoubts, under the protection of its artillery and its infantry.[32]

Scarlett's 300

With the Inniskillings leading, the 4th and 4th Dragoon Guards and the Scots Greys made their way back into the South Valley, formed in 'Column of Squadrons' i.e. a frontage two squadrons wide, making an oblique movement in echelon to their right to avoid the vineyard. It was during the oblique movement that the Inniskillings and 5th Dragoons 'took too much ground to their right,' which meant that when the order 'Change front to the Left' was given it,

> caused them ... to be some distance to the right of the parallel, and when we Wheeled into Line our regiment was next to the Greys; and the Inniskillings finding no space to act in front.[33]

Captain Forster (4th Dragoon Guards) suggests that: 'At the bottom of the vineyard ... we wheeled left' and then passed over 'some broken ground' before being ordered to 'Front-Form my squadron.'[34] Major Forrest (4th Dragoon Guards) says that the brigade was in confusion 'worse than I had expected, the men of all regiments were mixed together' due to having crossed 'very bad ground' and were 'scarcely reformed' when ordered to charge.[35]

Upon seeing the two regiments of Russian Hussars heading toward him, 'Lord Lucan, immediately ... ordered our Heavy Brigade to front and oppose the enemy' and,

> when the enemy saw that their superiority in numbers had no influence over us, they halted for a few moments; but, I suppose, tantalised by our small numbers, they began to advance – they did so in the form of a semi-circle, with a heavy square behind them; our men also slowly advanced.[36]

Sergeant Sherwin of the Inniskillings recounts what happened next:

> When they were within six hundred yards of us we got the order to advance, and directly they saw us they halted; the second squadrons of the Greys and Enniskillens then trotted up to within a hundred

yards of them, when we raised a cheer, and charged them. In about five minutes we broke their ranks, and the whole plain was covered with dead and wounded. Poor [Private Alexander] Lattimer and [Private Robert] Elliot were shot dead; Lattimer was close to me at the time, and I put my sword through the man's body that shot him, so that they both went to their last home at the same time. I am happy to tell you that I only received a slight wound in the right arm, but it did not prevent me from sticking to my work, which lasted all day.[37]

Charging first were the Scots Greys and the Inniskillings. One Mancunian trooper of the Greys wrote:

We got the order 'wheel in to line;' and the trumpet sounded 'gallop.' We have a hurrah and dashed at them in a charge, without any command, and rode over them and through them and back again, cutting and hacking them. Completely frightened, they galloped helter skelter, and never stopped till they were on the other side of the hill.[38]

Sergeant John Henson (Scots Greys) wrote to family in Nottingham that:

Paul Clifford was amongst the first that fell. Poor fellow he was chatting to me in his usual comical style about the manner in which the Turks had evacuated the redoubts, when the regiment was ordered to advance, wheeled into line, and before I knew where I was, I found myself surrounded by about a dozen of our friends the Cosssacks, however luckily there was assistance at hand, and after about ten minutes hard fighting, we succeeded in making them go over the hill a deal faster than they came. We had a good many wounded very severely, several (10) mortally and two killed outright.[39]

Corporal Benjamin DeCarle of the Inniskillings wrote to his family in Bury St. Edmonds:

The Russian cavalry, composed of the 11th and 12th Hussars (or Imperial Guard), and two regiments of Cossacks, came towards our position as fast as they could gallop, little thinking of the reception they would meet with. We wheeled into line, and, supported by the Scots Grays [sic], met them at the charge, and I may say not a man met his adversary without putting his sword through his body, and in many cases lifted completely from the saddle! ... The result was that the portion left (and numerous it was) immediately ran away; and as they were retiring they were helped on the road by a shot or two from our Horse Artillery.[40]

A sergeant-major of the Inniskillings wrote home to family in Leeds that:

The Inniskillings were the first to attack the Russians, and not the Scots Greys … The Squadron that I was in was the first, and I believe I was the first man that struck a blow. The Greys were next to us …I had some very narrow escapes for my life, and I had to fight hard for it. I came in contact with a big fellow, and I thought I would have a go in at him. He was a powerful fellow and shouted and bawled like a good one, but not smart enough with the sword for me, and I killed him dead with a tremendous cut on the side of the neck, which nearly took his head off; not, however, before he gave me a cut on the right arm, which cut my coat, my stripes, and two shirts right through. Thank God he did not cut my arm. Such cutting and slashing never was seen before![41]

Lieutenant Hunter notes that his (the left) squadron of the Greys was faced by an entire regiment ('their right regiment') and one squadron from the second.[42] An anonymous officer of the Greys wrote that:

They regularly surrounded us. I belonged to the left squadron (likewise the left of the line), and had two squadrons, each double our strength, who tried to turn our flank, opposed to us. We went clean through them and back again, and you never saw such a fight. They say you could not see a red coat, we were so surrounded, and for ten minutes it was dreadful suspense; but they couldn't stand it, and were soon cutting away like anything … I mercifully escaped without a scratch.[43]

Galloping to the help of the Greys and Inniskillings came the 4th and 5th Dragoon Guards. A corporal in the 5th Dragoon Guards described the charge in a letter to his parents:

A lot of Russian cavalry came to attack us. I suppose they thought we would run. At first we thought they were our Light Brigade, till they got about twenty yards from us; then we saw the difference. We wheeled into Line. They stood still and did not know what to do. The charge sounded, and away we went into the midst of them.

Such cutting and slashing for about a minute; it was dreadful to see. The Rally sounded, but it was no use – none of us would come away until the enemy retreated; then our fellows cheered as loud as they could. When we were in the midst of them, my horse was shot; he fell, and got up again, and I was entangled in the saddle, my head and one leg on the ground.

He tried to gallop on with the rest, but fell again, and I managed to get loose. A Russian Lancer was going to run me through, and I could not help myself. [Private Michael] Macnamara came up at the time, and nearly severed his head from his body; so thank God I did not get a scratch. I got up and ran to where I saw a lot of loose horses; I got one belonging to one of the Enniskillens, and was soon along with the regiment again. When I had mounted again I saw a Russian who had strayed from the rest; he rode up to try and stop me joining the regiment again.

As it happened, I has observed a pistol in the holster pipe, so I took it out, and shot him in the arm; he dropped his sword, then I immediately rode up to him and ran him through the body, and the poor fellow dropped to the ground.[44]

Our Leeds-born Sergeant-Major of the Inniskillings was eager to inform his family that:

> The Inniskillings were the first … the Greys came next to us; then the 1st Royals, and the 4th and 5th Dragoon Guards; but, mind it was nearly over when the two latter came up, for we had broken the Russian ranks and turned them.[45]

Firing in support of the Heavy Brigade was 'C' Troop RHA, commanded by Captain John Brandling who took up position on the right flank of the Brigade. Brandling notes that even though the Russian hussars had been driven off there were still 'seen holding up their swords and rallying their men.'[46] He opened fire at 700-800 metres and Lieutenant Temple Godman (5th Dragoon Guards) recalled,

> the troop of Horse Artillery firing into the retreating mass almost before some red-coats were clear of them, and going over the ground the next day I saw they did good work.[47]

Charge of the Light Brigade
The first phase of the battle was over: the Russians had assaulted and taken the redoubts on the Causeway Heights. Their cavalry had

attempted to pursue the fleeing Turks into Balaklava but had been driven out of the South Valley by the Heavy Brigade. The Russian force was now concentrated in the North Valley and on the Fedioukine Heights. *Capitaine* Charles Alexandre Fay, Aide de Camp to *général* Pierre Bosquet, observed the Allies disposition from his position on the heights:

> The Allied troops ordered to reinforce had arrived on the plain; they were established in two lines: the first, formed by the English cavalry, was between Redoubts No. 4 and 5, and directed to the right, towards Balaklava; our *Chasseurs d'Afrique* formed the left, to the north of the redoubts, in the plain of the Tchernaya. The second line is composed of infantry; the English (the First Division, with the Fourth in reserve, behind their cavalry, and the first brigade or our first division to their left, at the height of Redoubt No. 5. During this time, the Brigade of General Vinoy (second brigade of the first division) followed to the south, to the pass of Balaklava, and occupied Kadikoi.[48]

One French observer thought: 'The Russians captured and occupied this position [Causeway Heights], because, from there, they could menace at the time the line on the Tchernaya and the communication of the English and the port, where they drew their armaments, their munitions and their provisions.'[49]

The Causeway Heights had to be recovered to secure the Woronzoff Road which led from Balaklava to the heights upon which the Allies were camped, but the Allies were outnumbered and had limited forces at their disposal. Whilst *général* Bosquet's *2e Division* was spilling on to the battlefield, General Cathcart's 4th Division was slow to arrive, unlike that of the Duke of Cambridge. When Cathcart's men did start to arrive, they took up position at the western end of the Causeway Heights with the Guards Brigade at the head of the South Valley. As soon as Cathcart arrived, Raglan ordered him to 'Advance immediately and recapture the Redoubts.' But, with a 'maddening slowness' Cathcart only advanced as far as Redoubt No. 4 and then halted.[50]

The 1st Battalion Rifle Brigade under Colonel Horsford deployed in two wings along the Causeway Heights, with the 68th (Durham) Light Infantry formed in line on its right. In support was a battery of artillery commanded by Captain Barker.[51]

It was obviously with a sense of frustration that Raglan sent his 'Third Order' to the cavalry, as the only troops available to him that could move swiftly enough:

Cavalry to advance and take advantage of any opportunity to recover the Heights. They will be supported by infantry which has been ordered. Advance on two fronts.[52]

Often discussed as being 'vague' and poorly-worded, the third order, when read in conjunction with the order sent to General Cathcart, it is clear Raglan wished his cavalry *and* infantry to recover the heights. The second half of the order suggests he wanted them to make a simultaneous move down the North and South valleys.[53] General Richard Airey thought the orders were perfectly clear:

The Brigade of Guards was ordered by Lord Raglan to advance to the redoubts, and Lord Lucan ... was directed to hold the ground with the cavalry till they came up.[54]

Despite British infantry now being present, by 'some unaccountable wilfulness ... the cavalry never moved' which necessitated Raglan to send his now infamous 'Fourth Order.'[55] Lucan admitted later that he had not moved because he was waiting for the infantry and had intended 'to give all support possible to the infantry in the recapture of the redoubts' but since they were slow to arrive ignored the first part of the order, which instructed him to advance.[56]

That Lucan believed he was to wait for the infantry to arrive is confirmed by Captain William Morgan (17th Lancers) who wrote on 27 October that 'We waited about two hours for some infantry to come to our support.'[57] *Capitaine* Fay thought that the 'Russian cavalry were in disorder' and that the 'Third Order' made logical sense: the cavalry was to drive off the confused Russian cavalry, allowing the infantry to make their move along the Causeway Heights.[58]

It was with growing impatience at the lack of any activity the Raglan dictated his 'Fourth Order' to General Airey who hastily scribbled it down using his sabretache as an improvised desk:

Lord Raglan wishes the Cavalry to advance rapidly to the front – Follow the Enemy and try to prevent the Enemy carrying away the guns – Troop Horse Artillery may accompany – French cavalry is on your left. Immediate.[59]

According to Airey, Lord Raglan was 'amazed at the inaction of the British cavalry' as he watched 'the light squadrons of the enemy scouring over the ground.' However, by the time the 'Fourth Order' had reached the Earl of Lucan 'the time of action had gone by.'[60] Even the

French detected anxiety in the usually calm and unflappable Raglan.[61] Similarly, the French also expressed astonishment that the 'Third Order' had apparently not been obeyed. *Général* MacMahon was surprised at the sluggishness of the British cavalry, and agreed with Airey that by the time Captain Nolan had reached Lucan with the 'Fourth Order' the situation on the ground had changed considerably.

Nolan, however, transmitted his written order 'taking no account of events which had altered the situation' because 'Lord Raglan ... would not have forgiven his [Nolan's] taking any initiative upon himself.'[62] *Général* Canrobert believed that the plan of action was simple: the British would advance along the Causeway Heights whilst the French would attack the Russians on the Fedioukine Heights. Lord George Paget, albeit with the benefit of hindsight, believed that the Light Brigade was intended to have mounted the heights to recapture the guns, but owing to the 'difficulty of the ground' it would have been 'attended with great difficulty.'[63]

One French cavalry officer agreed with Canrobert: the French were to attack the Russian positions on the Fedioukine Heights whilst the British were to advance down both valleys, clearing the Causeway Heights and threatening the Russian rear which pivoted around the village of Kamara and the stone Tratkir Bridge – which would be the seen of one of the bloodiest battles of the war in August 1855 – which gave passage over the Tchernaya.

Lucan later wrote in his despatch: 'Being instructed to make a rapid advance to our front, to prevent the enemy carrying guns lost by the Turkish troops in the morning, I ordered the light brigade to advance.'[64] Lucan had expressed 'consternation' in reading the order from Raglan 'at once seeing its impracticality for any useful purpose whatsoever' – Lucan had probably failed to understand that the 'Fourth Order' was corroboration of the 'Third Order' (cavalry to advance ...) rather than a new order in itself. He urged Nolan, who had delivered the written order, of the 'of the uselessness of such an attack' to which Nolan, according to Lucan, replied that he was to 'attack immediately.'

Lucan and his ADC, Captain Walker, both contend that Nolan spoke to Lucan in a 'most disrespectful manner' and allegedly pointed to the end of the valley: 'There, My Lord, is your enemy, there are your guns.' This conversation, however, is not supported by the writing of members of the Light Brigade in the immediate aftermath of the battle, which may cast some doubt on whether it took place.[65] Indeed, in support of this argument, Lucan later denied that any 'altercation' between himself and Nolan ever took place.[66] It is not clear whether the redoubts cresting the Causeway Heights were actually visible from the valley floor.

Furthermore, it is also unclear whether the Russian battery ('Light Battery Number 7, 12th Artillery Brigade') at the end of the North Valley was visible to Lucan and his staff. *Général* Canrobert asserts that the guns were visible from the heights where he and Raglan were situated but not from the valley floor, and if this is the case it makes the subsequent action of the Light Brigade all the more confusing as Raglan, and therefore Nolan, knew the guns were there. Raglan, Airey or Nolan may have mistaken the Russian guns at the end of the valley as being those withdrawn from the Causeway Heights, which would explain why Nolan possibly pointed at the guns in the valley.

Lucan claimed that the guns were not visible from his position whilst another officer 'who knows the ground' agreed, saying that the guns at the end of the valley were not visible due to the valley rising toward its middle and then dropping rapidly away down to the Tchernaya.[67] Cardigan, however, suggests that guns *were* visible from the valley floor and most letters home written immediately after the battle confirm that the Light Brigade knew they were charging into the face of Russian guns.[68]

It is clear that in order to make sense of his orders Nolan went to reconnoitre, as recorded by a private from the 11th Hussars:

> Captain Nolan was sent to reconnoitre the hills on each side. Whatever report he took to Lord Raglan we know not, but I expect he reported they were all clear, as he came back with an order to Lord Lucan for the Light Brigade to charge and take the field guns, and the ammunition taken from the Turks.[69]

This is confirmed by a trooper of the 1st Royals,[70] and by an officer of the Light Brigade who watched as Captain Nolan:

> who had gone to the redoubts, now halted. I next heard heavy fire, and then he galloped back towards us. We were by this, in motion, and Lord Cardigan was preparing to act. The Trumpet sounded 'Stand to horses!' then rapidly followed 'mount, walk, trot, gallop!' and again the trumpet finally sounded the 'charge!' and we were off. I had just time, and no more, to see the effect of the first fire of the Russians. Captain Nolan, who had lifted up his hands, as I thought, in a signal, was then close upon us. His right arm was outstretched.[71]

Lucan trotted over to Cardigan, and ordered him to 'advance very steadily': Cardigan admitted that he received the order with trepidation, indicating the 'Russians have a battery in the valley in our front, and batteries and riflemen on each flank.' Lucan is believed to have replied 'I know it, but Lord Raglan will have it.'[72] W. H. Russell of *The Times* reports that the Light Brigade began its 'steady advance' at 11.10 hours precisely.

Thomas Dudley of the 17th Lancers wrote from his hospital bed at Scutari on 18 December:

> When we received the *order* not a man could seem to believe it. However, on we went, and during that ride what each man felt no one can tell. I cannot tell you my own thoughts. Not a word or whisper. On – on we went! Oh! if you could have seen the faces of that doomed 800 men at that moment; every man's features fixed, his teeth clenched, and as rigid as death, still it was on – on! At about 300 yards I got my hit, but it did not floor me. Clash! Oh God! What a scene! I will not attempt to tell you … what we did; but we were Englishmen, and that is enough. I believe I was as strong as six men – at least I felt so; for I know I chopped two Russian lances in two as if they had been reeds.[73]

Thomas Williams of the 11th Hussars informed his parents that:

> We got the order to advance. I could see what would be the result of it, and so could all of us; but of course, as we had got the order, it was our duty to obey. I do not wish to boast too much; but I can safely say that there was not a man in the Light Brigade that day but what did his duty to his Queen and Country. It was a fearful sight to see men and horses falling on all sides. Thank God, I and my poor horse got through it all without a scar, although I had two or three very narrow escapes. My sword scabbard had two or three very severe knocks; in fact a ball caught it about the centre, and cut it very nearly in two. How my leg escaped seems to me a miracle; but, thanks to a kind Providence, I did escape, and hope, by God's assistance, once more to return to the bosom of my beloved family.[74]

Samuel Walker (8th Hussars) wrote to his family in Leeds that:

> [I got] a severe wound in the calf of my leg from a cannon ball … which entered my horse's side and knocked out his entrails. The curious character that you used to speak about when I was in England – I mean the man with the 'bald head' – was riding next met at Balaklava on my left, and a cannon ball caught him on the

right ear and took his head clean off, without scarcely altering his position in the saddle, and the next man on his left had his horse killed from under him the same instant, and had to shove him off the saddle and mount his horse. This was done, I may term it, almost in a twinkling of an eye.

I am very sorry to inform you that Serjeant McCauley and his brother were both killed… I think no one can say that we (I mean the Light Cavalry) have done our duty. On that day 610 of us beat back about 25,000 Russians manfully … Lord Cardigan was entirely surrounded by Russian Hussars, and would have been killed but one of the 17th Lancers came up and ran one of them through the neck with his lance and beat the others off, so as to allow of his escaping.[75]

Watching from the Heights, the French could not understand why the Light Brigade had not turned and mounted the Causeway Heights; indeed, the Russian infantry on the heights had formed square believing that they were the intended target of Cardigan's men. *Général* Pierre Bosquet famously exclaimed 'What are they doing? It is superb but it is not war – It is madness! Where are they going?'[76]

Another French officer retorted 'They are the finest cavalry in the world. But the worst led.' It was clear to all on the Heights that the Light Brigade was galloping into a trap and they were powerless to stop it:

600 English horsemen charged before a formed Russian infantry square, it opened suddenly and unmasked a strong battery that vomited on them a rain of shot; the English then performed prodigies of valour, but when they managed to reform, approximately four hundred of them were missing.[77]

It is likely Nolan had seen the Light Brigade was deviating from its intended path and had been attempting to wheel it to the right so it could mount the Causeway Heights.[78] Sadly, Nolan was the first to be killed: 'He seemed to real in his saddle; out of his breast poured forth a red streaming tide; he looked as is his chest had been broken in. I saw him no more. The brave fellow – none braver in the army, nor a bolder horseman – was killed!'[79] Because Nolan was killed, he became (and still is) an easy scapegoat.

One newspaper editor caustically remarked: 'Dead men tell no tales,' whilst Lawrence Godkin, special correspondent of the *Daily News*, was more forthright: 'Dead Men cannot defend themselves; and this fact seems to have suggested the idea of casting the blame on a dead and voiceless man.' The *Morning Chronicle* called the charge 'wilful murder' and was sure of Nolan's innocence whilst *Reynolds's Newspaper* laid the blame for the disaster squarely on Raglan for his poorly worded and often ambiguous orders.[80]

As the Light Brigade – with the Heavies moving up in support – advanced down the North Valley, they came under intense artillery and infantry fire. Private George Gowings (4th Light Dragoons) informed his father that:

> Our men fell by dozens – horses and men blown into the air, and we ran every one through we could get at; we had to cut our way through thousands of them. I cannot tell you the horrors we went through, but all I can say is we only have about fifty left out of the regiment; we have lost half of our officers. Poor [Corporal Henry] Spence was killed – and in fact dozens that you have seen before we left Old England.[81]

Having reached the Russian guns, the Light Brigade found itself outnumbered with Russian cavalry preparing to counter-charge. A trumpeter of the 8th Hussars wrote how:

> men were falling on both sides. It was worse for us, for our light cavalry had to charge their cavalry between two batteries and they were firing on us for two miles and a half. As we were coming back, our regiment and the 17th Lancers were attacked by another lot of Russian cavalry, so we had to make the best of our way through them. Their artillery and infantry were firing on us all the time. Our regiment lost 38 men and two officers killed. Seventeen men and two officers wounded …
>
> It was an awful sight to see our men falling on ever side of me, but, thank God, I was spared. I had my horse shot under me, but I was no sooner down than I mounted a Russian's horse. I had not, however the pleasure of riding it more than half an hour when one of the Russian Lancers ran his lance through the horse's body. Then I was left without any, so I had to run for my life, which I did for three miles, until I came to the French cavalry, where I remained until our regiment came back. You may guess I had a narrow escape of my life. Our Trumpet Major [William Gray] was wounded in two places, and a trumpeter in three places … We had 60 men killed and wounded and 80 horses. We could mount more than that in my own troop when we left Exeter.[82]

A troop sergeant-major of the 8th Hussars wrote to family in Dorset that:

> No men could work better, and their line in advance through the Russian artillery, as well as through their cavalry, could not be surpassed on Hounslow Heath. After we had sabred and passed their artillery at the end battery the word was given, 'The Russian cavalry are in our rear: make ready to charge.' Some officer gave the word 'Retire by threes from the right' Our brave Colonel [Shewell] shout out immediately 'Steady, my brave men!' in a cool and determined voice, followed by 'Right about wheel.'
>
> We were all this time in full gallop, and this movement brought the officers and front rank facing the Russian Cavalry; and when we were well in line, the brave fellow said, 'Follow me – Charge!' He led us on, and how he escaped is a miracle, for he was the first who came up to that tremendous mass of horsemen. We followed close, and went through them like the wind, making clear way for the others to follow, after which our handful of men broke, and each, as best he could, cut his way to his original ground.[83]

One of those men cutting their way back was Wakefield-lad Private Richard Palfreyman of the 8th Hussars:

> There were the fellows cheering and cutting everything in front of them and just at that moment we saw the enemy lancers forming up at our rear to cut off our retreat. Then our colonel gave the order 'Right about wheel and charge' and at them we went cutting our way right and left. We managed to get through them when a cannon ball struck my horse. She gave a bound and fell right on top of me and she was such a heavy horse that I could not get from under her and there I lay until two Russian soldiers came and disarmed me and took me from under my horse. So there I was in the hands of the enemy so, By Jove, I thought it looked bad for the oldest of the family but it proved different, I was taken and imprisoned where I found a good many of my comrades placed in the same situation as myself ad instead of being ill-treated as I expected I was treated very well.[84]

Charge of the *Chasseurs*

Galloping to the rescue of the Light Brigade were two regiments of *Chasseurs d'Afrique* – regiments of ultra-light cavalry raised from French volunteers for service in North Africa, dressed in celestial blue jackets and riding their hardy little Barb horses. One *escadron* of the *1e Chasseurs d'Afrique* had landed back in September along with one *escadron* of *Spahis*; the remainder of the *1e Chasseurs d'Afrique*, together with the *4e Chasseurs d'Afrique and 1e Hussards* had landed on 4 October.

The officers of the French cavalry could not have been more different from their Allies. Unlike Lucan, Cardigan and Scarlett who had had no formal military education, all French officers had to have studied at the *École Militaire* in Paris. Furthermore, every officer and NCO in the French cavalry had to have studied at the prestigious *École de Cavalerie* at Samur. Unlike in Britain where promotion was by purchase, French officers were promoted by merit. The *Chasseurs d'Afrique* had recent combat experience and were trained equally well to perform the charge, or to fire their long rifled muskets dismounted or from horse back.

Overall command of the French cavalry was vested in *général de division* Louis-Michel Morris (1803-1867), a career soldier who was the antithesis of the Earl of Lucan. He been commissioned in 1829 and had served as an instructor at the *École de Cavalerie*. Promotion, through active service in French North Africa had been rapid: *capitaine* 1832; colonel 1843; general 1847. As colonel of *4e Chasseurs d'Afrique* he had led them in a charge against the religious fanatics of Abd el Kadir at the Battle of Smala (19 May 1843). Command of the brigade of *Chasseurs* was vested in *général de brigade* Armand-Octave-Marie d'Allonville (1809-1867), of whom Captain Valentine Baker (10th Hussars) wrote:

> No one could ever serve for day under General d'Allonville without feeling implicit confidence in him, and recognising a commander of consummate ability.[85]

D'Allonville had spent his career serving with the *Spahis* in North Africa, eventually rising to command of *1e Spahis* in 1839, and *général de brigade* 1851.

Général Canrobert watched as the *Chasseurs* sabred the gunners of 'Number One Battery, 16th Artillery Brigade' formed up on the Fedioukine Heights:

> They reached the heights where the batteries were, passed through them, made an about-turn, and fell upon the Russian gunners from the rear. *Capitaine* Dancla, at the head, was knocked stiff dead; but in a flash his horsemen, without stopping, entered the battery, whose gunners, sabred and hustled, however managed to throw themselves upon their guns, bring the horses and to couple them up, and to make them slip away at the gallop.[86]

The *colonel* of *1e Chasseurs,* the *vicomte* de Noë recalled:

> The combat of Balaklava is begun, but we remain only spectators for all of the first part of the action. Suddenly an aide de camp arrived, speaking on behalf of general Morris to descend into the plain. We left at a quick trot, in column by pelotons; our two regiments of *chasseurs d'Afrique,* because the 4e had joined us, we went into battle. As soon as our first movement was finished, a shell burst over the eagle of the *1e Regiment,* but did not hurt anyone. A terrible tumult is heard in the bottom of the plain, musketry and cannon fire salute the heroic, but absurd… charge of the English light cavalry. A little after, a dust cloud, with British hurrahs, advances on us: it's the unfortunate cavalry who are returning wounded and decimated. The Russian artillery, which is established on the heights on our left, commenced to fire case shot at this noble debris. The general Morris did not hesitate to launch the *4e chasseurs d'Afrique* against the Russians. Two squadrons bravely sabred two lines of skirmishers and came upon Russian squares [Odessa Jäger Regiment]; they opened their retreat in good order. The Russian artillery, so nimble, had soon limbered-up their pieces, retreating in haste before the chasseurs. [87]

The two squadrons of *4e Chasseurs d'Afrique* had been led by thirty-nine-year-old *chef d'escadrons* Louis Alexandre Desiré Abdelal who wrote in his after-action report:

> The brigade of *general* d'Allonville, were present and witnessed this veritable massacre [of the light brigade] … It was necessary at any cost to silence these pieces of cannon, at least for a moment to allow the debris of the English cavalry to rally and to retrace his steps. The two regiments of *Chasseurs d'Afrique* were formed in column by squadrons … we advanced at a quick trot; arriving at the heights with the batteries, the left hand squadrons are thrown on the Russian Artillery.
>
> I had command of the 3e and 5e squadrons of the *4e Chasseurs d'Afrique;* but I had on that day only one of my squadrons under my orders (the *3e escadron, capitaine* Mouton, was on service with general Bosquet). I was on the left flank of the line of battle. As soon as the enemy devined our intentions, they directed all their fire on us and left a moment of respite for the English …
>
> We climbed at a trot the slopes of the plateau on which the Russian batteries were in position, and, arriving at the crest, I

launched resolutely at the charge with the single squadron with me. The battery on the right had limbered-up before we arrived on the plateau. The other battery, which saw us ready to charge, was trying to follow their example, and take the road to Sebastopol, covered by their infantry which were forming square … My squadron, vigorously conducted, over-ran their guns, crossed the first battalion, which was marching in double columns, and fell on the second battalion already formed in square…

General d'Allonville, who was at the head of the rest of the brigade … sent in support a division of *2e Escadron*.[88]

The two Russian batteries on the Fedioukine Heights had been silenced at the cost of two officers and thirteen other ranks killed with a further seven wounded. Sixteen horses were killed and twelve wounded. The British casualties were far higher. The human losses from the Light Brigade were surprisingly light: the official loss was 110 killed or died from their wounds (*The Manchester Times* estimated 124 killed[89] whilst Kinglake suggests 113 killed and 134 wounded[90]); 129 wounded and returned to unit; 32 taken prisoner.[91] In other words, less than twenty per cent of the Light Brigade had been killed.

It was, however, the equine deaths that had the biggest impact on the Light Brigade's operational effectiveness. The official Return suggests an initial strength of 643 horses, of which 332 were killed; eighty-five wounded; and forty-three destroyed.[92] Conversely, Somerset Calthorpe, ADC to Lord Raglan puts the figure killed at 335;[93] and Kinglake as high as 475 of which forty-two wounded horses were subsequently destroyed.[94] Lord Lucan estimated 472 horses were killed or destroyed,[95] whilst Cardigan suggested 397.[96] Kinglake suggests that at the first muster only 195 *mounted* men could be found.[97]

The Light Brigade was destroyed not because of the human casualties, but that of the equine and that figure would continue to mount. The Earl of Lucan estimated the Cavalry Division had some 1,752 horses at the end of October 1854, but by 16 January this number had fallen to 847.

In other words, forty-eight per cent of his horses had died due to sickness (there had been an outbreak of glanders in the 'Sick Horse Depot' resulting in all the animals therein being destroyed) as well as through over-work (horses being seconded for commissariat duties) and exposure. On Christmas Day 1854, the Light Brigade could only find 200 horses and the Heavies 549.

NOTES

[1] Bapst, *Canrobert*, p.203.

[2] Dawson, *Light Brigade*, p.14.

[3] D. Thomas, *Charge! Hurrah! Hurrah! A life of Cardigan of Balaklava* (London: Futura Publications Ltd, 1976), pp.222-225.

[4] ibid.

[5] ibid, p.70.

[6] Dawson, *Light Brigade*, pp.48-53 and pp.65-67.

[7] ibid, p.66.

[8] ibid, p.13.

[9] ibid, p.158.

[10] 'Letter from a Soldier, a native of Aberford, near Leeds', *Leeds Intelligencer* (14 April 1855), p.10.

[11] Lincolnshire Archives (LA), Lincoln, Acc. 1-Dixon 22/12/3/5, Hunter Mss., Hunter to Sister, 27 October 1854.

[12] 'A Sebastopol correspondent of the *Patrie*', *Cork Examiner* (20 November 1854), p.3.

[13] 'The Scots Greys at Balaklava', *The Morning Post* (23 November 1854), p.2.

[14] Pascal et al, *Histoire de l'Armée*, pp.268-269.

[15] General Sir C. P. Beauchamp Walker, *Days of a Soldier's Life* (London: Chapman and Hall Ltd., 1894), pp.130-131.

[16] 'The Battle of Balaklava', *Manchester Examiner & Times* (22 November 1854), p.2.

[17] 'The Affair of the 25th October', *Manchester Examiner & Times* (22 November 1854), p.2.

[18] Anglesey, *A History*, pp.63-64.

[19] 'Letter from a Corporal in the 5th Dragoon Guards', *The Morning Post* (21 November 1854).

[20] FRO, Acc.D/E/1330, Erddig Mss., Yorke to Etheldred Yorke, 5 December 1854.

[21] 'Letters from a Serjeant-Major in the 6th Inniskilling Dragoons', *Leeds Intelligencer* (13 January 1855), p.8.

[22] 'Letters from the Seat of War', *Daily News* (16 November 1854), np.

[23] Paget, *Light Cavalry Brigade*, pp.165-6.

[24] LA, Acc. 1-Dixon 22/12/3/5, Hunter Mss., Hunter to sister 27 October 1854.

[25] Paget, *Light Cavalry Brigade*, pp.165-166.

[26] Angelsey, *Little Hodge*, p.47.

[27] ibid.

[28] Dawson, *Light Brigade*, pp.75-76.

[29] ibid, pp.76-77.

[30] Anglesey, *A History*, p.64.

[31] 'The Ninety-Third Highlanders at Balaklava', *Stirling Observer* (28 December 1854), p.2.

[32] De la Fay, *General Lacretelle*, pp.87-88.

[33] 'Letters from a Dumfrieshire Dragoon', *The Morning Post* (1 February 1855), p.3; 'Letter from a Dumfries Dragoon', *Glasgow Herald* (29 January 1855).

[34] Anglesey, *Little Hodge*, p.47

[35] National Army Museum, London, Acc. 1958-04-32, Major W C Forrest, Mss., Forrest to Brother, 27 October 1854.

[36] 'The Scots Greys and 93d Highlanders', *Paisley Herald and Renfrewshire Advertiser* (16 December 1854), p.1.

[37] 'Letter from Sebastopol', *Coventry Standard* (17 November 1854), p.4.

[38] 'The Scots Greys at Balaklava', *The Morning Post* (23 November 1854), p.2.

[39] 'From the Royal Scots Greys', *Nottinghamshire Guardian* (15 March 1855), p.7.

[40] 'Letter from Sebastopol', *Bury and Norwich Post* (29 November 1854), p.20.

[41] 'Letters from a Serjeant-Major in the 6th Inniskilling Dragoons', *Leeds Intelligencer* (13 February 1855), p.8.

[42] LA, Acc. 1-Dixon 22/12/3/5, Hunter Mss., Hunter to sister 27 October 1854.

[43] 'Extract from a letter of an officer in the heavy brigade', *Manchester Examiner & Times* (25

November 1854).

[44] 'Soldier's Letters', *Bath Chronicle and Weekly Gazette* (23 November 1854), p.4.

[45] 'Letters from a Serjeant-Major in the 6th Inniskilling Dragoons', *Leeds Intelligencer* (13 January 1855), p.8.

[46] L.W. Crider, 'Captain J. J. Brandling RHA – Forgotten Hero of Balaklava', *The War Correspondent* (vol. 32 no. 1 December 2014), p.39.

[47] ibid, p.40.

[48] Fay, *Souvenirs*, p.90.

[49] Comte de Margon, *Le General Abdelal* (Paris: Calman Lévy, 1887), pp.235-236.

[50] Anglesey, *A History of British Cavalry* (Barnsley: Pen and Sword, 1998), Vol. 2, pp.80-82; *see also* G. Cadlwell and R. Cooper, *Rifle Green in the Crimea* (Bugle Horn Publications, 1994), pp.143-144.

[51] Caldwell and Cooper, *Rifle Green*, p.144.

[52] Dawson, *Light Brigade*, p.123.

[53] ibid, pp.123-124; Angelsey, *A History*, pp.81-82.

[54] Anon, 'Sir Richard Airey in the Crimea', *The United Service Magazine for 1856*, Part I (1856), p.521.

[55] ibid.

[56] Anglesey, *A History*, p.82.

[57] Dawson, Light Brigade, p.138

[58] Fay, *Souvenirs*, p.90

[59] Dawson, *Light Brigade*, p.124.

[60] Anon, 'Sir Richard Airey', p.521.

[61] Bapst, *Canrobert*, pp.319-320.

[62] 'Marshall MacMahon on the Charge of Balaklava', *Freeman's Journal* (22 May 1888), np.

[63] Paget, *Light Cavalry Brigade*, p.205.

[64] Anglesey, *A History*, vol. 2, p.84.

[65] Dawson, *Light Brigade*, chapter 5. The Marquess of Anglesey also casts doubt on whether this conversion took place (Anglesey, *A History*, vol. 2, p.84).

[66] Dawson, *Light Brigade*, p.125.

[67] 'The Light Cavalry Charge at Balaklava', *The Morning Chronicle* (6 March 1855), np.

[68] Dawson, *Light Brigade*, chapter 5.

[69] 'The Balaklava Charge. From the letter of a wounded Dragoon in Scutari Hospital', *Cheltenham Chronicle* (23 January 1855), p.4.

[70] Dawson, *Light Brigade*, p.125.

[71] 'The Charge of the Cavalry at Balaklava', *The Morning Chronicle* (15 April 1856), p.6.

[72] Anglesey, *A History*, vol. 2, p.86.

[73] 'Letters from the Crimea', *Morning Post* (1 February 1855), p.3.

[74] ibid.

[75] 'Extracts from a letter from a private in the 8th Hussars ...', *Leeds Intelligencer* (13 January 1855), p.8.

[76] Dawson, *Light Brigade*, pp.128-129.

[77] ibid.

[78] Dawson, *Light Brigade*, pp.125-129.

[79] 'The Charge of the Cavalry at Balaklava', *The Morning Chronicle* (15 April 1856), p.6.

[80] Dawson, *Light Brigade*, p.126.

[81] 'The Cavalry Charge – Letter from One who was in it' *Taunton Courier and Western Advertiser* (29 November 1854), p.7.

[82] 'From a Trumpeter in the Eighth Hussars', *Taunton Courier and Western Advertiser* (29 November 1854), p.7.

[83] 'Letters from the Crimea', Dorset County Chronicle (25 January 1855), p.8.

[84] Kate Taylor, *pers comm.*, Email 24-2-2015.

[85] Captain V. Baker, *The British Cavalry with remarks on its practical organisation* (London:

Longman, Brown, Green, Longmans & Roberts, 1858), p.93.

[86] Bapst, *Canrobert*, p.324.

[87] Vicomte L. R. J. Noë, *Souvenirs d'Afrique et d'Orient: les Bachibozouks et les Chasseurs d'Afrique* (Paris: Michel Levy, 1861), pp.232-233.

[88] Comte de Margon, *General Abdelal*, pp.239-242.

[89] 'The Cavalry Attack at Balaklava', *Manchester Examiner and Times* (9 November 1854), p.2.

[90] Kinglake, *The Invasion of the Crimea*, vol. 5, p.326.

[91] T. Brighton, *Hell Riders* (London: Penguin, 2005), pp.293-294.

[92] Paget, *Light Cavalry Brigade*, p.341.

[93] S. J. G. Calthorpe, *Letters from Headquarters: Or, The realities of the War in the Crimea by an Officer on the Staff* (London: john Murray, 1857), p.132.

[94] Kinglake, *Invasion of the Crimea*, vol. 5, p.326.

[95] *Proceedings of the Board of General Officers …*, p.180.

[96] ibid, p.199.

[97] Kinglake, *Invasion of the Crimea*, vol. 5, p.326.

Chapter 5

Inkerman

Balaklava was a strategic defeat for the British: not only had they lost control of the Woronzoroff Road between Balaklava and the Chersonese Plateau, but their cavalry force had been decimated. The attack on Balaklava had shown how weak the British defences were: indeed, most French officers thought that the battle would never have been fought had the British been more prepared and in greater strength. Having tested the defences in the British rear, the Russians next probed the Allied defences on Mount Inkerman the following day. Sergeant William Morris jnr (63rd) recounted that whilst he and his comrades were eating their evening meal, 'we were suddenly turned out; nearly 4000 men had made an attack on our right flank; but Sir De Lacy Evan's division kindly took them in hand for us.'[1] Corporal Samuel Weale (30th Foot) wrote to his wife, Emma, that

> The left of our army was attacked by the Russians on the 25th Octbr. in which we lost a dreadful number of our cavalry. On the 26th Nov. [*sic.* October] they attacked our right flank which is defended by our (the 2nd) Division the 30th Regiment was on outlying picquet [*sic,* piquet] and we completely drove the enemy back into Sebastopol without any other assistance except the artillery who displayed their skill admirably. The poor handful of the gallant 30th totally defeated some seven thousand Russians, leaving the field covered with their dead and wounded while we lost but 31 men killed and wounded of our regiment.[2]

There is little evidence to suggest that Raglan took this reconnaissance in force seriously. Whilst he did express some anxiety about the weakness of his right flank, he is said to have replied to one officer of engineers who advised him to strengthen his position 'Nonsense! They will never dare come again.' The French, on the other hand, had been busy entrenching themselves. Colonel Herbert, De Lacy Evan's Assistant Quartermaster-General, suggested the construction of a rampart to be built, but in 'in the teeth of Headquarters' opposition.' Nor were any measures taken to clear the position – as the French had – of brushwood.[3] Years later Field Marshal Sir Garnet Wolseley indicted Raglan:

> The battle of Inkerman could never had taken place had any ordinary care and intelligence been shown by those who selected the positions for our outposts … I do not know of another instance of such culpable neglect … of the well known and long established precautions that should be taken by troops in the field against surprise.[4]

The following night *général* Pierre Bosquet reported that:

> Around midnight … at the first redoubt occupied by the Russians (the one closest to us), there is a brisk fusillade, seven or eight cannon shots, the whole preceded by shouts of alarm. At this cannonade, the batteries of Balaklava responded with several shots, and the Turkish artillerymen near the Telegraph, also fired on their side, three or four shells, after having distinctly seen cavalry in the plain. I called to arms, and I sent into the plain several small patrols … and I called for my reserves. At four o'clock in the morning, the posts at the Telegraph, those of the English (later the Redoubt Canrobert), and the first posts of the Zouaves in the middle of the line, between the Telegraph and the Col de Balaklava, are engaged in a fire of musketry … intermixed with several cannon shots. Here is why: there had been truly, all along the line, a movement of horses at the gallop, and a group of about forty, and others … on the main road (Voronzoff), and has entered out camp, leaving several dead on their way; but all this cavalry is without riders.[5]

Preparations for an Assault

By the beginning of November, the French had sapped to within 150 metres of the 'Bastion du Mat' (or 'Flagstaff Battery'); *général* Forey, commanding the French siege lines, concluded that the Bastion du Mat was the weakest of the bastions guarding Sebastopol and resolved to assault the city on 6 or 7 November, proceeded by a heavy artillery bombardment.[6]

The French had amassed a force of 41,789 men organised in five infantry divisions (Bouat, Bosquet, Napoléon, Forey, Lavaillant) and one cavalry division (Morris). *General* Pierre Bosquet (*2e Division*) was placed in command of the *Armée d'Observation* of 14,000 men tasked with guarding the approaches to the Allied lines from the 'Col de Balaklava' to the 'Redoubt Canrobert'.

The divisions of Napoléon (*3e*) Forey (*4e*) and Lavaillant (*5e*) – totalling some 17,000 – were engaged in the siege operations. Lord Raglan, by comparison commanded 24,000 men organised in four infantry divisions, plus the cavalry. The brigades of Generals Eyre and Sir Colin Campbell were detached on siege duties and to garrison Balaklava respectively. In addition, were 5,000 Turks, who were nominally under French command.[7]

The Russians Attack

To the surprise of the French, at 'the first rays of daylight' they came under 'sudden and fierce' Russian artillery barrage; one French officer thought the Russian shells 'fell like rain.' The Russians launched three simultaneous attacks: the first with 40,000 against the British on the Inkerman Heights (with a smaller column detached to pin-down Bosquet); a general attack all along the French siege works and an attack in the Allied rear against the Franco-Turkish positions around Balaklava.[8]

Using the cover of thick fog, two Russian columns were directed against the British position: the first 16,000-strong commanded by General Paulov, crossed the causeway and the River Tchernaya, allowing them to scale the Inkerman heights whilst a second 20,000 men under General Soimonov column sallied out of Sebastopol and climbed the heights via the Carénage ravine.

Paulov's men fell on the camp of the British 2nd Division (De Lacy Evans), surprising the pickets of the 21st and 41st Foot. Private Squire Wood (41st Foot) wrote to his grandfather in Micklefield (near Leeds) that:

> We were within one and a half miles of Sebastopol, and that we and the Russians can fire at each other when we are on picquet, if we are let do so. Our out piquet is close to the Russians ... They advanced on us ... and came on in columns on us, when our company was on outline piquet, and then we gave the alarm, and the other picquets came up to our aid, and we commenced firing on them and them on us; but we put our men in skirmishing order, and theirs came on in columns, so that their shots went through our men and very little harm, but our shots could not miss them, but they were all drunk, and they all ran on us like madmen, but they were soon made to retire.

When we started firing I could not get my piece to go. I tried it three times to go before I could deliver the shot, and was sat under a rock priming it, when some of the Russian sharpers saw me, and fired on me, and one shot took a piece of stone off the rock and not a foot from me. As soon as I got my piece to go I fired at them below, and killed two of them and wounded one. I charged again and fixed my bayonet and run the other two, and shot one of them, and run the other through the heart, but when I looked round there was not one of our men in sight, and the Russians were coming up the hill, and I had to run, and some of the Russians after me, and the shots fired after me took a piece out of the butt of my firelock and broke the bayonet in three pieces.[9]

One officer wrote how the muskets refused to fire:

I was sent to support the advance; on trying the muskets, to my horror I found that only about fifteen out of the company would go off, and out of those fifteen only about six men would follow me to the front. However, there was nothing to be done but to push to the front, and I soon joined the advanced picket, which I found much in the same state, with regard to arms, as my own. We retired gradually before them, as they were coming on in masses of columns, supported with a very powerful artillery, and soon had most desperate work, almost hand to hand, in the thick brush wood.[10]

A surgeon of the Brigade of Guards wrote to family in Newcastle a week after the battle:

At six o'clock on the morning … I was outside my tent, about to visit the sick, who at that time numbered 30. The fog was so dense and heavy that I could scarcely discern any object 50 yards in front of me. There was some little firing of musketry, toward the hill overlooking the encampment of the 2nd division, but not very rapid. However, it was quite evident that something more than ordinary was about to occur; for independently of a good deal of file-firing, a sharp cannonade had commenced, and we could see the flash of the shells through the fog as the explosion took place over the hill of the 2nd division.

I took a bit of biscuit, mounted my horse, and, giving direction that the usual preparations might be made for the reception of the wounded, rode off to the battalion … I found the tents empty, and only one company of the battalion left; three others were on outpost duty, and the remaining four had advanced to meet the enemy ... the firing was now most severe, and the shells were bursting ahead of us in every possible direction, about 250 yards in advance ... the whiz of the shot and explosion of shell were at this moment incessant. While in the act of turning round to remount my horse, a shot passed through the leg of my trousers, and at the same instant my poor horse fell, having been shot through the head, his brains sprinkling my face.[11]

Support in the shape of the 30th and 55th regiments soon arrived, holding back the Russian advance for around thirty minutes, during which time Captain Rowlands (41st) 'begged' Colonel Haly to charge the Russians. A swift melée ensued but Colonel Haly was dragged from his horse and received no fewer than fourteen bayonet wounds, being rescued by Captain Rowlands and Private McDermond. One officer wrote:

Our poor Colonel was shot in the thigh, and when down a Russian shot him in the back, clubbed his musket, and struck him on the mouth ... I saw death in his face when he was brought in at half-past twelve ... He was perfectly resigned, and he said he had made his peace with his Maker; and bade me tell his wife and son they were in his last thoughts; thanked me for my kindness to him ...No one ever on a bed of down died a calmer death ... he said to his servant 'Cochrane, cover my head; I am going to sleep,' shook him by the hand, and wished him good bye ... [he was] lying on his side, wish his hands in an attitude of prayer, his countenance calm and placid as a child's.[12]

Many of the British troops had just returned to camp from their period of duty in the Trenches. William Outing of the Coldstreams reported to his father that 'most of our regiment was coming off duty that morning at daybreak; so instead of going to camp to take breakfast ... [we] commenced fighting for our lives.'[13] Sergeant William Morris Jnr (63rd) wrote in his journal:

On the night of the 4th of November, a heavy, cold, drizzling rain fell. We were in the trenches and about two or three hours before daylight heard a considerable bustle and ringing of the bells of Sebastopol, but thought nothing more of it, than to urge our sentinels a more vigilant look-out. About an hour afterwards we were relieved, and marched to camp. Being wet through, and cold, some of us were rekindling the camp fires, to enable us to get some hot coffee, when the alarm was given that the enemy was advancing by way of Inkerman. Our division was ordered to fall in, but on its being reported to the general that our regiment had only just returned from the trenches ... we were dismissed with the exception of sixty-four men who had not been in the trenches ... This small portion of our men, with some of the 20th, under Lieutenant Curtis, was dispatched ... toward Inkerman. Soon afterwards (not yet daylight) another alarm... and orders came, that every man of our division, should advance to the support of the 2nd Division's camp ... Dark, foggy, with a thick rain falling, up to our ankles in mud, on a road not admitting more than four men abreast ... The flashes of the enemy's guns, gave us occasionally a glimpse of the dense masses of men advancing against us.[14]

Lieutenant Newenham (63rd) wrote that he had been seriously ill with dysentery but upon hearing cannon fire:

Put on my sword and pistols and felt better, and off I started in search of the Regiment, such a search, I never wish to undergo again. I somehow got in rear of the line and show and shell came tumbling about in a most unpleasant manner. I could not find the Rgt. For they and all the rest were in a low brush wood and such a smoke. I at last sat down tired and in despair. However I started again and at last found them lying down waiting for a start.[15]

The camp of the 2nd Division came under pressure from Soimonv's column. Command was temporarily vested in General Pennefather as De Lacy Evans had been thrown from his horse and injured few days before. Pennefather rallied the 47th, 49th, 77th and 88th Foot – in all about 3,000 men – against 10,000 from Soimonov's column. The Brigade of Guards held fast at the head of the Carénage ravine with the 4th Division (Cathcart) holding 'the Barrier'.

One sergeant of the 77th wrote home that,

about seven o'clock a.m., our regiment drove up in line on the extreme left; the ground was thickly covered with brush-wood, and there was a pretty thick fog, which prevented our seeing a powerful force of about 3,000 men, who almost completely surrounded our poor devoted regiment. We had only four companies of the regiment present ... Our four companies did not amount to over 300 men. General Buller exclaimed, 'My God! we are surrounded!' He ordered a volley to be fired into the then, and charged them with the bayonet; which was done in excellent style, and ... routed the cowardly Russians in disorder and confusion.

Steady the Guards!

Quickly coming to the aid of the 2nd Division was the Brigade of Guards under the Duke of Cambridge. Colour-Sergeant P. F. Davies (3rd Battalion, Grenadiers) wrote to friends in Manchester:

> We had not time to get into order before the whole force was upon us, and many were killed in our own tents. But, however, every man did his duty bravely; and, although overwhelmed by numbers, we fought them for hours. We could not have been over five thousand at any one time engaged against them, and they numbering fifty thousand. They had at one time got into our ground, but our handful rallied, and again became masters by driving them off ... Our loss is dreadful. The Brigade of Guards was cut up very much, and the poor third battalion all to pieces. It is no longer a regiment, but a *skeleton* ... we have lost four out of every of the brave fellows the called in the London 'papers of that date 'the flower of the country'.[16]

Davis was,

> one of a devoted band of 200 Grenadiers, in the midst of thousands of the Russian infantry, and without ammunition, having fired their last charge, yet determined to sell their lives as dearly as possible. Davis defended his colours with the utmost tenacity, and literally mowed down the enemy, who made a rush to capture them. On this occasion, Colonel Hamilton, who commanded this fag end of the heroic Grenadiers, seeing that there was nothing left for his men but the bayonet, ordered them to four deep and charge ... in a few minutes a clear gap was visible in the Russian columns ... Amidst dead and dying, first using the bayonet, then the butt-end of his musket, with his arms unnerved from sheer fatigue of striking down the enemy, this sergeant ... towered like a giant.[17]

Lord Raglan and his staff arrived on the scene soon after the Guards.

Alarm in the French Camp

The thunderous cannonade against the French siege works had been heard up in the camp of the French 2e *Division*. *Général* Bosquet

111

immediately called his men to arms and despatched ADCs to report what was occurring. The Russians were seen advancing,

> on three points; on the side of the Bridge of the Inkerman, in front of the right of the English corps of observation; in the plain of the Tchernaya; and in front of an elevated point upon which is constructed a ... wooden telegraph, at the spot where the Woronzov Road debauches from the Plateau.[18]

Colonel Félix de Wimpffen, commanding the *Tirailleurs Algérien* noted:

> The English were taken by surprise just as their dawn reveille was being sounded. Several of their badly defended posts were overrun and the enemy was in among their tents while they were still tumbling out of them alarmed by the noise. Across the North Valley of Balaklava, Russian cavalry, supported by artillery were menacing the French defence line along the edge of the cliffs and firing at us although they were too far away to do much harm. General Bosquet saw that this was only a decoy to stop us going to the help of our allies.

Following the loss of the redoubts on the Causeway Heights at the Battle of Balaklava, the French had established a series of new batteries, armed with twenty-two guns and manned by Turks to protect their rear. A fifth battery manned by French sailors was established at the Telegraph.[19]

Capitaine Herbé (*20e Légère*) recalled that the Turks abandoned two of the redoubts as soon as the Russians approached; the French *6e Dragons* were ordered down into the plain along with the British cavalry to guard against another cavalry attack. They were soon joined by French horse artillery.[20]

Zouave Chantaume (*2e Zouaves*) informed his father that,

> the Russians made a general attack on all of the line on 5 November; they put most of their troops on Mount Inkermann, against the camp of the English. It all commenced at daybreak; it was very foggy and we could not see two paces. They arrived with at least 60,000 men and 40 pieces of cannon that they had with them on the positions, which the English were holding. There were many English who were killed in their tents; they had not time to awaken; their horses were killed at their picket-ropes ... The Russians were to walk through the English camp.

Colonel Le Breton (*74e de Ligne*) reported how:

> The Russians had, during the night, formed up on the mountain dominating the English position. At daybreak they surprised them in their camp. The English, in disorder, abandoned their camps and retired some distance.[21]

Général Bosquet was indignant that his Allies had been surprised in their own camp: he believed that their pickets must have been asleep and that they had not taken the simple precaution of entrenching their position with a simple bank and ditch as was French practice. He fumed '[it was] a massive negligence, contradicting the Military Code, punishable by death, allowing the enemy to rapidly penetrate the position.'[22] He later challenged William Govett Romaine, the Judge Advocate General: 'why do you sacrifice your good soldiers and these fine troops?' by not taking the simple expedient of 'entrenchments and cover in front.'[23]

Confusion reigned as to where the main thrust of the Russian attack was directed; Prince Napoléon (commanding *3e Division*) was gravely ill but was able to mount his horse and 'his presence … in the middle of his soldiers was an act of courage and devotion.'[24] He despatched the first brigade of his division (2nd battalions of the *20e* and *22e Légère*) under *général* de Monet towards Inkerman.[25] *Colonel* Cler (*2e Zouaves*) pleaded with the Prince to march in support with one battalion of his regiment:

> Towards 9 o'clock, de Monet's brigade streams over the ridge of mount Sapoune, on a line with the windmill of Inkerman, *général* Canrobert at once gives it orders, to line the crest of the heights which overlook the valley of the Tchernaya, and to keep in check the Russian corps which, arrayed upon the slopes of the Fedioukine Hills, as well as in the plain extending between the aqueduct and the river, threatens momentarily an attack upon that position of our line.
>
> *Général* de Monet takes with him the 19th battalion of *chasseurs à pied*, two battalions of the *20e* and *22e légère*, and directs the colonel Cler to put himself at the head of the *Zouaves* and three companies of *Infanterie de Marine*.
>
> 'Spread out your pants' cries the colonel to his *Zouaves*, 'and make a big a show as you can.' For, such, indeed, and no other was the mission of this little troop, consisting of a thousand men at most.[26]

De Monet's brigade was, at this moment, the only reserve *général* Canrobert possessed and he ordered Cler to 'check the ardour of your

Zouaves' who were impatient to attack. Canrobert ordered de Monet to fall back, forming a second line, in support of the Brigade of Guards but soon found themselves exposed to heavy Russian artillery fire.[27]

Defence of the Barrier

General Cathcart's 4th Division was 'ordered to … support on their [2nd Division's] left … and took up position opposite the Sandbag Battery, in support of the 1st Brigade … this position, however, was not tenable.'[28] By now it had started to become light and the Russian troops could be seen advancing to out-flank the Sandbag Battery:

> The Russians, still advancing, drove before them the pickets of the 55th and 88th Regiments, who were gallantly disputing every inch of ground with the enemy's skirmishers, but sadly out-numbered… The enemy were advancing directly in front of our regiment, and General Torrens, placing himself just in rear of our colours, gave word to charge: a loud and simultaneous cheer burst from the men, as they sprung to their feet, having for some minutes been lying down, and they bounded through the intervening brushwood with a ferocity and alacrity truly astonishing; and now, in reality, commenced the Tug of War! The strife was, indeed, fearful. If we had been charging merely two ranks, the same as our own, then our work would have been soon done; but we had no sooner disposed of the first two or three ranks than we found behind them other ranks densely packed together … at length we threw the enemy into confusion, and they rapidly retired down the ravine. Captain Harris, who took the lead in this bloody affair, was, with his Lieutenant Newenham, severely wounded … The gallant 21st on our left, were at the same time hotly engaged against great odds.[29]

Bandsman William Watts (21st Foot) wrote to his family in Leeds that he had been employed 'in dangerous duties' as a stretcher bearer:

> Henry Flannery and John Enwright are both killed. Poor Enwright's head was blown off. I am thankful I am now living and able to write this letter, for we had a dreadful day of it on the 5th. It was an awful day's work. The Russians came out of Sebastopol the night before, and at six o'clock in the morning they were upon us while we were in our tents. They were 80,000 strong. We were fighting one hour before the French came up. The Russians fought desperately. They blew all our tents to the devil. I suppose Waterloo was nothing to it. The bands of the regiments have very dangerous duties to do: we

114

follow the regiment and pick up the wounded, and take the Russian prisoners to the rear, and then they are taken to the camp … Our regiment has lost 200 in killed and wounded. Nearly all our officers are killed or wounded.[30]

No sooner had one Russian column been repulsed than a second column was seen trying to scale the heights, having 'gained a hill in rear of our [4th Division] flank, and this placed us in a most critical, as well as dangerous, position.' Bombardier George Haigh of Wakefield was one of the gunners sent in support with heavy artillery:

It was a near case with me, for our company was sent up to a hill with two eighteen-pounders, and we did very well with them, till at length a shell came over and burst, and killed one sergeant, one corporal, and wounded two bombardiers, three gunners, and I was one of the bombardiers that was wounded.[31]

An anonymous artillery officer wrote:

The crest of the hill was covered with smoke, and the entire ground there thickly clothed with brushwood, through which we with the greatest difficulty moved the guns. Suddenly the smoke cleared away, and we discovered the Russian infantry in great force within 10 yards of us. I shall never forget the aspect of those fellows, dressed in their long grey coats and flat glazed caps, firing most deliberately at our poor gunners, and picking them down like so many crows.

We at this time were under a very heavy fire of shot and shell. Major Townshend saw at once the critical position of the guns, and most wisely gave the order to retire, as we were quite unsupported – but too late; the enemy's skirmishers had come up to the guns. However, five out of the six escaped; and one of the poor men, seeing the last, as was then supposed, certain to be taken, judiciously spiked it.

The gun belonged to a division of our battery, to which was attached young Miller, one of our lieutenants; and poor Major Townshend, turning round his horse, seeing what was likely to occur, cried out 'You won't disgrace me.' The words were hardly out of his mouth when a shell burst in among us and … one fragment struck him on the head and literally crushed it to pieces … Miller drew his sword, and single-handed galloped his horse toward the gun, riding down one and cutting down a second

115

Russian … He returned with his gun, without having received even a scratch.[32]

A drummer of the 47th witnessed the melée around the guns:

> They [the Russians] came on cheering at the charge, and they beat us off the hill and took two of our guns, when the Artillery office came to us and said, '47th, will you let them take our guns from us?' and we gave a shout to charge them. When we got the order to charge the Russians we charged them with a shout of determination that carried everything with it. We capture our guns back again, and drove them down the heights. It was a regular hand-to-hand fight. My sword was broken in my hand, and I worked away with the bayonet of one of our poor fellows that was killed by my side.[33]

Give them a Volley and Charge!

By now the whole of the 63rd, and a wing of the 21st were stationed well in front of Home Ridge; they were supported to the left of the Post Road by elements of the 55th and the 47th. On their extreme right were 150 Guardsmen and a similar number of the 57th. Lieutenant Newenham (63rd) recounts how the Grenadier and Number 1 companies of the 63rd were posted in open order in front of the battalion in skirmishing order and that very soon:

> We blazed away as hard we could, where we saw the shots from the Russian skirmishers. At last we were recalled and going in a man of my Company said, 'There are two of them Sir' so I said 'Shoot them', he fired and one fell. I then looked round and all ours were gone. So I ran after them, and such a shower of shots came after me I wonder I was not riddled. Only one hit me in the leg. I hardly felt it at the time. But just as I pass thro' the line, by the Colours of the 21st N.B.F. [North British Fusiliers] the loss of blood and pain stopped me. I luckily came across two of ours Drs and a stretcher. They bandaged my leg and sent me home on a stretcher. There was the end of my fight.[34]

The Adjutant of the 63rd, Lieutenant Robert Bennet, was unsure as to the viability of their position:

> The Russians would have turned over our position, and that all would have been lost. They opened up a tremendous fire of artillery on us... It was evident something must be done, or the enemy would

116

be in the camp of the 2nd Division. Colonel Swyny (whether by order or by Brigadier I cannot say) ordered the 63rd to halt and Front ... and meet the enemy ... and immediately came to the charge, rushed over the crown of the hill, and sent the Russians, in awful confusion, into the valley below.[35]

Sergeant-Major Morris remembered seeing 'General Cathcart place himself in the midst of his division' and 'spoke very encouragingly to them.' 'When he was reminded that our ammunition was expended he replied, "Well, you must use your bayonets". The men were 'hemmed in on all sides and exposed to a heavy fire. Volley after volley, was poured in upon us, and in one of these, Sir George [Cathcart] was killed.'[36]

Sergeant-Major James Slack wrote home that:

Brigadier-General Pennefather... rode up, called for Colonel Swyny, and said, 'Let me see what metal the 63rd is made of; the enemy will be soon upon you, be ready to give him a volley and charge.'

Colonel Swyny had formed his regiment in line and ordered the men to lie down, as they were exposed to a terrific fire from the enemy's artillery. The morning was foggy, and the enemy, rushing up the ravine in columns, were close upon us before they could be seen. The colonel gave the order to fire a volley and charge. A volley was fired, when the regiment, with its usual cheer, charged with the bayonet and drove the Russians down to the Barrier; they however disputed every inch of ground with incredibly fury and determination ... Colonel Swyny charged at the head of his regiment, but one barrel of his revolver only had been discharged before he fell in this murderous melée ...

Sergeant Prouse ... [was] severely wounded on the road above the Barrier ... Major the Honourable Dalzell ... rode up, when his horse, being shot, galloped a considerable distance down the road towards Sebastopol before he fell dead with Major Dalzell under him ... Lieutenant Curtois was a promising young officer, and a favourite in the regiment... he was unfortunately killed by a roundshot... Lieutenant Twysden was mortally wounded by a shell and immediately afterwards Ensign Clutterbuck was killed in the charge; both these officers were carrying the colours.[37]

Sergeant-Major Morris remembered how:

Poor Clutterbuck was the last officer who carried the Queen's Colour ... and, when he was killed, Sergeant Brophey had some trouble in releasing the colour from his death-grip. Brophey then, while waving the colour and cheering on the men, was shot through the left thigh; but as he lay on the ground, regardless of the pain from his wound, he continued to wave the colour as a rallying point for them ...

Brophey had nearly two miles to creep along before he could hope to get surgical assistance, and every moment getting weaker from the loss of blood, and suffering also from hunger, thirst, and excessive fatigue ... Worn out he was giving up all hope of safety, ... when he was fortunately induced to shake the canteen of a dead 41st man, and found it nearly full of water ... he bound up his wound ... but... was again obliged to give up from sheer exhaustion, when fortunately two men of our regiment came by, and removed him to the Windmill.[38]

One anonymous Rifleman thought that colours were 'dangerous incumbrances':

I was out from five o'oclock in the morning until six at night, without time to eat. I was two hours in a hole firing as fast as I could, and I believe every shot told ... We exhausted our ammunition several times, and had to use the bayonet, which is unusual with us Rilfes. My comrade (we generally go in pairs), was shot in the arm. A bullet just graved my neck, scarcely ruffling the skin ... After I had used my powder... I went, with some others, to protect the colours of the 77th, which were nearly taken, but we succeeded in keeping them. I do not like these colours: they only serve to draw the enemy's fire upon the men. The Rifles have no such dangerous incumbrances.[39]

En Avant Bosquet!
The first French troops on to the field were those of the brigade of *général* Bourbaki: two battalions each of the *6e de Ligne*, *7e Légère*, four companies from *3e Chasseurs à Pied* and two batteries of horse artillery. They took post to the left of the Telegraph Redoubt. The *7e Légère* had been on trench duty all night and, having just returned from camp and instead of getting their breakfasts, strapped on their knapsacks and 'marched to the sound of the guns.'[40] The French troops were greeted with 'loud hurrahs.' Bosquet, however, was lucky to escape being a victim of 'friendly fire.' According to *serjeant* Morris Jnr:

At this moment that brave general was, perhaps, never so near his death, for we had a man in our light company, an American, named

118

Warrant', who was armed with a Minié, and was considered one of our best marksmen, and, as he saw the French advancing on our left, mistaking them for Russians, he said to his sergeant, 'Brophy, see me bring that Russian officer down.' The sergeant, by a motion of his hand, turned the piece away, and in all probability saved the general's life.[41]

Général Bourbaki was joined by *Général* Bosquet and his staff and mounted escort at the Windmill at 07.30 hours.[42] It was at the Windmill where Bosquet encountered General Cathcart (commanding the British 4th Division) and General Brown (Commanding the Light Division). A brief conversation took place between the three generals, Bosquet offering the British his full support. To this offer, either Brown or Cathcart (it has not been recorded) responded with a fatal confidence that 'Our reserves are sufficient to guard against all contingencies; be good enough to cover our right a little, in the rear of the British redoubt.[43]' Bosquet sent an ADC, Colonel de Cissey, to order Bourbaki to rapidly move to the front, to support the British right and the beleaguered British 2nd Division. Bourbaki sent forward the *6eme de Ligne* and the *7eme Légère*. They were supported by the two reserve batteries of Horse Artillery of Thoumas and Toussaint. In addition, were three heavy 30-pounder Paixhans guns manned by French sailors.[44]

Personally led by *général* Bourbaki, the *6eme de Ligne* and *7eme Légère* and the 1st Battalion *Tirailleurs Algérien* charged with the bayonet the Russian troops advancing onto the heights:

> The three battalions assembled with the *7eme*, charged together the Russians, and overthrew them with the bayonet in the belly to the bottom of the Inkermann Ravine, and pressed them one against the other to present a compact mass for the musketry fire, and they were crushed and put into complete rout.[45]

Capitaine Adrien was at the head of his company of *voltigeurs* of the *6eme*:

> We arrived at the critical moment …we marched with confidence into the Inkerman ravine, and fell against the right flank of the Russians, who we pursued hotly, I heard a constant whistling of [musket] balls. Several cannon balls ricocheted at my side and covered me with earth. Several men were killed and wounded beside me.

My sabre was covered in blood; the terrain was literally covered with Russian bodies ... In the middle of this butchery, I was found to be perfectly calm, always master enough of myself to lead the men around me. You have never seen such confusion: *7e Légère, 6e de Ligne, Zouaves*, English, *chasseurs*, riflemen, *turcos*, all of them mixed up...

Two times, during this affair, we have to retreat, and, two times we come back to the charge ... the Russians are definitively beaten and our success is assured.[46]

Eagle of the 6e

At the Barrier, a position designed to cut off access to the Inkerman Heights, officers of the 21st and 63rd Regiments noticed 'five columns of the beggars advancing upon us, so we retired'. The Russian infantry attacked in 'a profound column,' advancing like 'a human hurricane' against the French line where they were met by a hail of fire. The Russians had the superior numbers, however, and the French were 'thrown back by the ever-increasing throng; but they retired step by step, fighting like lions.'[47].

As the melée developed, the *porte-aigle* of the *6eme*, Sous-Lieutenant Rotté, was cut down by a member of the Ochkost Regiment and the precious emblem fell to the earth.[48] Lieutenant Colonel Francois-Auguste Goze, the second in command, rushed forward to recover it, waving the standard over his head shouting 'The Eagle, the Eagle' but was shot in the right arm. As the eagle fell for a second time the '*sous-officiers* and ordinary soldiers ... rushed forward' to retrieve their standard.[49] The eagle was extricated and passed 'hand over hand, into the rear ranks of the battalion' and presented to the colonel by lieutenant Biggotte.

No sooner had Camas received the eagle, than he fell from his horse, mortally wounded. The stricken colonel was immediately surrounded by members of the grenadier company of the *6eme* to protect him; *sergent* Ricci (*6e*) and a soldier of the *7e Légère* rushed forward to rescue the fallen colonel 'carrying him by his shoulders, over his back for about thirty paces' so that he was clear of the fighting. Sergeant Ricci insisted on trying to get the colonel to an ambulance, and had sent off his colleague from the *7eme* to find a surgeon.

Camas, however, was losing a lot of blood and knew he was dying; he told his rescuers to 'leave me here... for I have nothing to do but die.' He asked to see the colours but started to lose consciousness from lack of blood, yet 'continued to feel about, with his hand, repeating the words "my father's sword".' The sword was recovered by a sergeant who carried it 'suspended from his shoulder by the sword knot' but was later 'lost in the melée'. Just before he died, colonel de Camas recognised Riccis bravery by awarding him the *Legion d'Honneur.*[50]

Seeing the *6e de Ligne* wavering, the men of the *7e Légère* started to panic; they began to fall back in confusion, but *sergent* Padovani grabbed the eagle of the *7e* and 'advanced five or six paces in front, and planted the eagle in the ground, and rallied his braves, his face to the Russians.'[51]

À La Baionnette

It was at this critical point, with Bourbaki's brigade in difficulty, that *général* d'Autmarre's brigade (*3e Régiment des Zouaves, Tirailleurs Algériens, 3e Chasseurs à Pied*) joined the fray. The relief amongst the British and French troops was palpable:

> Our ammunition was expended, and we were supplying ourselves from the pouches of dead men, when the *Zouaves* came bounding down the ravine like deer and joined the fray.[52]

Another British officer wrote:

> The French behaved nobly. There was no coolness about them … they attacked the enemy with a fierce, reckless enthusiasm, which carried all before it. The 50th Regiment of the Line in particular 'Covered itself with Glory.' It was awful to see them charge the enemy's flanks, making a thousand killed and wounded at every charge.[53]

Zouave officer Eugene Perret later recalled:

> 'Come on my irresistible *Zouaves*! Come on my brave *chasseurs*!' he [Bosquet] shouted in a strong voice 'show yourselves the children of fire!' … Everyone rushes on the enemy… One looks at these Africans, a troop of tawny beasts, suddenly unleashed; the balls of the Russians do not touch or strike then … This heroic charge is the admiration of both armies.[54]

Capitaine Fay was at the side of *général* Bosquet:

> Nothing can compare with the effect of the arrival of these veterans of the African army, bronze complexion, a strange costume, carrying their bayonets forward; the *Tirailleurs Algeriens* leaping 'amidst the scrub like panthers'… Profiting from their [Russian] hestitation, four companies of *Tirailleurs*, four of *Zouaves* and the half-battalion

of *Chasseurs à Pied* pursued [them] up to the ridge which dominated the old post road, and extended on the right to the extremity of this ridge, while the *6e de Ligne* and the *7e Légère* charged with a new impetuosity on the post road. The reserve is formed at the sand-bag battery, by the remainder of the battalions of *Zouaves* and *Tirailleurs*.[55]

Capitaine Henri-Augustin Brincourt was a thirty-one-year-old company commander in the *3e Zouaves*:

> After an hour of a race, the battalion arrived at the English camp, at the moment when the Russians entered it for the second time. We did not even have time to make a proper deployment, and, without knowing anything other than this: we must repulse the Russians, we ran at them with the bayonet … A shiver than through the men like electricity, from their head to their feet; all were delirious. The officers knew to shout to augment the enthusiasm. One hears 'Zouaves! You are what you are today. Everyone has seen you at the Alma: the first soldiers in the world! Forward! My little jackals; with the bayonet, my children!'… The bugles sounded, each in his own way, [playing] different sorts of polkas, marches and charges and shouts deafened by the whistling of bullets, the shells, the case shot and the cannon balls … I put my *kepi* on the point of my sabre, and I ran like crazy …
>
> Hardly had they [the Russians] discharged their weapons, than they ran, without waiting to reload. Their long greatcoats embarrassed their legs; they had no time to return; they received two or three bayonet thrusts. I had an insolent happiness … After crossing an immense plateau, [we] descended a big ravine, and were going to cross another, beyond which was the Russian artillery …
>
> Before us, only several paces away, rolling like an immense herd, 3 or 4,000 Russians … We were in the middle of the Russians. They fired musket-shots, but avoided fighting hand-to-hand.[56]

At the head of the *Tirailleurs Algériens* was their colonel, Félix de Wimpffen:

> Our troops are forced to fold, and the Russians advanced into the English camp, several of them reach the first [line of] tents, when a battalion of *Zouaves* and one of *Tirailleurs* [*Algeriens*] rush on them. Two times the French troops chase our enemies … into the plain; at the second only, did the latter only abandon their project to capture the English lines.[57]

The French had attacked too well: they had chased the Russians down the ravine and found themselves trapped, fighting against overwhelming odds and coming under artillery fire from Russian batteries near the lighthouse and ships in the harbour. The melée dissolved into vicious hand-to-hand fighting, using musket-butts, and throwing rocks and stones. *Capitaine* Fay recalled:

> The march of the Russians, for an instant suspended by the resistance of commandant Dubos, is recommenced. The Okhotsk and Yakoutsk advanced in front, [the] Seleghinsk on the flank, towards the sand-bag battery. But, on our side, *général* d'Autemarre ... decided to repulse the enemy with a supreme effort, bringing, at this moment all of his troops to the charge, supported by his artillery ... Under their protection, *général* Bourbaki sent forward for the fourth time his intrepid battalions ... The Russians were pushed into the Quarry Ravine; the *Zouaves* and the *Tirailleurs Algeriens*, extending to the right, at the same time repulsed with the bayonet the battalions of the Seleghinsk into the ravine of the sandbag battery, and forced them to pass the aqueduct.[58]

According to *capitaine* Fay, the battle was beginning to swing in the Allies favour by 11.00 hours and by noon the Russians were retreating in disorder but they maintained a steady artillery fire until late in the afternoon.

Attack on the Siege Works

Whilst the drama on the Inkerman Heights was unfolding, two strong Russian columns attacked the French siege works. *Colonel* Le Breton reported:

> At daybreak, we were attacked with fury by around 6 to 8,000. The battalions on guard, of the *39e*, the *19e* and the *Légion Étrangère*, and also the workers, surprised in their trenches, folded; but in the meantime, we all descended from the camp. We filled the trenches with Russian bodies.[59]

Commandant Lacretelle of the *Légion Étrangère* wrote that at around 06.00 hours the heavy overnight rain stopped, only to be replaced by 'a fog equally intense, and it is impossible to distinguish anything at several paces.' It had started to dissipated by 08.30 (when the relief parties were getting ready to enter the trenches) when suddenly:

There was a fusillade which extends on our right. Suddenly, one of my *voltigeurs*, who was towards the bottom of the ravine … cried 'To Arms! The Russians are behind me!'. These were the scouts of *général* Timofeief, who led a column of 4,000 men, who was to turn our trenches, while … another column of the same force, was sent against our batteries … The fusillade grows in intensity in front of us; the voice of cannon is added …

The skirmishers of Timofeief were not a hundred paces from us; each of our shots takes effect but the strong Russian column was still climbing; our companies are weakened after the Alma, containing only about 65 effective men; I don't have 200 men with me, and I thought the Russians were too numerous to engage as they came between our lines. We had to quickly take a part; each instant made our position more critical … 'Forward! With the bayonet!' and the bugles sound the charge.

My 200 legionnaires, old soldiers of Africa, don't hesitate for a moment: they rush the enemy skirmishers, they push over the head of column, swirling in a moment, but the enemy opens a volley on us, and continues its forward march.[60]

Elsewhere along the line, French troops were coming under pressure:

Around nine o'clock … a column of five or six thousand Russians came out by the 'Quarantine Bastion' and preceded by numerous skirmishers, who bravely pounced on the left of our parallels, capturing the batteries 1, 2 and 3, and in an instant the enemy was master. *Général* de la Motterouge is in the trenches; the 1st battalion of the *20e* [*Légère*] under the orders of captain Moreno, is the guard of batteries 13b and 14b; the companies of the left support the batteries 8 and 9. The *voltigeurs* of captain Pouget and the *6e* company of lieutenant Morel are sent as quickly as possible to the batteries taken by the Russians and throw out the Russians with impetuosity. Captain Pouget falls, a ball through his thigh; his *sous-lieutenant*, Schwartz, surrounded by his brave *voltigeurs*, fights hand-to-hand; the enemy evacuates the batteries.[61]

The *Légion Étrangère* soon found itself hard-pressed:

At the start of the action, I had sent a few minutes away two corporals, to ask for support at the depot of the trenches at the clock tower, where I knew there were three companies of *chasseurs à pied* in reserve. I saw nothing coming from that direction and began to fear my corporals would not arrive. But the intensity of our fire had attracted the attention of our bivouacs and I saw movement on their side 'Hold fast, my comrades! We are coming to your aid!' But our bivouacs are in the rear, more than 1500 metres, and it is immediate relief we need.

Finally, I hear the sound of bugles, and in the direction of the clock tower, and I see a black mass rapidly advancing toward us. I distinguish the uniform of the *chasseurs à pied*; it's the support I asked for and impatiently waited … The brave captain X … arrived at the wall, sees a few paces before him and below him, the enemy column, stops astonished, and as soon, without hesitating, throwing off his cloak and drawing his sabre [cries] 'Forward! With the bayonet!' He crossed the wall, followed by a hundred or hundred and fifty *chasseurs*, and fell on the head and left flank of the Russian column.

It was the moment I had expected. I jumped onto the ledge of the quarry 'Stand up! With the bayonet!' My legionnaires follow me, and we fall on the right flank of the Russians, at the same time as the *chasseurs* on the left flank. Imagine the furious attack of 400 soldiers, veterans of the wars of Africa, habituated to the boldest raids, incapable of doubting their success … it's with thrusts of the bayonet and musket-butts which address the Russian column, throwing back the first ranks onto those who follow, and who, in several minutes, make a body of troops more than ten times their number about turn. The disorder is at its height amongst the enemy: the pursuit becomes butchery, the Carénage ravine in the direction of the Quarantine [Redoubt], is covered with dead and wounded.[62]

Help came from *général* La Motterouge and Lourmel:

At this moment, the sounding of bugles is heard behind us and rapidly approaching. It's the arrival of the brigade of Lourmel. It's chief, with his usual energy, heads to our right, going directly to batteries 1 and 2 which Timofeief had captured, he made him [the enemy] evacuate it …

In the flow of the battle, when at the moment I crossed the wall for the second time, I felt a strong sensation in my left shoulder; a ball had gone through my shoulder. I realised this wound was not serious, the clavicle was not broken, my arm was free, and I was able to remain in combat with my comrades. But the loss of blood made me weak. With the arrival of *général* de Lourmel … I was persuaded to quit the battlefield.

Captain Bounetou … who was in the same situation as me, a ball in the leg, had also been obliged to retire. We headed together towards our bivouacs, and, having met an ambulance mule, we were conducted to the ambulance of our divison.[63]

Capitaine Herbé wrote how,

Général de la Motterouge, commandant that day of the troops on service in the trenches, crossed the parapet, then rushed with our [20e *Légère*] companies on the Russian masses, which fell back, to rally under the protection of the guns of the city.

At the moment the enemy reformed, coming forward, a reserve brigade under the orders of *général* Lourmel, arrived at the run and threw itself on the Russians with such impetuosity that they returned in disorder behind their fortifications.

Général de Lourmel, did not have any doubts, and intended to enter Sebastopol in pursuit of the Russians, but at the moment he gave his orders, for this purpose, he fell, hit by a ball in the chest.[64]

The French troops ran on, almost out of control, chasing the Russians back into Sebastopol as Lieutenant Cullet relates:

Their shock is irresistible, the Russians retire in disorder, pursued with our bayonets in their bellies by the soldiers of *général* Lourmel and the companies of the *20e* [*Légère*], while the brigade of d'Aurelles, hastened to their side, covered on the left by a deadly fire.

The brave *général* Lourmel, has an ardour which he communicates to his soldiers, to advance beyond the houses, but just under the guns of the city, a ball passed through his chest. He died the following day … *général* Forey ordered the retreat; the troops engaged retired, but not without serious losses.[65]

Watching from the heights, *général* Forey saw the impending disaster with de Lourmel's men running straight into the face of Russian heavy batteries and 'immediately' sent orders for de Lourmel to retire. One of Forey's ADCs, *commandant* d'Auvergne, arrived soon after de Lourmel had fallen.

Command passed to colonel Niol (*26e de Ligne*), and supported by the *74e de Ligne* (colonel Le Breton) and two companies from the *5e Chasseurs à Pied*, Forey managed to extricate de Lourmel's and d'Aurelles' men. Colonel Le Breton reported:

Above: Allied soldiers were voracious readers – not just of letters home but of newspapers. Here relaxed British troops are listening whilst a more literate member of their band reads aloud news of the day, probably several months old by the time it reached the Crimea.

Below: British and French soldiers fraternise in camp whilst a *Cantinière* enjoys the hospitality of a group of British sailors. *Punch Magazine* joked that the *Cantinières*, who shocked much of British polite society by wearing trousers, were the '[w]hor[e]s de combat' when they were nothing of the sort.

Above: The French, like their allies, had to improvise clothing food and shelter during the dreadful winter of 1854-1855. This group of French officers, sketched in camp, are wearing a wide variety of far from regulation uniform.

Left: The French commissariat, perhaps even more so than the British, collapsed under the strain of wartime conditions. Here a *Zouave* is grinding his coffee in a shell fragment.

Left: A rather dejected-looking *Chasseur d'Afrique* on picket duty in the winter 1854. Note how the conical bell-tent has had a low wall built around its base to improve head-room, as well as the horses sheltering behind windbreaks, though this were later ensconced in dug-out stables. Despite these precautions, equine mortality was horrendous.

Below: One of the most unusual spectacles of the entire siege was the 'Theatre du Zouaves', or 'Theatre d'Inkermann'. Established by the French, soldier-performers raised money for their wounded comrades in arms, the shows being attended by British and French officers and men alike.

Above: *Cantinières*, females serving alongside their male counterparts to provide food, brandy, a few luxuries and tend the wounded, had been a feature of the French Army since the 1690s. During the Battle of Inkerman, one *Cantinière* fought off several Russian attackers, saving the life of her wounded husband.

Below: *Cantinières* were brave and loyal. Often called 'Mère' (mother) by the troops they served with, they tended the wounded off all sides, including this little drummer boy.

Above: The death of Captain Louis Nolan at Balaklava, sketched by a friend. A shell-splinter tore open his chest as he was in the act of giving the order 'Threes Right' to re-direct the ill-fated Light Brigade.

Below: The brutal, savage, close-quarter trench fighting in the Crimea is brought home in this French illustration, with bayonets, rifle-butts and fists being the order of the day.

Above: The final act of the eleven-month siege, the attack and capture of the Malakoff or 'Round Tower', the erstwhile 'Key to Sebastopol', by French troops under *Général* MacMahon. This was an attack which could have gone disastrously wrong when it was found, moments before the attack went in, that someone had forgotten the scaling ladders!

Left: No such luck for the British in their ill-fated attack on the Great Redan. Lead by General Charles Ash Windham, who was vocal in his condemnation of the British high command in the Crimea, it was poorly planned and, using too few troops, was a painful fiasco.

Above: Death is ever-present in war. Sketched in the field by Hippolyte Bellangé, this drawing depicts two brothers who were killed side-by-side at the Battle of Tratkir, only to be found together in an eternal embrace.

Below: French troops burying their dead. There was little 'nobility in death' for most casualties at the Crimea, for whom little more than a mass grave, a sprinkling of quick lime and a perfunctory Funeral Rite awaited.

Above: The French Imperial Guard, headed by its walking wounded, triumphantly enters Paris to the adulation of the crowds. There was no such celebration for the poor troops of the Line who remained camped around Sebastopol.

Right: Two French soldiers, a *Chasseur à Pied* and a *Zouave*, in company with a British Guardsman, celebrate the fall of Sebastopol amidst its ruins.

The two *chefs de bataillon* of the *26e* are killed ... I lost one officer (the *sous-lieutenant* Lemaire) and 5 soldiers killed; 47 wounded of which 5 were made amputees ... The struggle was unequal; not because of the number, which cannot overcome the admirable élan and intrepidity of our soldiers but because of unheard fatigues from such a colossal siege ... *Général* de Lourmal paid with his life for his fatal courage, his temerity which led the regiments of his brigade up to the mouths of the cannons. Hitting the head against a wall, and then back, crossing the cannon balls, the canister shot and shells. It was madness![66]

Aftermath

Inkerman was something of a pyrrhic victory – the 'soldier's battle.' The British had lost 2,816 killed or wounded and the French around 1,800. The French reported that the Allies buried 4,500 Russian dead, attended to 900 wounded and took 250 prisoners. *General* Bosquet, surveying the sand-bag battery, where bodies were heaped nearly as high as the parapet, exclaimed 'quelle abattoir' (what a slaughter-house). Amongst the British dead were Generals Cathcart and Strangeways.

Whilst the French had hurried to the aid of the British, some commentators in the British domestic press unfairly claimed Bosquet had been slow to respond which placed even further strain on the already tense alliance. Many British soldiers, however, expressed their admiration and thankfulness toward the French; Bombardier Weeks of Leeds wrote that:

If it had not been for the French reinforcements, the English would have been completely done for, as the Russians were so numerous, and advanced upon us repeatedly, but without success.[67]

The Rev. A. M. Lawless, Assistant-Chaplain to the 2nd Division, was exhausted, tending to the wounded and dying:

Oh! What a sad spectacle was now before my eyes! Groups every moment increasing of wounded men and officers of the several regiments of the division spread upon the ground, their respective surgeons with gory hands busily and anxiously performing their labours; many of the poor sufferers consoling themselves as best they could for the loss of shattered parts which had just been amputated ... Many a one ... joined fervently in prayer ...

Several, whilst conscious that their wound was mortal, exhibited the greatest patience under agony, and expressed meek and humble, but cheerful and hearty faith in their Lord… Colonel Haly, of the 47th, had several wounds, which he bore most cheerfully …. Colonel Carpenter, of the 41st, was dreadfully wounded … he … gave utterance to a long and fervid prayer … Poor Major Dalton was pierced through the stomach. He was very weak, expressed anxiety about his 'poor wife and children.' He joined fervently in prayer, casting his care upon God … General Adams … in great pain from a musket wound through the ankle ….

I found poor Colonel Blair in great pain … he had been wounded through the stomach. He was in deep concern for his soul … he joined earnestly in prayer Oh! how solemn to witness the soul's anxiety in its fast ebbing moments! And how anxious the ministerial task.[68]

The funeral of generals Cathcart and Strangeways took place with great solemnity on 6 November:

Shortly before the hour of sunset … a troop of Royal Horse Artillery, with a solitary gun-carriage. On the gun-carriage rested a rough plank coffin, enclosing the mortal remains of a good old soldier, General Fox Strangeways. There was neither knell nor band, no funeral pall, no decoration, no attempt to cloak over the rough work of death. The dull distant boom of cannon, as gun replied to gun … was the only music which accompanied the warrior to his last resting place. The troops of a whole division under arms gazed at the sad procession … in solemn silence … On the crest of this Russian hill … lies the corpse of another British soldier … Sir George Cathcart … by his side will be placed his brother in arms of yesterday; and there, amid prayers and tears both will be consigned to the common earth.[69]

The Russians had been bloodily repulsed: it was clear that they were unable to raise the siege whilst it was also equally apparent to the Allies that they would not be able to assault Sebastopol with the small force available to them, and, as autumn began to change into winter, the biggest enemy they would face would not be the Russians, but the Crimean Peninsula itself.

NOTES
[1] T. Morris, W. Morris, & W. Morris Jnr, *The Three Serjeants or phases of the soldier's life* (London: Effingham Wilson, 1858), p.212.

[2] 'Letter from a wounded soldier to his wife in Wakefield', *Wakefield Journal & Examiner* (1 December 1854).

[3] W. Baring-Pemberton, *Battles of the Crimean War* (London: B. T. Batsford Ltd., 1962), pp.121-122.

[4] ibid, p.122.

[5] General Fay, *Souvenirs de Crimee*, pp.95-96.

[6] Bazancourt, *l'expedition*, tome 2, pp.51-54.

[7] Fay, *Souvenirs de Crimee*, pp.97-101.

[8] Herbé, *Francais et Russes*, pp.126-128.

[9] 'A letter received from a young soldier from the village of Micklefield', *Leeds Intelligencer* (23 December 1854), p.3.

[10] 'Letters from the Crimea. From an Officer of the Second Division', *The Essex Standard* (8 December 1854), np.

[11] 'The Battle of Inkerman. Further Particulars' *Newcastle Courant* (8 December 1854), p.2.

[12] 'Letters from the Crimea. From an Officer of the Forty-first', *The Essex Standard* (8 December 1854), np.

[13] 'Extract of a letter dated December 14' *Morning Chronicle* (12 January 1855), np.

[14] Morris et al, *The Three Serjeants*, p.214.

[15] MRA, Acc. MR 1/16/2 Newenhamm Mss, Newenham to family, 24 November 1854.

[16] 'Another Letter from Colour-Sergeant Davis (From the *Manchester Guardian*)'. Preston Chronicle (9 December 1854), p.2.

[17] ibid.

[18] Bezancourt, L'Expedition, tome 2, p.62.

[19] Fay, *Souvenirs de Crimee*, p.102.

[20] Herbé, *Francais et Russes*, p.136.

[21] Devanlay, 'General Breton', p.87.

[22] Herbé, Francais et Russes, p.129.

[23] Fusiliers Museum, Bury, Acc. LFA FO.1, William Govett Romaine Mss., Diary. Entry 5 November 1854.

[24] Roche, *Un regiment de Ligne*, p.112.

[25] ibid.

[26] McClellan, *Zouave Officer*, p.150.

[27] ibid, pp.151-152.

[28] Morris et al, *The Three Serjeants*, pp.214-215.

[29] Morris et al, *The Three Serjeants*, pp.214-216.

[30] 'Letter from a Leeds Soldier', *Leeds Mercury* (2 December 1854), np.

[31] 'Letters from the Crimea to Relatives in Wakefield', *Wakefield Journal & Examiner* (12 January 1855).

[32] 'Letters from the Crimea. From an Artillery Officer', *The Essex Standard* (8 December 1854), np.

[33] 'Letters from the Crimea. From a Drummer of the 47th Regiment', *The Essex Standard* (8 December 1854), np.

[34] MRA, MR1/16/2, Newenham Mss, Newenham to family, 24 November 1854.

[35] L'Estrange, ed, *The Friendships of Mary Russel Mitford as recorded in letters from her literary correspondants* , (London, 1884). pp.298-9.

[36] Morris et al, *The Three Serjeants*, p.216.

[37] Major J. Slack, *The History of the late 63rd (West Suffolk) Regiment* (London: Army & Navy Co-Operative Society Ltd., 1884), pp.117-119.

[38] Morris et al, *The Three Serjeants*, pp.218-220.

[39] 'From a Soldier of the Rifles', *Cheshire Observer* (6 January 1855), p.8.

[40] P. Avers, *Historique du 82e Regiment d'Infanterie* (Paris: Lahure, 1876), p.241.

[41] Morris et al, *The Three Serjeants*, p.218.

42 Fay, *Souvenirs de Crimee*, pp.126-127.

43 Bazancourt, *L'Expedition*, tome 2, p.64.

44 Fay, *Souvenirs de Crimee*, pp.126-128.

45 Avers, *Historique du 82e*, p. 242.

46 Joppe, 'Commandant Adrian', pp.216-217.

47 Bazancourt, *L'Expedition*, tome 2, p.78; *Sabretache*, 1908, p.217; *Revue Contemporaine*, vol. 87, p.323.

48 L. Guerin, *Histoire de la dernier guerre de Russie* (Paris: Dufour, Mulat et Boulanger, 1859), Tome 1, p.383; Fay, *Souvenirs de Crimee*, pp.127-128; *Revue Contemporaine*, vol. 87, p.324.

49 Guerin, *Dernier Guerre*, p.383.

50 ibid, pp. 383-384; see also E. Jouve, *Guerre d'Orient* (Paris: Alphonse Delhomme, 1855), p.403; E. Woestyn, *Guerre d'Orient: les victoires et conquètes des armées alliés* (Paris: E. Woestyn, 1857), p.70; E. de Bedollière, 'Histoire de la guerre d'Orient: Inkermann', *Panthéon Populaire Illustré* (Paris: nd), p.6.

51 Guerin, *Dernier Guerre*, p.383.

52 Slack, *63rd*, p.118.

53 'Incidents of the Battle of Inkerman', *Burnley Advertiser* (2 December 1854), p.4.

54 E. Perret, *Récits de Crimée 1854-1856* (Paris: Bloud et Barral, 1896), p.161.

55 ibid, see also Fay, *Souvenirs de Crimee*, pp.131-132.

56 Commandant C. Brincourt, 'Lettres du General Brincourt', *Carnet de la Sabretache* (1923), pp.84 –86.

57 Anon, *Campagnes de Crimee, d'Italie,* Letter 79: Colonel de Wimpffen to Maréchal Castellane, 2 December 1854, pp.129=133.

58 Fay, *Souvenirs de Crimee*, p.134-135.

59 Devanlay, 'General Breton', 2e partie, p.87.

60 De la Fay, *General Lacretelle*, pp.91-92.

61 Roche, *Un Regiment de Ligne*, p.115.

62 De la Fay, *General Lacretelle*, pp.92-94.

63 ibid, pp.94-95.

64 Herbé, *Francais et Russes en Crimee*, pp.133-134.

65 Roche, *Un Regiment de Ligne*, pp.115-116.

66 Devanlay, 'General Breton', 2e partie, pp.87-88.

67 'Letter from a Leeds Soldier', *Leeds Mercury* (16 December 1854).

68 'Letters from the From the Crimea. From the Rev. George Lawless, A.M.', *The Essex Standard* (8 December 1854), np.

69 'Letters from the Crimea', *York Herald* (2 December 1857), p.7.

Chapter 6

'Generals December, January and February'

Despite their victory at Inkerman it was now clear to the Allies that they were unable to capture Sebastopol before winter set in. The second bombardment and assault proposed by *général* Bizot was postponed indefinitely. Neither the French nor British had anticipated a winter campaign: their planning had assumed a rapid descent on Sebastopol, which was to be captured in a 'grand raid' with their troops over-wintering in the city. This resulted in a series of linked crises: lack of shelter, clothing, food, and transport resulting in massive rates of sickness throwing the medical establishments into chaos.

The decision by Sir John Burgoyne to commit to a formal siege of the south side of the city gave the Russians ample time to bolster the weak defences of the city. Furthermore, given that the Allies had only invested the southern side of the city, it meant that the Russians were able to bring in supplies and reinforcements to the north. The Allies had neither the men nor materiel to completely invest Sebastopol and little attention had been paid to blockading the city or the Crimean Peninsula, with only a small Turkish force at Eupatoria. The failure of the first bombardment (17 October 1854) should have rung warning bells in the Allied camp that Sebastopol would not be easy to capture; indeed as one French officer remarked, it was the Allies who were besieged by the Russians, bottled up on the south side of Sebastopol, rather than the Allies besieging the Russians.

French reinforcements poured into the Crimea, however, bolstering the Allied force. The *6e Division* (*général* Paté: *6e chasseurs, 28e, 49e de Ligne, 23e Légère*) landed 19 November; the *7e Division* on 27 November (*10e chasseurs, 14e, 18e, 43e de Ligne, 4e Légère*) and the *8e Division* (*17e*

131

chasseurs, 10e, 57e, 61e de Ligne, 10e Légère) at the end of December. By 10 January 1855 the French had mobilised nearly a million men destined for the Crimea and the Baltic. Their army in the Crimea consisting of two Corps, each of eight Divisions and an 'Army of Reserve' consisted of the Imperial Guard and the *9e Division*. Two more divisions were dispatched in May, bringing the French strength to over 80,000 men. Because the French were clearly the senior partners in terms of manpower, and in order to take the strain from the much smaller British force, Lord Raglan requested that the French take over the part of the 'Right Attack' on the Inkerman Heights and in front of the Malakoff on 23 January 1855.

The Great Storm

The weather grew increasingly cold and wet from the beginning of November, but on 14 November the Allied camp – and fleet – were wrecked by a 'Great Storm.' One Captain of the Royal North British Fusiliers wrote to his family in Wakefield:

> It commenced suddenly, at 6 o'clock in the morning and lasted 'til 12 o'clock. The wind blowing from the south directly on this bold and rugged shore. We had 16 vessels outside the harbour, some of the finest transports and steamers in our service, amongst them the 'Prince', quite a new vessel, she broke in half right in the centre, and sunk at once with 150 souls on board and a valuable cargo. The effect of this disaster is most serious to our proceedings, and it has thrown gloom over us all.
>
> Every vessel had stores and warm clothing for our poor but brave soldiers, so you may imagine how it will throw us all back. When the storm had moderated, I climbed to the top of a cliff, and from thence beheld one of the most awful sights ever witnessed by man (a sketch of which I enclose). I counted 14 wrecks. Such a sea! The waves nearly equalled the height of the mountain on which I stood. You may guess the effect of this on the encampment. In a moment every tent was blown away: some were carried into the air like parachutes, those who indulged in sleep without their clothes were left in a state of nudity… The Colonel was carried inside his tent, down the side of the mountain; he was much injured, and was immediately taken to the hospital.[1]

A lieutenant of the Scots Greys described the chaos and confusion in a letter to his sister:

We turned out that morning as usual before day break in a storm of wind & rain, so violent that the parade had to be dismissed & just as we got off our horses such a blast suddenly burst on us as if by a cannon shot. The rain sleet & snow at the same time blowing so that we were obliged to lie down on our things wet as they were to prevent both them and ourselves from being blown away, for no mortal man could stand before it.

My troop was startled by the falling tents &c. & at night 25 were still missing but we have recovered nearly all of them now. The worst of it was that we could get nothing to eat till near evening when the storm moderated & we got some ration mutton cooked (half) on green wood. For some days previous we had a great deal of rain, but the storm quite polished us off & we got all our things wet & uncomfortable. Our work, in spite of all this, continues & the very next day I was on outlying picquet & had brought it on a black hill side all night, when I was nearly frozen. I stood on my feet from 12 at night to nearly ½ past 4 when I was so done and weak I could hardly stand & my right side was quite paralyzed. Ever since I have been all over acute rheumatism & yesterday & the night before had a good deal of fever, but today I am all right, with the exception of a very sore throat and pains in my left arm & shoulder. This is truly miserable work I can tell you & now we have real hardships to contend with.

A lot of our ships have been [illegible] anchor & wrecked, amongst them some of our men of war & a lot of transports, including all our horse forage for 27 days, an awful loss & one ship with all the men's warm winter clothing which they need much for our poor fellows. 30 men died of cold in the trenches the night of the storm, & every night night now our horses share the same fate, 2 or 3 per regiment. We cannot take this place now this year & so shall have to be here all winter.[2]

The devastation of the Allied camps was nothing compared to the fate suffered by the Allied fleet anchored in Balaklava, Kamiesch and out at sea. Fanny Duberly, on board *Star of the South* watched as: 'The spray, dashing over the cliffs many hundred feet, fell like heavy rain into the harbour. Ships were crushing and crowding together, all adrift, all breaking and grinding each other to pieces.'

On board *Retribution* was the Duke of Cambridge, who 'had a more dreadful 24 hours of it than we ever spent'. The steamer *Prince* was lost with all but six of her 150 crew; she had had on board 40,000 winter uniforms; joining her were *Progress*, *Wanderer* and *Resolute* which had on board a cargo of 10,000,000 Minié rounds. The French battleship *Henri Quatre* and the steamer *Pluton* were both lost together with two merchantmen carrying food and stores: losses that proved to be irreplaceable.

Life in the Camp

Bridget France, the wife of Private James France (68th Foot (Durham Light Infantry)), wrote to her relatives near Huddersfield that 'the greatest source of our misery … is the weather, which, since the early part of November, has been nothing almost but a succession of rain, hail and snow'. Christmas Day, however, 'opened bright and frosty … and up to the present time [29 December 1854] no frost or snow has fallen.'[3] Life under canvas was utterly miserable:

> Our camp ground … [is in] a state resembling very much a ploughed field, and you cannot move a dozen yards without being up to the ankles in mud – this, of course, the men cannot help carrying with them into their tents, which besides, often admits the water, and then are we not in a nice pickle? Picture to yourself for your bed a mud floor with about two inches of soft mud, your bedding consisting of your ordinary clothing, and two blankets. The men, however, in this case, generally scrape the soft part off, which is but little improvement, as the ground is so damp that to sleep with any warmth is impossible, and thus you perceive what a deadly enemy we have in wet weather. We hear numerous reports and accounts of wooden houses to be sent for accommodation; but these, like a great many other things, will, I think, arrive too late to be of that service they would have been had they been thought of two months ago. They would have saved the lives of many hundreds who now lay cold in their graves… and where many more will surely rest if not better covering is provided than canvass.[4]

Not only were the men – and their wives – cold and wet, but starving. She continues:

> Another hardship the men endure is the want of fuel to cook with, everything now being consumed but mere roots, which have to be grubbed up with great labour … The irregularity with which the commissariat furnishes the supplies – of the 4th Division I can only speak; of the others I know nothing; but we are but too often cut short of our rations – sometimes we have no beef, other days half allowance; the coffee and sugar are pretty regular; rice, a great

comfort to a man, has quite disappeared; and rum, we are very often docked, sometimes none and sometimes half.

The deprivation of this luxury (for it is a luxury) is felt more by the men than any other. People at home by a warm fireside may smile that a glass of this liquor will cause the wearied and harassed soldier to forget his trouble, and cause him to set about his duties with a cheerful heart and contented mind. Again, only fancy it a cold night, with occasionally showers of hail, snow and rain, and a poor fellow on an advanced post before Sebastopol, within 200 yards of a Russian. Here the devil must crouch for hours, spike of hail, snow or rain, nor daring to move for fear a storm of Minié rifle bullets should poor round his devoted head. Fancy the value of a glass of rum to that man on being relieved, powerless almost, from cold and wet. [5]

Corporal E. C. Davies (1st Royal Dragoons), writing to family in Preston, noted that whilst commissariat supplies were invariably not forthcoming, the men of the Heavy Brigade at least were able to go down to Balaklava and trade or barter with the merchants there, but for very exorbitant prices:

Now for the prices – flour 1s. to 1s. 6d ... raisins 1s., butter 2s. 6d. to 3s ... and cheese 2s. 6d. per lb. Bread we can only get about once a month, and there is such a run for it then, it is about 1s. per lb. Sugar 1s. per lb; yes, and their pounds are Turkish – about eleven English ounces to the pound. Everything is the same; and we cannot get these things when we like neither.[6]

Robert Crawford (28th Foot) wrote to his mother in Wakefield, describing the Crimea as:

A dreadful place. We are lying out in tents amidst frost and snow, and you would not be surprised to see six or seven dead in the morning. You are out of bed six nights out of the seven, and we are every second night on the trenches, and during the 12 hours we are on the trenches we have to lie on our bellies – if we did not do that we would be shot by the Russians; they are firing from their batteries all day and night. We have to go 10 miles to a place called Baliklava [sic] and 10 miles back for our rations, and the roads is so bad you would be up to your neck in muck. The men is dying like rotten sheep, but we have plenty of fine warm clothing. We get grog three times a-day when we are not on the trenches ... We are very badly provided for as British soldiers out in the Crimea ...

The Turkish Soldiers is no good whatever out here – the only good they are is sitting down on their hunkers and drinking coffee and smoking their pipes. The French soldiers is elegant soldiers, and well fitting for the campaign – better than <u>any</u> soldiers out here. You must excuse the price of the letter, for money we have not seen since we out to the Crimea, or no likelihoods of it.[7]

One 'dragoon officer' thundered in a letter to the *Manchester Examiner and Times*:

One of the worst and most culpable items of Lord Raglan's want of forethought has been, it appears to me, the little care he has taken to prevent sickness amongst the men. I wish you could see our condition at the moment I am writing. Yesterday we had rain all day, and it poured incessantly all night. Towards morning the wind became more northerly, and, instead of rain, snow fell. The ground is now white, notwithstanding the slush and mud, and it continues snowing heavily.

In the ravine the water is flowing with the noise and fullness of a considerable stream. An order has just been given for seventy men to go into Balaklava for the rations of salt pork and biscuit for the regiment; the bat horses, from neglect of shoeing, inattention, and overwork, have foundered days ago. These men have not been able to get any breakfast, because the little brushwood they have collected would not burn in such weather…

In general orders there appears a notification 'that, in future, the issues of fuel will be limited to the troops encamped above Sebastopol.' Now, would not anyone seeing this order imagine that we, in common with others, had had fuel issued to us? Yet, I assure you, upon my honour, we have never had an ounce issued to us since we have been here. And as to there being fuel at Balaklava for us, it might as well be in London; for the authorities know – or ought to know, if they cared to do so – that we have not the means of bringing it up.

We have hard work, from the fact of no roads having been attempted to be constructed until the weather was too bad to make them, and from the failure of our limited means of transport to get up the daily allowance of pork and biscuit for the men, and they are frequently compelled to subsist on half-rations.[8]

The failure of the British commissariat to feed the army was largely due to the lack of a working supply train. The Royal Waggon Train had been disbanded in 1833 and the British commanders in the Crimea had optimistically assumed that local drivers could be dragooned into transporting the army's stores, rather as the Portuguese had done during the Peninsular War. This aid, however, had not been forthcoming, leaving the British, in the words of General James Estcourt, Raglan's Adjutant General, 'perfectly helpless.' Even worse, many officers in the Crimea blamed the 'penny pinching' House of Commons for not purchasing remounts to help alleviate the transport crisis. Sidney Herbert in London thought the transport crisis was due the commissariat lacking the common sense or forethought to organise a working transport system whilst General Estcourt thought it entirely due to the incompetence of Commissary-General Filder.[9]

In comparison the French *Train des Équipages* appeared to be 'working like clockwork.' So successful were the French commissariat arrangements *believed* to be that Lord Hardinge, General Commanding-in-Chief at Horse Guards, argued that 'I cannot say I anticipate any improvements ... unless Departments such as Land Transport and Ambulances imitation [*sic*, imitate] the French.' The Duke of Newcastle sent a commission to Paris under Major-General Knollys to study the French commissariat, upon which it reported favourably.[10] Unnoticed by the British, however, the French *Train* was struggling to cope with the poor roads and bad weather; it lacked serviceable vehicles and remount horses, being forced to eventually use the bullocks for draught purposes which had originally been intended to provide fresh meat for the army.[11]

Predictably, sickness soon set in, as Gunner Edwin Peat (Royal Artillery) informed his sister in Barnsley:

> I have been very unwell from diarrhoea for the last ten days, but, thank God! I am recovering; it is the general disease amongst the troops at present time, and there is no wonder, being exposed as we are to such horrid wet weather as it has been for the last five weeks, night and day. I am surprised that I am living at all, for I am scarcely dry, and with no means of providing myself with any dry clothing. It is hard work, I do assure you, to get a shirt drawn through a pool of water, and getting it dry is out of the question, and we are all getting very hard-up for clothing of every description. God only knows what will become of us if Sebastopol is not soon taken, for there is no such thing as getting any rations cooked now-a-days, and if it was not for our rum ration it would soon be up with us. We had a dreadful gale the other day; it blew the whole of our tents away for miles, and nearly everything they contained. I will leave you to

guess what it was when it blew four waggons [*sic*] away off a plain for about two miles …

There are some parties who have brought some things out here for sale from Malta, and I can tell you that they do sell them – only fancy a shilling for two table-spoonsful of sugar; a penny for one onion; sixpence a-pound for potatoes; candles, one shilling each; four shillings for a small bottle of pickles; porter, three shillings per bottle, brandy six shillings per bottle; tea, six shillings per pound, and so on in proportion for other articles: so you see it is impossible for any one under the rank of an Officer to purchase anything he could fancy. Tobacco is very fair, at 1s. 6d. per pound.[12]

Exhaustion, exposure and malnutrition began to take its toll on many regiments. Lance Corporal Samuel Hyde (33rd Foot) wrote to his brother in Halifax, that:

I have had several severe attacks of diarrhoea, which is the prevailing disease, on account of the extremes of fine and wet weather, lying on the wet ground, and having wet blankets regularly, which are enough to almost kill anyone. All the troops out here now have not one night in a week in bed on an average, owing to the duty in the trenches being so hard, and outlying pickets, requiring to be reinforced so often. Since I last wrote, we have had two drafts of 160 men, but unfortunately they stand the climate worse than the old soldiers: 7 have died of cholera during the past week; 5 are now in a very precarious state with the same disease, and 27 in hospital suffering from dysentery, which in most cases of a violent character turns into cholera. In addition to the above we are on average sending to Scutari general hospital, 7 daily. The strength of the regiment at present is 540, including the drafts; it came out 1,000 strong.[13]

In direct contrast was the experience of John Brown one of the sailors manning the siege guns who celebrated Christmas 1854 in lavish style:

We have been cooking this last night or two for Christmas. We have four hams boiled; a plum <u>duff</u>, that is a plum-pudding, the weight of which is 48lb; two legs and two shoulders of mutton; three rounds of good English beef, weighing 32lbs, 31½, and 34 ¼ each; one gross of oranges, two stones of apples, nuts of all kinds, four dozen of mould-candles, two pounds of raisins, 10lb currants, 8oz. candied lemon-peel, 6 oz. of all-spice; two legs of fresh pork roasted; one sea-pie, weighing 32lb, two cwt. of potatoes, three apple-pies, and four pumpkin-tarts, grog and tobacco in abundance. I have and am enjoying myself pretty freely, and hope you have done the same.[14]

Corporal Davies spent Christmas Day drinking with the French:

The French came down from the hills with fine French brandy at 5s. a bottle, which we made very free with. We enjoyed ourselves very much, and had several French friends with us. They are very good company, and first-rate singers. The day was very wet, and, of course, out here every day is the same. But at night, if you stood anywhere near the cavalry camp you could hear singing going on in every tent. It was something like a country fair at night.[15]

Shortages in the French Camp

It was not just the British that were suffering, but the French too. Often thought to have been more successful than its British counterpart, the French commissariat – or *Intendance Militaire* – broke down under the strain of the Crimean Winter. It was unable to supply suitable tents, winter clothing or food leading to a high rate of sickness amongst the French troops. In turn, this placed massive pressure on the French army medical services (*Service de Santé Militaire*), which came close to breaking point. During the winter of 1854-1855, the biggest cause of death for French soldiers were 'fever', exposure and scurvy.

The French hospitals were designed to cater for up to 2,800 cases per month, but during the period December 1854 to February 1855 had to treat over 10,000. The *colonel* of the *74e de Ligne* lamented that by January 1855, 500 men under his command were *hors de combat* with frozen limbs, 18 of whom would have to undergo amputations, from lack of warm clothing.[16] *Capitaine* Pontgibaud (*57e de Ligne*) noted how five-sixths of the ill taken to hospital suffered from frostbite and frozen limbs, mostly feet and legs, due to the regulation French boot neither being waterproof or warm and often falling apart. Worse still, the *Intendance*, was unable to supply any replacements and soldiers had to bind their feet with rags or sheepskins. Many regiments replaced their boots with clogs stuffed with fleeces.[17] *Colonel* Breton notes that he, and many others, wore 'bizarre costume[s]' in order to keep warm:

My large pair of black clogs ... a sheepskin waist band, the hooded overcoat, the tunic, a waistcoat, a Turkish sash, trousers reinforced with leather, underpants, two shirts ... my small Bulgarian cap which looks like the bearskins of the sapeurs.[18]

Where the French did have an advantage over their Allies was in the supply of thick, hooded, caped, winter overcoats, dubbed by the soldiers as 'Criméenes'; French soldiers each received a sheepskin jerkin and gaiters, topped off with a fez as a gift of the Sultan of Turkey. Napoléon III lavishly sent wine, tobacco and chocolate:

> The poor soldier does not know what it is to have dry clothing, and yet the Emperor thinks of us with a maternal solicitude. He has distributed to all the officers and soldiers a good winter overcoat with a cape and hood and a waistcoat in sheepskin with its fleece left on … The Emperor has also sent to the officers cognac, about a dozen litres each, wine of Old Lamalgue called Bordeaux, about eight litres – And a gratification of 1000 francs for the colonels; 250 francs for the lieutenant-colonels, 200 francs for the superior officers, 150 francs for the capitaines and 100 francs for the lieutenants and sous-lieutenants.[19]

The camps and tents themselves were filthy and festering. Because the ground was frozen, offal and carcasses of butchered animals could not be buried to the regulation depth of two metres and due to the lack of firewood could not be burned either. This meant that stinking, rotting animal parts remained partially or even unburied but for a sprinkling of quick-lime. Latrines had not been dug to the regulation depth and had been dug too close to the tented lines so that human waist as well as animal seeped into the water table. Soldiers, contrary to regulation, had been urinating in their tents and the tents themselves had not been aerated. Few soldiers had had the time to wash themselves or their clothes.

In response to the Press reports and letters home, Napoléon III sent Jean-Baptiste Lucien Baudens as Inspector of Medical Services. He was to inspect and review the medical services and hospitals of the French army in the Crimea for the French War Ministry, who were expecting a glowing report, but instead he committed career suicide in presenting to maréchal Vaillant, the Minister of War, a report that utterly damned the French Service de Santé. Baudens was not alone in his condemnation of the Service de Santé in the Crimea.[20] Whilst Bauden's presence and his conclusions may not have been welcomed by the higher echelons of the French army, he was certainly considered beneficial by the rank and file. It was believed that by his 'true and sincere reports' to the Minister of War that the lot of the common soldier would be improved and many of the 'dangers and illness that follow our army' could be prevented.[21] Charles Mismer (6e Dragons) relates that during the winter many officers simply 'gave up' trying to implement discipline. The new regime of spring 1855 resulted in the imposition of strict discipline and 'doing things by the book'. This even included appointing new commanding officers:

> [Our new colonel] M. Ressaye is a man who is rude and hard, unsympathetic to the first degree. He does not in any fashion pretend after the reputation of an officer of the parade ground or salon.[22]

Instructions were issued to ensure that tents were aerated and 'cellars' were dug two feet deep to improve headroom; the men were to wash daily and clean their uniforms. Everything was done per regulation and the men's health, and morale, very rapidly improved.[23]

Things did not necessarily improve immediately, however: the *lieutenant-colonel* of *11e Leger*, wrote to his wife in March 1855 lamenting:

> The rest of the horses and the mules (we have lost a lot) is, in the Crimea, a very precarious existence; there are shelters for none, not even those of the of *Général-en-Chef*, who have their noses under a type of plank, above a hole dug for them. The others are there, in the open air, night and day, in the rain, in the snow … The means of transportation are very reduced, we can [only] make movements of 2 leagues only from our positions that we occupy, without being embarrassed by the question of food … our situation is … stationary …
>
> What a singular campaign! And yet we cannot hide that it is very hard for the poor soldiers; they do not have time to breath between the trench service three days [a week], and the fatigue details. They have to get the wood up to two leagues [distant] and carry it across their shoulders; for food [they go] a quarter of a league; all the rest is taken at Kamiesch, about a league away …
>
> For water, all the camps are not as good as our share; we have five water wells around us, and drawing it in the morning, we have very beautiful clear water. However, I serve it two or three times through a felt filter.[24]

The failure of the *Intendance* to supply winter clothing and food was perhaps in part due to circumstances beyond it's control. The harvest of 1853 had been very poor and there was a bread famine in France. Furthermore, their entire stock of tents, bread, biscuit and the mobile bread ovens were destroyed in a fire at Varna in August 1854. The

Intendance was also a victim of its own organisation: it was beloved of red-tape, penny-pinching and was hide-bound by protocol as much (if not more so) than the British Commissariat. *Capitaine* Thoumas (*7e Artillerie*) raged,

> Oh! Saint Paperwork! Patron of the French Army, welfare of the Intendants, foster mother of accountants, the despair of real soldiers! I have spent forty-five years with the army, we were going to lower your importance, and bring your size back to more modest proportions, and you are still growing ... as you devour time, money and men![25]

Maréchal de Logis Charles Mismer (*6e Dragons*) agreed, grumbling that the *Intendance* was every bit as pernickety on campaign as home service:

> During the entire campaign, the *Intendance* continued to place importance on paperwork and accounting, as meticulous as in garrison. For a trifle of no value, such as a pistol ramrod, or replacing a stirrup leather, I do not know how many statements, covered with several individual signatures, all controlling each other![26]

Général Bosquet had a radical solution for improving the French commissariat:

> Nothing will go well here until you have two gallows set up to the left and right of your tent, one bearing an *intendant*, and the other an *officier d'administration*.[27]

The weakness of the *Intendance* had been manifest even before the campaign had opened. *Général* de Martimprey had warned that 'we do not have artillery ... the engineers do not have the means of transportation. The train is insufficient, the same for carrying the wounded. Our magazines are also empty.'[28] In desperation, *maréchal* de Saint-Arnaud had written to Napoléon III back in May 1854 informing him that

> It is with some regret that I tell Your Majesty that we are neither constituted, nor in a state to make war ...We cannot make war without bread, without shoes, without camp kettles, without mess-tins ... I beg Your Majesty's pardon for these details, but they prove to the Emperor the difficulties which beset an army thrown 600 leagues from its positive resources.[29]

Despite the numerous complaints from Saint-Arnaud, and via albeit censored letters home in the French press, the French War Ministry consistently replied that there were no problems at the front; Saint-Arnaud was simply 'wrongly informed.'[30] This led to Frances' allies operating under a 'cruel disillusion, and in its effect disastrous' that Saint-Arnaud and his men were better able to take to the field than Raglan was, a myth perpetuated by the likes of W. H. Russell of *The Times*.[31] As the present writer recently stated, 'Russell was the best 'Public Relations guru' the French army couldn't afford.'[32]

Whilst each French soldier did have a tent, they were the tiny two-man *'tentes d'abris'* which were eminently unsuitable for a winter campaign. Indeed, some French officers had noted before the Crimean war that it was not well suited to a European campaign, and were also reluctant to use it in North Africa except in exceptional circumstances, because it did not protect its users from the elements who 'soon became sickly with fever, dysentery and rheumatism'.[33] *Général* Bosquet repeatedly wrote to the *Chef d'Intendance* asking for more tents, specifically the large 16-man tents as they were warmer and better suited to winter campaigning than the *tentes d'abris*. The response, however, was negative: the *Intendance* was unable to supply any large tents but could provide some *tentes d'abris* which meant that Bosquet's – and other – Divisions were to spend the winter of 1854-1855 in their totally unsuitable *tentes d'abris*. Denied large 16-man tents Bosquet blamed the 'useless' death of many of his men from cold on the incompetence of the *Intendance*.[34]

Bosquet's men were relatively lucky even to have tents, however: *Capitaine* Pontgibaud noted some regiments had none, and would lose between forty or fifty men per night from exposure.[35] Even where the large 16-man tents were issued, they may not have been warm or waterproof; one NCO of French engineers recounted how the rain came through his tent as if through a sieve.[36] Many French officers purchased their own tents, especially 'Turkish' ones which they described as vastly superior to their own, because they were 'double' (i.e. had an inner tent) and thus warmer, were waterproof, and from their dome shape were better suited to resisting strong winds and inclement weather.[37] What few tents the French did have were largely destroyed by the 'Great Gale' of 14 November, forcing them to improvise shelter as best they could. *Sergent-Major* Alfred Minart (*27 de Ligne*) wrote to his mother that,

> We had a terrible storm the other night. The wind commenced by blowing-down the three tents of our colonel, he cried like hell for us to come to his assistance, but no one could go out for fear or being

blown away by the storm. The *sapeurs* took pity on the colonel, and gave him a small tent where he passed the day. The tents of the other officers had the same fate. Only the tent of Charles resisted, and was soon overrun by the other officers who went to seek asylum. The others sought refuge at Balaklava, hoping that the 'myladies' would be seduced by their pitiable state: but the ladies did not have sensitive hearts as ours do, and the would-be conquerors returned crestfallen.

I saw several comic scenes occasioned by the storm: the *cantinières* took shelter in their wagons; they took post and without their horses descended into the ravines.

The following day the wind ceased and we reconstructed our dwellings. We have built hurdles to stop the wind, and also subterranean houses. The government is sending us jerkins in sheepskin, and we have the air of Eskimos.[38]

Lieutenant Coste of the Engineers notes:[39]

The storm [14 November 1854] demonstrated the insufficiency of the shelter the army possessed, immobilised for a long time before Sebastopol, it had a camp not inappropriate for the rigours of the climate, but the Intendance was unprepared, the few resources it did have, the planks and timbers, were reserved for the ambulances and hospitals.

The horses suffered more than the men, attached to their picket rope, in the mud, they presented a very miserable aspect, the English cavalry lost all its effectives, and the horses of the French were just as decimated, the Algerians resisted well, their endurance proved by the mode of their breeding. The Administration allowed several pieces of wood and four planks per horse to make stables. A declivity in the ground was used, the planks served to form the roof, and dry stone walls formed the three sides and a straw curtain completed this installation ...

The men received Turkish tents, conical in form, giving less wind resistance, more securely fixed to the ground and whose impermeability and hermetic closure offered better safeguards against changes in temperature. They slept in these tents in groups of ten or twelve, the feet in the centre, and each man disposing a sector for themselves and by their industry managed to make them as comfortable as possible.

For the officers, the primitive tents were equally replaced by the Turkish tents and each showed ingenuity in their installation. The process usually involved digging out 60cm of soil, but leaving a central pillar of soil to support the pole ... the most frivolous constructed a furnace with a chimney to the exterior, consisting of saggy shakos made of sufficient height to assure that the fire would draw ...

The Kitchen was established with the mess-tins on supports dug into the soil in the open air, the dining room was a large French tent, open at all the sides.

Thousands of improvised tents sprang up in the French camp: most soldiers improved the headroom of their *tentes d'abris* by digging down a metre or so and digging a drainage gully all the way around. One *Zouave* admitted to living in a 'large wardrobe, with double doors' which he buried in the side of a trench. *Colonel* Le Breton had his *sapeurs* 'construct and install a bunk, and a true chimney.' He later had a proper window and door installed. He was also thankful for his two faithful servants, Gaget and Hardi.[40] Chimneys and fireplaces were improvised from old food tins and some members of *2e Zouaves* stole the 'patent water closet' belonging to Lord Rokeby of the Brigade of Guards in which to boil their soup.

Rations failed to appear for days on end, and when they did they were generally considered 'detestable.' Conspicuous by their absence were any fresh vegetables, leading to a debilitating rate of scurvy amongst French regiments. The enterprising *cantinière* of *2e Zouaves*, Madame Dumont, hired at her personal expense a steamer to bring food and supplies from Constantinople, but even this did not stop the scurvy.[41] Like their British allies, the French could use their meagre pay in the shops and cafés in the shanty-town which had sprung up around the French port at Kamiesch:

> The streets were formed of barracks occupied by small merchants who were with us and we would find useful, but they are mostly big rogues. After long hours in the trenches, our poor soldiers arrive in this town en-masse invading the cabarets, and, with the fabulous sum of ten or fifteen or twenty sous, get a glass of brandy, and, under the excitation find time enough to make them forget fatigues, their past and future. The Kamiesch streets were crisscrossed in every direction by a motley crowd that looked as diverse as his costume and language.
>
> The French, soldiers and civilians, Turks, Bulgarians, some English, Greeks, came and went, pell-mell, bumping, jostling, regardless of neighbour, and sometimes as sharply separated by vans or trains of

long lines of arabas drawn by buffalo. The summer is heinous in Kamiesch, in winter it must be even more unbearable. Under the sun it is a furnace: in the rain, a marsh. This is the place of those people who live in the love of gold. It is for them that momentary destruction of the full self, everything for gold, of which the supreme example is the Californian *digger*. Moreover, it seems that this race of merchants is always and everywhere the same, even if the army travelled to the end of the world, they would still be there.[42]

Lieutenant-Colonel Hardy (*11e Leger*) notes that many French regiments took to growing their own vegetables and keeping livestock:

We have several chickens and the fresh eggs … Our small gardens (peas, beans, salads, radish, onions, cabbages) are found well … and the grass and flowerbeds. Our little camp has a most agreeable aspect.[43]

Colonel Grenier (*4e Leger*) 'established at Balaclava a section of loggers who prepared for me the wood of the regiment. I also organised a section of laundresses; every day my men have clean linen and, in this manner, avoid vermin' and ensured his men washed daily. One anonymous French soldier wrote home that:

Nothing can be seen at head-quarters but small houses surrounded with gardens, and little seats constructed by the soldiers for their officers. There are regular lines of stables erected, and also a number of wooden huts. The tents, which still exist, have all planks for flooring, and in many of them pretty mantelpieces made of wood. In a corner is a camp-bed, and the arms are arranged round the post in the centre. Such is the appearance of an officer's tent … What has given pleasure to everyone is a chapel which has lately been built: it is very pretty surmounted by a steeple – without a bell. It appears to us very fine, for it reminds us of our village, of France … Two masses are performed on Sundays … in France, the soldier who attends Divine Service is frequently pointed at, but here this religious act is regarded as quite natural, and no mockery takes place.[44]

Lieutenant-Colonel Hardy admitted that the officers of his regiment lived quite well:

A Turkish tent serves as my bedroom; a large French tent as my office; another the dining room. Our kitchen, surrounded by a good wall, is roofed with planks ... We have good tables in our tents. I sleep blissfully in my little campaign bed; my sheepskin serves me as a mattress; I have a pair of cotton sheets and I sleep naked ... our dining table has eight persons ... a lively ensemble. I also offer a comfortable dinner, with excellent white bread. We exchange with the *Cantinières* ... two loaves of ration bread for one of white. Between us ... we have eight rations of every nature, lard, salt, dried vegetables, rice, sugar, coffee and bread or biscuit. Occasionally we received fresh meat ... but this is often not sufficient ... In our mess we are reasonable and we are quite well off for three or four hundred francs; but there are some officers, very indiscrete from the majority, who have lived, up to the present, on pates de foie gras, petits pois, the wines of Bourdeaux and Champagne; and their pay for four months would not be enough to pay their share ... What ruins is the cost; the ordinary wine, which the *Cantinières* sell us for 1Fr 50. per litre... at Kamiesch or at Balaklava, we pay 2Fr 25 at least ... Eggs, very common 1Fr 50 per dozen. The mutton ... is detestable; the beef passable ... Milk is impossible to procure.[45]

Napoléon III was sufficiently concerned by the lack of winter accommodation for his army that, like the British, he ordered the construction of wooden barrack huts, to his own design. Most of these came from British manufacturers: Messrs. Potter & Price of Gloucester supplied the French with 450 *Baraques d'Officier* (officer's barracks) and 1,500 *baraques* because French suppliers could not meet the demand – French companies were only able to supply 150 officer's barracks and 950 barracks. In addition, were 210 wooden stables. In theory the French had winter accommodation for 70,000 men and 10,000 horses.[46]

Ironically, despite the French barrack huts coming from the same supplier and design as those for the British army, British soldiers naively considered the French designs 'superior'.[47] Many French officers, however, complained that the issue of the wooden huts was too late to save many of their men and instead of them being delivered to the hard-worked troops of the Line were instead issued to the newly-arrived Imperial Guard and the officers at Headquarters.[48]

In February *lieutenant* Coste and his fellow Engineer officers formed a '*Cercle des Officiers*' and ensconced themselves in a wooden barrack hut:[49]

Ceded by the Administration. It was divided into four rooms; one furnished the lecture room and library, well-stocked with books; one was a games room and two others were fitted up with forms and benches ... The inauguration of this Circle was *en fete*, with a grand musical soiree. The best singers gave us their repertoire; a comic note was offered as were monologues; the silly songs, the pantomimes and burlesques. The soiree ended with the *Deux Aveugles* in song and a chorus of 'God save the Queen' by two English officers, invited to this debut, and, to our great surprise they sang with great respect the air of Queen Hortense.

Brigadier [corporal] Henri Choppin of the *Chasseurs d'Afrique* notes that the tinned 'preserved' food was detestable, and even years later when he was writing his memoirs the 'tinned meat', 'the macaroni, rice, Gruyère cheese and other commodities' still 'fill me with horror.' He recalled that:

We had very little time to ourselves, in the service of numerous reconnaissance, of which we always took part, the pickets and the guards, and talking about scientific discoveries to make the frozen potatoes [edible] and Turkish wine [drinkable] which were distributed by the Administration.

I was famous. I had a reason to be proud! Everyone knew, from the General Staff to the other regiments, that there was a brigadier lucky enough to receive in each mail arriving from France, a letter of eight, even twelve pages, written large and lengthy, by my mother, furnishing me with an exact bulletin of what was happening in Paris ... My mother sent me the four volumes of 'The History of the French' by Thomas Lavallée. I think, without a drop of smugness, that this has been the literary event of this glorious campaign ... My book was passed from hand to hand around the entire squadron ...

The biggest attraction in camp was Lotto. In fact, there were two rival groups. One of the buglers of the Chasseurs à Pied called the numbers according to the received usage. As the tenant was from Marseille, it was difficult to understand them. Following the established reclamations, he obviated this inconvenience by recalling the first digit. He said: '34 by 3, 55 by 5, 60 by 6.' When the other fancy ran a game it was thrust until the last limits. Instead of saying numbers, the owner, our Corporal replaced the numbers with a definition that was applied to them. As far as I recall 'on the gallows meant 7', 'the legs of James 11', 'two tin pots, 22'.[50]

Wives and Children

One of the major scandals was the treatment of the wives and children of soldiers serving the Crimea. Under Army Regulations, only four wives per hundred men were allowed to accompany their husband to war. It has been estimated that approximately ten per cent of an infantry battalion; twenty per cent of the Guards and twenty-five per cent of cavalry troopers were married. Around half of the wives lived in the barracks with their husbands – as there were no married quarters, they had to make do with part of the barrack room screened off with old blankets. The wives were entirely dependent upon their husbands and were not, in theory, allowed to take in work such as sewing or washing because that was thought to be immoral.

Those wives who were not selected to go had to travel to their home parish and seek 'Outdoor Relief.' The problem with this situation was that unless a soldier had been 'Married with Leave' (i.e. with permission from the Commanding Officer) their wife and any children simply did not exist in the eyes of the Army and they were left destitute. Even those soldiers who had been 'Married with Leave' soon discovered that their family left at home fell into poverty.

One such wife was Emma Weale, the wife of Corporal Samuel Weale. She had had to return to her home Parish of Wakefield to claim 'Outdoor Relief' from the Parish in order to look after herself and her three children all aged under nine. She lodged with her brother, William Hartley and was in receipt of 5s per week from the 'Central Association in Aid of the Wives and Families of Soldiers Ordered to the East.' The 'Central Association' had been established in March 1854 to provide for the wives and children – usually by providing temporary accommodation and then employment. In the Cheshire town of Stockport, twenty soldier's wives were put up in the Heaton Norris Workhouse. They were given cash handouts and 'encouraged' to take in sewing or washing or enter domestic service.

If the life of the wives and children left at home was hard, it was perhaps preferable to life in the camp. Margaret Kerwin, wife of Private John Kerwin (19th Foot) wrote how,

> The men were dying so fast with the cholera, and what they call the black fever, that they had to be buried in their blankets ... There was one sergeant in particular of the 19th, Murphy was his name, and he had come in from a long march with the colours. Mrs Murphy, his wife, a nice respectable woman, came to me for the loan of a frying-pan, and before she had the beef-steak fried, her poor husband was dead ... From my hardships in Turkey, standing in the river washing, I took two internal complaints and I thought I was dying, and the men made a little shade for me with boughs ... When my husband left me on going to the battle of Alma, what must have been

my feelings so see him going away from me, and I dying and thinking that I never would see him again. It was a hard feeling thing. The day my husband went away from me I was left on the beach of Turkeyland ... I was carried off to the Hospital under the care of a very good doctor, who kept the Hospital at Varna. I lay sick till after the battle of Alma, until I got a letter from my husband, saying he was safe ... This good news recovered me very quickly.[51]

Margaret Kerwin was one of the lucky wives – many more were less fortunate than she – as one Assistant-Surgeon raged in a letter to the *Leeds Mercury*:

When Government determined to allow a certain number of soldiers' wives to come out with the expedition, one would have thought that a proper provision would have been made for them, but this has never been the case. They were landed here in showers of rain, without a place to lay their heads, and persons were actually obliged to go to some of the ships to borrow a little tarpaulin to cover them with.

They have ever since been the opprobrium of the whole establishment, every body gave them the cold shoulder, and considered them a nuisance; their comfort or accommodation was made to give way to anything. It as the same at Varna, where they were attacked by Cholera and many of them died by the road-side [*sic*]; everybody hated to have anything to do with them. The army medical officer required to attend to the women considers is a nuisance that he ought not to be subjected to; their very commonest wants are often not supplied. In child-birth the medical men exhaust all sorts of excuses to escape attending them. They are treat in the same way by the military authorities; in this hospital there are huddled together in rooms that are quite unfit for any other purpose. This morning I was in a room about sixteen yards long by twelve wide, that contains twenty-five married women, most of them with husbands and families. Of course with such crowding there are many sick, some recently confined, and others, whose confinement is approaching; for it is one of their peculiarities that every woman either has a child in her arms or appears as if she very soon would have. They all lie upon the floor; in some parts of the room they have hung up gowns and blankets to make a screen from other parts. In one place, about nine feet square, I found one woman in acute fever, another far advanced in dropsy, and two other women recently confined. All the cooking is done in the same room, on little wood fires, without any chimneys, making an atmosphere of smoke difficult to see things through.

I have several times been urgently requested to visit women very dangerously ill, who had no medicine or attendance for days; the other two of them came to me, begging me to see a woman in great pain with a gathered breast, as they day not pass the night with her without some relief; the doctor had seen her in the morning and told them to get warm water, &c., and he would open it, but had never been near them again. I opened it, and let out above a pint of matter. Many cases of gross neglect have been brought to my notice. The result of all this treatment has been what might be expected, - most of the women have become intemperate; this has in many cases been followed by worse vices, and the place has become a thorough pandemonium. Unfortunately for me, some of them are placed just under me, separated by a double [floor] boarding, so that I can hear the words made us of, the evening orgies carried on by the side of the sick and dying, the drunken quarrels of men and women, the obscene and blasphemous expressions; the carouses and singing parties have often been kept up until one or two o'clock in the morning. All these sounds come up to my ears with fearful vehemence.

Were this the only fault or neglect committed by the managers of this expedition, it would be quite to enough to prevent us from expecting God's blessing would go with us; and until something is done to put a stop to it, we can scarcely pray or hope for any success in our undertakings. It appears to me that the only way of procuring any remedy for this crying evil is through the medium of the Public Press; private representations of the matter have been frequently made, and the only answer is abuse and abhorrence of the women, by those who do not pause to think who and what it is that has made them such as they are. This congregation of women, men, and children, is quite sufficient to make this place, which many do not now hesitate to call it – 'a pest house.'[52]

The Hospitals

Lack of adequate winter clothing and accommodation, coupled with the failure of the commissariat led to a high rate of sickness, which stretched the hospitals almost to breaking point. British sick and wounded were transported to the [in]famous Barrack Hospital at Scutari, a three- or four-day sea voyage away. Often considered to be 'hell on earth' by W. H. Russell or Thomas Chenery – who, it has to be noted, never visited Scutari – letters from surgeons and the sick and wounded, on the other hand, paint a less damming picture. Surgeon Scott (57th Foot) noted that the Barrack Hospital was as 'comfortable as can be expected.' The wounded were all in 'wooden cots' and 'well supplied with good rations and warm dress.' The high rate of mortality was not due to incompetence of hospital staff but because the sick were 'already dead'; 'mere skeletons' from exposure and starvation brought on in the 'Crimea, that land of death': victims of the failed commissariat.[53]

The Rev. William Whyatt, formerly Curate at Leeds Parish Church serving as a Chaplain at Scutari, was 'much pleased with all I saw there, and felt assured that all was being done for them that could be done. Such of the soldiers as I inquired from expressed themselves in most grateful language for all their comforts.'[54] Dr Michael Hinton has recently demonstrated that the high rate of mortality was not due to poor or mis-management of the hospitals, but rather due to conditions at the front: 'Decrease in the rate of mortality was due principally to the beneficial effects of improved living standards for the troops at the front.' Thus, the decrease in mortality at Scutari – for example – was due to changes at the front line, rather than primarily the activities of Florence Nightingale *et al*, the Sanitary Commissioners or the prompting of the newspapers.[55]

The voyage from Balaklava to Scutari was arduous and often proved fatal to the wounded, already weakened from exposure and malnutrition. Private Edward Edmonds (4th Light Dragoons), wounded during the Charge of the Light Brigade, wrote to his wife that:

I left the Regimental hospital, under the walls of Sebastopol, or rather the tent appropriated for the sick, on the 28th last month [November], and went on board ship at Balaklava, where we left on the 4th December, and arrived here on the 13th. We had on board 250 – I was going to say men – but I do not know what to call them, unless I call them the wrecks of good men – but our number was sadly reduced on our arrival at Scutaria [*sic*, Scutari]. Oh! What a tale might be told – it would defy my poor, simple, abilities to give the least idea of such a scene. Scarcely a morning came but two or three bodies were sewn up in a blanket and carried on shore while we were in harbour, or thrown overboard at sea.

I must now tell you something of our reception at Scutaria Hospital. On our arrival we were put into a clean, warm room, stripped of our – I mean worldly – rags; our poor bodies were washed of their filth; we were put into clean beds, with plenty of clean good clothing, and supplied with arrow-root and wine by the charitable Miss Nightingale and her Christian band. No one could sufficiently describe the kindness and attention of that lady to the unfortunate. Every man can get a flannel shirt, a pair of drawers and socks from her, by requisition signed by the Surgeon of the war, and there is no stint of anything on her part to make the sick and weak comfortable. Oh! what a pattern she is to the ladies in England. I fear you will think this is a strange letter; but I have been called away very often, for as I am convalescent, it is my duty to render assistance to the helpless which I have received from others.[56]

Private Samuel Weale (30th Foot) was badly wounded at Inkerman. He wrote to his wife Emma in Wakefield from his sick bed at Scutari:

My dear wife, I am sorry to have to inform that I am among the wounded who fell on Sunday the 5th Nov [Battle of Inkerman]. A musket shot entered the front of my left thigh and came out at my hip. I received a second wound near my left hip bone from a shell and while I lay wounded upon the field, the Russians came upon me and beat me upon the head with the butts of their muskets and bayoneted me in a frightful manner until they thought they had killed me quite dead. But thanks am yet alive and out of danger. My wounds are: 1 shot wound through the left hip; 1 wound left hip from shell; 1 sabre wound left groin; 2 bayonet wounds right thigh; 2 bayonet wounds right hip; one bayonet wound small of back, 1 bayonet wound right shoulder blade; 1 bayonet wound left breast; 1 bayonet wound left arm, fracture in the head from blows inflicted, making a total of 12 wounds. But I hope, my dear wife, that you will not be too anxious about me, as I assure you that I am progressing most favourably, but am still very weak from the great loss of blood. I arrived here on Friday last – Mrs Holmes is here and the children came to see me and are very kind to me, I am inclined to think my soldiering is over; and I hope that, as soon as I get a little round, I shall be sent to England. A great number of men who have been wounded set sail for England on Saturday last.[57]

Weale wrote again a month later:

The wounds inflicted by the bayonet are nearly all healed, but the others will be a long time healing, though they are doing very well; the bone of my left hip is fractured, which will, I think, render me incapable of serving with my Regiment again. I am totally unable o move, and have therefore perpetually to lay in one position (on the broad of my back), which is very severe to me. The doctor who attends me is a very kind you man, and does all he can for me; he allowed me half a pint of port wine per day.

My appetite has been very bad since I was wounded until a few days since, but it is quite good now, and I have fell [*sic*, fallen?] away very much. Our wounded received horrid treatment until we arrived here. We were three days without tasting food or nourishment of any kind, and on the fourth day I got a few ounces of fat salt pork and some hard biscuit presented to me, though I had fasted so long I could not touch it. I felt myself sinking very fast, but when a soldier's wife took compassion upon me, and but for her kindness I don't think I ever should have reach Scutari. Many of our poor fellows sank under their sufferings, and whose bodies became a prey to the waves; Corporal Young died by my side on board ship. You will see in the papers the names of our poor men who fell, but many who were wounded are since dead: I will give you a few of their names, viz., Colour-Sergeant J. Thompson (was, Ensign),[58] Colour-Sergeant Gallagher, Corporal Young, Privates W. Cook, J. Luton, and J. Allen; and poor Jos. Geddes died of fever. There are more than 2,000 patients in this hospital among whom are some awful sights, and there are from twelve to twenty die every day; a great many officers die too. Sergeant Holmes has got a fine berth – he is fairly going; he can sell anything to the patients, and has great pay besides. They send me a dinner every Sunday. Little James has been very ill, but is much better. My dear, I am very unhappy at your long silence … I don't know when I shall send more money, as I cannot get as much as will buy a sheet of paper; a little money would be very useful to me, as I could get many a thing I require. I have not received a farthing since 31st of August.[59]

Not everyone was convinced by 'Miss Nightingale and her Christian band'. Amongst them was Lieutenant Hunter of the Greys:

I hear Miss Nightingale has done good already there, but everyone says that her staff of young Lady nurses have not been judiciously selected, & that when once the enthusiasms of the thing wears off they will sicken of their work, wounds are things which new Doctors dislike to dress on account of the horrible Effusions, the wounded wards are dreadful in spite of the ventilation, & I cannot think that young ladies of 25 & 30 will or can stick out – you rather want some more <u>matronly</u> nurses, who tho' not quite so enthusiastic would understand it much better. They <u>will not</u> however look at the officers as they are considered <u>able</u> to pay for attendance & <u>therefore</u> confine their good offices strictly to the men.[60]

The attacks on Nightingale were not just because she was a woman who had dared enter a man's world, but for her Unitarian faith, which, according to hard-line Protestant Evangelicals, was putting the immortal soul of her patients in danger. They urged for Nightingale's recall and that Protestant, Trinitarian nurses and missionaries be sent – despite proselytising in the hospitals being banned.[61]

The controversy surrounding Nightingale's religious persuasion became something of a national scandal. One senior Anglican clergyman accused Nightingale of trying to make converts by distributing Unitarian bibles, pamphlets and books. The Rev. James Martineau of Liverpool replied that Unitarians used the 'Authorised Bible' and that the banning of Unitarian books would mean the removal of volumes by Newton, Milton, Locke and Charles Dickens. Nightingale's close friends, Sidney and Elizabeth Herbert (Sidney was Secretary of State for the Colonies) became embroiled; Elizabeth writing an open letter to the press stating that Florence was a member of the Church of England. It is no wonder Florence suffered what amounted to a nervous breakdown.[62]

One volunteer assistant-surgeon from Leeds Medical School wrote the following on 1 February 1855:

Undoubtedly there has been great mismanagement here; at the same time the English public cannot in any way appreciate the difficulties that have to be overcome: you may easily imagine some of these experienced in accommodating 6,000 or 7,000 persons in a country where bedsteads, chairs, tables, fire-places, chimneys, knives and forks, are not known, and where all these things have to be made for us, or sent out from England.

The medical men who have been ill here have mostly suffered from a bilious remittent fever, with great tendency to delerium [sic, delirium] and head affections. Dr McG[63]showed me a beautiful specimen the other day, that I tried very hard to beg for the Leeds School of Medicine; it was a musket ball firmly impacted in the head of the humerus. Dr. McG. Had performed excision of the shoulder join in the case.

I have got some fresh patients to-day from the Crimea, very ill with scorbutic affections. This is a common cause of sickness, and which could not have happened had the managers done their duty; it is a well-ascertained fact that scorbutus is produced by the prolonged use of salt diet. So well is this known, than an Act of Parliament has been passed to compel a daily allowance of lime juice to men on board ship, when living upon salt provisions; and the proper authorities ought to have seen that the same allowance of lime juice was made to the troops when placed under similar circumstances.[64]

He continued four days, later noting that the Press and 'authorities at home' were busy trying to 'cast blame' upon the medical staff in the Crimea for the high rate of mortality:

> I quite agree with what you say about any attempt to throw all the blame upon the medical men, but you must be aware that in the army they are all obliged to take whatever blame may be laid upon them patiently without answer. There can be no doubt that the great majority of them have worked very hard and suffered great privations, but the active, energetic men, have not been the managers ... Dr and Lady Alicia Blackwood[65]are both of them working very hard, and very patiently here. Lady Alicia has undertaken the superintendence of the soldier's wives, who are in a very sad condition, and she has to be their doctor and everything else; she comes to me for medicines and occasionally for advice; they appear both of them very nice people. They have two Swedish young ladies with them.
>
> Some of my patients applied to me to-day to give them something to poison rats with, complaining that they were so much infested with them that they would even fetch the bread from under their pillows. I told them they had only to put up with the same inconvenience I had, and they must make the best they could of it.
>
> A poor man I saw the other day with frost bitten feet, and had just made up my mind he would not live twenty-four hours, when he told me he should soon be well again as, as 'his feet were getting quite stunning'. We are landing fresh sick everyday, from 100 to 300, and have now in the hospitals here upwards of 5,000 patients, and 27 new medical men have arrived from England this month ... fresh medical men arrive with nearly every mail. I saw nine dead bodies landed at the Pier yesterday, and their deaths must have occurred whilst the vessel was in harbour, for if they occurred in the voyage from Balaklava they are thrown overboard. Each set of sick as they arrive appear in more feeble and miserable condition than those which preceded them.
>
> The abuse of Miss Nightingale and Co. in the English papers is very disgusting and the grounds upon which it is based show the

complete ignorance of the writers on the subject. I have no hesitation in saying that Miss Nightingale and her party have done more to <u>humanise</u> this place, to give the poor invalids some appearance of comfort, and to save heir lives, than any other class that has had to do with them. This, at least, the evidence of an impartial observer, for I have once of twice interfered to attempt to keep her nurses in what I consider their <u>legitimate</u> sphere of duty, when I have seen them inclined to intrench upon that of the medical men: in some cases the medical man has been more to blame than the nurses in willingly relinquishing to them duties he ought to have performed. It really makes me quite savage, knowing all I know, to read such attacks on Miss N.[66]

Assistant-Surgeon Thomas Park (attached to C Troop RHA) was also keen to defend the surgeons and 'Medical Men' at the front from the Press in a letter written to his friend William Raynor MD (the Mayor of Stockport):

We all know that in many respects there are alterations necessary, but it is extremely hard to throw the blame upon the poor unfortunate doctors, who have no authority whatever, and individually do everything they can. It would be extremely convenient to commanders if they could do without us, but it is not quite fair to blame us for not doing that which we have no power to do. I hope that it may lead to a searching inquiry, and I am sure that it will be found that, as far as individuals are concerned, there has been the utmost devotion to duty: and it is the system only which is to blame.[67]

By early February he reported that:

[Despite] our [sickness] having been less in us than most, I have been, and still am, very busy here, having a vast portion of duty. I found great numbers of sick requiring hospital, and, by dint of perpetually working, the authorities have succeeded in getting a good many away. During January, the deaths in camp were very numerous. We hope that, during February, they will not be more than one-third or one-fourth of what they were. All this, and the sending away of the worst cases, and [thus] being able to take better care of those remaining. I am glad to say that there are now a good many huts erected; but, even so they are no means sufficient for the <u>sick.</u> Of course, we should expect such a luxury for ourselves; and I hope we shan't go all through the winter without.

The Commissariat arrangements have improved of late, and the men get their food – unfortunately, too often the ration being 'Salt' meat – and the consequence is that scurvy has appeared and in some cases badly, and this, combined with dysentery, produced a truly-developed disease. I must mention here that of late I have been well supplied with wine, soups, preserved meats, and good things for the sick. In fact, there is a very general opinion, I believe, among the men, that the worst is past and I must again advert to their extraordinary endurance amidst all their sufferings and privations. No [illegible] here can fully understand or appreciate this: but which brings with it the melancholy reflection, that many of their lives might have been saved by timely fore-thought [sic].[68]

Solving the Transportation Crisis: The Grand Crimean Central Railway

To alleviate the transport crisis in the Allied camps, the British turned to the richest man in England – Sir Samuel Morton Peto MP, senior partner of Peto, Brassey & Betts – and the 'wonder of the age': the railway. In just twenty-five years from the opening of the 'Liverpool & Manchester Railway' (the world's first inter-city railway, and the first to be run by steam from the outset) the railways had mushroomed from around 100 miles in 1830 to 8,335 miles in 1855, with fortunes being made and lost in the process; the dramatic rise and subsequent disgrace of the erstwhile 'Railway King' George Hudson being the most notorious example. As Olive Anderson has identified, the Crimean War was part of the mid-century crisis where 'overt class bitterness and impatience with prevailing institutions' as the newly enriched (but not enfranchised) middle classes demanded a say in the running of the country.[69] The failure of the British army in the Crimea was linked to its being perceived as a last bastion of the aristocracy and old ways of thought. To the largely middle class newspaper readers who were agitating for reform, via such organisations as the Administrative Reform Association that argued, 'to bring Public Management to the level of Private Management in this country', it was the example of the likes of Peto ('the right man in the right place') that provided a better 'working model' than the 'jobbing aristocracy'.[70]

Ironically, however, it was the least aristocratic branches of the army – the Commissariat and Medical Departments – which had failed. Thus, it is not surprising that in January and February 1855 those reformers turned to big business and to new technologies to win the war.[71]

The Crimean War was the first time that the railway had been used in a combat theatre – Britain and France had both appreciated the strategic advantages of the railway to move troops and materiel almost from the very beginning. During the opening stages of the war it had been proposed to ship the British Cavalry Division by rail across France using the recently completed *Chemin de Fer de Paris a Lyon et à la Mediterranée* which linked Paris to Marseilles rather than send them by sea; similarly troops were moved around Britain to their embarkation points by rail. The Scots Greys marched from Nottingham to Liverpool, but their stores and baggage went by train. The contribution of the railways in Britain and France cannot be understated in the ability of the Allies to win the war with Russia economically.

Peto – who had hade his fortune building the railways – suggested the idea of a railway to link Balaklava to the camps on the heights in front of Sevastopol back in November 1854. After meeting with the Duke of Newcastle and the Prime Minister (Lord Aberdeen) he promised to build 'seven miles of railway in seven weeks'.[72] The *Railway Record* opined that such a railway was entirely 'novel' and that the Government and Army would never have approved of such a scheme due to '"Rules of the Service" [being] ... too stringent [to allow] our suffering soldiers being promptly saved from cold, wet and hunger.' The railway – and private business – was therefore the cure for 'the drivelling traditions' of the Army.[73]

Other prominent industrialists and inventors with schemes for the solving the various crises in the Crimea included Isambard Kingdom Brunel who designed a prefabricated a cast-iron hospital which was erected at Renkoi; Sir Joseph Paxton (designer of the Crystal Palace) organised a labour-force under the title of 'Army Work Corps', and the celebrity French chef of the Reform Club, Alexis Soyer, travelled out to the Crimea to teach the troops how to cook and, *inter alia*, invented the Soyer Stove.[74]

The first railway navvies landed in the Crimea on 1 February 1855. The *Journal des Chemins de Fer* was 'amazed' by this feat of engineering:

> This enterprise for the transportation of materiel and the workers for the construction of a railway ... to Balaclava, and to any other work which can be regarded as necessary for the siege and the destruction of Sebastopol ... The immense resources of Messieurs Peto and Betts has been massed together, organised and expedited, without great effort, in a space of time inconceivable ... Indeed when the first order was given, three weeks ago, the biggest part of the rails were not rolled, the bushings were not made, the steam engines were on their journey to Victoria Docks.[75]

A fleet of twenty-three ships were needed to transport the 550 navvies who had volunteered from across the railways in Britain as well as 1,800 tons of rails and fishplates; 6,000 sleepers; 600 'loads of timber' and

> fixed [steam] engines, cranes, pile engines, trucks, wagons, barrows, blocks, chain falls, wire rope, picks, bars, capstans, crabs and a variety of plant and tools; besides sawing machines, forges, carpenters' and smiths' tools.[76]

There was much controversy surrounding the treatment of the Navvies, due to their relative high pay (compared to the soldiers at the front) as well as their superior clothing, accommodation and victuals:

> Each man is supplied with ... one painted bag [to make it waterproof], one painted suit, three coloured cotton shirts, one flannel shirt (red), one flannel shirt (white), one flannel [cholera] belt, one pair moleskin trousers, one moleskin vest lined with serge, one fearnought slop, one Lindsey drawers, one blue cravat, one blue worsted cravat, one pair of leggings, one pair of boots ... one bed and pillow, one pair of mitts, one portable stove for every ten men, one rug and blanket, one pair of blankets, one woollen coat, one pair long waterproof boots, one pair fisherman's boots, one pair gray stockings.[77]

Unlike the soldiers freezing in the trenches in 'rotten old bell tents' the Navvies had heated wooden huts that slept forty men; the Navvies also had their own medical staff and two chaplains.[78] Peto later recalled that:

> It was in the midst of the dreary winter of 1854, when the British army was suffering unparalleled hardships before Sebastopol, that it was resolved to construct a railway ... the idea emanated from the Duke of Newcastle ... we accordingly placed at the disposal of Her Majesty's Government the whole of our resources ... The works (nearly seven miles of railway) were executed in less than one month – an incredibly short space of time, considering the season of the year, the severity of the climate, and the difficulties to which, considering our distance from home, we were all of use exposed ... On the day the Railway was opened, it carried to the camp ... in twenty-four hours more shot and shell than had been brought from Balaklava for six weeks previously.[79]

Work on the railway was rapid. Construction commenced on 8 February 1855 and the first train of commissariat stores was run to Kadikoi on 23 February. Three days later the railway had reached the British HQ and started transporting shot and shell for the guns. By May 1855 it had transported some 1,000 tons of shells, 3,600 tons of commissariat stores (fuel, and forage) and was carrying 112 tons of food up to the front each day. But despite the railway being in full operation, there was considerable friction between Commissary-General Filder and the Railway Board:

> The biscuit, salt-meat, and groceries, Commissary-General Filder has not made any arrangements about issuing it … The Commissariat have now at their disposal every day 30 wagons or more, and these might be filled on average twice a day, sufficient to take up everything in the shape of stores; but the Commissariat Men will not work before 8 in the morning nor after half-past 5 in the evening, and the Commissary-General does not seem disposed to take any steps … in fact he will not put himself out of the way one step to forward the comfort of the army as far as the railway is concerned.[80]

Whilst the Commissariat may not have been particularly warm towards to the Railway, 'The Royal Engineers are very friendly… Indeed I may say every department works cordially with us.' Despite this, friction remained between the entirely civilian railway and the 'Military Men' because it 'show[ed] the Army that there are other and better means of transport … they may yet derive some assistance from the skill and science of civilians.'[81]

Balaklava was transformed by the railway, as one member of the 42nd informed friends at home:

> Our Railway from Balaklava to Sebastopol is very nearly finished. Guns, shot, &c., &c., can be got up to the front quite hand. The navvies sent out here are working well. The town of Balaklava is greatly changed, now that the railroad is right through it. Wood-sawing goes on by steam, &c., &c., which makes a great change in this little town.[82]

The Railway was initially worked by horses and stationary engines on incline plains. By Summer 1855 the system had become a victim of its own success and was struggling under the strain of maintaining the siege. New, heavier, rails were laid in August and the first steam locomotive 'Victory' arrived the following month.

The second, named 'Alliance', was volunteered for service by Sir John Lister Kaye from his colliery at Denby Grange, near Wakefield. It was a virtually new, 0-6-0 tank engine, having been built by E. B. Wilson of Leeds. It was returned to its makers in Leeds and overhauled for service at the front.[83] The *Leeds Mercury* reports:

> The engine which leaves here for Southampton today has had a thorough renovation, and repainting at the Railway Foundry. Her 'Iron Sides' are adorned with the English, French Turkish and Sardinian flags conspicuously painted thereon, and she is called the 'Alliance'. She will be embarked for the Crimea by the middle of next week, so that her whistle may in two or three weeks be blended with the other notes of defiance hurled against the common foe, and her shrill voice shall not be the least emphatic declaration of the Allies to carry on this war with the utmost vigour.[84]

'Alliance' made her way to Southampton under her own steam and made quite a stir passing along the rails as the *Leeds Mercury* notes:

> On Thursday Morning, a beautiful little engine, decorated with the flags of England, France, Turkey and Sardinia passed through Pontefract Station en-route for the Crimea.[85]

'Alliance' arrived in early October, after the fall of Sebastopol, to join her sister 'Victory' (also a product of E. B. Wilson of Leeds); W. H. Russell of *The Times* thought the railway locomotives, and particularly their names 'recalled to us the familiar sounds of Wolverhampton or Swindon, and made us believe for a moment we were in a civilised country.' In total four locomotives worked on the 'Grand Crimean Central Railway', the two additional locomotives being purchased second-hand from the London & North Western Railway due to 'Alliance' and 'Victory' being of insufficient power.[86] These latter two locomotives had been built in 1842 by the Liverpool & Manchester Railway, to a design ('Bird' Class, 2-4-0) by John Dewrance.

The railway solved the transportation problem and explains why during the winter of 1855-56 that the roles between the French and British armies were reversed – it was the French who were starving and having to beg for food and clothing from the well-fed, well-clothed and hutted British soldiers whilst their own soldiers were starving and still living in tents.

Philanthropy on the Home Front

The letters home and reports of the 'Special Correspondents' not only urged the businessmen and Merchant Princes of Britain into action, but all classes and sections of society to 'do something'. This led to an orgy of domestic philanthropy; towns and cities competed with each other to send the largest amount of 'comforts' to the troops at the front. The 'Royal Patriotic Fund', destined to raise money for comforts for the troops and to provide support for the 'widows and children of the British Soldiers Sailors' ordered east at the request of Queen Victoria.

Local committees were formed across Britain: in Manchester, a public meeting on 26 October chaired by the Mayor, Benjamin Nichols, was attended by the 'great and the good.' But it was a meeting which attracted controversy: Rev. Canon Hugh Stowell of Manchester Cathedral was vehemently opposed to the formation of a local committee as he believed it was the government's responsibility to look after it's soldiers, not philanthropists; it was an 'unjust tax' upon the well-to-do. His colleague, Rev. Canon Clifton, was concerned that the funds raised would only aid the other ranks and urged the establishment of a special fund for the officers, but this was voted-down as being divisive. John Bright – Quaker MP for Manchester – was opposed to the fund as he believed it would prolong the war. Rev. William Gaskell (Unitarian Minister of Cross Street Chapel) was of a similar belief, and was compelled to write:

> O God! the darkness roll away
> Which clouds the human soul,
> And let the bright, the perfect day,
> Speed onward to its goal.
>
> Let every hateful passion die,
> Which makes of brethren foes;
> And war no longer raise its cry,
> To mar the world's repose.

Gaskell's wife however, the novelist Elizabeth, unlike most of her co-religionists, was in favour of the war as being 'just' and supported raising money for the troops at the front. Controversies aside, in just three months Manchester raised a staggering £27,500 – over £2,000,000 in today's money. Over the Pennines, the 'Ladies of Leeds' responded magnificently sending out to the Crimea:

1,254 linen shirts
300 pairs woollen drawers
2,028 pairs sheets
403 towels
504 flannel shirts
½ ton "Old linen for bandages"
130 down pillows
552 pocket handkerchiefs
9 bundles lint
8 sacks of bandages
9 ½ dozen bottles Amontillado Sherry
10,000 needles, thimbles and reels of cotton
5cwt of tow for pillows

Down the road in Wakefield, formation of a committee to support the troops and their dependents became highly charged: Alderman George Washington Harrison – a Quaker –raised three questions for the council regarding the Royal Patriotic Fun. Firstly, he wished to know who would be distributing the funds raised through collection and subscription; secondly what had happened to the funds raised for the Central Association at the start of the War and finally he stated that it was not the Council's business to be involved in charity work.

Both he and Councillor Holdsworth were both opposed to the war; Harrison was opposed to the Royal Patriotic Fund because he believed the 'war was un-Christian' and the fund 'got up by those with a War-Spirit' to prolong the conflict. He addressed the council stating that, 'The War Spirit has been so scandalously and cunningly got up in this Country' and that saw the war not only as a great waste of life but also of money. He further stated that the State Funeral for the Duke of Wellington in 1852 had been a total waste of money and that the Duke's assertions that the nation's defences were in a parlous state of disrepair in 1848 were the ramblings of a tired old man who was losing his faculties. For this he was vilified by the Tory, Anglican, press in the north.

The Wakefield Town Council, however, voted unanimously that it was not its business to be involved charity work and that the Patriotic Fund should be administered by the Townsmen, and by the end of October had raised some £513 8.s and at a cheque for £700 was sent to the Royal Patriotic Fund in the middle of December.[87]

In Newcastle, the 'Ladies' Balaklava Fund' raised £420 15s 6d and was able to dispatch some 473 flannel shirts; 121 flannel vests, 111 pairs of drawers 'Newcastle Hoods … Knitted Caps … Shetland Nightcaps …

Dressing Gowns ... Mittens ... Muffs' as well as newspapers and books.[88] In Stockport, Mr Downe, a prominent cheesemonger, furnished:

> Two Prime Cheeses ... They are both enclosed in strong boxes, and hoped with iron, and now lie at the [Stockport] courthouse...The First is Directed as follows:- 'For the Band, Drummers and Pipers of the 79th Highlanders... from Edward Cunningham, late 79th Highlanders.' The other is 62lbs of best Cheshire Cheese for the army in the Crimea, from Mrs Scholey, Greek Street, Stockport.[89]

The publicans of Nottinghamshire formed a committee to send out beer and ale to Nottinghamshire Regiments, notably the Scots Greys who had been barracked there 1853-1854. More than twenty publicans sent a barrel of Nottinghamshire ale to the front at the suggestion of Thomas Dickinson, landlord of the 'Old Black Lion Inn', Nottingham.[90]

The committee was established at a public meeting at the 'Three Wheat Sheaves' Old Lenton, Nottingham:[91] some eight barrels had been despatched by January 1855 – much to the joy of the Scots Greys.[92] Other publicans made their own gifts: Philip Henry Lees (Shakespeare Inn, Nottingham) sent 'a fifty-gallon barrel of his prime strength ale ... He has also most liberally sent a barrel of ale to Sergeant Dawson, at the depot of the regiment.'[93] Meanwhile 250 boxes containing four one-gallon bottles of Nottingham ale were sent from Welbeck Abbey estate;[94] in addition were 200 boxes of 'potted meat, clothing, &c.' as well as a 'large quantity of pheasants, and as many rabbits as can be killed ... five bullocks, 25 deer, 400 hares.'[95]

In the Manchester area, Ashton-Under-Lyne raised £1,800; Dukinfield £220; Salford £3,000 and Stockport £2164 6s 4d. The Police in Stalybridge and Hyde each donated a days' wages. The 'heart of the nation' went out to the ordinary soldier as 'never before': across the country towns and villages all did their part to raise money for the troops and send comforts for the front.

War and Peace

The divisions and acrimonies raised over the question of the necessity, and indeed legality, of the 'Great War with Russia' did not end once war had been declared. As the Siege of Sevastopol ground on into stalemate, both the conduct of the war, and its necessity, were called into question. The war also unleashed xenophobia and bigotry: the *Morning Advertiser* (a 'Red Top' of its day) attacked Prince Albert simply for being German, and therefore in the eyes of many indistinguishable from a Russian. He was accused of treason by the popular press, with the *Morning Advertiser* calling for his execution:

> Better than a few drops of guilty blood should be shed on a scaffold on Tower Hill than that a country should be baulked for its desire for War![96]

In Manchester, where there was a sizable community of Greek and Russian traders, the *Manchester Guardian* reported known members of those communities were denied service in shops, and in one case, 'thrown off' an Omnibus! *The Times* censored the Russian community in Manchester for 'celebrating the triumphs of their Countrymen' at the Battle of Balaklava. One letter-writer to the *Daily News* could not understand the *volte-face* of public opinion which in 1853 had been 'in favour of the Greek race'. In reply, the *Daily News* poured scorn on the Greek and Russian communities in London and Manchester, describing their 'actions' at the Manchester Exchange as 'Indecent', darkly referring to them as enemies within.

The Times, in a thinly veiled attack on John Bright, the Quaker MP for Manchester, thought that a single pacifist in the House of Commons was the equivalent of a hundred Russian spies at Horse Guards. Bright – and other pacifists – were pilloried by the popular press. One Irish paper referred to the Tsar as 'John Bright's dog in Petersburg' and that 'his heart has been there since long ago.' When Bright published an open letter in *The Times* the jingoistic press exploded in a shower of vitriol. He was burned in effigy 'wearing his ludicrous Quaker costume', 'mocking the peace-at-any-price Gentlemen'.

A total of 613 of his outraged constituents in Manchester petitioned the Mayor, the Unitarian philanthropist Benjamin Nicholls, to hold a public meeting in the Town Hall on King Street. The riotous meeting was duly held on Monday 18 December, allowing Bright to defend his actions. The Town Hall was 'densely filled' with many waving anti-Bright, pro-war placards, with further placard-bearing demonstrators outside, hustling one another of their opposed positions. The meeting was held to decide whether or not Bright should be censored. It was moved that 'it was unfair, unjust and tyrannical' to censor Bright for expressing his deeply held convictions – which many of his constituents had 'well known' for years. Speaking in defence of Bright was William Rayner Wood esq., but he was 'rendered perfectly inaudible' and was 'received with a perfect storm of disapprobriation.' He was supported by Alderman W. B. Watkins and Mr Alexander Henry and both were booed off stage with a shower of rotten fruit.

The attacks on Bright centred around his pacifism – and therefore his patriotism, reliability and his purely fictitious links to the Tsar – and the status of Manchester on the world stage. Bright finally rose to speak, but 'was unable to be heard, on account of the row, for a full ten minutes.' He was greeted with chants of 'Go Back to Russia.' The vote to censor Bright was taken three times, and eventually Sir John Potter had to call for the Constabulary to clear the Town Hall and those outside.

Letters home from the troops, and reports of the likes of William Russell and Lawrence Godkin, revealed the appalling conditions at the front and apparent mis-management of the war provided renewed impetus for calls for peace, or at least an armistice. Leading the charge was the 'Peace Society' and George Thompson MP, editor of *The Empire* newspaper. Public meetings and rallies to end the war were held across Britain in the New Year and spring of 1855.

That in Manchester was held on Wednesday 24 January at the Mechanic's Institute, chaired by Alderman Abel Heywood. Heywood was a life-long Radical, a Chartist and anti-Corn Law agitator, who campaigned for the incorporation of Manchester and via his publishing concerns, printed most of the material for the chartists. He served as Mayor of Manchester twice.

The institute was filled to capacity, the press reporting 2,500 to 3,000 persons being crammed inside. Thompson didn't even get a chance to speak. Heywood was almost immediately booed off stage by the 'tumultuous crowd' (whom the *Manchester Guardian* believed had been seeded agitators by the Tory press and 'filled with strong drink'). Heywood believed that the war had 'Grossly mismanaged' and had 'sent thousands of brave souls to an unnecessary grave.' On those grounds alone, an armistice should be declared and peace talks started.

He was booed and jeered off stage, eventually the Constabulary being called to defuse the situation.[97] Thompson met a similar fate elsewhere: in Oldham, Stockport and Wakefield near-riots ensued. That said, new branches of the Peace Society sprang up across the country, revealing some, perhaps, unexpected alliances. In Wakefield it included the Unitarian Rev Edward Higginson, Quaker George Washington Harrison, but also Anglican clergy such as Thomas Kilby and Rev. William Bowditch.

Mirroring the Peace Society in the town was a 'War Society' headed by the Rev. Taylor, headmaster of the Grammar School. Wakefield also had the unique distinction of sending a petition to Parliament for 'Dispatching Without Delay, conjunction with our Allies, an Overwhelming Force to the Crimea.' A public meeting was held at the

Court House on Wood Street, addressed by many town notables, including G. W. Harrison who argued that 'War was false' and an 'un-Christian doctrine.' The Tory, Anglican *Wakefield Journal & Examiner* interpreted Harrison's opinion as an attack on the troops at the front and was tantamount to treason.

A week later the same 'paper stated that they did not 'quarrel with Mr Harrison's Peace Principles, but rather his lack of support and friendliness displayed towards widows and orphans.' One enraged correspondent suggested Mr Harrison take a lesson from his friend the Quaker MP John Bright who had recently lost his seat in Parliament for his pacifist stance. In fact, Bright had what would be now described as a nervous breakdown as a result of the jingoistic hatred he (and many others) had received from the press and at public meetings. The Rev. Edward Higginson proposed that the Petition be amended as it was

> perfectly idle to be urging government now to take further measures
> to reinforce the army, when they are doing everything in their power
> … the petition is uncalled for, and there is no necessity to get up the
> excitement about it.

He proposed amending the petition, postponing it *sine die* (indefinitely). He was seconded by Alderman Boston who expressed his own abhorrence to war and proposed amending the petition to read, 'Necessity of sending reinforcements *together with the medical stores and comforts for the troops.*' It was universally carried. The petition was presented to the House of Lords by the Duke of Richmond, and the 'Noble and gallant Duke expressed a warm eulogium' on the townsmen.

Not to be out done, Rev J. Taylor and the 'War Party' held their own meeting, to consider and vote upon the conduct of the war. The meeting considered that the government had mismanaged the war and called censure upon Lord Aberdeen (Prime Minister) and Lord Raglan. The meeting concluded that there were not enough men at the front; they were chronically over-worked, and 'God for shame' the British had to rely on the French to carry their sick and wounded to the transport ships, to bake their bread and take over their duties in the trenches. Despite this, the meeting 'Expressed its admiration of the unparalleled bravery of the Allied forces … its sympathy is with them in the severe losses the have suffered'. This second petition was signed by Rev. Taylor and passed to the Mayor to send to the House of Commons.

NOTES

1. 'Letter from the Crimea', *Wakefield Journal & Examiner* (15 December 1854).
2. LA, Acc. 1-Dixon 22/12/3/7, Hunter Mss., Hunter to Sister, 17 November 1854.
3. 'Letter from a Berry-Brow Man in the Crimea', *Huddersfield Chronicle* (27 January 1855), p.7.
4. ibid.
5. ibid.
6. 'Christmas in the English Camp', *Huddersfield Chronicle* (27 January 1855), p.7.
7. 'A Soldier's letter from the Crimea', *Wakefield Express* (31 March 1855), np.
8. 'Letters from the Crimea', *Manchester Examiner & Times* (13 January 1855), np.
9. A. L. Dawson, *British Army Perception of French Support Services during the Crimean War* Unpublished M.Res Thesis, University of Leeds, 2013, pp.73-74.
10. ibid, pp.74-76
11. ibid, pp.87-88.
12. 'Letter from the East', *Wakefield Express* (30 December 1854), p.8.
13. 'From Another Yorkshire Soldier', *Leeds Intelligencer* (20 January 1855), p.3.
14. 'Christmas in the Crimea', *Wakefield Express* (13 January 1855).
15. 'Christmas in the English Camp', *The Huddersfield Chronicle* (27 January 1855), p.7.
16. Commandant Devanlay, ' Lettres de Crimée du General Breton. 2e Partie', *Carnet de la Sabretache*, vol. 18 (1909) p.96 and p.150.
17. Anon, *Campagnes de Crimée, d'Italie, de Chine et de Syrie 1849-1862* (Paris: E.Plon, Nourrit et Cie., 1898), p.154: Letter 89: Capitaine Comte More de Pontgibaud du 57e de Ligne au Marechal de Castellane, 1e Fevrier 1855.
18. Devanlay, 'General Breton', p.152.
19. ibid, p.96 and p.145.
20. 'Army Medical Organization', pp.572-573.
21. H. G. Gilbert, ed, *Campagne de Crimée. Lettres écrites par le Capitaine d'État-Major Henri Loizillon à sa famille* (Paris: Ernest Flammarion, ND), p.275.
22. C. Mismer, *Souvenirs d'un Dragon en Crimée: avril 1854-juillet 1856* (Paris: Hachette, 1887), pp.113-114.
23. ibid, pp.114-117.
24. General Hardy, *11e Legere*, pp.103-105.
25. C-A Thoumas, *Mes Souvenirs de Crimée* (Paris: La Librairie Illustrée, 1892), pp.14-15.
26. Mismer, *Souvenirs d'un Dragon*, p.118.
27. P. Chalmin, *L'Officier Français de 1815 a 1870* (Paris: Librairie Marcel Rivieres, 1956), p.282.
28. Goutmann, 'Objectif: Sebastopol', Napoleon III, no. 1 (Janvier-Mars 2008), pp.27-28.
29. C. F. M. Rousset, *Histoire de la Guerre de Crimée* (Paris: Librairie Hachette et Cie., 1878), vol. I, pp.73-74.
30. Dawson, *British Army Perception*, p.53; see also A. L. Dawson, 'The French Army and British Army Crimean War Reforms' in *19: Interdisciplinary Studies in the Long Nineteenth Century* 2015(20), DOI: http://dx.doi.org/10.16995/ntn.707.
31. Goutman, 'Objectif: Sebstopol', p. 28. See also Dawson, 'The French Army and British Army Crimean Reforms.'
32. A. L. Dawson, 'The French Army and British Army Reform', Conference Proceedings *Charting the Crimean War: Contexts, Nationhood, Afterlives*, National Army Museum, London, 28-6-2013.
33. 'The French Army. To the Editor of the Morning Post', *The Morning Post* (15 September 1853), np.
34. Fay, *Souvenirs de la Guerre de Crimee*, pp.168-169.
35. Anon, *Campagnes de Crimée*, p.149.
36. 'Hardship in the French Camp', *The Morning Post* (13 January 1855); G. Bertin, 'Les 6eme Dragons', pp.368-369; Joppe, 'Commandant Adrien', p.215; Anon, *Campgnes de Crimée*, p.344; Herbé, *Francaises et Russe*, p.144.
37. Molènes, *Commentaires d'un Soldat*, pp.136-137; Devanlay, 'General Breton', 2e partie, p.91;

Boppe, *General Vanson*, pp.85-90 and pp.105-106.

[38] Minart, 'Les Freres Minart', p.233.

[39] 'Souvenirs de la Guerre de Crimee par le General de Division Coste' *Revue de Midi* Tome XXXXI (Decembre 1908), pp.726-727.

[40] Devanlay, 'Genera Breton', 2e partie, p.91.

[41] Lieutenant J. Spitz, *Histoire du 2eme Regiment de Zouaves* (Oran: Paul Perrier, 1901), p.177.

[42] Author's Collection.

[43] Hardy, *11e Legere*, p.105 and p.132.

[44] 'The Homes of the French Soldiers', *Leeds Intelligencer* (12 May 1855), p.11.

[45] Hardy, *11e Legere*, pp.132-134.

[46] 'Affairs d'Orient', *Journal de Toulouse* (3 Fevrier 1855); 'Siege de Sebastopol', *Journal de Constantinople* (21 Janvier 1855).

[47] Dawson, *British Army Perception*, pp.60-61.

[48] Anon, *Campagnes de Crimee*, p.156.

[49] 'Souvenirs de la Guerre de Crimee', pp.729-730.

[50] H. Choppin, *Souvenirs d'un Capitaine de Cavalerie 1851-1881* (Paris: Berger-Levrault et Cie., 1909), pp.19-21.

[51] Margaret Kerwin, 'In the Crimea with the 19th Regiment', *Green Howards Gazette* vol. IV (1896-1897), pp.94-95.

[52] 'The Soldiers' Wives at Scutari', *Leeds Mercury* (3 March 1855), np.

[53] NAM, Acc. 1993-07-39, Surgeon J. J. Scott, Mss., Journal, entry 26 January 1855, 28 January 1855, 1 February 1855 and 7 March 1855.

[54] 'Extracts from Letters of Assistant Chaplains recently sent by the Society for the Propagation of the Gospel to the Seat of War', *The Colonial Church Chronicle and Missionary Journal*, No. XCIV (April 1855), pp.379-381.

[55] Dr Mike Hinton, 'Pitfalls in the Assessment of Hospitals: Can lessons be learnt from the Crimean Campaign', Conference Proceedings, *Charting the Crimean War: Contexts, Nationhood, Afterlives*, NAM, 28-6-2013.

[56] 'Extracts of a letter dated Scutaria Hospital …', *Hampshire Telegraph & Sussex Chronicle* (6 January 1855), np.

[57] 'Letter from a wounded soldier to his wife in Wakefield', *Wakefield Journal & Examiner* (1 December 1854), np.

[58] Probably Ensign Horatio J. Thompson, who died from wounds received at Inkerman on 10 November 1854.

[59] 'Letter from a Wounded Soldier in Scutari Hospital', *Wakefield Express* (30 December 1854).

[60] LA, Acc. 1-Dixon 22/12/3/8, Hunter Mss., Hunter to Sister, 26 December 1854.

[61] 'Good Testimony', *The Evangelical Repository*, vol. 13 (1854), pp.424-425; 'The Bible Society at Constantinople', *The Manchester Examiner and Times* (14 February 1855).

[62] Dawson, *William Gaskell, Manchester Unitarians, and the Crimean War*.

[63] Probably Staff-Surgeon Dr Alexander McGrigor; a staunch ally of Florence Nightingale who said he 'was the only surgeon not wedded in everything to what had been done in the Peninsula.' He is buried in the cemetery at Haydarpasa, near Istanbul.

[64] 'Extracts from the letter of a volunteer surgeon at Scutari', *Leeds Mercury* (24 February 1855), np.

[65] The Blackwoods were allies of Florence Nightingale. Lady Alicia was a nurse – she recorded her experiences of the Crimean War as 'A Narrative of personal experiences & impressions during a Residence on the Bosphorus throughout the Crimean War' (1881) – and her husband Rev. James Stevenson Blackwood was a Chaplain to the forces in the Crimea.

[66] 'Extracts from the letter of a volunteer surgeon at Scutari', *Leeds Mercury* (24 February 1855), np.

[67] 'Letters from the Crimea', *Stockport Advertiser* (12 January 1855), p.3.

[68] 'Another letter from the Crimea', *Stockport Advertiser* (2 March 1855), p.3.

[69] O. Anderson, *A Liberal State at War* (New York: St. Martin's Press, 1967), p.97.

[70] ibid, pp.105-107.

[71] ibid, pp.116-118.

[72] M. Robbins, 'Balaklava Railway', *Journal of Transport History* vol. 1, no. 1 (1953), pp.29-30.

[73] 'Balaklava Railway', *The Railway Record* (20 January 1855), p.40.

[74] I. F. W Beckett, *The Victorians at War* (London: Hambledon and London, 2003), p.174. See also Anderson, *A Liberal State*, pp.116-118.

[75] 'L'enterprise de chemin de fer de Balaklava', *Journal des Chemins de Fer* (6 Janvier 1855), p.4.

[76] 'The Balaklava Railway Corps', *Manchester Courier* (30 December 1854), p.9.

[77] ibid.

[78] 'The Balaklava Railway Corps', *Newcastle Journal* (30 December 1854), p.5.

[79] 'The Balaklava Railway', *The Northern Whig* (9 January 1862), p.4.

[80] 'The Balaklava and Sebastopol Railway', *The Railway Record* (12 May 1855), pp.3-4.

[81] ibid, p.4.

[82] 'Letters from Balaklava', *Inverness Courier* (10 May 1855), p.6.

[83] 'A Leeds Locomotive for the Balaklava Railway', *Leeds Mercury* (8 September 1855); 'A Locomotive for Balaklava', *Wakefield Express* (15 September 1855); see also Robbins, 'Balaklava Railway', pp.36-38.

[84] 'A Leeds Locomotive for the Balaklava Railway', *Leeds Mercury* (8 September 1855).

[85] 'Engine for the Crimea', *Leeds Mercury* (22 September 1855).

[86] Robbins, 'Balaklava Railway', p.40.

[87] A L Dawson, *Wakefield and the Crimean War*, Unpublished Paper presented to Wakefield Historical Society.

[88] 'The Ladies' Balaklava Fund', *Newcastle Courant* (15 December 1854), p.2.

[89] *Manchester Courier* (30 Dec. 1854)

[90] 'Christmas Box for the Scots Greys', *Nottinghamshire Guardian* (7 December 1854), p.8.

[91] 'Nottingham Ale for the Crimea', *Nottinghamshire Guardian* (14 December 1854), p.5.

[92] 'The Present of Ale to the Scots Greys', *Nottinghamshire Guardian* (19 April 1855), p.5.

[93] 'Magnificent Christmas Gift to the Scots Greys', *Nottinghamshire Guardian* (21 December 1854), p.5.

[94] Approximately 1,000 gallons of ale.

[95] 'The Comforts for the Troops from Welbeck Abbey', *Nottinghamshire Guardian* (21 December 1854), p.5.

[96] Dawson, *William Gaskell, Manchester Unitarians, and the Crimean War.*

[97] ibid.

Chapter 7

Spring Assaults

Les Ouvrages Blancs (23-24 February 1855)

The French, who had become the senior partners of the Allied force, had taken over the 'Right Attack' on Mount Inkerman and in front of the Malakoff on 23 January. But almost under their noses, during the night of 22-23 February the Russians constructed a battery on the Inkerman Heights, to enfilade their right flank. Known to the French as 'Les Ouvrages Blancs' (the White Works) because of the light-coloured spoil used to make the embrasures, to the Russians it was the 'Seleghinski Redoubt.' It was with 'great stupefaction' that the French awoke on 23 February to find that a new battery had appeared only 1,000 metres from their position.[1] Cler describes it as a 'gabionade' i.e. made from wicker-work gabions, filled with stones which was then covered with earth.[2]

Général Adolphe de Monet was charged by Bosquet to capture the Ouvrages Blancs and to silence the enemy guns. He led his brigade (two battalions of the *2e Zouaves*, 2nd battalion *4e Régiment Infanterie de Marine* and one battalion each from the *6e* and *10e de Ligne* in reserve) in a night attack on 23 February.[3]

Colonel Cler wrote:

> On February 23, the colonel of the 2nd *Zouaves* was ordered to be ready to march at eleven in the evening, with the available part of his regiment who held the camp Moulin. The Anglo-French muster-point had been indicated to him as a meeting place of a column to make an attack on the work raised by the Russians in front of the port. About a thousand *Zouaves*, divided into twelve platoons, were gathered to take part in this expedition, which was to be supported by five hundred men of the *Infanterie de Marine*. Orders were given to occupy the Russian works only for a short time and to abandon

them when the signal for retreat was given. The timing of this signal was to be left to the commander of the troops engaged.

Around midnight, the column was directed to the *place d'armes* on the second parallel; the two battalions of the regiment were placed behind two large ditches on the right and left of this work; the marines in the centre, with *général* de Monet, who was to command the operation.

Between one and two o'clock the battalions left the parallel arranged in column by sections, they were set in motion soon after, on the order that was sent to them by *général* Monet. Colonel Cler and *commandant* Lacretelle were with the right column, and *commandant* d'Arbois had command of the left column.

The companies of each battalion of *Zouaves* had been arranged in the following manner: a vanguard company, placed a hundred yards in front of the column, was supported by another company established fifty paces further back; the other four companies of each battalion formed the main the columns.

At the agreed signal, the two columns marched. The night was very dark; the left column, led by an engineer officer, at first went too far to the left, into a deep ravine, and then they regained the direction to the main work.[4]

Commandant Lacretelle, recalled the sense of doubt that pervaded the French camp:

I commanded the 1st Battalion of the *2e Zouaves*; Darbois, my colleague, commanded the 2nd. In the afternoon of the 23rd, we received the order from the *général* to make ready, with *commandant* Marmier, of the *4e régiment d'infanterie de marine*. The *général* announced that, this evening, we will attack the Selinginsk redoubt on the right, with Darbois seeking to turn the works by the left, while *commandant* Marmier, marching between us … forming a support which should operate with the brave *général* Monet. Colonel Dubos was to form the main reserve with a battalion of the *6e* and the *10e de Ligne*. The *général* added that in order not to expose ourselves to the converging fire that would certainly [be] directed at us, the attack would take place at night. It was a regrettable precaution, which was to make us fail.

My colleagues and I both felt at the time, but none of us said anything that might be seen as showing weakness. The order also said, as soon as we were master of the redoubt, we had to destroy it, filling the ditch and then retire into our parallels, at the signal to retreat, which would be sounded in our trenches, at the order of the general of division. This order was impossible to execute. We could not destroy the parapet, or fill-in the ditch, without taking several hours' work.

At ten o'clock we were at our posts; it was a beautiful moonlit night, which would have allowed us to see and effectively lead our battalions, and we would have some chance of success. But believing that such an attack would benefit more from darkness than light, they wanted to wait for the darkness to be complete and we were allowed to languish for three and a half hours in the trenches half filled with a mud mixed with snow, and freezing cold. It was enough to cool the ardour of any soldiers ... Finally, at half past three, the moon set, the darkness became complete: We were given the order to attack.[5]

At 03.30 hours, the attack went in: 1st battalion of *2e Zouaves* on the left, 2nd battalion on the right, proceeded by their skirmishers. At the head of the 1st battalion, *commandant* Lacretelle jumped onto the parapet shouting, 'Stand up, *Zouaves*! Go straight ahead':

We run to the trench work; but nothing is so difficult as keeping the right direction in the dark. We got lost and wandered beyond the redoubt without seeing it; the *Infanterie de Marine* mingled with *Zouaves*: our confusion was complete. Neither soldiers nor officers could see each other or knew where the other was.

The Russians had guessed our attack would take place, and waited for us; in a short time, they welcomed us with a barrage. But their fire had the advantage to indicate their positions to us. We ran hither and thither, but were faced with ... rifle pits and sharpshooters positioned in front and around the redoubt. We ceded the field: we were in complete disorder, and had no hope of success; soon a rain of rockets ... illuminated the field.

The scene shown was hellish and indescribable. Several hundred braves swirling aimlessly, and uselessly displaying the most admirable courage; bombs and shells crisscrossed the air by hundreds and many of us are wounded; the destruction of the *Zouaves* comes quickly; but they had orders not to retire until a signal is given and this signal not being heard, these braves were left unprotected on the plateau.[6]

The 2nd battalion of *2e Zouaves* had crept up to the Russian trenches in silence, bayonets fixed, without firing a shot, only to discover that they were surrounded:

Assailed on both flanks and in front by a fusillade fired at very close range … Under the most heavy fire from the left, the four companies supporting the first column changed direction to the left, strongly attacked the advanced trenches with the bayonet, and in a few minutes, the middle of the defended ground was swept away. Some prisoners were taken in the first fight. During the attack, the head of the left column, which had to wade through a ravine, debouched from it, and formed line with great composure.

The advanced guard companies of the two columns, which had been allowed to pass through the forward trenches by the Russians, continued marching on the work; they arrived on the small squares arranged in front and on the flanks, and there, with bayonets and musket-butts, they engaged in a furious silent struggle. Two officers, Messrs Baratchard and Bartel, and several soldiers received their first wounds but did not stop their march.

Towards the end of the first fight, *général* de Monet, who had pressed too far to the left with the battalion of *Infanterie de Marine*, arrived at the forward trench. He was hit five times and asked colonel Cler to take over [overall] command This change is made, the brave *général* telling the troops who marched behind him [in the centre column], 'Your salvation is in the trench works; forward! follow me!' Electrified by such courage and selflessness, several officers and soldiers of the *Infanterie de Marine* followed the *général*, which he directs to the centre of the entrenchment …

Colonel Cler gives the direction of the attack: on the right *commandant* Lacretelle, and on the left, *commandant* d'Arbois, then he rushes with a few companies in the ditch of the retrenchment.

After climbing the ditch and the parapet, the centre column jumps into the interior of the structure, while those on the right and left penetrate the flanks. The heads of column attack, received by the fire of Russian battalions established in close column holding on to the entrance of the retrenchment; we see falling seven of our officers, two adjutants and a large number of NCOs and soldiers. The position of the *Zouaves* became very critical, the colonel ordered his men to get onto the berm and the gap left between the outer slope of the parapet. The colonel gave the order to his men to stand in the gap, which was only one meter deep and was protected on the side of the ground by a gabion mask. The batteries of the square, those on the right of the port and those of Tchernaïa, the guns of large vessels and steamboats, fired a hail of shells and shrapnel that was to inflict great losses on the Russian troops, so to speak, without reaching the *Zouaves*.

In the darkness, the Russians found it difficult to see where to shoot. Some of their boldest soldiers were being killed with bayonets inside the entrenchment of stones and gabions ...

Having supported this unequal struggle for twenty minutes, the colonel, hearing for the second time the signal for retreat, decided to abandon the field, where he has lost the elite of his regiment. It brings with it the few men who still occupy the ditch, and, before throwing himself headlong on Russian bayonets, he addresses them these words: 'I do not want to give these Jean-Foutres[7] satisfaction of promenading a captive *Zouave* colonel through all Russia. It is better to die.'[8]

The French attack had stalled and confusion reigned; no one seemed to know where *général* de Monet, or even colonel Cler was. Lacretelle took the initiative:

We had to take control; I stopped some *Zouaves* ... 'Do you know where the general de Monet is?' – 'Injured. Returned to our trenches' – 'And *colonel* Cler?' – 'He followed *général* de Monet.' – 'So it is for me to take command. Call all the officers and buglers and tell them to come here to me, *commandant* Lacretelle.'

Darbois was near, he said: 'Do we leave?' I said 'it is not for me alone to make such a decision.'

'My friends, be quiet and listen to what I have to say'. Several officers and buglers were already with me. 'Darbois, you see something to do, something to try?' – 'We have nothing to do here except die, my opinion is we retire.' – 'Gentlemen, are you of the same opinion of *commandant* Darbois? Have any one of you something to offer?' – 'We believe in retiring' – 'Well, it is also mine. I'm going to sound the retreat; and that everyone head back to our bivouacs.'

I ordered the buglers to sound the retreat ... Darbois and I stayed until the last moment, and got back together. Nothing can give an idea of the rage of this old soldier, who was renowned for his bravery. He was not likely to soften and yet could not hold back his sobs: 'Where are my old *Zouaves*, my brave soldiers? They died needlessly, victims of an absurd conception of their leaders.' I agreed and tried to calm him; but I also thought of what he said. It was certainly a glorious combat; it showed once again the courage of our soldiers, and, at the same time, the spirit of the Russians, on whom the moral effect was considerable.[9]

After the battle, *colonel* Cler wrote bitterly:

> If at the time of the taking of the entrenchment, the furious and
> desperate attack of the *Zouaves* could be supported by fresh troops,
> the reserves the Russians could not have held and all those to the
> rear, would have been completely swept away. Unfortunately there
> were no reserves, and the *2e Zouaves* had lost several of their officers
> and bravest soldiers. The Russian battalions, seeing the weakness of
> the attack, sallied out of the work by the right and the left, in an
> instant, they roughly handled the *Zouaves* who occupied the face of
> retrenchment, and surrounded them.[10]

Did the *Infanterie de Marine* 'run away'?

The failure of the French at the 'Ouvrages Blancs' was the first major
set-back suffered by the Allies. So what had gone wrong? Many British
observers believed the *Infanterie de Marine* 'ran away.'[11] *Colonel* Cler
suggests that the *Zouaves* had never fought a losing battle; that this
failure came as a massive psychological shock, and they needed
someone to blame.

The *Infanterie de Marine* – who had a poor reputation amongst the
French army – were an easy target.[12] French accounts do not indicate
that the *Infanterie de Marine* ran away and, furthermore, their officers
were mentioned for bravery in official despatches.[13] *Commandant* Adrien
of the *6e de Ligne* states that:

> We encountered a very strong, unexpected resistance. In vain the
> *Zouaves* made prodigies of valour; evil seconds! It is said by the
> *Infanterie de Marine* that the enemy numbers and the amount of
> grape shot fired overwhelmed them. They beat the retreat only after
> taking very heavy losses.[14]

The staff-officer Emile Vanson, suggests the reserves (*6e* and *10e de
Ligne*) 'would not attack' to which he attributes the failure of the attack.[15]
Neither *commandant* Adrien, nor the Regimental History of the *6e de
Ligne*, confirm this.[16] Other French eyewitnesses indicate that the
Zouaves attacked and captured the position but were taken by surprise
by a very strong Russian counter-attack and artillery fire from Russian
naval vessels.[17] Moreover, they believed the Russians had been made
aware an assault was to be made,[18] and many British officers agreed,
believing that the Russians were 'better acquainted with the intentions
of the French than we are.'[19]

The *Zouaves* came out of the battle with an enhanced reputation.[20] Cler recounts how Lord Rokeby and officers of the Brigade of Guards visited him to,

> Compliment him upon the glorious manner in which his regiment had fought … and to assure him of the very true and deep sensation of regret, with which they hard of the death of so many of their gallant comrades among the *Zouaves*.[21]

To the consternation of the French, however, a second redoubt was thrown up by the Russians – the 'Volnya Redoubt' flanking the Seleginksi – a mere 500 metres from the French lines during the night of 27-28 February.[22]

Arrival of the Imperial Guard
The French ranks were swelled with reinforcements during early spring, with the arrival of the remainder of the Cavalry Division (*7e Dragons*; *6e* and *9e Cuirassiers*), two new infantry divisions as well as the Imperial Guard.

The Imperial Guard had been re-established by Imperial Decree of 1 May 1854, consisting of two regiments each of *Grenadiers à Pied* (wearing their tall bearskin caps and red epaulettes) and *Voltigeurs* (in their jaunty shakos and yellow epaulettes), a battalion of *Chasseurs à Pied*, a regiment of *Guides à Cheval, Cuirassiers, Gendarmes d'Elite* and *Artillerie à Cheval*. Command of the Imperial Guard Expeditionary forced was vested in *général* Regnault Saint-Jean d'Angely, a veteran of Waterloo. The first elements landed in the Crimea in January 1855; the remainder arrived in mid-May.

Paul de Molènes watched the Grenadiers march into camp:

> The uniforms of these warriors were consecrated by many glorious events in our history, and recalled many great patriotic emotions, being symbols as powerful as our flags … our grenadiers, I see with joy, under the hazy sky… the bearskin cap which speaks to me of Austerlitz and Moscow.[23]

One young officer of *Voltigeurs* left his impression of arriving in the Crimea:

> The 19th, in the dawn, a large black line, but still lost in the fog, appeared on the horizon.

'There,' I said to a sailor who was on watch, pointing to the land 'Is that Balaklava? And Sebastopol?'

Walking over to me, he answered: 'Wait a moment, and you will hear: listen.'

I cupped my ear, and soon a deep, unknown, booming came to me. It is the cannon of the city. My soul felt troubled: for us, the prelude of this gigantic struggle, which was to be the source of so [many] new thoughts, of such strong emotions, the memory of which will end only with life – war! It was there, we heard it, we were going to see it, and in a few days, make it ourselves.

Little by little this black line took shape: dog-toothed, high red cliffs were outlined on the horizon, and the cliffs formed an uninterrupted line to the sea, terminating with a very tall lighthouse. 'There it is! Kamiesch' continued the sailor. 'And this,' he added, pointing to a big, black, round, wide and low, tower barely out of the water, 'is Fort Constantine.' – Sebastopol was behind, completely hidden to us. The cannon's roar only shows us its presence. In front [of us] we saw the allied warships, of France and England, formidable engines of war that the English denote such with an expressive name 'Menowar'. They are immobile, set at anchor, rather like sleeping lions.

We continued to advance under steam and discovered, on our right, a large bay, filled with ships of every tonnage, and crossed in every direction by innumerable little boats. It was Kamiesch Bay … The bay contained over a thousand ships: a few months ago it was a wild refuge, housing no more than a few boats of fishermen. At ten o'clock in the morning, a splendid sun, crossing the boom, the *Cacique* entered the harbour and dropped anchor. We had arrived. We, the first soldiers, all part of the Guard. There were different regiments: about twelve hundred of the *1e Regiment des Grenadiers*, and two or three hundred of the *1e Regiment des Voltigeurs*. We were carried on land by twenty-five, wide, flat-bottomed barges with a metal bottom.

The soldiers were happy: there were jokes, quips without end, the '*Veste à Paul*' (Sevastopol), The Emperor Nicholas, '*Gross Schako*' (Gorschakoff) and about a hundred others like this. In less than an hour all were landed with weapons and baggage. After supervising the landing of our horses, we, the officers, went in a boat to a wooden landing-stage located at the bottom of the bay, opposite which were two small huts pompously named 'Office of the Port'. Touching the shore, we are surprised by all its particular physiognomy. To the right and left were vast stores of boards, trucks, and gun carriages, cannon barrels, mortars, and piles of cannon balls. In the middle of all this perpetually running back and forth [were] small fiery horses and men of all nations and dressed in all colours.[24]

Marching with the *Voltigeurs* was a little wire-haired terrier dubbed *Thouton* who was the regimental mascot. He had attached himself to the regiment in Paris and had been smuggled out to the Crimea. *Thouton* survived the campaign and the NCOs attached miniature versions of the British and Turkish Crimean medals to his collar. Sadly his habit of chasing after cannon balls got him killed during the Italian Campaign of 1859 – but he was stuffed and mounted and preserved in the NCOs mess. The Guard was entertained by *général* Canrobert, who hosted a dinner for the officers:

> What joy! What embraces, what handshakes were exchanged! And interwoven questions of the homeland and the Crimea, of friends present and absent! Finally, veterans and recruits retired to their tents or chatted through the night. With his staff at his side, general Uhrich gave us the most generous hospitality. The first person we met when arriving there was a general officer whose frank and martial air, intelligent and expressive physiognomy, struck us all. It was general Canrobert, who came to welcome us.
>
> The presentations were made, and, after half an hour, we all reunited around a table and were splendidly served. General Canrobert is a man, who managed, if it was possible, to make the evening more pleasant than usual. He spoke to us in a very interesting way of all that was left to do. We saw him and thought him highly tense but he was calm with us … The general, amongst other things, spoke with praise about the Russian engineer officers, and their chief Totleben, whom we hear is a famous engineer.
>
> These words, in the mouth of such a man, showed the nobility of his soul. He was not afraid to do justice to an enemy, he proclaimed his greatness, he glorified his opponent. Does this not add to glory? This evening left me eternal memories. So I was at the camp in the Crimea, near an illustrious leader, Sebastopol was before me. The shifting red light, which appeared and disappeared constantly, each in turn, followed by a low booming, that was repeated in echoes, was the struggle of the East and the West.[25]

Enter Pélissier

The arrival of Jean-Jacques Aimable Pélissier (1794-1864) as the new French commander-in-chief in May 1855 renewed the energy of the

Allied armies. *Général* Canrobert, exhausted from struggling to keep his army together during the terrible winter, and exasperated by political interference from Paris, had resigned on 19 May, and resumed command of his old *1e Division*.

Commandant Lacretelle thought that Canrobert was popular with his men; he always visited them in their bivouacs and trenches but was unable to make 'big resolutions'. At the last minute, he had ordered the cancellation of the proposed Allied assault on Sebastopol in April 1855 as well as the expedition to Kertch. Pélissier was far more ruthless, and, unlike Canrobert, was willing to 'sacrifice' his men. He famously joked 'one cannot make an omelette without breaking eggs.'

One of the first acts of the new French commander-in-chief was to order an attack on Russian trenches in front of the Quarantine Redoubt and the cemetery on the west side of Sebastopol. Selected to lead the attack was *général* la Motte-Rouge. The French were to attack in two columns, with the newly-arrived *Voltigeurs* of the Imperial Guard forming the reserve. *Capitaine* Richard – an officer of the Imperial Guard who became its historian – records:

> As the night fell, all our troops were prepared, all waiting for the signal, which would be given at nine o'clock in the evening.
>
> Our Column of Attack on the Left is launched with resolution; they cleared the advanced trenches crowning the escarpment which bordered the right bank of the Quarantine Ravine. After an obstinate combat, they remained masters of the position.
>
> On the Right, the column of *général* de La Motterouge first seizes the gabionade. The Russians return in great number, and the companies of the Foreign Legion are ejected, onto the *28e Regiment de Ligne*. These recover and soon go back to the combat. But a fresh Russian regiment makes a new offensive, at around half past ten, and forces our troops to retire again. One battalion of the *18e Ligne* stopped the enemy with its violent fire and forced it to retire in its turn. Two companies of the 1st Battalion of the *1e Regiment des Voltigeurs de la Garde* are also sent, to the extremity of the cemetery, on the side of the Quarantine, to defend against an approach by the Russians to outflank our troops where they were able to hold their ground after a fierce combat.
>
> In front of the cemetery they found two apparently unoccupied trenches, because they were silent as the enemy approached. A solitary brave, *Voltigeur* Beaupoil, volunteered to his Captain, Mr. Borel, to scout the enemy trenches. Beaupoil advanced resolutely and fell into the middle of some Russian Grenadiers who ran out of

their hiding place. 'To me! *Voltigeurs*! It's the enemy!' he cried to his comrades as he died, his chest pierced by a bayonet.[26]

One anonymous officer of the *Voltigeurs* left his account of the '*Affaire du 22e Mai*':

At eight o'clock in the evening, on the 22 May, all the dispositions had been made, and the troops posted in the trenches, waiting for the signal to attack. They would be led by *général* Patté, assisted by *générals* La Motterouge and Beuret. For us, who were waiting, this night was to be fixed eternally in our memoirs. Until the time fixed for the attack, only the artillery was to be heard. Gradually came a few bursts of gun-fire whose light is stretched out moment by moment like wildfire that follows gun-powder. Soon the noise increases; [the] shooting is sharp, strong on all points. The cannon roars incessantly, and it seems that its repeated boomings announce the approach of the invisible angel of death, spreading his already expansive wings in the night [in which all] these men will die. Gradually the funeral noise slows by degrees, but soon to be heard more heartbreaking and more terrible: the silence.

These are the notes [which] vibrate on the heart in these harrowing minutes. We would fly into danger, brave oneself this terrible death rather than remain the motionless spectator of heroism. The love of glory, fighting fever, has captured us …

At the agreed signal, the columns of attack began to move and, in less than a quarter of an hour, these brave troops were decimated by a terrible fire. They called for the reserves to come their aid, [and] the *voltigeurs* appeared. But the Russians, who were in large numbers in a ravine located behind the entrenchment, had also brought up reinforcements. Our men were welcomed by the most murderous fire. The crackling of the musektry, the whistling of bullets, the shells exploding, and dominating all, the cry of '*en avant*!' given by heroic officers and sub-officers, which the Russians responded with savage jeers. What a spectacle! What a stage for these men sent thus, in their first action, in the middle of the night, in this storm of fire and iron!

Soon, the third [reserve] column itself, which was held ready in the event of failure, received orders to cross the fields and into the scene of action. They took about twenty minutes to arrive at the entrance of the cemetery. There, after a momentary pause, the head of the 1st Battalion of the *2e Voltigeurs* is directed in the fourth parallel, facing the front of the *place d'armes*.

The order is given to the men to cross the earthwork, and as they leave, they did so flat on their stomach. They crawled under a sheet of grape-shot, and reach the foot of the slope of the work without a shot being fired. They half rise into a crouch, steeling in, cross the Russian bayonets, [and with] helping hands they throw the gabions into the interior of the entrenchment, turning it against the defender. They make some breeches [in the trench] and passing through, driven by a young officer, M. Boscary, they penetrate, in the darkness, the middle of the most appalling fracas, while the air and land are seemingly all churned up. They are committed, furious and fierce, fighting man to man.

The Russians ceded to our irresistible momentum; they sought to move away, but strengthened by the flood of reinforcements arriving, they are closely packed, and forming in a circle in front of these breeches, they oppose [us with a] heroic resistance. Three times, like the ebb and flow of the sea, the *voltigeurs* of the Guard are repulsed, and three times they return to the charge, and finally entered with fury into the entrenchment.

The Russians cede ground, disorganised, moving away. They were defeated. But not all is finished. Soon, we are forced to abandon the place: the fire of [the Russian] artillery decimates our ranks, and forces us to leave the dearly-fought ground.[27]

Capitaine Richard conveys the chaos and vicious hand-to-hand fighting faced by *2e Voltigeurs* as they held firm in face of an overwhelming Russian force: it was here that *colonel* Boudeville muttered the immortal words *'La Garde mort et ne se rend pas!'*:

Around half an hour after midnight, the struggle started over with renewed and terrible intensity. In the left-hand Column, a Battalion of the *2e Regiment des Voltigeurs* victoriously resisted the efforts of the Russians to turn and re-enter their trenches. The soldiers of the Guard charged with the bayonet at the backs of the enemy who were formed in compact groups, and pushing on with loud 'Hourahs!' captain Vichery is wounded in one of these pursuits. At his side, captain Bouton is remarkable for his courage: he communicated an indomitable energy to his company; they cling to the ground and hold the trenches they have captured throughout that terrible night until dawn of the 23rd.

Sergeant Bessin killed two Russians with the bayonet ... *Sergeant* Conté killed with his bare hands a Russian Colonel, and brings back, to the cheers of his comrades, two Russian prisoners from the trenches. *Voltigeur* Cartellier is surrounded by four enemies, he quickly kills them but falls grievously wounded ... Corporal Caer is wounded three times and still charges at the enemy with his bayonet.

Voltigeur Bollenger, surrounded by Russian Grenadiers, kills two of them, evades the others and runs back to his comrades. Corporal Durand receives his first wound but refuses to be taken to the ambulance; wounded for a second time by a bayonet-thrust, he continues to fight with valour and does not abandon his post. Corporal Han is suddenly faced with two Russians, one of them shoots him which smashes his shoulder, but the valiant corporal still has the strength to kill his assailant with a bayonet thrust and drag the other assailant by the collar into our ranks ...

The two companies of the *1e Voltigeurs* detached at the cemetery resist heroically against all the most furious assaults. The officers fall one after another. Captain Devoge has his arm broken by a gun-shot; lieutenant Niel and *sous-lieutenant* Fariau are wounded. But not a man retires. The only remaining officer, *sous-lieutenant* de Sommyevres, is remarkable for his sang-froid and his courage through the whole ordeal. His clothes are ragged with holes from musket balls and bayonet thrusts; finally he too is wounded.

The neighbouring company is commanded by sergeant Jeantrelle, a veteran sub-officer who has taken command of his company because all the officers are dead. When the enemy counter-attack he is the first of our men to stand against them them. He fights hand-to-hand with the Russians, and kills three of them but he stumbles and falls onto the ground and is carried off to the trenches. His sang-froid never left him, and in the blink of an eye, he escapes from his agressors, and rejoins his company.

With the aid of two elite companies from the 2nd Foreign Legion, the *Voltigeurs* push the Russians into the ravine. Repulsed on this point, the Russians fall on our Right, trying to pierce our Line.[28]

At this crucial point, *général* La Motte-Rouge ordered two more battalions of the *Voltigeurs* into the desperate struggle:

Commandant Boulatigny, who had only been promoted to lieutenant-colonel the day before, would not abandon his battalion during the first time it saw fire. It was with remarkable ardour that he inspired his men, who were electrified by his attitude. He quickly fell, terribly mutilated; he had an an arm and a leg missing, and a hip shattered. After him fell the brave captain Genty, hero of the affair of 2nd May and the brave captain Chicard, who later died from his suite of wounds. The fight is terrible; the struggle man-to-man where the bayonets thrust and the sabres cut with repeated shocks ...

It is about one o'clock in the morning and we have been fighting since nine in the evening. Our troops are overwhelmed. It is now that the troops of the General Reserve are called forward: it's the *1e Régiment des Voltigeurs*, commanded by their Battalion Chiefs Farine and Gremion, who receive the order to go forward to retake the gabionade that our troops had been driven out of.

The 1st Battalion of the *2e Voltigeurs* is directed towards the Fourth Parrallel, facing and in front of the *place d'armes* of the Russian work. There, the troops crossed the breastwork and, as they emerged, lay flat on their stomach. This was how they advanced under a blanket of case-shot and reached the foot of the scarp of the work without firing a single musket-shot. There they half-rise, under the Russians bayonets, and with their hands and shoulders, they throw the gabions into the works and overcome the defenders.

They thus make an entrance, and driven on by the lieutenant Boscary, penetrate into the gabionade. There, they engaged the enemy in the dark, fighting man to man, in which the brave lieutenant falls seriously injured among his *Voltigeurs*. *Voltigeur* Rondet, is among the first into the work, he makes the space around his injured officer, defending him with the bayonet with an unequaled ardour, but soon the others arrive. Faced with this sudden irruption of our *Voltigeurs*, the Russians fold, but they return with reinforcements, and reject us out of gabionade. Three times, the *Voltigeurs* of the Guard are thrown back, but three times they come back and charge with indomitable energy.[29]

In total some twenty-seven officers and 1,000 NCOs and men from both regiments of voltigeurs were killed or wounded, but the French were masters of the approaches to the Quarantine Redoubt and the cemetery.[30] British staff officer Somerset Calthorpe believed that:

> The conduct of the French troops cannot be too highly extolled: the Voltigeurs of the Garde displayed the greatest bravery, and earned for themselves a name worthy to be classed with the Old Garde of Napoléon I.[31]

Crossing the Tchernaya

Under the cover of darkness on 25 May, the French cavalry and the infantry divisions of *générals* Canrobert and Brunet, led by the *6e*

Dragons, surprised the Russian sentries on the Tratkir Bridge – which would play an important role in the battle of the same name in August. The *Journal du Marche* of the *6e Dragons* notes:

> 25 May, at three o'clock in the morning, infantry and cavalry strongly massed, in silence, on the left bank of the Tchernaya, in front of the redoubts abandoned by the Turks at the Battle of Balaklava.

Sous-Lieutenant Silbert de Cornillon (*6e Dragons*) related to his father two days later that,

> the combat was not really serious … The expedition, conducted with spirit, was all done by the cavalry. We were launched with great rapidity on the enemy, because the infantry had arrived too late to take part. They only took part after we had returned. The Cossacks were surprised and fled after one of our batteries fired several shots into them. We passed over the bridge of the Tchernaya at the gallop, and mounted the hills and scarp of the right bank of the river with the same zeal. After thus chasing off the enemy, we returned to our post, after having re-crossed the Tchernaya.[32]

In a letter dated 14 June de Cornillon wrote the following:

> We were ordered to leave our camp before Sebastopol on 25 May last. We left in a minute and were ordered to quickly march for the Tchernaya. The River Tchernaya flows through a magnificent valley and we started out on its left bank. On the right bank, it is defended by a series of hills which the Russians have guarded with cannons. Our march was, naturally, very rapid because they [the Russians] instead of defending their batteries, are limbering-up their guns and moving-out, leaving behind a line of skirmishers to secure their retreat. So we did not run any sort of danger. The Tratkir bridge which we passed over was enfiladed by a battery, but we galloped on to escape its fire, and my squadron was touched by cannon shots. The only serious danger was from a French battery, which, mistaking us for the Russians, fired on us two or three times, precisely at the officers. Luckily, they saw their mistake and ceased fire before one man of ours was hurt.[33]

During the night of 5-6 June, the *6e Dragons* were ordered to attack artillery batteries commanding the Tratkir Bridge. Because the Russian guns were firing at long range (estimated to be 1,000 metres) the French soldiers in the trenches simply 'watched them [the round shot] descending, stepped aside to let them pass and then dug them up to construct into trophies. After several months' firing not a man was hurt.'

Nevertheless, it was decided that the Russian guns should be taken, and this was attempted by the cavalry but, according to *sous-lieutenant* de Cornillon, it was an attack that should never have been ordered:

> The coup de main was a beautiful as it was serious; it was executed by the *3e Escadron* of the *6e Dragons* of which I was a part ... We found a Russian trench at the foot of one of the hills situated on the right bank of the Tchernaya. This hill, on the bank of the river, is very steep, and crowned by a battery which our soldiers call the Bilboquet, a battery which fires into the valley of the Tchernaya and enfilades the Tratkir Bridge ... The crest of this hill is, in addition to the battery, guarded by Russian soldiers, who gave a prolonged fire as we approached ... Our captain, who led us himself, had seen the day before how imperfect this position was.
>
> We departed somberly and in silence, passing the Tratkir bridge without alerting the enemy, or the Bilboquet, which is silent, giving no alarm. After the bridge, we separated: the *3e Peloton* sent round to the left; the *1e* to the right; the *2e*, which is mine, marches to the right to attack in front. The *3e Peloton* is commanded in person by the captain ... After about five minutes, the captain sent a Sub-Officer who ordered me to leave the *Peloton* and with a few men take shelter in an arbour ...
>
> Then all the shots, a fusilade ... coming from the hill I have spoken of before. Meanwhile, the Bilboquet Battery is also awake, and sees my *Peloton* in the valley manoeuvring, and fires at them. 'Come to this side, away from their fire,' I cried to my *Peloton* 'Forward!' We left at the gallop and arrived before the hillock. There, the fire continued as I have already said ... It was impossible for my comrades to get up there, to silence the Bilboquet, because the hill is too steep. Infantrymen could barely climb this hill. So I left this fatal place, crawled back down to the valley ...
>
> During this time, the Russians had brought up troops to the crest and they fired on us: but the projectiles passed over our heads without doing us any harm ... 'The dragoons won't be able to get up there,' I thought; 'it is a folly to think that.' Alas, we were trapped in a sort of funnel formed by two arms of the mountain, cutting and slashing with our sabres in the dark at an unseen enemy. The fire from the ridge was all against us ... This butchery was held in the shadows in this hollow which we had not previously discovered.[34]

Maréchal de Logis [sergeant] Charles Mismer of the *6e Dragons* remembered how:

> The *3e Escadron* of my regiment, where you will find myself and my friend Jaquillon, was in a serious affair. This *Escadron* was ordered, at eleven o'clock in the night, to cross over the Tratkir bridge with the point of the sabre, and, by the light of the moon, to attack the outposts of the Gringolet battery. It was to be taken by a coup-de-main, in the African style. The mysteries of Gringolet and its surroundings were penetrated through a Lunette battery. They killed a few of us; we killed a few of them in return …
>
> After several moments, we heard the clatter of sabres in scabbards, and hooves on soil. The appearance of the moon was saluted by a discharge of musketry. At the same time, the cannons of the Gringolet, added their voices to the fusilade …
>
> After passing out of column, I came upon wounded men, among whom was my friend, two comrades of the saddle. In between his groans, he recognised my voice. He had hardly the strenght to reply to my questions. The ground was all broken-up, the horses were forced to walk. 'Halt!' came the order, 'Dismount.' We tried to go forward on foot. 'This is not working. Disentangle yoursleves. Back into the saddle.' These were his last words. Several minutes laters, a poor widow lost her only son …
>
> This night affair was absolutely unncessary and was the death of many men and 30 horses. Only three *Pelotons* took part in this affair. The fourth, which got lost in a swamp, attempting in its march to turn the enemy's flank, was commanded by a young officer, M. Silbert de Cornillon.[35]

The Mamelon Vert

Eager to maintain the momentum of the Allied attacks, Pélissier held a Council of War on 1 June: he fixed 7 June for an attack on the Mamelon Vert and the Ouvrages Blancs. The British were to attack the quarries in front of the Redan. *Général* Mayran was to attack the Ouvrages Blancs over on the French extreme right whilst *général* Camou was to simultaneously attack the Mamelon.

At the same time a smaller French force under *lieutenant-colonel* d'Orion was to take post in the Quarry Ravine to prevent the Russians from using it as a means of escape.[36] The attack began with a sustained five-day long artillery barrage: the French fired more than 1.5 million rounds of ammunition, including some 510,000 cannon balls and 350,000 mortar rounds.[37]

Sergeant James Parry (49th Foot) wrote to William Shaw of the 'Waterloo Vaults' Ashton-under-Lyne that:

> At three o'clock on the 6th of June were opened a dreadful siege, and on the 7th we stormed two mud batteries, and took them from the Russians, but with great loss on both sides. Our batteries played on them until the 18th. [38]

One artillery officer informed a friend in Sheffield on 9 June that,

> [On the 6th] the batteries were due to open at two o'clock p.m.; at three, the batteries opened, and kept up a terrible fire. I was in the trenches, when a roundshot came through an embrasure, taking away a man's chest and the arm of another, wounding me slightly on the forehead; and, annoyed at being ordered to leave the trenches, accompanied by the lieutenant-colonel throughout the postern, when a volley of Minies came in.
>
> Yesterday evening it was determined to assault the Mamelon and Quarries, as well as a couple of Russian forts on the right; accordingly, at six o'clock, on the rockets giving the signal, the batteries all along the line opened with awful effect – I may say, crushing the enemy's fire. Two columns of 10,000 French in each, crossed the parapet at a run, and dashed upon the Mamelon; unfortunately, however, they pushed on to the Malakhoff, when the ditch stopped them. The Malakhoff opened a terrific cannonade, and out rushed a column of Russians, driving the French right through the Mamelon to their trenches. There the reserve turned out, and without a shout, drove Russians again before them, and secured the Mamelon, keeping it.
>
> At the same time, our army took the Quarries on the left, and although these attacks were made on them in the night, yet we have held them. On the extreme right, the French stormed and carried the two redoubts, the Volthynian and Selingkuisk ... There is a great deal of firing this morning, but nothing compared to the night of the 7th, which appeared as though [redacted] had broken loose; such a terrific cannonade and fire of musketry, the heavens appeared lit up, and in flame – every moment interspersed with vivid flashes. To add to the awful grandeur, like a ball of fire, the sun set that night over the devoted city. [39]

The Quarries were attacked by the 2nd brigade of the Light Division commanded by Colonel Shirley (88th or Connaught Rangers).

189

Sergeant Usherwood (19th Foot) recounted in his journal that:

> Later in the evening, the British attacked the Quarries which being
> done at a time when the enemy did not expect them they carried the
> Work tho' the Russians several times counter-attacked the place but
> only to be driven back with loss.[40]

It was during the attack on the Quarries that John Lyons, a private in the
Grenadier Company of the 19th 'performed a daring and gallant act' by
throwing a 32-pounder shell out of the trench, winning the Victoria
Cross:

> A 32-pounder shell, sent from a battery near the Round Tower,
> struck the ground short of the work, and thence, by ricochet,
> alighted on the parapet. From the parapet it rolled down to the inner
> side, among a group of men who were lying under its cover – some
> belonged to the Rifle Brigade, some to the 19th Regiment. There was
> seemingly no escape. The fuze was burning and hissing with that
> peculiar rushing noise which few can hear close to them without
> some degree of alarm ...
>
> 'My God! we're all murdered,' cried out one of the men; but, on
> the instant, Lyons, who is a tall and exceedingly powerful man,
> started up, rushed to the shell, and, grasping in both hands the
> threatening missile, hurled it over the parapet. What a moment of
> suspense! But it was gone, and all danger was over. A second
> scarcely elapsed after it reached the ground on the opposite side
> when the explosion took place, the men who saw the thing could
> scarcely believe their eyesight, and only felt secure after the shell
> had burst. You may imagine there was no want of gratitude to the
> deliverer.[41]

The attack on the Mamelon Vert was led by troops of *2e Corps*, with the
Imperial Guard held in reserve.

Capitaine Paul Menessier (*4e Chasseurs à Pied*) recounted his
experiences in a letter to his father:

> Arriving at the depot of the trenches, we massed in column on the
> right flank of the ravine, and before us are massed the *6e de Ligne*
> and the *82e*; we knew they constituted the second party of the
> assault column. The assault on the Mamelon Vert was to be made
> by three columns marching on the same line: the *3e Zouaves* on the
> left, the *50e* [*de Ligne*] in the centre and the *Turcos* on the right ...

The second column is furnished by the *6e de Ligne* and the *7e Légère* (now the *82e*), then us [*4e Chasseurs*] and finally the Grenadiers of the Imperial Guard.

You would have seen a show worthy of note: the fact that the cannon balls arrive randomly precisely to the right and not to the left of the ravine; our *Chasseurs*, despite this, were sitting at the base of their stands of arms, saluting each cannon ball with jeers…

Several instants later, there arrived a group of Russian prisoners, officers and soldiers: the escort announced that the Mamelon Vert had just been beautifully taken by the bayonet. The Russians had abandoned this terrible redoubt, and had set fire to two salients of the bastion: the *50e*, unfortunately, heard the cry 'Beware of Mines': a panic sets-in, the *50e* retreat, their Colonel, Monsieur Rageut de Brancion, is killed. If the panic spreads, all is lost. We received an order to attack at the Karablenaia Ravine with another brigade. This is when the second assault is made: in a misunderstanding, general Brunet is given the order, but not general Camou … our bugles sound as loudly as possible the march of the *chasseurs*, the *11e légère* sound their stirring march …

During this time, the *Zouaves* and the *Turcos*, letting themselves get carried away with their ardour, cry 'To the Malakoff! To the Malakoff'. The *Turcos* gave their Arabic war cry … the *50e* re-enter the fight without hesitation … all is folly, losing their formation passing through the rubble of the Mamelon Vert, they rush headlong in a crowd in the direction of the Malakoff: *Zouaves*, *Turcos*, *50e*: all of them, pell-mell, without commands, without order, they throw themselves like a hoard, crying 'To the Malakoff! To Sebastopol! *Vive l'Empereur!'*

The space is crossed like the wind, but they are received with a terrible fire of canister shot. Despite this they arrive at the ditch of the Malakhoff which they cannot cross; there, in the abyss, they are butchered. The remainder flee pell-mell to the Mamelon Vert, but the Russians dared not to pursue them.[42]

The second assault column was ordered forward into the Mamelon, but their officers found their men uncontrollable, and they too surged forward to the Malakoff:

But then the *4e Chasseurs à Pied*, followed by the *11e Légère* alone, came out of the Karabelnaia Ravine, and arrived there at the run. Leaving our trenches, our buglers sounded the charge: the battalion, with a terrible élan … crossed our three parallels and the Russian parallel, and arrived at the ditch of the Mamelon Vert, on the parapet floated the fanion of the *Zouaves* ... scrambling to the top, we could see the attack of the *Zouaves* on the other side of the Mamelon Vert and they were carried along with them the *50e* and the *Turcos*.

The first soldiers we met cried: 'To us, the Victory!' Nothing could hold back our battalion, my men shouted 'To the Malakoff! To the aid of the *Zouaves*! Forward the *4e*!' The buglers picked up the charge ... [without orders] we ran from the Mamelon Vert ... the whole battalion ... and threw itself, head over heels and with an incredible speed, in the direction of the Malakoff.[43]

As shattered remains of the of first two French columns were chased back through the Mamelon Vert, *général* Camou, with the Grenadiers of the Imperial Guard, was ordered to counter-attack:

Our Grenadiers were remarkable for their ardour, they lost many of their own ... *capitaine* Desmerliers de Longeuville, at the head of the first three companies of Grenadiers, threw themselves on the Russians with the bayonet, and occupied the position.

The three other companies, led by *commandant* Peyssard, flocked to their comrades and the Grenadiers were installed in the redoubt, ready to repulse any counter-attack by the enemy. The French flag flies victoriously over the Mamelon Vert which definitively remained in our possession.[44]

The attack on the 'Ouvrages Blancs' was more successful and far less bloody. The *19e Chasseurs, 2e Zouaves* and *4e Infanterie de Marine* were to revenge themselves by attacking the Volynia Redoubt; the *95e, 97e de Ligne*[45] and the *Gendarmes* of the Imperial Guard were to attack the Selenghinsk Redoubt. *Commandant* Lacretelle (*2e Zouaves*) noted that:

At half past six [in the evening], general Bosquet, established in the Lancaster battery, gave the signal. We crossed the parapet and ran towards the works which we are to capture. My battalion quickly crossed the 250 metres which separated us from the redoubt, under fire of canister shot and Russian musketry. We jump into the ditch, while some of us climb the scarp to enter via the embrasures, the others, with the cover of the ditch ... are rendered its masters.

The Russians have no way out: a terrible struggle ensues in the interior, a struggle without mercy ... but it does not last a long time; no more than ten minutes, the ground is covered with bodies, and the wounded tumble one amongst the other. Those Russians who had survived, threw away their arms and surrendered, under the guard of several *Zouaves* and a sub-officer. [46]

The second column, directed against the Seleghinski Redoubt, was the 'baptism of fire' of the *Gendarmes* of the Imperial Guard:

> The battalion, led by the *chef d'escadron* Baudinet, advanced in the most admirable order, leaving the dead to mark its glorious passage. But, little by little, led on by their officers ... the *Gendarmes* of the Guard, arrived, irresistibly, crossing the parapets, and received a terrible fire as they leap into the works despite the desperate resistance of the enemy.[47]

The attack on the Mamelon Vert – and the subsequent disastrous rush on the Malakoff – was another pyrrhic victory. It had cost the French some 5,443 men *hors de combat*: 697 dead and 4,363 wounded. Sixty-nine officers were killed, including *général* de Lavarande. The British lost only 639 in comparison.

Some French regiments were decimated: the *2e Zouaves* had seven officers killed, twenty-one wounded and around 650 other ranks killed or wounded, and the *4e Chasseurs* lost sixteen officers (three killed, two taken prisoner, eleven wounded) and fifty-nine other ranks killed with a further 190 wounded.

NOTES
1 General J. J. G. Cler, *Souvenirs d'un Officier des Zouaves*, pp.195-196.
2 ibid, p.196.
3 C-L de Bezancourt, *L'Éxpedition De Crimée Jusqu'a La Prise de Sébastopol. Edition Spécial pour l'Armée* (Paris: Amyot, 1857), Tome 2, pp.186-188; Lieutenant J. Spitz, Histoire du *2eme Regiment de Zouaves* (Oran: Paul Perrier, 1901), chapter 5.
4 Anon, *Campagnes de Crimée, d'Itale, d'Afrique, de Chine et de Syrie 1849-1862* (Paris: Librairie Plon, 1898), pp.169-170: Lettre 97: Colonel J. J. G. Cler au Maréchal Castellane, 7 Mars 1855.
5 De la Fay, *Souvenirs du general Lacretelle* (Paris: Emile-Paul, 1907), pp.101-102.
6 De la Fay, *General Lacretelle*, pp.103-104.
7 French slang: Good for nothing, layabout, blackguard.
8 Anon, *Campagnes de Crimee*, pp. 170-173: Lettre 98. Recit historique du combat...dans la nuit 23 au 24 fevrier 1855.
9 De la Fay, *General Lacretelle*, pp.105-106.
10 Anon, *Campagnes de Crimee*, p.173: Lettre 98. Recit historique.
11 NAM, Acc. 2002-05-2, T. Bell, Mss., Bell to father, 5 May 1855; NAM, Acc. 1994-03-153, E. Maxwell, Mss, Maxwell to father, 25 February 1855; NAM, Acc. 1973-11-170, N. Kingscote, Mss., Kingscote to father, 26 February 1855; NAM, Acc. 1982-02-18, Captain Tower, journal, 24 February 1855.
12 Cler, *Souvenirs*, pp.191-192.
13 Bezancourt, *L'Éxpedition*, Tome 2, pp.193-194.

14 Capitaine Joppé, 'La Campgne de Crimee, d'apres les letters du Commandant Adrien au Capitaine Joppé', *Carnet de la Sabretache*, vol 16 (1907), p.259.

15 Commandant P. Boppe, *Crimée, Italie, Mexique: Lettres de Campagnes 1854-1867* (Paris: Berger-Levrault et Cie., 1905), p.100.

16 Capitaine Joppé, 'Capitaine Adrien', p.259. Capitaine M. Méjécaze, *Historique du 6eme Régiment d'Infanterie* (Paris: Henri Charles Lavauzelle, 1891), p.102.

17 E. Flammarion, ed, *Campagne de Crimée: Lettres écrites de Crimée par le Capitaine d'État-Major Henri Loizillon à sa famille* (Pars: E. Flammarion, ND), pp.35-36; Commandant Devanley, 'Général Breton', *Capp*, pp.201-202; Capitaine Minart, 'Lettres écrites pendant la Campagne de Crimée' pp.88-90.

18 Anon, *Campagnes de Crimée*, pp.168- 173. See also Cler, *Souvenirs*, pp.176-187; Spitz, *2eme Zouaves*, Chapter 5; Lieutenant Burkard, *Épopée des Zouaves. 4eme Zouaves et Zouaves de la Garde* (Paris: Ernest Flammarion, 1897), Tome 1, pp.150-153. Cler estimated the French forces totalled no more than 1,500 and the Russians at least 6,000.

19 Queen's Lancashire Regiment Museum, Preston, J. B. Patullo, Mss., Patullo to wife, 26 February 1855; Duke of Wellington's Regimental Museum (DWM), Halifax, Major Mundy, diary, 24 February 1855; D. C. Boulger, ed, *General Gordon's Letters from the Crimea, the Danuve and Armenia* (London: Chapman and Hall, 1884), p.21.

20 NAM, Acc. 1994-03-153, E. Maxwell Mss., Maxwell to father, 25 February 1855 and Maxwell to father, 4 March 1855. See also DWM, Major Mundy, diary, 18 March 1855.

21 Cler, *Souvenirs*, p.187.

22 E. Perret, *Recits de Crimee*, p.248.

23 Molènes, *Commentaires d'Un Soldat*, pp.137-138.

24 Author's collection.

25 ibid.

26 Capitaine A. J. C. Richard, *La Garde 1854-1870* (Paris: Librairie Furne, 1898), pp.34-35.

27 Author's collection.

28 Richard, *La Garde*, pp.36-38.

29 Richard, *La Garde*, pp.38-39.

30 L. Guérin, *Histoire Dernier Guerre de Russie, 1853-1856* (Paris: Dufour, Moulat et Boulanger, 1858), pp.208-210.

31 Somerset Calthorpe, vol. II, second edition, p.257.

32 G. Bertin, 'Les 6e Dragons en Crimée', *Carnet de la Sabretache*, vol. 10 (1902), pp.497-98.

33 ibid, p.501-502.

34 ibid, pp. 502-504.

35 C. Mismer, *Souvenirs d'un Dragon de l'armee de crimee, avril 1854 – juillet 1856* (Paris: Librairie Hachette et Cie., 1887), pp.182-187.

36 E. Perret, *Recits de Crimeé 1854-1856* (Paris: Bloud et Barral, 1890), pp.310-311.

37 ibid, p.313.

38 'Letter from a Sergeant in the 49th at the Seat of War', *Ashton Weekly Reporter* (7 July 1855), p.4.

39 'Private Letters from the Crimea', *Sheffield & Rotherham Independent* (7 July 1855), p.12.

40 Usherwood, Service Journal.

41 'An Act of Courage', *Sheffield & Rotherham Independent* (7 July 1855), p.12.

42 'Le 4e Bataillon de Chasseurs à Pied en Crimée: Lettres du capitaine Mennessier', *Carnet de la Sabretache*, vol. 12 (1903) pp.14-15.

43 ibid, pp.15-16.

44 Richard, *La Garde*, pp.42-43.

45 On 24 October 1854, the twenty-five regiments of Light Infantry (Infanterie Légère) were converted to Line Infantry (*Infanterie de Ligne*), taking effect 1 January 1855. Thus the *1e Légère* became the *76e de Ligne*; the *20e Légère* the *95e de Ligne* etc. A. L. Dawson, *French Infantry of the Crimean War* (Nottingham: Partizan Press, 2011), p.20.

46 Lacretelle, *Souvenirs*, pp.114-115.

47 Richard, *La Garde*, pp.43-44.

Chapter 8

The Malakoff and the Great Redan

Eager to maintain the momentum gained by the capture of the Mamelon Vert, Ouvrages Blancs and the Quarries, Raglan and Pélissier held a council of war on 15 June to plan the next stage of operations. It was resolved that the French would assault the Malakoff and the British the Great Redan. The date for the attack was to be 18 June – the fortieth anniversary of Waterloo. Captain Hugh Robert Hibbert of the 7th Fusiliers hoped that by 'mixing their blood' 'the English and French ... [would] have wiped out all the Old Scores of Waterloo.'[1]

Sadly, all was not well at French HQ. The prickly Pélissier had quarrelled with Bosquet – the two had been fierce rivals in Algeria – and after Bosquet had failed to present to Pélissier a plan of the Russian defences which had been found in the uniform of a dead Russian officer, coupled with a string of messages back to Paris criticising his superior, Pélissier had no qualms about sacking him. In his place was *général* Regnault Saint-Jean d'Angely, commandant of the Imperial Guard who had only been in the Crimea five months. Pélissier also managed to quarrel with *général* Mayran who had been designated to lead the French assault on the Malakoff.

The loss of Bosquet was felt by the whole of *2e Corps*, leaving them unsettled and demoralised; even worse their new commander was unknown to them and had very little local knowledge. The bombardment opened at dawn on 17 June with 600 guns; one Russian officer admitted later 'I don't remember any of the preceding bombardments having been even a little bit like this ... this time it was pure hell.' Crucially, Pélissier changed the time of attack on 18 June to 03.00 hours (daybreak), and it was in a state of confusion that the Allied armies filed into their trenches.

195

The pre-arranged signal for the start of the attack was to be the firing of a rocket – but *général* Mayran's staff mistook the trailing flames from the fuse of a shell and ordered his division (*1e Brigade* under *colonel* de Saurin and *2e Brigade* led by *général* Failly) to attack prematurely, launching them at the Russian defences of the Carénage Ravine, towards the 1st and 2nd Bastions.

To Mayran's right, the division of *général* Brunet – which had only just arrived in the trenches and was not ready for the attack – seeing Mayran's division surging forward started their own ragged advance against the 'courtine' which linked the Malakoff to the Petit (or Little) Redan. Finally, the division of *général* d'Autemare – which had only three days earlier returned from the successful expedition to Kertch – attacked the 'batteries Gervais' and 'redoubt Korniloff'. The Imperial Guard was held in reserve, along with seven batteries of artillery (including two from the Imperial Guard).[2]

Lieutenant Marie Octave Cullet (*95e de Ligne*) serving under *général* Mayran, recalled:

> Throughout the entire day of the 17th, the fire of our batteries was redoubled, the enemy only replied occasionally. This silence is suspicious: they are reserving their fire and resting their soldiers for the decisive moment that perhaps they are waiting for.
>
> At 8 o'clock in the evening, the division is under arms ... we depart in silence and descend the long *ravin du Carénage*. After a pitiable march for an hour and a half, we halt almost at the extremity of the ravine, in front of the lime kilns. The Petit Redan is on our left; a road which descends to the Malakoff passes several hundred metres from the Redan and diagonally traverses the ravine: it is below this road, in the long grass growing on the steep slope that the enemy will ambush the 1,600 men of *général* Failly's Brigade.
>
> Throughout the night, our batteries *du Carénage* give a terrible fire on the Russian works; several French shells bursting as they pass over our heads. The enemy does not respond with cannon shots. It is obvious to us that the march of our columns could be arrested, and that the enemy rather than wasting time in a useless cannonade, is saving his ammunition, repairing his parapets, gatheing their troops behind their defenses: in other words, perparing a vigorous defense.[3]

Lieutenant Cullet and his regiment were only 300 metres from the Petit Redan but found that they could not advance:

The *97e* rush forward and commence to climb the slope which separates us from the Redan; but we had hardly started, when our brave soldiers are met with a storm of canister shot and balls; the enemy parapets are covered with defenders whom we attack bravely. The head of the column is crushed by this terrible fire and is halted in its advance. The enemy follows up with a bayonet charge which the *97e* and the *bataillon de marin* meet without ceding a single step.

In the middle of us, behind the gabionade, *général* Maryan is shouting out to us that all is well; but soon the noise of the fusillade of the *97e* is for us a sign for sure that our column is arrested. *Général* Mayran quickly recognises his error, and proceeds to send support in aid of our vanguard. But at this moment he is wounded by a shell fragment in his arm, the officers around him try to induce him to retire, and give *général* Failly command of the division; *général* Mayran refuses to quit his post, he is dominant, heroic, and in a voice loud and piercing shouts 'The *95e*! Forward!'

Lieutenant-colonel Paulze d'Ivoie and *commandant* Giacobbi scale the parapet; they are followed by our elite grenadier company, and then by the rest of the battalion; hardly had they covered a hundred paces when our brave colonel falls at our head, hit by a bullet in the heart. The battalion continues its march and in several moments we are with the *97e*. It is three o'clock; it is with difficulty that, in the middle of the burning light of the morning, we perceive the parapet of the Redan. Our ranks are thinning, ploughed by grape shot. The officers, their *kepis* on the ends of their sabres, setting the example. The cry 'Forward!' comes from all their chests, and our three battalions, which are very reduced, continue their advance, by littering the ground [with their bodies]. On the parapets, the Russian soldiers, formed in thick ranks … Under this terrible fire, our column is halted for a second time …

A regiment of the *Voltigeurs* of the Guard, held in reserve behind us, came up with shouts of '*Vive l'Empereur!*' Each soldier had his *bonnet de police* on the end of his bayonet; our intrepid soldiers acclaimed their comrades of the Guard with cries of '*Vive la Garde!*' But, soon, like us, there are decimated by the fire of the enemy, and the *Voltigeurs* are halted in their tracks: their commander, who sees the folly of continuing his attack, orders an about-turn and his men return to their trenches

Finally, *général* Failly gave the order to *commandant* Giacobbi to beat the retreat, and to carry away as many of the wounded as

possible. For a long time our fire had ceased; we were immobile …
The fire from the steam frigates in the harbour was the most
destructive. The order arrives, our soldiers flowing back, each one
with a wounded man on their shoulders.[4]

Capitaine Richard records that not even the elite Imperial Guard could
advance into the furious Russian fire:

> The columns were assailed by a fire of such violence that our men
> cannot leave their trenches. *Général* Mayran orders the *95e de Ligne*
> and two battalions of the 1st Regiment of *Voltigeurs* of the Guard,
> commanded by colonel Boudeville, marched in front of them, sword
> drawn. The artillery fire is crushing, the cannon balls arrive in fatal
> numbers, the gaps in the ranks are large; the regiment swirls for a
> moment and halts, sheltering behind a fold in the ground. It is not
> possible to reach the battalions they are meant to support and they
> begin to retreat.
>
> Soon the brave colonel Boudeville rallies them, rushes forward a
> second time to encourage his men; but only after a few paces falls
> mortally wounded. *Sapeur* [Lambert] Debs rushes to the aid of his
> colonel and in the middle of a storm of shot carries him on his
> shoulders. A ball strikes the brave *voltigeur*, and he tumbles over,
> bloody, under the body of his colonel.[5]

At the head of his battalion of *2e Zouaves*, *commandant* Lacretelle led the
attack against the 'Batteries Noires', but found himself unable to cross
the defensive ditch, becoming pinned down by musket and artillery
fire:

> We had before us a narrow path on the side of the ravine, through
> the impenetrable thistles and in which my *Zouaves* were following
> me one by one. It was the worst condition to give an assault. But
> enjoying a form of favourable terraine, I stopped 80 meters from the
> ditch, and there I massed 150 or 200 men. Then, continuing as before,
> we discovered the ditch, under a terrible fusilade. The ditch was
> wide and deep; it had not been filled in by our artillery; it was
> impossible to cross; the only thing to do would be to descend down
> there but we could not find a ramp to leave on the the other side.
> My men fell under fire at almost point blank range; I gave the order
> to retreat …
>
> At this moment, a shell splinter hit me tangentially in the chest,
> on my cross of the *legion d'honneur*, and met resistance from the

padding of my tunic ... it picked me up and threw me fifteen paces backwards. Several *Zouaves* picked me up [and carried me] to the shelter of the ravine ... I had a chest ploughed with a large, deep, wound, the two sides of the skin pressed up; I was covered in blood from head to foot.[6]

Capitaine Paul Menessier (*4e Chasseurs à Pied*) wrote to his mother the day after the attacks, lamenting the 'fatal 18th of June, anniversary of Waterloo':

After the most horrible of combats, after receiving all that the human spirit could endure, in one of the most terrible of days ... after being literally buried under a blanket of canister shot, we re-entered our trenches. I estimate our losses in dead and wounded at 5,000 men. We received entire broadsides of canister shot from the Russian ships in the port, which rendered the Malakoff impenetrable ... Our battalion is, today, composed of only four officers and 174 men ... The *5e* battalion of *Chasseurs*, which entered the Malakoff, and which could only remain there twenty minutes, now only musters two hundred men and two officers.[7]

Seeing the French in trouble, Lord Raglan ordered Sir George Brown, commanding the Light Division, to attack the Great Redan. Led on by Sir John Campbell and Colonel Lacy Yea, they had to cross fully a quarter of a mile of open ground under a concentrated fire of grape and canister shot. The 'Forlorn Hope', accompanied by sailors carrying scaling ladders and woolsacks, was drawn from the Rifle Brigade and the 33rd (Duke of Wellington's) Regiment. Barnsley-lad Corporal James Wallis (2nd Rifles) wrote to his brother that:

It was a very remarkable day, being Waterloo Day, but we made a very bad attack of it. We commenced bombarding two days before we made the attack, and the Russians fired scarcely a gun in return, and we thought that their batteries were silenced, but they knew that we were going to attack them, and reserve their ammunition for us, and on the morning of the 18th we marched soon after twelve o'clock, so as to be in a position to attack them by daylight, and we all knew that we had our work to do.

It was our duty to carry the scaling ladders and wool-bags, and 100 sailors volunteered to carry ladders for us, and I am sorry to say that they nearly all were killed, for we cannot take their batteries without scaling-ladders, as they have a trench round them from 18 to 20 feet deep, and we have 3,100 yards to run with the ladders before we can get to attack them, and they had their guns loaded with grape and canister up to the muzzles, and as soon as the signal rocket went up for us to charge, they opened fire with all their guns at one time, and I am sorry to say that the poor sailors were nearly all killed to a man, and a great number of our regiment shared the same fate, and other regiments beside.

It was impossible to reach their batteries, for as soon as a man attempted to get on, he was cut down with grape shot. I should have shared the same fate, but an officer would not allow any more to go in front, as the men who had already gone were all killed. It was like driving sheep to the slaughter house … Our force was not sufficient to take the battery… These places are built so strongly that it is almost impossible to take then. What put a great check upon us was, on account of our general and a great number of our officers being killed at the onset. I was employed the whole day in carrying off the wounded, and they were terribly mangled, poor fellows.

I saw one man belonging to us who had got shot through the arm and thigh. He was a tall powerful man; he said he would be revenged for his wounds, and he came a little closer to the Russian batteries to fire a gun at them, when a round shot came and took off both his legs in such a manner that they only hung on by a piece of skin. It was heart rending to see this poor fellow lying in agony, and it was two hours before I could get a stretcher to carry him away. Both his legs were taken off by the doctor, but he died. The same shot took off the leg of an artilleryman, and also killed an officer.[8]

One anonymous Aberdonian Colour-Sergeant of the 57th (West Middlesex) Regiment thought there was a 'screw loose' with the whole attack:

Early in the morning down comes an order for 400 of the 57th to form a storming party under Major-General Sir J. Campbell. The order was received with the greatest enthusiasm, and banished (from me at least) all signs of fatigue. We fell in at midnight, and after a few words from our brave old Colonel (Shadforth), we marched off. We had not got well into the batteries when I saw there was a screw loose; instead of quietness and regularity (for it was meant to be a surprise), Staff Officers were shouting at the top of their voices, – 'Stand clear the stormers'; 'This way the men with the ladders'; 'Go to the left, the men with woolsacks', &c. &c. Johnny Russ, of course, knew something was up, for they could hear every word, and they opened a most tremendous fire of grape, shot and shell upon us, very soon silencing our Staff Gents. Well, we kept close, and on the lookout for our signal, which was given just at daylight.

Well, away we went by companies from the left, but by the time we got near the Redan, there was hardly enough left to carry ladders and woolsacks, to fill up the ditch. General Campbell was killed; our poor Colonel was, alas! also killed by this time. Colonel Warre of ours then ordered us to find good shelter as we could, and fire away. In the meantime, he sent for reinforcements *twice*, but not a man was sent. Was it not provoking to lie as we did (some holes where a shell had exploded behind a big stone, aye, and some behind the dead bodies of their comrades), and see thousands of men, with Lord Raglan amongst them, within a few hundred yards of us, and not one sent to assist us?

To advance would have been madness, for we were reduced to a mere handful, and we could see the Russ well prepared for ten times our number. So the Colonel very prudently ordered us to retire gradually; this was not easy matter. However, by 10a.m., all that was left except eight and Captain Forsyth got into the trenches again – they eight men did not get away till dark, for they were right under the chevaux de Frieze. I was left to see the wounded into a place of safety... I managed to get all sent in that I could reach; and I returned myself, bringing Capt. Snodgrass (General Campbell's Aide-de-Camp) under my arm: I found him lying behind a stone, severely hurt; and never did I see a more grateful look than I got from him ... we reached camp about 1 o'clock, and between fatigue, excitement and vexation I was knocked up. But I had not got my belts off, when I was sent for by Col. Warre, complimented for my conduct, and though junior Colour-Serjeant, in the Regiment, appointed Serjeant-Major.[9]

One anonymous NCO of the 19th (Green Howards) Regiment wrote home the day after the assault, expressing the sense of foreboding that pervaded the British camp:

During the whole of Sunday there was a continuous firing from the batteries on the right attack; and it was stated, but I have heard it since contradicted, that the French had made a breach in the Malakoff ... However, the enemy's fire was considerably slackened from all the works facing us in the afternoon. Towards evening we could see that something grand was about to be undertaken – Aides-de-Camp and orderly cavalrymen were passing to and from camp and thence to head-quarters; ambulances coming up from the rear, and all the premoultory appearances of a move were on foot.

It was nearly ten o'clock, when Peter, poor fellow, came to me and whispered, 'We are for the assault to-morrow; prepare yourself, and remember there is the same Being to protect us as at Alma.' He left me. I could sleep no more; and when the day had began to dawn, turned to and burnished my arms and accoutrements, but in the midst of my work we were called to fall in; a few words passed, but it was here and there said that we were going to have a second Waterloo.

Our old General, Sir G. Browne, took the command, and we marched direct for the trenches; it must have been then three o'clock, or nearly that hour, when we reached the advanced works, and at a preconcerted signal the troops rushed to the plateau before the fortress. Here the whole body was almost in a moment exposed to a galling and murderous fire of grape, canister, round shot and musketry ... The shot pelted on us like a hail shower; the men advanced only to be cut down, never to rise ... Where men were cut down, others rushed forward to fill their places, although almost certain of instant death – the chasms made by the enemy were immediately filled up by living masses, which were as frequently mown down by the incessant fire from the enemy's guns. Poor Peter met his death in a singular manner – a man having stumbled on reaching the level ground, he, being behind, stopped to assist him on his legs, when the upper part of his head was taken off by a round shot; he never spoke more. As true a heart was in the regiment fell.[10]

Colonel Burton (7th (Royal Fusiliers) found he and his men could not advance under the weight of the Russian fire and had to shelter on the battlefield until nightfall:

I had but time for one glance at the position, but that was quite sufficient to show me that it was a regular Balaklava Charge which was expected of us. However, there was nothing for it but to obey, so, having whispered my view of affairs to E-, and told him the part I wished him to play, we sprung over the ridge and went at it. How I blessed my stars at having a good pair of legs to take me like the wind over the vines which entangled the path between me and a house on which I had fixed as my head-quarters. Even Ferozeshah was a joke to it.

Grape, canister, and roundshot swept round me like hail; and for encouragement, just as I reached the cover of the building, surprised to find myself with a whole skin, one of the latter crashed through the building as thought it had been paper. E. had taken a line to my right, and I was gratified to see that he also had reached the cover of some walls safely; but determined to join me, I almost immediately saw him spring from his lair, and with uplifted sword call on his men to advance.

Again the battery opened, and it was with most intense interest that I watched his charge down the hill. The vine holes – for they are partially sunk – made the footing very uncertain; he suddenly turned an awful somersault, and I thought it was all over with him, as with many others – but no, again he was on his legs – 'Forward, men' – and again reached the Russian battery, and a few more strides placed him by my side. And did not we, then devotedly wish we were back again?

However, there was nothing for it but to pack close, dodge the shot as best as we might, and aggravate the enemy as little as possible. And there we spent 14 dreary hours, the enemy at one moment bringing down our house with roundshot, burying the wretched wounded beneath the ruins; then, throwing shells among us, which, owing to the softness of the ground, fortunately penetrated deep, and, in bursting, only formed craters big enough for one's grave; and, if a leg was injudiciously allowed to protrude for a certain limit, it instantly furnished a target for a dozen rifle balls.[11]

Pinned down behind the wrecked house, Colonel Burton had to send runners to the rear explaining his predicament – and to fetch water:

I had no difficulty in finding volunteers ... The knowledge that they would get a drink of water was sufficient inducement, though certain to have some 50 rifle balls fired at them during their transit both ways. Many escaped through this ordeal almost miraculously, but one of my messengers came to grief. He was laden with commissions for water, and reached the general in safety; at length he re-appeared, loaded with his precious freight, and broke cover cheered on by the thirsty crowd.

As usual, he was twigged in a moment, a volley of balls cut up the dust around him, and, when within 50 yards or so ... the poor fellow was winged and dropped heavily. For a time he was so still that we feared he had got his *quietus*, but shortly the arms began to move, and he soon appeared dragging with him a wounded leg, two tins of the precious water, and my note between his teeth, like a good retriever. I found the poor fellow's wound was slight, the ball having only grazed the knee-joint; and you may imagine my sorrow when part of the wall afterwards fell upon him, and hurt him a good deal.

You will hardly credit the numbers begged of me immediately afterwards to be allowed to go and bring in the water which he left on the ground when he began to travel on all fours. A positive veto alone stopped them, for my homily to the text, that water was not worth blood, was not much thought of ... At nightfall, when the riflemen fired wide, we gradually got our wretched wounded to the rear, scorched and parched by the burning sun; my men filed off, and at ten, P.M., choked with the dust of ages which had arisen from the ruins, and bespattered from head to foot with blood and brains, it was with a sense of no slight thankfulness that I again reached my hut.[12]

Amongst the wounded was Private Robinson of the 7th (Royal Fusiliers) from Cleckheaton:

It was a sad affair, in short it was open murder, and I wonder that a man escaped with his life on that morning. There were upwards of 70 guns laid for us the moment we made our appearance from behind the trenches, charged with grape and canister shot. We had 300 men of our regiment engaged that morning; we had 11 officers killed and wounded: amongst the killed was our gallant Colonel Yea (who had braved every battle before,) and the Adjutant ...

I received a very curious wound on the lower part of my body, and it must have been Providence that guarded me, or I should have been cut in two; as it was I fully expected to lose the use of my legs, but am glad to inform you that such is not the case, as I can now walk about, but the lower part of my body is much discoloured. I feel great pain in my legs, and think my soldiering is done for some time. I fully expect to be sent home soon, as they send a great many from here [to Scutari].

I have to inform you that I have a bed to lie on, (being the first I have had since I left England) and very good treatment and all sorts of nurses, both gentle and simple. Miss Nightingale and her women are very kind to the wounded here; you would scarcely believe the attention that is paid to us here by the better class, who have come here at their own expense for that purpose. On the whole I am very comfortable at present, considering how I am situated, but hope to be soon along with you at home.[13]

The assault had been a disaster: the British had been repulsed at the Redan and the French at the Petit Redan and *Batteries Noires*. There was a bright note, however: troops under *général* d'Autemarre had managed to gain entry – albeit briefly – into the Malakoff and make a breach in its walls.

The *5e chasseurs à pied* and *19e de Ligne* 'without being stopped by the shrapnel ... these brave troops rushed onto the battery and commenced a fierce combat with the bayonet against the Infantry Regiment Poltaw, who they forced, after a rude melée, to cede to the superior enemy.'[14] *Zouave* officer Eugene Perret remembered that the '*5e bataillon de la chasseurs à pied* covered themselves with glory.'[15]
Despite such glory, the reality was that the losses were unacceptably high. The French had suffered 3,500 dead or wounded and the British 1,500. Five days later Lord Raglan would be added to this number.

Death of Lord Raglan
The failure of the attacks on 18 June had left Raglan tired and demoralised: he wrote to his wife the following day that, 'You may imagine my disappointment at this failure! It is a great misfortune.' He had felt 'duty bound' to make the attack to support the French, advancing against a 'murderous' fire which 'no body of troops could face.'

Three days after the abortive attack, his friend and colleague Sir George Brown was taken sick, and on 21 June the Adjutant General, Sir James Bucknall Bucknall Estcourt fell ill with cholera, dying three days later. Raglan was prevented from attending the funeral (25 June) due to his own ill health – having been reported to be suffering from diarrhoea, 'weakness' and 'anxiety of the mind caused by the death of General Estcourt.' He never recovered from this final illness and died at 21.00 hours on 28 June surrounded by his friends and family (his nephews Somerset Calthorpe and Francis Lord Burgersh).[16] *The Times* said of him:

> Although Lord Raglan did not possess the highest qualities of military genius, and although the enormous magnitude on the enterprise in which it was his fate to be engaged, may have demanded a degree of energy and a vehemence of character which is often found in younger men, the reputation he leaves behind him is one which the bravest might be proud to enjoy, and the best might envy.

The Duke of Cambridge who commanded the Guards Brigade at Alma and Inkerman, and was ultimately General Commanding-in-Chief 1856-1895, thought Raglan had been 'an honourable man and gallant to a fault, but he is no general.'[17]

The *York Herald* approved of the appointment of Major General James Simpson as Raglan's successor, opining that:

> Major General Simpson has risen in the Army, not by wealth or high Aristocratic influence; but, solely, on his own merit, great experience, and good conduct – a mode of advance, which ought to be universally adopted, and which would render the British army unequalled by any other military power, of similar numbers, in the world.[18]

Simpson (1792-1868), had been sent out to the Crimea in February 1855 by the government, both to act as Chief of Staff to Lord Raglan and to report back to them about the supposed mismanagement of the army, reports of which had been so lustily taken up by the domestic Press.[19] Upon arrival, however, Simpson quickly found that Raglan would not and could not delegate, and that there were two existing and competing Chiefs of Staff – Generals Estcourt and Airey who were constantly feuding. Thus, Simpson had found himself 'the fifth wheel of the coach, without the power of working.'[20]

Raglan's body was placed on the steamer *Caradoc* to be transported to England for burial, sailing for Malta 3 July, finally steaming up the River Avon to Bristol Docks on 26 July. 150,000 people lined the streets as the cortege passed en-route to Badminton House where Raglan's body laid in state (28 July) before burial at a private service the following day.[21]

Battle of Tratkir (16 August 1855)

The French were well ensconced in the Tchernaya and Baidar valleys by high summer 1855; the fertile valleys afforded the French access to clean water, and good pasture for their horses. They were joined by the 10,000 men of the Piedmontese-Sardinian expeditionary force commanded by General Alphonso de la Mamora who had arrived in May. Mamora had served in the Piedmont-Sardinian army for nearly thirty years and had recent combat experience fighting the Austrians in 1848 – a war which ended disastrously for Piedmont-Sardinia but which taught its army a great many lessons. His brother, Allesandro, founded the famous *Bersaglieri* corps of light infantry, inspired by the French *Bataillons des Chasseurs à Pied*, in 1836. Piedmont-Sardinia had thrown its lot in with the Allies in spring 1855 with the hope of international recognition and support for the 'Risorgimento' to create a unified Kingdom of Italy, under Piedmontese-Sardinian leadership.

The French cavalry set up camp on the plain outside the village of Baidar, where there was excellent pasturage for the horses. In the village the *6e* and *7e Dragons* were able to obtain a plentiful supply of eggs, honey, cereals and poultry. The valley 'possessed a natural richness beyond the imagination.'[22] The *6e Dragons* moved camp on 11 June and bivouaced at Varnoutka, an abandoned village set amidst some beautiful countryside. *Sous-lieutenant* Silbert de Cornillon thought, 'it is a beautiful valley: to the right and left are wooded hills, green and fresh. The hillsides are meadows enamelled with flowers. Between the two hills are rather pretty little villages.'[23] The advance guard and pickets of the *6e Dragons* found an abandoned hunting lodge where they managed to ensconce themselves comfortably.

On 21 June Omar Pacha with 10,000 Turks established his HQ at Baidar.[24] On 24 June the Piedmontese Army took up positions covering the Mackenzie Road, and its advanced scouts located the Russians in the Chouliou Valley.[25]

There were constant skirmishes between the French and Russian cavalry. On 28 June the *Chasseurs d'Afrique* fought-off a strong force of five squadrons of Russian Lancers and Cossacks and on 7 July the *7e Dragons* skirmished with Cossacks.[26] On the same date, the *6e* and *7e Cuirassiers* under *général* Forton arrived. The Cossacks made sorties against the French cavalry outposts on a nightly basis, causing the *Dragons* and *Hussards* to be in an almost constant state of alert and readiness, which became increasingly tiring for men and horses alike. Things got to a point that *général* d'Allonville ordered the camp be moved. The camp of the *Cuirassiers*, however, was behind the river and they remained inactive, eventually becoming bored and insubordinate, a situation made worse by cholera breaking out amongst them.[27]

Prelude to Battle.
For several days prior to 16 August, French scouts, and information from Polish deserters, had warned of a build up of Russian troops in the Tchernaya valley. The French and Piedmontese forces had taken up a strong defensive position on heights on the left bank commanded by *général* Emile Herbillion (1794-1866), who like other French generals in the Crimea was a veteran of the Napoleonic Wars, having served in the élite *Chasseurs à Pied de lu Gurde Impériale* as a '*gentilhomme volontier*' (1813) being promoted to *sous-lieutenant* (1814) and fighting at Waterloo (1815). He later had a glittering career in North Africa. He thought 'the

positions we hold are very favourable for defence' and urged his divisional commanders not to 'lose their advantages by too much forward movement. It is necessary to study the movements that the enemy make, and to profit by the moment that may appear the most propitious to attack vigorously.'

On 15 August, the *6e Dragons* and *3e Zouaves* were chosen to reconnoitre in force the Tchernaya valley, the *Zouaves* marching ahead as scouts and guides. It wasn't before long that men and horses began to suffer from parched throats and the 'suffocating heat.' At about noon the *Zouaves* had detected a force of Russians who opened fired on the *Zouaves* killing several of their number. The *6e Dragons* were hurried to the front whilst the *Zouaves* buried their dead comrades, digging their graves with their sabre-bayonets.

The *Dragons* could find little trace of the Russian skirmishers who were well hidden amongst the rocks. The *Dragons* soon found that the sun glinting from their brass helmets made them highly conspicuous to the enemy, 'making fine targets' to Russian snipers: 'The bullets whizzing thick past our heads forced us to dismount and go on foot to avoid unnecessary losses. The *Zouaves* were ordered to respond.' After several more *Dragons* were wounded, the party had to beat a hasty retreat.[28]

About an hour later they returned to the camp, which had been ordered to be hurriedly struck because the Russians were believed to be advancing in force. It was cleared in twenty minutes and belongings and rations hurriedly packed into a rolled cavalry cloak, strapped to the saddle. As the *Dragons* fell back to the left side of the river, they could see marauding Cossacks burning and looting what remained of their old camp.[29]

Towards evening, Herbillion received an incomplete telegraphic dispatch from *général* d'Allonville who warned him that the Russians were massing for an attack, but it was interrupted by the heavy fog that had fallen.[30] During the night a lone cavalryman brought the following message from D'Allonville:

> The information that I received from both sides [of the river], and by from reliable men, indicate a concentration of infantry on Ozenbach and of cavalry on Cardonebell.
>
> I will take precautions, but I am very weak and very short of troops and ammunition. Send me some infantry and get the cavalry ready to march.[31]

Herbillon immediately sent a copy of the despatch to *général* Pélissier, who ordered d'Allonville to 'double your surveillance' and to report everything to him. If d'Allonville was attacked in the Baidar valley, he was to evacuate and not start a separate action.[32]

First Moves

Overall command of the French was vested in *général de division* Emile Herbillion. Under his command was the 'Army of Observation' consisting of three divisions (Herbillion, Faucheux, Camou) totalling 18,000 men and forty-eight guns. The lack of artillery, according to *général* Lebrun, nearly cost the French the battle – only two days before *général* Pélissier had withdrawn half the divisional artillery from Herbillion's command to supply fresh gunners for the siege works.[33] To make matters worse, the artillery horses and been to out to pasture overnight, and in order to move the guns, officer's horses had to be put in the harness.

The French occupied the Fedioukine Heights and 10,000 Piedmont-Sardinians with thirty-six guns under de la Marmora gathered on Mount Hasfort. Arrayed against the French was Prince Gorchakov, commanding around 50,000 infantry, 7,000 cavalry and 226 guns comprising the 7th, 12th, 15th and 17th Divisions.

The Russian right wing (7th and 12th Divisions) was commanded by General Read, who was to attack the Traktir Bridge; the left under General Liprandi (6th and 17th Divisions) was to attack the Piedmont-Sardinian positions. The 4th, 5th and 11th Divisions were drawn up in reserve.

The First Attack

At 04.00 hours, using the cover of thick fog, the Russians approached the French and Piedmont-Sardinian positions on the right bank of the Tchernaya, simultaneously attacking the French held-*tête de pont* which controlled the only river crossing and the Piedmont-Sardinians who held the right flank of the Allied position. *Général* de la Marmora wrote in his despatch:

> At break of day our outposts stationed on the Mamelon which commands Tchorgoum were enveloped in a well sustained fire of artillery, which preceded from three batteries posted opposite the breastworks, by which our outposts were covered, and on the two Mamelons further to the right, which form the two banks of the Schouliou. They were at the same time vigorously charged by three Russian columns, who came on with fixed bayonets, and attacked our breastworks in front and rear … I begged His Excellency Omar Pasha to bring up the Turkish troops, who were stationed furthest

off; and I ordered the fourth battalion of riflemen (Bersaglieri) to the support of our outposts, which only consisted of three companies …

Attacked in the rear by the enemy's artillery, and charged by three columns of infantry, the outposts, after an hour's fighting, fell back, the reinforcements I had sent to them, greatly facilitating their retreat. At the same time, I made every effort to silence the enemy's guns. In this endeavour, I was assisted by the Turkish field-pieces from Alson and by an English field battery … several of the enemy's ammunition wagons exploded.[34]

As his men fell back on the extreme right, de la Mamora's men in the centre and left flank came under increasing Russian pressure: 'The Russians had, without loss of time, crowned the heights of Tchourgoum with artillery' and 'lower down, deployed numerous batteries in front of all the positions of the French.'

The Sardinians could clearly see the Russians advancing on the French *tête du pont* and the division of General Trotti was sent forward to reinforce them, taking up 'a position close to the canal' 'on low ground, beyond the bivouac of the French cavalry' with the artillery so deployed as to 'take the advancing columns of the enemy flank and rear.'[35] The guns soon opened a 'rapid fire', and coupled with the well-aimed shots of the Bersaglieri and General Mollard's brigade, the Russians 'soon began to waver and fall back in disorder.'[36]

Capitaine Jules Francois Herbé, *adjutant-major*, *95e Ligne*, wrote to his wife from his hospital bed on 21 August that at around dawn on 16 August:

> *Commandant* Giacobbi, of my battalion, without getting off his horse, approached the tent of the *général* [Herbillion]: 'The 3e battalion is returned, there is nothing new, my general' [he reported] when at the same instant boum … A cannon shot! The *général* quickly left his tent. 'My horse!' he said, 'and you, *commandant*, make the men have their coffee and quickly go to the bridge … take both of your first battalions to the bridge.'[37]

The *95e* and *97e* were commanded by *général* Failly, and formed the 2nd Brigade of the division of *général* Faucheux. The *2e Zouaves* and *19e Chasseurs à Pied* formed the 1st Brigade. It was 150 men of the *97e* who guarded the bridgehead of the stone bridge crossing the Tchernaya on the morning of 16 August:

It is a detachment of 150 men of the *97e*, under the orders of *capitaine* Morel, who are the guard of the *tête de pont*. The platoon of *Chasseurs d'Afrique*, who every night keep watch over the foothills of the Chouliou, and had, as was customary, made a reconnaissance into the plain. The battalion of the *97e* behind the river, is the one of *commandant* Giacobbi …

At four o'clock in the morning, we were barely out of our tents when we asked some of our comrades who had returned to camp, how their night had passed, [when suddenly] several cannon shots [are heard] on the right, on the other side of the Tchernaya, made us prick up our ears: it's in the direction of the redoubts on the Chouliou [Hills], occupied by the Piedmontese; the white smoke pierces the fog; and in several minutes this cannonade grows, and the noise of musketry increases.[38]

Capitaine Fay remembered:

In front of the River Traktir, the companies on picket, descended at the first gun shot towards the aqueduct to support the advanced guards …We had before our eyes the Russian army corps of general Read; he was advancing, under the protection of a formidable fire of artillery, and the smoke, for the want of wind to dissipate it, enveloped the enemy like a cloud.[39]

The *95e* and *97e*, recalled *capitaine* Herbé, were ordered to, 'Cross the river at the ford, upstream of the bridge; establish yourselves in the ditches and undergrowth bordering the right bank.'[40] Lieutenant Cullet (*95e de Ligne*) recalled the chaos of the unfolding drama:

We descended the hills at a run, we crossed the river via the ford and we rushed to occupy the position which was indicated to us. Hardly had we taken several paces, when thousands of Russian caps appear on all sides, from the midst of the fog. Taking advantage of the fog, the enemy had advanced, and covered all the approaches to the bridge; we are met by a tenfold fire …

At the same instant, we perceived the position at the bridgehead assailed by an enormous mass; captain Morel defended it energetically: he was killed sabre in hand, and his lieutenant taken prisoner, and the bridge was carried by sheer weight of numbers …

On the other side of the river, our situation is most critical, enveloped by an enemy ten times our number, we are pushed back into the Tchernaia which we wade through, its waters up to our bellies.

Arriving on the other side, *commandant* Prevost thought he would attack the Russians with the bayonet who surrounded the bridge, but seeing that the number of Russians is increasing every minute, and whose battalions were also crossing the river upstream using pontoon bridges, carried by their heads of column, he rejects this idea as folly. [41]

Coming into action with the *95e* and *97e* was their attached artillery, the battery of *capitaine* de Sailly:

> The artillery battery of the Division of Faucheux, established behind the Tractir Bridge … This battery produced unimaginable ravages in the ranks of the long column of Russian infantry. They opened fire, and one could trace, every ten seconds, furrows marked by quantities of killed or wounded men …
>
> Almost as soon as the action commenced, *capitaine* de Sailly … and his lieutenant were grievously wounded, one after the other. As the battery was missing its *capitaine-en-second*, *commandant* Buadoin gave command to his adjutant, *capitaine* Contamine.
>
> Although decimated by the fire of this battery, the Russian battalions continue marching onto the Tractir Bridge unchecked.[42]

The *tête de pont* was soon taken the 7th and 12th Divisions under General Read:

> The Ukraine Regiment … Attacked the small Redan, the ordinary post for 150 men, which had been reinforced by one company of the *2e Zouaves*… *Général* Failly was charged with the defence of this important position, and called to him the 1st battalion of the *95e de Ligne*, supported behind by artillery, and at the same time the *2e Zouaves* … but, despite their efforts the defenders of the *tête du pont* are overwhelmed by the mass of assailants, and obliged to retire just up to the aqueduct, where they joined the rest of the brigade of *général* Failly.[43]

The *95e de Ligne* surrounded

Capitaine Herbé thought that the situation for the *95e* and *97e* was now desperate; if they remained between the canal and the river they would be surrounded by the Russians and taken prisoner. *Lieutenant* Cullet continues:

The 1st battalion of the *95e* was joined by groups who had crossed the battlefield, from right to left. The whole ensemble arrived at the river, where we reform the ranks of our brigade ... During this, the *2e Zouaves* are reformed behind the canal, in front of the lock-keeper's house ... The *tête du pont* is formed from a simple parapet around a metre high, with a ditch in front; it has a face and two projecting salients, ... to the left and to the right ... The *97e* cover the left-hand parapet, the 95e the right hand, several companies of the regiment are lodged behind two small breastworks raised on the left bank ... Behind us the two hills are occupied by the division of [général] Herbillon ...

Each man had that morning 60 cartridges in his giberne [cartridge pouch], but had only spent a small number; nobody pays attention to the fire on our flank which decimates us; we see only the Russian grenadiers, our balls penetrate the thick ranks, and who, against this fire of musketry, seem to hesitate; they stop and turn, they close ranks, filling gaps, always gaining ground on the right and left of the line, their skirmishers approach and we are enveloped.

Our small troop continues to fire at this vast semi-circle, not a single ball misses its mark, our men aiming with a marvellous coolness and no-one thinks of giving up. The cartridges begin to run out, *colonel* Danner orders more; *général* Failly sends down an artillery caisson; it shelters under an arch of the bridge and our gibernes are refilled.[44]

Charge of the Guard Horse Artillery

The 'Russian horde hurled themselves savagely' at the beleaguered French, crossing the ditch, climbing the parapet and driving them slowly back.[45] Galloping down the hill came No. 4 Battery of the Horse Artillery of the Imperial Guard, commanded by *capitaine* Lafaille, and *lieutenants* Berge and Jamont. They deployed at the gallop at the edge of the canal and opened fire with canister shot at 400 metres range.

Under a heavy fire of Russian artillery and musketry, 'the gunners of the Guard served their pieces as if on parade'. *Capitaine* Lafaille was wounded twice (first by a musket ball, then by a shell splinter), *lieutenant* Berge was shot in the neck, and *lieutenant* Jamont in the foot. All three were awarded the *Légion d'Honneur* because they did not quit their post and stayed with their guns despite being badly wounded. In total the Artillery of the Guard won eight crosses of the *Légion d'Honneur* for their role at Traktir and thirty-five men and forty horses were killed or wounded.

One of the most conspicuous acts of gallantry was performed by *Maréchal de Logis* Jeanne whose gun had one of its wheels broken: 'with great calm, the gun captain [Jeanne] commanded the manoeuvre as though on parade, under a heavy fire, to change the broken wheel.' The gun commanded by *Maréchal de Logis* Hachotte had its crew reduced to two men, yet they 'continued to fire at the columns of the Russian infantry' albeit 'firing at very large intervals, and very slow.' Hachotte and Jeanne were both awarded the *Médaille Militiare* and cited in Orders of the Day, along with seventeen of their comrades. The suicidal bravery of the Guard halted the Russian column in its tracks.[46]

One French officer remembered:

> The artillery… poured in an incessant fire, which made terrible gaps in the enemy's ranks. A battery swept the bridge over which the Russians were obliged to pass the waters of the Tchernaya were filled with bodies.[47]

Général Failly ordered the shattered Guard Artillery to retire to the heights. It was whilst conveying this order to colonel Danner that Herbé was shot and wounded by a ball in the hip. He was one of the few mounted officers and had presented an easy target for Russian sharpshooters. *Lieutenant* Cullet describes the retreat of the *95e*:

> *Commandant* Prevost and his adjutant-major, captain Herbé, the only two on horseback amongst us, are a good target for the Russians. On this side, the slope almost has a peak, the canal is passed and on the summit of the first slope, a company of the *2e Zouaves* lay in ambush. Rallying with us, we fire an ineffective volley on the Russians, who follow us; on our left the hill is covered with all parties, we will be cut off if we don't make haste. We gallop pell-mell after the Russians on the steep slope … we are in the middle of the *2e Zouaves* where we take refuge.[48]

The *Zouaves* counter-attack
In his after-action report, *Capitaine* Pierre (*2e Zouaves*) wrote:

> Almost immediately, the order came to detach the left-hand half-battalion of the 2nd Battalion at the *tête de pont*; as for the rest of the regiment, they were formed in column, to support if necessary. The regiment was put in march by *commandant* Darbois, who led the battalion, and arrived behind the hill on the right and established its advanced units, having marched at a forced pace to arrive quickly at their destination, following the slopes that form the left side of the hill…

The regiment opened a very rapid fire on the left flank and the [enemy] force was halted. But *commandant* Darbois sees a second Russian column climbing the hill, which we are behind, [that was] preparing to turn us on our right. He orders us to the crest of the hill, to be there before the Russians: this means making an oblique movement to the rear. The slope is very steep. Arriving at the summit, the regiment is met by the Russian infantry which opens fire and continues to advance ... The *Zouaves* slowly cede their ground, but seeing behind them reserves marching purposely towards them, they spontaneously return to the attack with *commandant* Darbois and the eagle at their head.

The Russians quickly retire and are thrown into the canal, and have to cross the river, with considerable loss. Skirmishers open fire on the Russians as they cross the river. They leave behind 400 bodies.

During this movement against the Russians, *commandant* Darbois, along with several officers and a great number of men, jump into the canal, cross it, and reach the opposite bank. He calls the *Zouaves* to him, but falls grievously wounded in the thigh by a shell splinter.[49]

On the summit of the hill was the remainder of the Faucheux's division and *lieutenant* Cullet recalled hearing the order '*À la baionette*' and seeing the French fall on the Russians 'like an avalanche, our eight hundred braves rush head over heels onto the profound masses; which collapse one onto the other, like dominoes. The Russians, in an inextricable disorder, retire, at the run, with the bayonets of our intrepid comrades in their bellies.'[50]

Arrival of General Cler

Coming up quickly in support were troops under *général de brigade* J. J. G. Cler – formerly colonel *2e Zouaves*. He wrote:

The 16th, an hour before daybreak, the Russians, who had received strong reinforcements via forced marches from Poland, profiting from the fog which covered the hills and the plain, dislodged the advanced-posts the Sardinians had established on our right ...

At five a.m., I left my camp taking with me three battalions (first and third of the *63e de Ligne* and first of the *73e*), to the hill occupied by fifteen hundred men, part of the division of *général* Faucheux, at the right of the defile of the Tracktir. I had just arrived on the reverse of the hill when I received orders to push on my advance, and very promptly my three small battalions were very hotly engaged ... I immediately ordered the two battalions of the *62e* commanded by colonel de Perrussis to deploy. This line arrived at the extremity of the plateau meeting the heads of the Russian column, although stopped with great difficulty by a party of the *19e bataillon de chasseurs* and several companies from *2e Zouaves*; they resumed immediately the offensive, and after a short combat with the bayonet, the Russians were thrown to the bottom of the hill.[51]

Attack on the French left

As the battle for the bridge raged, a strong Russian column attacked the left of the French position, held by troops commanded by *général* Félix de Wimpffen (*Tirailleurs Algériens, 3e Zouaves* and *50e de Ligne*). In reserve was *général* Verge commanding the *3e Chasseurs à Pied, 6e* and *82e de Ligne*. *Lieutenant* Cullet thought that the *50e* 'with a bayonet charge, maintained their old reputation.'[52] An anonymous French soldier wrote home on the day of battle:

> At five o'clock this morning (16 August) the cry of 'To Arms!' was suddenly raised in camp … Our men notwithstanding the surprise of this attack, and the number of assailants, offered a furious resistance. They were, however, overpowered by numbers, and the enemy crossed the river … But at this moment they were attacked by two regiments of infantry, the *50e* and *97e*, who fell on them front and flank with unexampled impetuosity.[53]

Capitaine Herbé remembered seeing,

> On our left, a Russian brigade has crossed the Tchernaya at the ford around three kilometres upstream from the Bridge of Tractir, in front of the division of [*général*] Camou, despite the presence of a half-battalion of *Tirailleurs Algériens* who guard this point.
> The *Turcos* were equally obliged to retire, and they reformed on a small hill, half-way to their camp; *général* Camou came rapidly to their aid with a battalion of the *3e Zouaves*, a battalion of the *92 de ligne* and a battery of artillery. This force was sufficient to arrest the progress of the Russians on this side, and soon after, to throw them on the right bank of the river.[54]

Capitaine Fay recalled the resistance made by the *Turcos* and the *50e*:

> Two regiments of the 7th Russian Division crossed the river, despite the resistance of four companies of the *Tirailleurs Algériens*, and

marched towards the Maison-Blanche, located near the aqueduct; but *général* de Wimpffen quickly directed the 1st battalion of the *3e Zouaves*, who stopped them with their fire and under that of the outposts of the same regiment and the *Tirailleurs Algériens*, posted on the flank of a hill, between the canal and the river …

The situation became critical when *général* de Wimpffen, under the orders of *général* Camou, attacked with vigour with the *50e de ligne* against the last Russian column, and at the same time sent the 1st battalion of the *82e de ligne* in support of the battalion of the *3e Zouaves*, who were struggling… in front of the Masion-Blanche; the 4th battery of the *13e* [*Régiment d'Artillerie*] effectively came to the aid of these last two battalions, which overthrew the enemy beyond the canal and the Tchernaya, they forced them to rally behind the Uhlans and the Cossacks and under the protection of the artillery batteries of the Gringalet and Bilboquet, and prepared to make a new attack.

At the side of the bridge arrived the *50e de ligne*, and *général* Failly attacked vigorously and managed to push back the Russians; then he established colonel Danner at the *tête du pont* with the *95e* and *97e* and a company of grenadiers from the *50e*. While that was happening, *général* Cler, after having posted two battalions of the *73e de Ligne* in reserve, took the 3rd battalion of that regiment and all of the *62e*, onto the emplacement of the 1st Brigade of *général* Failly. At the same time *général* de Failly re-opened the offensive, a part of his 1st Brigade [*2e Zouaves* and four companies of *19e Chasseurs à Pied*], to which was attached a company of *voltigeurs* of the *95e*, rushed, on the right, on the Regiment d'Azov and forced them back beyond the Tchernaya … *général* Read and his chief of staff, *général* Weimarn, are amongst the dead.[55]

The Final Attack

The Russians, however, maintained pressure on the French centre, pushing forward battalion after battalion over the stone bridge. *Général* Cler recalled:

During this combat, a strong Russian column crossed the stone bridge of Tracktir, won the ground and pressed against the main body of *2e Zouaves*, which guarded the left side of the entrance to the ravine. Already, the enemy columns with flags flying, appeared on the crest and re-formed at the entrance to the plateau. I immediately supported the *2e Zouaves* with the battalion of the *73e*, and, after a swift engagement, the Russians were thrown back …

A new enemy column, which had crossed the Tchernaia below the ford of the cavalry, moved towards the slope, turned right and climbed the plateau to come face to face with the Sardinians. I immediately oppose this movement by turning one of my battalions, commanded by *chef de bataillon* de Lavoyrie, of the *62e*. This brave commander is gravely wounded engaging the troops … which were repulsed in its attack on the plateau.[56]

Despite having failed to dislodge the centre, a third column was sent in attack, only to meet a very similar fate:

At this moment, the head of the enemy column was reformed in the very mouth of our cannons. I made them fire one last salvo, and immediately after I went forward with the 3rd battalion of the *62e* (*commandant* Cotta), and supported this movement on the left by the 1st battalion of the *73e*, in close column of divisions, and on the right by the remains of the *19e bataillon de chasseurs*. In one minute, the head of the column was thrown back to the foot of the hill and pursued with our bayonets in their backs. They left on the ground numerous bodies, many wounded, including a colonel and two *chefs de bataillon*, and left in our hands, one hundred unwounded prisoners.[57]

Staff officer Barthelemy Lebrun recalled:

One of the battalions of the *62e*, opened an intense fire at the head of the enemy column, that made it change direction; instead of continuing its march forward, it was directed obliquely toward the battery of [*capitaine*] Armand, forcing it to go to the rear. But this battery riddled them with case shot. Then soon after, another battalion of the *62e*, the four companies of the *19e bataillon des chasseurs à pied*, who were close to the battery, and the right-hand battalion of the *2e regiment of Zouaves*, all ran together in support of the battalion of the *62e* already engaged; engaged and fell upon the Russian column.

So overwhelming was their fire that after one or two minutes of resistance their soldiers were in a dangerous disorder, fleeing towards the canal to regain the plain. The two regiments of *général* Cler, the right-hand battalion of the *2e Zouaves* and the companies of *chasseurs à pied* of *capitaine* Versini pursued the enemy with the bayonet in the belly up to the edge of the canal.[58]

Capitaine Fay describes the fate of this last desperate assault:

> Three regiments from the 17th Division, descended on the west ...
> threatening to cross the bridge... the cannon smoke which had
> masked these movements, had dissipated by 7 am ... we could see
> on the heights, three columns of the 5th Division, supporting the
> regiments of the 12th Division which were rallying and moved
> towards the *tête du pont*. The enemy attack on the left failed because
> of the fire of the *2e Zouaves* and our artillery; but that in the centre
> dislodged colonel Danner, but success on the right by the *50e* ...
> enabled Colonel Danner to return to the offensive with the *95e* and
> *97e*, supported by two battalions of the *73e*.
>
> During this advance the *50e*, supported by a battalion of the *82e*
> on the left, were sent forward with the same vigour; the Russians
> could not stand and were thrown back in disorder... the brigade of
> *général* Sencier arrived at this moment... the three regiments of the
> 17th Russian Division had crossed at the cavalry ford, and had
> attempted to turn the *2e Zouaves*; but this solid regiment, aided by
> the *14e bataillon de chasseurs à pied*, part of the 1st battalion of the *73e*,
> and four companies of *14e Chasseurs à Pied* (Brigade Sencier), was
> thrown onto this column, which had already been badly treated by
> our artillery, and it was thrown over. The *62e* were ordered to
> pursue.[59]

By 09.00 hours the battle was over. The Russians were in retreat, the
French line having held fast. *Général* Pélissier was criticised for not
pursuing the defeated Russians with his cavalry: indeed, *général*
Faucheux instructed Morris to pursue the retreating Russians with his
Chasseurs d'Afrique. Staff-officer Lebrun believed *général* Pélissier should
have launched his cavalry after the Russians – citing the example of the
Hussars which captured the Dutch fleet trapped in the ice at Helder or
the *Chasseurs d'Afrique* in Algeria, where an audacious, surprise attack
brought complete victory – but Morris was concerned about the fire
from the heavy Russian batteries (Gringolet and Bilboquet) and he
didn't want a French version of the Charge of the Light Brigade.[60]
After nearly half-an-hour of lively debate, Pélissier was 'content to
order *général* Morris to go to the front ... charged with a reconnaissance
of the terrain.'[61] Several of Pelissier's officers disagreed with their
commander-in-chief, believing that the French victory would have been
complete had the cavalry been let lose on the routed Russians. But,
général Morris' concerns about the Russian batteries were proved correct

when the French soldiers who descended into the valley to recover their dead and wounded came under heavy artillery fire. One British officer wrote:

> On every side the French were assiduously administering to the wants of the Russians, and on the hills were carefully dressing their wounds. The vile Russians actually began firing on the French as they removed the wounded from the field. A wavering shot came flying over my head, and fell near to where I was, from a Russian masked battery on the Northern Hill, and other shots followed in such quick succession, that I was glad to gallop from a sight so truly revolting and hazardous.[62]

Following the battle there was a two-day armistice to recover the wounded, and bury the dead, amongst which was General Read. The Russians had lost a staggering 5,000 *hors de combat*: the French collected some thirty-eight wounded Russian officers and 1,620 other ranks and buried 3,329 during the two days of the armistice.[63]

The French official losses were eight 'superior officers' wounded; nine subaltern officers killed and fifty-three wounded; 172 other ranks killed and 1,163 wounded and the Piedmont-Sardinians 250.[64] The firing upon the parties collecting the dead and wounded caused considerable controversy; Pélissier wrote to *Maréchal* Vaillant, the Minister of War in Paris that,

> the Russian batteries on the Mackenzie Heights inexplicably fired upon our flying ambulances when they came to collect those of our adversaries which still lay on the battlefield, well after our *Tirailleurs* had ceased fire. The commanders of these batteries have given, in consequence, an inadmissible explanation to their general, to whom I have signalled their misconduct. This conduct is not honourable for the enemy artillery.[65]

Prince Gorchakoff replied to *général* Pélissier:

7/19 August 1855
I pray, your Excellency will receive all my thanks for the care you have shown to our wounded, but I must declare to you, at the same time, that the commanders of the batteries on Mackenzie declare to me that they did not fire on your advanced posts of the Tchernaya, but following the fire of the French *Tirailleurs*, they did, in spite of the energetic and sustained efforts of their officers, fire against those of

your men who were on the banks of the river removing their wounded and their dead from the battlefield.

It is impossible to be precise over who fired the first shots. The commanders of the advanced posts cannot depart from their general instruction (to always fire on the enemy) without receiving special orders to the contrary. It is only the superior officers that can alleviate, by exceptional measures, the useless sufferings of war.[66]

Aftermath

Despite the arrival of fresh reinforcements, the Russian defeat showed that they could not dislodge the Allied right and raise the siege. Losses on the Russian side were massive, including General Read, who showed little tactical flair.

Whilst French losses were comparatively light, some units such as *2e Zouaves* or the *95e* ceased to exist: both had been previously severely mauled in the stalled attack on 18 June. The *95e* could muster only 500 men on the morning of 15 August, and by the afternoon of the following day, 256 were *hors de combat*. Out of thirty officers three had died in battle and sixteen were wounded. All five mounted officers had had their horses killed under them. The brigade of *général* Failly, perhaps only about 800 strong at the start of battle, was reduced to 550. The *19e Chasseurs à Pied* and the *2e Zouaves* could only muster 450 between them.

On 18 August the remains of the *95e* was reviewed by *général* Espinasse, who asked *colonel* Danner where the rest of his regiment was; the *colonel* replied, 'Alas! *mon général*, I had a big regiment, but now can only form a small one.' Espinasse replied 'console yourself, *colonel*: it is worth three regiments.'[67]

NOTES
[1] Chester Archives and Local Study Services (CALSS), Chester, Acc. 2618 Ref. DHB/27, Captain R. H. Hibbert, Mss., Hibbert to Mother18 June 1855.
[2] Général Fay, *Souvenirs de la Guerre de Crimée* (Paris: Berger-Levrault et Cie., 1889), 2e edition, p.260.
[3] L'Abbe S, Roche, *Un Regiment de Ligne Pendant la Guerre d'Orient: Notes et souvenirs d'un officier d'infanterie 1854, 1855, 1856* (Lyons: Librarie Generale, Catholique et Classique, 1894), pp.183-184.
[4] Roche, *Une regiment de Ligne*, pp.185-187.
[5] La Capitaine Richard, *La Garde* (Paris: Librairie Furne, 1898), pp.46-47. Debs, born 1818 in Altenheim (Bas-Rhine), survived from this wound and retired from the Imperial Guard in 1866 after twenty-five years and six months' military service.
[6] De la Fay, *Generale Lacretelle*, pp.123-124.
[7] 'Le 4e Bataillon de Chasseurs à Pied en crimée. Lettres du Capitaine Mennessier', *Carnet de la Sabretache*, vol., 12 (1903), p.70.
[8] 'The Crimea', *Halifax Courier* (21 July 1855), p.3.

9   'The Attack on the Redan', *Aberdeen Journal* (8 August 1855), p.5.

10 'The Attack on the Redan', *Enniskillen Chronicle and Erne Packet* (19 July 1855), p.1.

11 'The Attack on the Redan', *The Belfast Daily Mercury* (16 July 1855), p.4.

12 ibid.

13 'Letter from the Crimea', *Halifax Courier* (11 August 1855), p.5.

14 Fay, *Souvenirs*, pp.261-262.

15 E. Perret, *Récits de Crimée 1854-1856* (Paris: Bloud et Barral, 1890), pp.337-338.

16 J. Sweetman, *Raglan, from the Peninsula to the Crimea* (Barnsley: Pen & Sword, 2010), pp.315-320.

17 ibid, p.278.

18 'The Death of Lord Raglan', *York Herald* (7 July 1855), p.7.

19 A. L. Dawson, *British Army Perception of French Army support services during the Crimean War* Unpublished M.Res Thesis, University of Leeds, 2013, p.24

20 ibid, p.25.

21 Sweetman, *Raglan*, pp.331-332.

22 C. Mismer, *Souvenirs d'un Dragon de l'armee de Crimee. Avril 1854 – Juillet 1856* (Paris: Hachette, 1887), p.192.

23 G. Bertin, 'Le 6e Dragons en crimee', *Carnet de la Sabretache*, vol. 10 (1902), p.505.

24 P. E. A. Ducasse, *Precis Historique des operations militaire en orient, mars 1854 a septembre 1855* (Paris: E. Dentu, 1856), p.307.

25 ibid, p.308.

26 ibid, pp.309-310.

27 Mismer, *Souvenirs d'un dragon*, pp.193-196.

28 ibid, pp.197-201.

29 ibid.

30 Colonel Herbillon, *Quelques pages d'un vieux cahier. Souvenirs du General Herbillon (1794-1866)* (Paris: Berger-Levrault, ND), p.202.

31 ibid, p.203.

32 ibid, pp.203-204.

33 General B. L. J. Lebrun, *Souvenirs des Guerres de Crimée et d'Italie* (Paris: E. Dentu, 1889), p.92.

34 'Sardinian Army', *Morning Chronicle* (4 September 1855), p.5.

35 ibid.

36 ibid.

37 J. F. J. Herbé, *Francais et Russes en Crimée. Lettres d'un officer français à sa famille pendant la campagne d'orient* (Paris: Calmann Lévy, 1892), p.311.

38 Roche, *Un regiment de Ligne*, p.199.

39 Fay, *Souvenirs*, pp.276-277.

40 Herbé, *Français et Russes*, p.312.

41 Roche, *Un regiment de ligne*, p.204.

42 Lebrun, *Guerres de Crimee, d'Italie*, pp.95-97.

43 Fay, *Souvenirs*, pp.276-277.

44 Roche, *Un regiment de ligne*, pp.207-208.

45 ibid, p.209.

46 Richard, *La Garde*, pp.53-55.

47 ibid.

48 Roche, *Un regiment de ligne*, pp.204-205.

49 Lieutenant J. Spitz, *Histoire du 2e Regiment de Zouaves* (Oran: Paul Perrier, 1901), pp.167-169.

50 Roche, *Un regiment de ligne*, p.205.

51 Anon, *Campagnes de Crimee, d'Italie, d'Afrique, de Chine et de Syrie, 1848-1862* (Paris: Librairie Plon, 1898), pp.270-271: Lettre 156: General Cler au Maréchal Castellane 20 Auot 1855.

52 ibid.

53 'French accounts of the Battle of the Tchernaya', *Sheffield & Rotherham Independent* (1 September 1855), p.7.

[54] Herbé, *Français et Russes*, p.315.

[55] Fay, *souvenirs*, pp.277-279.

[56] Anon, *Campagnes de Crimée*, p. 272: Lettre156, Cler au Castellane, 20 Aout 1855.

[57] ibid, p.273.

[58] Lebrun, *Guerres de Crimee, d'Italie*, p.105.

[59] Fay, *Souvenirs*, pp.279-280.

[60] Lebrun, *Guerres de Crimee, d'Italie*, pp.109-117.

[61] ibid.

[62] 'Letters from the Seat of War', *Wakefield Journal & Examiner* (7 September 1855).

[63] 'Depeche No. 93', *Moniteur de l'Armée* (6 Septembre 1855), p.2

[64] 'Rapport du general Pélissier', *Moniteur de l'Armée* (1 Septembre 1855), p. 2; Fay, *Souvenirs*, p.282.

[65] 'Le géneral commandant en chef l'armée francaise au ministre de la guerre', *Moniteur de l'Armée* (6 Septembre 1855), p.2.

[66] 'Le Prince Gortchakoff au general commandant en chef l'armée francaise en crimée', *Moniteur de l'Armée* (6 Septembre 1855), p.2.

[67] Roche, *Un regiment de Ligne*, pp.213-218.

Chapter 9

The Battle for Sebastopol

The victory at Traktir showed that the Russians could not relieve Sebastopol by attacking the Allied rear; it also showed to the Allies how strong the Russians still were. The defeat of Prince Gorchakov, however, paved the way for the final assault on Sebastopol on 8 September 1855. The fourth and final bombardment of the city commenced on 5 September and lasted four days.

The work in the Allied siege lines increased to a frenetic pace, in order that Sebastopol might fall before the winter. Sadly, this meant that accidents happened all too frequently. On 29 August, at 01.00 hours:

> In the Mamelon Vert, a powder magazine exploded, and immediately the Russians, for two hours, fired on us with all their batteries in a most terrible way. It was a Russian bomb that fell on the shield of a powder magazine, and set it on fire, the concussion was terrific and looked like an earthquake, all the men who were in the Mamelon Vert were knocked over; everyone was excited, and everyone believed that the entire Mamelon Vert had been blown up. One thing especially was awful; it was the dead silence which reigned for a few moments after the huge detonation. Luckily the loss was much less than previously thought.
>
> The Battery 15b, in which the powder which exploded was stored, was actually undamaged; two neighbouring batteries have also suffered greatly, but the others, whose guns had only been disturbed, resumed their fire on the spot: with the first round they fire, there was general relief, all hearts are relaxed, because, as I have told you, we thought the Mamelon with all the batteries, had been overturned, from top to bottom. The number of victims was quite considerable, although it isn't written in the report or talked about at the time.

224

In the Battery 15b, by great providence, the Captain, the *Maréchal de Logis* and two artillerymen have escaped the disaster. What caused the most trouble were the strong beams forming the shielding of the magazine; they were launched into the air, landing in the Karabelnaïa Ravine, and fell on a company of *Voltigeurs* of the Guard wounding several. The English, at the same, in their trenches, had thirty men killed or wounded.[1]

The powder magazine in the Mamelon had contained 7,000kg of powder; some thirty-one men were killed, eighty wounded and 113 suffered from bruises, light cuts and contusions. Some of the debris fell onto the camp of 2nd battalion *1e Voltigeurs de la Garde*, killing a further three officers and five *voltigeurs*, wounding two officers and 110 *voltigeurs*.

The Allied trenches had got so close to the walls of Sebastopol, that Pélissier reported he was losing a hundred men a day from Russian snipers. Sergeant Hinchliffe (2nd Battalion Rifle Brigade) wrote to his mother in Wakefield that:

We are at them then (the Russians) day and night. The big guns knocks their houses and batteries about, and the shells burn their buildings. Our Minie balls pick off their gunners, and those who show us their phiz [sic].[2] It is like playing with a rat in a hole. If we retire out of our advanced trenches they jump into them. Then we have to rush on them again, and there is a heavy slaughter on both sides.

Our trenches are got so near their walls and batteries, that when we are in our works, we fire a volley on them, and charge them right into traps at the same time. We have to return the way we came, and then Johnny Russ sends grape shot and canister at us as thick almost as the hairs on a donkey. Our batteries dare not fire on those occasions, or they would down every one of us if they (the Russians) could fire …

Until their shipping can be destroyed, we can't get in at all. Their shipping is close under the rock on the north side, and our vessels can only send a chance shot into them. Our batteries can't touch them at all, only when they pop out, one at a time. Fort Constantine stares our shipping in the face with 400 heavy pieces of cannon mounted, which would sink every one of our ships as fast as they could go in, as the entrance is narrow …

The French walked into the Black Batteries the other night, and took it like smoke; not one single Johnny left in it. As soon as they were there away goes a fireball, and then every battery and the shipping opened on them with a murderous fire. All the town seemed on fire for a time, and the French were compelled to retire to the trenches again as fast as they went … We had a great many of our battalion killed on the Glorious 18th of last month …

We get pretty well off for grog. We have two gills in the trenches, and the same at home. Men are told off to carry it in a barrel, and send it out at stated times. We get everything here very <u>cheap</u>. One rotten egg (never sound), 2d; one oz. of butter (palm oil), 3d; half an ounce of cheese (made of goats milk), 3d.; a lemon, 3d; an orange, 3d, bacon (very bad), 4s per lb; a small onion, 1d; a bottle of Alsopp's Stoute [*sic*, Allsopp's Stout] (very good), 2s;[3] ditto Ale, 2s ; tobacco, per oz., 1d.; a short pipe, 2d.; a glass of brandy or rum, 6d. The French wines are cheap, but if you drink it long, it will kill you.[4]

Corporal John Swift (34th Foot) informed his mother in Barnsley that:

We are constructing some monster batteries close to the enemy's works, and when we do open fire again it is computed that 30 shells per second will be thrown into the enemy's works. There is more shot and shell in our batteries now than there has been during the three preceding bombardments. There is <u>no doubt</u> that Sebastopol – that devoted City – is a strong place, but if it were twice as strong, it must yield next time we open fire, which will not be, I should suppose, for two or three weeks yet.

The Russians last night made an attack upon some new works of the French. As soon as the French saw them coming they retired and allowed them to enter, but no sooner had they got in than the French pounced upon them like hawks, and drove them out at the point of the bayonet, and I am of the opinion that none of them were left to tell the tale. One of our own men this evening had both his arms blown off by the bursting of a shell.

Cholera is disappearing from amongst us, thank God! Diarrhoea still prevails, but is not so virulent. Fifty-two or our men have died in the hospital this month, exclusive of those we lost on the 17th and 18th June, and in addition to those killed in the trenches.[5]

The Final Assault

The British were to attack the Redan whilst the French were to launch several simultaneous attacks. Of the latter, MacMahon was to attack the Malakoff; Dulac and La Motterouge the Petit Redan, the Courtine (which joined the Petit Redan to the Malakoff) and 'Batterie de Gervaise' (which flanked the Malakoff). *Générals* Levaillant and Paté were to assault the 'Bastion Central', whilst *général* d'Autemarre was to attack the works to the right of the 'Bastion du Mât'. The assault was to be led by the French at midday exactly; the signal for the British to start their assault was to be the Tricolour flying from the Malakoff.

On the morning of 8 September, Charles Bocher, *officier d'ordonnance* to *général* Bosquet remembered:

> All the watches were set to mine, which is a good one, to mark the hour of the start of this terrible drama. The unfortunate [*général*] Saint-Pol, who, by nature, did not have much confidence, told me on leaving the meeting 'When orders are so much given, and everyone knows what he has to do, success is already half assured.' Poor *général*, who I was never to see again!
>
> Each made his preparations to fight as if we were to go to a review. I never noticed in the faces of the men any traces of worry. They were also saying that there were very glad to have done with it all, at whatever cost. Past sufferings we had experienced elsewhere combined singularly in this last solemn ordeal. I took the time to write two letters saying my goodbyes … At nine o'clock all the Staff of *general* Bosquet were ready to leave. Then breakfast, but as was my habit, I did not take any. It was neither happy nor sad. My brother Alfred was marching past with his troops as they silently went into the trenches. He detached himself and embraced me, we surrounded each other with good wishes and he told me 'We will do all that we can to win the [Marshal's] Baton'. We wished the same desire on all the other officers who passed through our camp.[6]

At around 10.00 hours the French started to defile into the forward trenches:

> We mounted our horses to take us down to the entrance of the trenches which were a long way from the camp. We formed a very brilliant and numerous staff, one of the first among us were attached to the *générals* de Cissey, Bueret, Fossard, and many other officers belonging to various arms, all brave and strong, and with good looks. We encountered on our way the Sardinians, with General Cialdini at their head; and the English troops: those who commanded the closed ranks in the Full Dress uniforms with their large starched collars, as if they were going on parade; their men were stiff, upright, without emotion. They appear that they should do well under fire; there is a lack of enthusiasm for the attack; but

they have courage, are strong and tenacious and energetic in resistance.

Our French troops, officers and men were all slovenly-looking for the forthcoming battle. In the morning, most were gathered in the trenches, taking advantage of the half-darkness of the dawn in order not to awaken the enemy. I met along the way, many friends, including *général* Bourbaki, colonels Maussion [and] Chabron, who I embraced, because it is proper to be affectionate in these solemn moments, so close to death! Colonel Chabron had his sleeves rolled up to the elbow and his fists clenched like a madman. A little before midday, we were all ready for the assault, everyone was at their post.[7]

At 12.00 hours the French artillery barrage ceased. All along the line a great cry of '*En avant! Vive L'Empereur!*' was heard, accompanied by the playing of 'the Charge' on drums and bugles:

At noon precisely, the time kept secret, but agreed in advance with the other Generals, the [artillery] fire ceased instantly, and General Bosquet who was in the 6th parallel, the one closest to the city at the side of the Petit Redan, and surrounded by his staff, drew his sword and commanded with a voice strong and menacing 'Drummers and Buglers, [sound] the Charge! My friends, Forward! *Vive l'Empereur!*'…

This command was repeated at the time down the entire line, the air is rent with the sound of all our bands and fanfares. Immediately the troops leave their trenches, officers at the head, swords drawn. This is the signal for this solemn moment! The bloodiest battles of which it is possible to attend, which lasted one day, and whose details will you read in the official reports. In the case of such a battle so large, embracing an extended space – over several leagues – we only see what is happening close to us, within sight.[8]

The French attacks on the Bastion Central and Bastion du Mât failed. French staff officer, *sous-intendant* Jean-Henri le Creuzer watched as,

the *1e* Corps (the Divisions of Levaillant and Paté) was to attack the Bastion Central, and by a turning movement, use the work against the enemy; *général* d'Autemarre was to attack the works to the right of the Bastion du Mât. The companies of volunteers, which were formed for this purpose, attack with the 9th Battalion of *Chasseurs à Pied*. Despite the great difficulties, they entered in a moment the bastion, where they found a lot of Russian troops waiting an assault

… *Général* Trochu came in support with his brigade, and rushed forward resolutely. An artillery captain assured me that he had been magnificent. Young solders, recently arrived from France, believing that everything was going to fail, ran away in to the trenches, abandoning [their] generals, officers and NCOs. That's when the brave Trochu, who was shot in the middle of the last 27 minutes, received a very serious wound, a shell splinter tearing off his calf. He suffers a lot and has a high fever that causes us great concern.[9]

The attack on the Bastion du Mât was headed by the *9e Bataillon des Chasseurs à Pied* who formed the head of the assault column. *Capitaine* Paul Mennessier of the *4e Chasseurs à Pied* recalls how in desperation the Russians exploded a mine under the bastion:

This unfortunate battalion had a very frank deal with the enemy, they fell on the *Chasseurs*, who, it must be said, were alone, the *42e* was holding-back. The *Chasseurs*, assailed from all side, make a heroic defence, they take huge losses, are under a terrible fire, but they still stand. Suddenly, a cloud of terrible fire, of smoke, earth, stones, human flesh rises into the air, the Russians cannot dislodge this noble and too unfortunate Battalion, so they explode a mine: poor *9e* are almost destroyed entirely; honour them. Today, there are only two officers and I do not know how many soldiers.[10]

Battle for the Malakoff

The French met with more success at the Malakoff – but even there, events did not go according to plan. With only fifteen minutes before the assault was to take place, it was discovered that the engineers of MacMahon's division had not brought up the scaling ladders or gabions with which to cross the ditch of the Malakoff.

MacMahon's Chief of Staff, colonel Lebrun, was sent to fetch them:

The scaling-ladders that the officers had had the engineers to build had not yet arrived, and *général* MacMahon showed himself somewhat impatiently. I ran to meet them in the trench where they were to be carried. Soon I found *commandant* de Marcilly of the Engineers who was responsible for transportation of the scaling-ladders. He explained to me that in his despair, he was late, which was because the trenches were crowded with troops, and he had experienced the greatest difficulties in ordering his soldiers carrying the ladders and boards forwards, mainly at the points where the trenches crossed, forcing them to pass through narrow defiles.

I took out the scaling ladders of the trench and ordered *commandan*t de Marcilly to carry the scaling-ladders, the men walking on the side of the trench, even if they by this, by putting themselves in the open, were exposed to Russian rifle fire. Then, casting a glance at my watch and saw that 10 minutes later it would mark the noon hour: 'I leave you,' I said to the commandant, 'I must go and join *général* Mac Mahon; by God! Arrive as soon as possible!'

In coming to the *général*, I learned that they had to depend on the scaling ladders they expected, but they were too far away for them to arrive before noon. This was one of the most unfortunate set backs, because they alone could affect the success of the assault. *Général* MacMahon, all with regret, however, thought that it was impossible to delay the time of the operation, and he decided that he would run to the minute indicated, whatever might happen.[11]

As his watch chimed noon, Lebrun watched as thirty-three-year-old *capitaine* Léopold Sée led the forlorn hope of *Zouaves*:

The *Zouaves*, leaping like lions over the crest of the parapet, rushed at full speed towards the gap in [the] Malakoff. It's who of them will arrive first. Our engineer officers said that they would have a little distance of 25 to 30 meters in order to achieve this. But instead, there is more than 75 meters between the parapet and the ditch, and they have to run under very heavy Russian fire. That's not all, the area of land they have to cross was deeply ploughed-up during the last attack, the bombs have created deep holes, so that our brave soldiers are tumbling at every step they make, and that their advance is very slow. Finally! now, after more than one minute, they arrive breathless at the edge of the ditch. But such is their amazement and disappointment when they recognize that, far from being filled with earth, as they had hoped they would find, the moat has a depth of 6 to 7 meters, and its slope of scarp and counterscarp are of perpendicular rock.

Capitaine Sée, who in this moment received the order, trembled. But his soldiers, themselves, are not dismayed and, without hesitation, at the risk of death or to break arms and legs, they throw themselves over the precipice before them. The majority of them remain there, they know it, but the fellows who can get on their feet do not continue their business less heroically.

Of all the *Zouaves* who had jumped into the ditch, some had been mortally wounded, many others seriously enough to not be able to fight. But among those who were unwounded, the men who had been carefully selected to carry workmen's tools had cunningly used them, digging their pickaxes in the wall of the scarp to climb to the top of the ditch ... Once at the top of the scarp, the *Zouaves* carrying picks as well as those that went up without this tool, picked up their rifles, which they had carried slung over their shoulders.[12]

Whilst the *Zouaves* fought hand to hand with the Russians at the top of the ditch, the Chief Engineer, Ragon, had managed build a solid bridge to cross the ditch of the Malakoff. The bridge was 'drawn up in two or three minutes at most, the last companies of the battalion of *Zouaves* under *capitaine* Sée could soon go to join the first that was mounted to the assault.'[13]

But the battle for the Malakoff was not over quite so easily. For one thing, the French had over-estimated the efficacy of their counter-battery fire, which had lulled them into a false sense of security:

> The fire of our artillery ... demolishes the embrasures of the batteries Russians, whose fire was significantly slowed, which could make us believe that we had demounted many of their guns. Unfortunately... we saw that the evil we have done is not as great as we suppose.[14]

Colonel Lebrun reports that despite the French Engineers claiming to have had a plan of the Malakoff, their knowledge of its layout was very hazy, and it was far stronger than they had believed:

> MacMahon realized, as soon as he took a look at all the defences, just what the Russian engineers had constructed behind the entrenchments. Indeed, he found that this retrenchment, the rampart of the Malakoff tower that his soldiers were occupying right now, was nothing but a bastion, part of a larger work, a real fort, which was enclosed and protected throughout its development, by very strong trenches and ramparts. He realized then that the real strength of the fortress of Sevastopol were the defences behind the Malakoff tower.

The Russians launched a desperate counter-attack against the French, but found that they were being taken in the flank and rear by fresh troops under *colonels* Collineau (*1e Zouaves*) and Théodore Decaen (*7e de Legere*). Decaen wrote to his wife:

> My regiment displayed an admirable spirit and intrepidity; I counted them and I had prepared, and although I had 450 new young soldiers arrived from France last week, they fought like veterans.

I told them a few words passing down the ranks. All my senior officers are wounded, the Lieutenant-Colonel very seriously and a Battalion Chief as well. Four officers killed, 17 wounded and three having to undergo amputations, then 431 NCOs and soldiers out of action, with killed 110 or so. When you see returns of such a fight, we should be thankful and thank God. I received a shell splinter on my belt plate, but it was stopped by my red sash, my two flannel waistcoats and my underpants etc. ... It only produced a strong contusion, which I do not suffer from; my shirt is torn and cut to ribbons.

Another thing, my good friend, everyone complimented me on my success, my regiment and my brigade. What soldiers! What *Zouaves*! I was happy to fight with them, and my fine regiment, and if you could see how all these young soldiers raise their heads today: they have received a beautiful baptism [of fire]![15]

According to Lebrun, by 13.15 hours MacMahon was 'definitely master of the Malakoff' but, at that moment,

The enemy's batteries, which were established over the arsenal of Sebastopol began to fire on the inside of the structure occupied by our French troops, a huge amount of shells that killed or wounded many men. Certainly, the *général* could say he was absolutely in possession of the position he had just conquered, after the last fight that decided the retreat of the defenders of [the] Malakoff, and yet the battle was not over.

A quarter of an hour had passed since the *général* had made his great display of the tricolour flag on the top of Malakoff, when a British officer, sent by his general came to him, to ask if he thought he could hold his ground. 'Tell your general,' said MacMahon, 'I am here, and it is here that I stay.'

Suddenly, however, panic gripped the French in the Malakoff: sappers had uncovered electric cables and batteries, set to explode a mine under the Malakoff remotely. Even worse, in order to dislodge the Russians from the underground bomb-proof shelters beneath the Malakoff, one French officer had had the idea to 'smoke them out' by setting them on fire, only to discover to his horror that,

The ground inside the bomb-proof shelter was covered with a huge number of cartridges and no doubt there would be the same in the small tower. The fire of the gabions, communicating itself to a heap of cartridges and producing an explosion, would set fire to the fougasses and mines, already prepared in the small tower.

I rushed to the few sappers who were not far from me, carrying their tools, shovels and picks, 'Follow me quickly', I tell them, 'come put earth onto the gabions that are burning, we must extinguish the fire.' The sappers began at once to dig the ground, throwing soil over the gabions, and this stopped the fire. What would have happened without it? I still shudder just to think by writing these lines!

Leading his men on, *général* Bosquet was severely wounded by a shell splinter; his aide was so panicked by this that he thought 'we had lost the battle.' Bosquet refused to be removed from the battle or have Pélissier '[send] for a replacement':

It was only later when his strength quite abandoned him that he consented to be removed from the field of carnage. At that time we had to get [him] out of the trenches. They were blocked by the defenders, [by] dead and wounded. We had to take thousands of precautions, stopping at every pace, obeying the general who suffered cruelly. We walked slowly, leaving the trenches under a rain of fire. A battery of mounted artillery crossed our path descending to the city, was almost annihilated before our eyes.

It was night when we arrived at our headquarters, and we placed in the barrack on a bed of planks our poor wounded [general]. If only he could find some relief for his mortal sufferings. What a horrible night for us! When we left the battlefield, the battle was not won, and we were not reassured about the existence of one who was doubly dear to us.

We had no news from the theatre of the action since we had left it; the troops engaged since the morning had been repulsed and forced to seek shelter in the trenches.[16]

The 'Grand Courtine'

Linking the Malakoff to the Petit Redan was the Courtine or curtain wall that was assaulted by the division of *général* Dulac. Success at the Courtine was linked inexorably with success at the Petit Redan because its guns swept the line of the Courtine. One French officer watched the attack go in:

Général Dulac had under his command *général* Saint-Pol and *général* Marolles, the *17e Bataillon Chasseurs à Pied*, the *75e, 85e, 10e* and *61e régiments de Ligne*. The position was bravely tackled in front and by the right flank right, whose configuration was better suited to the attack. It is here that the fight was the hardest. The artillery of the Petit Redan thundered at our approaches to the work so as to discourage the very bravest. Also, one battery in the rear of the Courtine had a very murderous fire and was joined by the Batteries Noires, crushing with its shells those [who] approached the Petit Redan. However, it was finally captured by the *17e Chasseurs à Pied*, the Grenadiers of the Imperial Guard ... fought like lions.

Entering the work, the soldiers were faced by an enemy who met them vigorously, and an artillery cross-fire of extreme violence. It was impossible to remain there. *Général* Pélissier tried to fight the Courtine with horse artillery, and two batteries were brought, but soon forced to withdraw ...

A counter-offensive, that killed *général* Saint-Pol, brought us back the Petit Redan, without our being possible to stay there. The Grenadiers of the Guard have been very brilliant. In sum, the Petit Redan was impregnable, since even troops like ours could not be maintained there. We suffered at this point our most significant losses.[17]

Capitaine Paul Menessier (*4e Chasseurs à Pied*) wrote home that:

The 5th division which did not arrive at the Russian parallels at the same time, had jumped over the trench, and ran towards the Courtine. The Russians gave a very feeble resistance and fled back to their second line, which vomited grape-shot and an atrocious fusillade. *Commandant* Clinchant of the *4e Bataillon des Chasseurs*, although wounded by a bayonet in the Russian trench, continued to fight; he slashes left and right, his Adjutant-Major, Grandjean, arrives at the first parallel, but fell mortally wounded. The *Chasseurs* block every attack with sword cuts, rifle-butts and bayonets and continue until the Russians fled to the second line. They are met by a hail of large stones, from which the trench was constructed.[18]

Many French officers watched in admiration of the 'useless heroism' as two batteries of horse artillery, (*6e* under *capitaine* Rapatel, and *9e* under *capitaine* Deschamps, of the *10e regiment d'artillerie*) under *chef d'escardon* Souty galloped forward:

Men, horses, caissons and guns crossed the parallels, I do not know how but they crossed at the gallop, and come to form a battery under a murderous fire of grape-shot. They fired seventeen rounds per piece, on the seventeenth time, they had 80 horses and 150 gunners [dead] on the ground, but their grape-shot played on the Russian; crushed by these unfortunate batteries, they retreated to their second line, and continued until the Karabelnia suburb and made no more resistance than that at the Batteries Noires.[19]

Of the twelve guns, 150 men and 150 horses engaged, only four guns remained serviceable; ninety-five men were killed or wounded and 131 horses. *Chef d'Escadron* Souty and *capitaine* Rapatel were both mortally wounded; two lieutenants (Renaud and Schriener) were killed and a third, Marsal, gravely wounded.

The staff officer Henri Loizillon wrote home:

> We set off from our parallel, we have taken as if by magic a space of five hundred metres encumbered with abatis, fox holes, fougasses and chevaux-de-frise, and, arrived at the ditch, everybody jumps down the counterscarp, which was a vertical slope, to climb the steep scarp, which was all loose earth and stones, the result of the damage from our shells. At our approach, the Russians fired at us on all sides, bullets, stones, bombs, shells, cannon balls, everything was raining down, but nothing stopped the storm that carried us. We were thus masters of the Courtine, and we killed the Russians which did not want to escape.[20]

Fourier Numa-Pichot of the *16e Légère* wrote home graphically about the assualt:

> From our trench the Colonel led us up the last parallel. Just [as the] Malakoff was invaded we marched forward, certain that we [would] follow. The cries: 'Forward the *16e*!' was heard on all sides, 'avenge the 18th of June'.
>
> On that fateful day we crossed the trench full of ardour and resolution. In two bounds we arrived at the curtain or the Postern, the formidable battery to the right of the Malakoff. At that time, some of the *25e* [*Légère*], [who] we left a few moments before, were beginning to retreat. The Russians leaving the Malakoff had taken refuge there, and they menaced us with their reinforcements, resolved to get revenge on us. 'Do not run away, my children,' said our Colonel, seeing that there were still men fleeing 'Come on the *16e*, forwards my children, do not let them in your ranks, they are cowards.' These words stung our self-esteem and they rally us.

Enduring the most terrible fusillade, we arrived at the battery ... with no bullets left, we used stones to good effect to crush the enemy. Seeing us take the advantage, the rest of the division and the Imperial Guard arrived in haste as reinforcements. We redoubled our efforts, the enemy finally retreated and our flag with that of the *25e Légère* soon flew from the battery.

All this was done with such speed that the Grand Redan, in the care of the English, and the batteries to the rear of Malakoff and Batteries Noires had not had time to fire at us.[21]

Sensing they were not able to hold the Courtine, the Russians exploded a powder magazine under it, killing both French attackers and Russian defenders:

In a wink of the eye, it swept us up, threw us around. I was next to the general: we are flung backwards one on top of the other, but not hurt, under all the stones and rubble. Having escaped the first stones, believing we had already been saved, we put out our heads, when we see a huge wooden beam coming straight towards us. It knocked one of its ends against a large stone behind which the general had hidden his head. The stone was broken and cut all his face.

Fortunately, although his wound is very painful, it is not very severe, and he will soon be well. As for me, when the beam completed its fall, I rolled with it, along with the general and all those who were near us. I got up again bruised all over and my first impulse was to help the general, but as our men then entered a new panic, and abandoned the position, I ran toward the men, and it took everything I had, with the officers, and with the NCOs, [even] taking my sword in my hand to stop them fleeing, and I managed to make them remount the parapet.

From that moment, I, a captain, took the command of the entire division, because in this explosion, *commandant* Tellier of the *16e Légère*, was crushed with four of his brother officers of the regiment. The *colonel* of the same regiment had frightful wounds, which will heal though. I kept the command until I met with the *lieutenant-colonel* of the *16e Légère* who was in our sixth parallel, and that's when I passed it over to him.[22]

The magazine exploded directly under the *16e Régiment Légère* virtually wiping it out. Pichot graphically describes the destruction of his regiment:

Suddenly, the earth heaved like a flood, a terrible explosion was heard, succeeded by a gloomy silence, broken only by debris that fell to earth on all sides, and the stifled cries of the dying. The magazine had exploded, and the trench had collapsed for a length of 15 metres. Everyone fled in terror, believing that everything was mined. The Russians redoubled their fire, but order was restored and we come back to this place; everyone is trying to bring succour to the many unfortunates who were buried alive; we could only save a few, as we did not have enough time to save them all.

Placed a few meters on the right, I was happy to receive only a little contusion. Some were killed or wounded by debris, beams, stones. Our colonel's left shoulder was fractured. Evening came, we gave the order to return to the parallel to rest a bit and recuperate.

However, we left a guard over our flag, which was still buried. Soon the Russians began to explode the powder magazines and set fire to the city in several places. They began their retirement in the morning and burned the vessels that remained in the harbour. At midday, we were surprised to see all positions evacuated. After unearthing some sixty soldiers, eleven officers, and our mutilated flag, we went back to camp. It was a sad spectacle to see us march through the camp in silence … The fringes of the flag were loosely attached, the staff was broken and tied together with a rope, and the eagle was dismembered, and was carried by a non-commissioned officer next to the *porte-drapeau*. One adjutant-major, two captains and three lieutenants, and about 200 men formed the procession. We lost about 700 men, 200 died from wounds in the field hospitals; most of them were lost when the mine exploded. Despite everything, we marched proud and happy from our victory. We defiled into the camp. We were all pressing to see our flag. Everyone wanted to see it and hailed it as the honour of France and the Glory of the *16e Légère*. The English especially showed the greatest enthusiasm.[23]

The Petit Redan

The Petit Redan was assaulted by the Division of *général* Dulac, but because the attack was not simultaneous with the attack on the Malakoff, the Russians were well aware of the intentions of the French. *Capitaine* Menessier was under no illusion that the attacks on the Petit Redan and Batterie Gervaise were doomed to fail:

We knew so well that six guns, loaded with grape shot, stood on the ditch of the Petit Redan, and that the six embrasures of the Malakoff had their guns facing in that direction. There was not a compromise; it was the same salient [of the] Malakoff to be attacked with the bayonet. But if we attacked the Malakoff alone, and if we took it, the Russians would have easily brought their reserves back, this being the only point to attack.

Thick and compact masses of our enemies would rush on the points we had taken, and the space in the work is limited: you can, after all, place in a work a small number of men – soldiers cannot be placed on the shoulders of each other – and then we were about to have a very pronounced numerical inferiority in this respect. The counter-attack could be resumed and everything would be lost. That is why they decided to attack two other points: the Courtine and Petit Redan. In this way, the Russians were being given the alternative to divide or unite their reserves ...

It is important to appreciate exactly in taking the Malakoff why the other two attacks were necessary. Many people look at things superficially, saying, 'But since the Malakoff is the only important work, the one which commands the other works, why sacrifice these soldiers to the other attacks?' I repeat, this was to divide the reserves that were sure to come and strongly attack us. The Russians knowing that because the Malakoff is Sebastopol, as the mountain of Sainte-Geneviève is Paris ... But by the same means, the Petit Redan which is completely under the [protective] fire of the Malakoff, you must attack there, and when you have captured that place, then you will see the French flag flying on Malakoff, but, for example, as soon as you throw in, you'll see *inter alia*, that the reserves will be forced to divide. This is actually what was ordered ...

We were obliged to make the assault because it was becoming necessary; we were losing around 100 men per night in the trenches ... it was agreed that the English would attack the Grand Redan, and a powerful diversion would be made on the left.[24]

Capitaine Menessier watched as,

The 17th Battalion of *Chasseurs* headed the column of the 4th Division; they are the child of the 4th Battalion [the 17th was formed from a cadre of the 4th in 1853]; they arrived at the Petit Redan, the proud battalion of *Chasseurs* overthrowing everything before them. But the Russian reserves, formed in large masses, advanced rapidly in dense and compact columns. The Malakoff was secure, the position was less difficult to defend, the work being formed with a ditch but it was not the same at the Courtine and Petit Redan ... The

Troops were exposed to a horrible fire of musketry, assaulted by huge columns, they could not all fit in or make the work secure.

The Imperial Guard attacks ... and immediately its regiments take their place among the fine regiments of the siege – the *Zouaves* and *Voltigeurs* of the Guard - who march on the Malakoff to support the troops who are defending it. The Grenadiers of the Guard arrive at the run ... to support the 5th Division, which, thanks this help, returned into battle and drove back the Russians for the second time, but the 17th Battalion of *Chasseurs*, on the right, was not reinforced, and had lost the Petit Redan. It was then seen, like an avalanche of steel, the admirable battalion of *Chasseurs à Pied de la Garde*, composed of the cream of the *Chasseurs* of the Line. This fine battalion of 1,300 men rushed at full speed, the Battalion Chief at the head (de Cornulier de la Lucinière, killed) in full dress, his Adjutant-Major at his side (Gaullier de la Grandiere, also killed); the bugles, under the grape-shot, sound the charge. These magnificent troops arrived at the ditch, which they descended, they crossed, and climb through the embrasures. But these struggles of man to man were fatal to us, our troops being too few in number.

Dulac's men had swept into the Petit Redan but were soon overwhelmed by the Russian counter-attack. *Capitaine* Pistouley of the *Chasseurs de la Garde* graphically describes their attack:

'*En Avant!*' The battalion left in column of divisions and we crossed six parallels at the run and jumped over the parapets, under a storm of bullets and canister shot. Commandant [La Cornelier-Lucinière] was always in the lead, not allowing any obstacle to impede him.

Our race was very rapid, having arrived at the last parallel, which is in front of the Batterie Noire, we were no more than a few.

The commandant crossed the last parapet; we follow him and we take at the run the last eighty metres, which separates us from the enemy under a storm of bullets and shrapnel. Many men fall before reaching our goal. We arrive at the ditch ... [and] mount the assault on the Courtine. The commandant is on the right and I on the left with several men ... The commandant raises his sword in his right hand and points to the enemy with the left hand. No sooner had he articulated '*en av ...*' than he is hit at the same time by a shell splinter and a bullet at point blank range, and he rolls into the ditch. I took his hand, he was dead.

His sword, to which an officer had tied a piece of our flag, was placed on the parapet as a rallying sign. Many times the Russians made desperate attempts to remove us, but without success.

Out of 1,000 combatants the battalion had in its ranks at half-past noon, we lost fifteen officers *hors de combat*, of whom 4 were killed and 450 sub-officers and men killed or wounded.

Although injured, I took command of the battalion, which was heroically led against the enemy by its young chief who had a glorious death, which robbed us much too soon![25]

The *Chasseurs* of the Guard, 'after having swept the Petit Redan' managed to rally 'the debris of their battalion and pounced on these batteries; the Old Guard could not have done any better.'[26] Two battalions of *2e Voltigeurs* of the Guard, led by *colonel* Douay, were sent to re-take the Petit Redan, but when the mine under the Courtine exploded, they,

feeling the earth tremble, decamped and nothing could make them return. 400 Russians, who came to them to lay down their weapons, seeing them fleeing, instead fired on them … they found themselves under the guns of a steam frigate which fired canister shot at them, killing 39 officers and several hundreds of men. It is said that it was during this circumstance that *général* Saint-Pol was killed; being abandoned by his soldiers, he told his aide 'We will die here.' These words could well be from a novel, the fact remains that the Petit Redan was very difficult to regain.[27]

The *2e Voltigeurs* were driven back in confusion, having five officers and 107 other ranks killed and twenty-three officers and 558 other ranks wounded. To their rescue came the *1e Voltigeurs* under colonel Montera (who was killed). One French officer wrote home two days later that:

The Russians wanted to keep the Petit Redan; we do not want to leave it with them; it was captured and re-captured three times. The *généraux* de Marolles, and de Saint-Pol were killed there, with the colonels Javel, Dupuis, Kerguern. Until nightfall the fire of the enemy was terrible, incessant: from then it is weakening; at 11 o'clock it was silent. Repairing to our parallels, then, about midnight, a terrible detonation, which made us fall on to the ground, and covered us with debris. It was the Petit Redan, which exploded. Since this time, hour-by-hour, an enemy work is blown up, and the English, then occupied the Grand Redan, the possession of which had been so keenly contested.[28]

Attack on the Redan

Simultaneous with the French attack, the British Light and 2nd Divisions were to attack the Redan. They still had not properly recovered the shock of the failed assualt of 18 June. Orders were issued on the evening of 7 September:

> The Redan shall be assaulted after the French have attacked the Malakoff – The Light & 2nd Divisions will share this important duty and finding respectively half of each party.
>
> The 2nd Brigade Light Division, with an equal number of the 2nd Division will form the 1st body of attack; each Division furnishing first a covering party of 100 men under a Field Officer.
>
> 2nd a Storming Party carrying ladders, of 160 men under a Field Officer – these men to be selected for this essential duty will be the first to storm after they have placed the ladders.
>
> 3rd a Storming Party of 500 men with 2 Field Officers
>
> 4th a Working Party of 100 men with a Field Officer.[29]

The covering party of 100 men was to be provided by the 2nd Battalion Rifle Brigade under the command of Captain Fyers. The first Storming Party consisted of 160 men under Major Wellsford from the 97th Foot; the second storming party was 200 men of the 97th under Lieutenant-Colonel Hancock and 300 from the 90th under Captain Grove. The Support consisted of 750 drawn from the 19th and 88th. The reserve was formed by the remainder of the Light and 2nd Divisions.[30]

Sergeant Usherwood of the Green Howards (19th Foot) wrote:

> As daylight appeared the batteries on the left again opened as before; on the right the bombardment was anything the reverse to rapidity – With it came also a strong and cold wind carrying over and to the directin of the camps clouds of dust, while at the same time being unfavourable to an attack. Shortly after the men had breakfasted in camp the Corps assembled in their respective parades in order to move off to the trenches ...
>
> So soon as the French troops had entered the works of the Malakoff ... the British moved out of their parrallels, the covering party then the ladder men, and in quick succession the remainder of the attacking forces, but as the Russians had had ample time to collect a vast body of men to the defence of the Great Redan ... they met the leading troops with showers of grape and matching musketry which cut down great numbers 'ere they could cross the wide space over which they had to go before replying to the enemy's

fire being 260 yards in extent and flanked by various batteries. Nothing daunted, however, onward the troops went and reaching the ditch which was wide and deep instantly descended, some by ladders (which unfortunately proved to be too short to be of any use) while the greater number did not and scrambled up the face of the work where they opened on the enemy a rapid and well-directed fusilade entering at the same time the work as well as circumstances permitted, the enemy having blocked up all entrances by the embrasures by screens of sheet iron and plaited rope ...

The Supports having now arrived and entered the ditch, the enemy from all the batteries that would bear on the face of the Great Redan opened up, doing immense mischief ... while too at the same time the Russians brought into play some guns that were ingeniously planted in the work of the Redan itself to sweep the several parts of the ditch, being entirely hidden from sight ...

Immediately on the attack being delivered, the enemy rushed down from molesting the French in the Malakoff to assisting their brethren in the Great Redan ... Four o'clock having now passed and no reinforcements coming to assist the few still holding the work, tho' Colonel Windham, who had succeeded to the Command in lieu of Lt. Col. Unnett, [of the] 19th Foot [who was] badly wounded, had recrossed the plain to ask for them and finding that it was utterly impossible to remain any longer opposed to such a force as the Russians now had at their disposal, the remnants of the attacking British retreated to their own lines.[31]

Private James Evans of the 97th Foot wrote to his brother in Barnsley describing his part in the assault:

The French stormed the Round Tower first [the Malakoff], and all the Russians were driven out of it in no time, and they all flocked into the Redan battery, which our brigade was told off to storm, and our regiment had to go in first. There was one party had to take the scaling ladders, because the Russians had a deep ditch dug in front of each of their batteries, and because of the ground being softer in front of the Redan than in front of the other batteries, the ditch in front of it was deeper; and you must know that the party with the ladders had to go out first, with the ladders on their shoulders, and the enemy firing on them with their cannon at the same time.

Our Major [Augustus Welsford] volunteered to lead this party, who were to carry the ladders and put them into the ditch, and when they were placed there, the storming party had to rush over the ditch in the best way they could. They, however, got into the battery without many lives being lost; but when they got there the support could not be got up, and the Russians were coming up out of the other batteries in large columns against us. The bugler was ordered to sound the 'retreat', and when our chaps heard it, they began to curse and swear, and told him to sound the advance, but it was no use, the Russians were flocking in, and we had to retire. Then there was the rush to get across the ditch back again, in which our men got killed in great numbers.

Our regiment suffered most, because it was the first regiment that attacked the battery. Our Major – a gallant little gentleman – got the back of his head knocked off. The Colonel [Hancock] was killed, and the Lieutenant also. In the taking of Sebastopol we had out of our regiment above 200 killed, wounded and missing, besides officers, and we had only about 350 men fit for duty before that, out of the 1,130 we had when we left England, besides about 500 we have since had from England. We have only now about 150 men fit for duty; so you may think what a cutting-up we have had.[32]

Leeds-born George Kershaw was convinced that the order 'retreat' had been sounded in error:

The 90th Regiment was the first to get in, and they drove all before them, but at last they were overwhelmed with numbers, and were forced to retire; but they renewed the attack again, the 88th Connaught Rangers leading. They got in again, when some cowards from the ranks cried out 'Retire'. The bugler thought it was from the officers' word, and sounded, when they all turned to the right about again, and beat a retreat. But not before they left some thousands dead and wounded. Of course we had heavy losses too, as must be expected.[33]

Kershaw was also quick to the blame the French for the disaster at the Redan:

If the French had not been so quick in taking the Malakhoff Tower, we should not have had to retire; but they began the attack too soon. Of course they took the Russians by surprise, but they fled from the Round Tower to the Redan, and we had four times the number that we should have had against us. But anyway, we were repulsed. The French, however, kept the Round Tower, and the Highlanders were warned to storm the Redan again the next morning at six o'clock.

But judge our surprise, when at about eleven o'clock at night, the Russian began to blow up the whole of the south side of the town, beginning with the Round Tower; but the French had discovered the train that led to the principal magazine, so that only part of it blew up … Our regiment lost 15 men wounded, and 4 killed. My rear rank man was one of the killed.[34]

Private Henry Firth of Dewsbury opined that attacking the Redan was 'a hundred times worse than the [Malakoff] tower':

We made a rush at it, but we had a field to cross, and the grape came amongst us like hailstones, which killed and wounded a good many of our men. When we got up to the parapet our work was to be done, and some of our men fell into their deep ditches and could not get out for some time, the Russians throwing stones on them. We hammered away at them for an hour, when we were forced to retire. We held it as long as we could, but we were overpowered by numbers.[35]

Sergeant James Wallis of 2nd Battalion Rifle Brigade wrote to his brother in Barnsley that,

the French attack[ed] the Malakoff at the same time, which was the easiest place to take. They were far superior in number to us, and they took the Malakhoff in ten minutes, and drove the Russians out of the batteries in all directions, and as they came out we sharpshooters cut them down in all directions.

I am sorry to say that the English could not take the Redan, for the ditch round the battery was so steep that it was impossible to any man to get up it. We got all round the battery in thousands, and great numbers got into the battery, but were cut to pieces by the Russians, and to advance up to the battery was like going to a slaughter house. I saw hundreds fall around me; but thank God! I never received a scratch. Some dozens of my poor comrades, that a few minutes before were in good health and spirits together, I saw cut to pieces with grape and canister. It was enough to bring tears to one's eyes, hardened as we are to these scenes of slaughter. This was the most awful sight I have seen yet. Our regiment lost one hundred and forty, and some of the regiments lost double that number. I know some regiments that have suffered very severely; one in particular I know that lost all their men except about 100. Such awful scenes of killed and wounded were never seen before.[36]

The British assault on the Redan was a bloody failure. One French officer thought that the failure was because 'The English, as usual, who pretend to attack the Grand Redan with a few hundred men, instead of ten thousand.'[37] General Sir Colin Campbell bitterly remarked:

> Was it supposed, that such a work, defended by Russian soldiers, could be carried by 40 men, presenting themselves on the ramparts from 40 ladders, even allowing that we had succeeded in bringing the whole 40 to the scarp of the work and placing them against it? – a most impossible event under the fire of artillery and musketry to which our troops would be exposed in passing over the distance of upwards of 200 yards.[38]

One French officer had watched with disbelief as the 'English troops: those who commanded the closed ranks in the Full Dress uniforms with their large starched collars, as if they were going on parade; their men were stiff, upright, without emotion.'[39] *Capitaine* Mennesier wrote to his father:

> The English left their trenches, which were a distance of 300 metres from the Grand Redan; no closer than 250 metres. They had only one way to offset this disadvantage – it was to run fast, but the English do not run, they walk, as in a bygone era, in the good old days, in their red coats, but the bullets and shells fell thickly on their compact battalions with their obvious outline, but they filled the gaps immediately, it's true.
>
> I cannot better compare the march of this English column than to a snail, this animal, with its horns in front and his big shell, he leaves behind a sticky trail; the English with their crossed bayonets and their solid battalions, leaving behind them a hideous trail of blood and corpses. They were not cowards, but they could not get the batteries as they [the Russians had] spiked a few pieces, and they were forced to fall back after losing a lot of people, and their best troops.[40]

Another French officer blamed the British defeat at the Redan on the 'system' of the British Army:

> The English, who because of their works of approach, were still several hundred metres from the Grand Redan, however, managed to seize it and took their time to spike the guns, without thinking that it had to be covered by other works against a countre-attack by the

Russians. They came, in effect, after one hour and the English, despite the efforts of their officers, were swept off almost without resistance.

I say all of the English, it is no longer the soldiers of the Alma and Inkerman, but mercenaries recruited from everywhere, not only in England but on the Continent also. They do not do much honour to their Queen's flag. The officers are brave, but many of them, who owe their rank to their social position or their wealth, are incompetent and ignorant of the the first notions of the Military Art, and their soldiers do not know enough.[41]

The Aftermath

The Malakoff was the 'key' to the south side of the city and overnight the Russians retired to the north side via a bridge of boats built across the harbour. *Zouave* Chantaume described the Russians blowing up their magazines and defences as like a fireworks display:

> In the night of 8 and 9 of this month, the Russians set fire to their powder magazines, and their flammable projectiles. This was like a magnificent fireworks display to watch, and have set fire to the whole city; it was now evacuated. It is tranquil in the trenches; we do not fire a single cannon shot …
>
> There are still several vessels to be destroyed, but we have already started the batteries before the Malakoff tower to sink them, if the Russians do not sail them off, as is very probable. As soon as Russians evacuate the city we can say Sebastopol is ours. We treat the Russians as cowards for abandoning such strong positions.[42]

Conscious that 8 September was the anniversary of the entry of the French into Moscow during the ill-fated Russian campaign of 1812, the Imperial Guard camped in the ruined Malakoff:

> The [Imperial] Guard of Napoleon III spent the night in [the] Malakoff, just as Guard of Napoleon I spent the night in the Kremlin, the first night of the occupation of Moscow. The new Guard is magnificent, its sangfroid, its discipline and élan. It proved worthy of its forebears. What officers! What soldiers! They had under fire 5,700 combatants: they suffered 500 killed, and 2,000 wounded. At the end of that memorable day, all the regiments of the Line were shouting *'Bravo la Garde!'*[43]

Considered to be 'merely Praetorians' at the start of the campaign, the Imperial Guard had shown itself an inheritor of the traditions of its forebears for which it paid a heavy price: 4,950 officers and men perished, of whom 2,471 (out of a total strength of 6,700) were killed or wounded during the final assault.[44]

French Naval Officer Henri Dieudonné Garreau awoke with astonishment on 9 September to be informed by his valet that,

'All Sebastopol is on fire. The Russians vessels are sunk.' … A rather intense fog made it impossible to distinguish the harbour, yet in the clouds, it seemed empty and as to the city, flames were seen in ten different places, explosions in several others, gave no doubt. The Russians ended their admirable defence by destroying, as always, everything they could not keep.

At one moment, we see everything clearly. The maritime power of Russia in the Black Sea no longer exists; a single vessel sinking down to its bulwarks but floating yet. Seven steamships have withdrawn against Fort Constantine; they were the last scrap of this fleet, which flattered so many ambitious hopes! The Russians came to hoist the flag of truce to Fort Constantine. What do we want?

The explosions follow one another in the city … just sounds reverberating in the gloomy weather, heavy, cold. The spectacle was something grand but infinitely sad. The joy of this day is limited by the memory of those who died yesterday and that would greet this day of glory. We regret especially those who perished in the fatal attack on the Bastion Central.[45]

In a letter dated 15 September, Garreau continues:

Every quarter of an hour, we heard explosions and they told us stories of marauders that had been blown up with their loot. I had not left the Bastion Central ten minutes when it exploded for the third time this morning. It is believed that we lost 300 men at least from accidents of the day. To prevent the soldiers entering the city, we always made them discard what they had brought, furniture, weapons, effects, women's hats and soldier's helmets. As I write, the fire is still burning, but heavy rain will contribute to put it out and I hope, yet, by the end of the week … it will be safe to visit the city in all its parts, unless that the fight starts between North and South.

It is believed that the Russian army will concentrate at Simpheropol, others say they will evacuate the Crimea, and that the movement is begun. The Navy, which was unable because of the bad weather, to take part in the affair of Saturday, is now not to let the big steamers that form the Russian squadron in the Black Sea escape. If they fail to deceive our surveillance, some howitzers drawn up in the city will soon force them to sink next their vessels. What a bouquet for the party of the Emperor Alexander, who, following the Greek calendar, arrives tomorrow![46]

Despite the danger posed by the Russian batteries on the north side of the city, and the constant detonation of magazines, the French troops who entered Sebastopol indulged in an orgy of looting. *Capitaine* Thoumas reported seeing:

> *Zouaves* wearing Russian helmets, artillerymen in huge overcoats carrying large tables, chairs, pictures, statuettes, in short loot of all kinds. Several soldiers were seated tranquilly on chairs, and were going to sell to the English what they had found. The crowd of new arrivals increased at every moment, and it was not just the cantinières who were stocking up. It was an ignoble spectacle: Piedmontese, Turks, English, French, all were more or less drunk and you could see then fall down beside the dead bodies of fighters [from] the day before who were not yet removed.[47]

Another French officer thought that the trenches were 'like a fête':

> Someone who was a stranger to war and was there at 10 o'clock in the morning of September 9 would have thought they were dreaming by seeing what was happening; around 5,000 or 6,000 men back from Sebastopol, with a chair, an arm chair, a piano, a mirror, a frame, a mattress, with a Russian hat on the head, a coat on his back, a pair of chickens, a turkey, a cat, rabbits, all laughing like crazy.
>
> One thing I was most amused by; a few metres in front of the Quarantine Bastion, on the plateau, we saw a soldier dressed as a Russian riding a cow, playing the flageolet and followed by 7 or 8 pigs and escorted by a score of troubadours. This was a matter for laughter; the plain looked like a fête, since for a long time we in the trenches had been very depressed.[48]

There was little sense of joy in the British camp. Their attack had, one again, been bloodily repulsed. Judge Advocate General William Romaine confided:

> Sebastopol has fallen! Thanks to the French! ... I am also doubtful whether to tell you my opinion of the <u>contemptible</u> position we

occupy out here, I am perfectly ashamed of the share we have had in the result … we are fallen to be a mere contingent of the French.[49]

NOTES

1. G. Gilbert, ed., *Lettres écrites de Crimée par le Capitaine d'État-Major Henri Loizillon à sa Famille* (Paris: Ernest Flammarion, ND), pp.179-184.
2. Phiz, fiz: slang for face.
3. Samuel Allsopp & Son was founded c.1740s in Burton-upon-Trent. It was famous for its 'Milk Stout' and 'India Pale Ale'.
4. 'Letter from the Crimea', *Wakefield Express* (18 August 1855).
5. 'Letter from the Crimea' *Wakefield Express* (28 July 1855), p.8.
6. C. Bocher, *Lettres de Crimée: Souvenirs de Guerre* (Paris: Calman Lévy, 1877), pp.136-149.
7. ibid.
8. ibid.
9. Anon, *Campagnes de Crimée, D'Italie, D'Afrique, De Chine et de Syrie, 1849-1862. Lettres Addressées au Maréchal de Castellane* (Paris: E. Plon, Nourrit et Cie., 1989), pp.289-290.
10. '4e Chasseurs a Pied en Crimee', *Carnet de la Sabretache* (1903), pp.199-209.
11. General B.L.J. Lebrun, *Souvenirs des Guerres de Crimée et d'Italie* (Paris; E. Dentu, 1889), pp.145-167.
12. ibid.
13. ibid.
14. G. Gilbert, ed., *Lettres écrites de Crimée par le Capitaine d'État-Major Henri Loizillon à sa Famille* (Paris: Ernest Flammarion, ND), pp.179-184.
15. Commandant R. Duplessis, 'Lettres du General Decaen (extraits)', *Carnet de la Sabretache*, vol. 8 (1900), pp.76-79.
16. C. Bocher, *Lettres de Crimée: Souvenirs de Guerre* (Paris: Calman Lévy, 1877), pp.136-149.
17. 'Correspondance Particulière', *Moniteur de l'Armée* (26 September 1855), p.3.
18. 'Le 4e Bataillon de Chasseurs à Pied en Crimée: Lettres du Capitaine Mennessier', *Carnet de la Sabretache*, vol. 12 (1903), p.204.
19. 'Le 4e Bataillon de Chasseurs à Pied en Crimée', p.205.
20. G. Gilbert, ed., *Lettres écrites de Crimée par le Capitaine d'État-Major Henri Loizillon à sa Famille* (Paris: Ernest Flammarion, ND), pp.185-193.
21. Commandant E. Martin, 'Souvenirs et Lettres du Capitaine Pichot', *Carnet de la Sabretache*, vol. 22 (1912), pp.27-30 and pp.80-82.
22. ibid.
23. Commandant E. Martin, 'Souvenirs et Lettres du Capitaine Pichot', *Carnet de la Sabretache*, vol. 22 (1912), pp.27-30 and pp.80-82.
24. 'Le 4e Bataillon de Chasseurs à Pied en Crimée', pp.199-209.
25. Richard, *La Garde*, pp.62-63.
26. 'Le 4e Bataillon de Chasseurs à Pied en Crimée', p.205.
27. Commandant E. Martin, 'Souvenirs de la Guerre de Crimée: Lettres du Commissaire de Marine Garreau', *Carnet de la Sabretache*, vol. 21 (1912), pp.348-349.
28. 'Correspondance Particulière', *Moniteur de l'Armée* (26 September 1855), p.3.
29. Usherwood, Service Journal.
30. ibid.
31. Uhserwood, *Service Journal.*
32. 'Yorkshire soldier's letters from Sebastopol', *Leeds Mercury* (2 October 1855).
33. ibid.
34. ibid.
35. Letter from a Crimean Soldier', *Wakefield Express* (6 October 1855).
36. 'The Fall of Sebastopol – letter from Sergeant Wallis', *Wakefield Express* (29 September 1855), p.8.

[37] Gilbert, *Henri Loizillon*, pp.185-193.

[38] General Sir Colin Campbell, cited in W. Baring-Pemberton, *Battles of the Crimean War* (London: B. T. Batsford, 1962), pp.222-223.

[39] C. Bocher, *Lettres de Crimée: Souvenirs de Guerre* (Paris: Calman Lévy, 1877), pp.136-149.

[40] 'Le 4e Bataillon de Chasseurs à Pied en Crimée', pp.205-206.

[41] Martin, 'Souvenirs de la Guerre de Crimée', pp.348-349.

[42] Anon, *Expedition de Crimee. Lettres d'un Zouave* (Paris: Libraire de Firmin Didot Freres, Fils et Co., 1856), pp.93-98.

[43] 'Correspondance Particulière', *Moniteur de l'Armée* (26 September 1855), p.3.

[44] L. Delperier, 'Les Grenadiers de la Garde', *Napoleon III*, no. 12 (Octobre- Decembre 2010), p.40.

[45] Commandant E. Martin, 'Souvenirs de la Guerre de Crimée: Lettres du Commissaire de Marine Garreau', *Carnet de la Sabretache*, vol. 21 (1912), pp.348-349.

[46] Commandant E. Martin, 'Souvenirs de la Guerre de Crimée: Lettres du Commissaire de Marine Garreau', *Carnet de la Sabretache*, vol. 21 (1912), pp.349-350.

[47] General C-A Thoumas, *Mes Souvenirs de Crimée, 1854-1856* (Paris: 1892), pp.241-245.

[48] J. Colnat, *Lettres d'un Combattant de Sebastopol (1855-1856)* (Editions de Loraine, 1965), pp.4-7.

[49] C. Robins, ed., *Romaine's Crimean War: The letters and journal of William Govett Romaine* (Stroud: Tempus, 2005), p.212.

Chapter 10

The Importance of
the Siege of Sebastopol

News of the fall of the south side of Sebastopol was received in Britain within twenty-four hours. In the Yorkshire town of Wakefield, the news was 'met with no ordinary enthusiasm. A complete holiday almost throughout the Town.' During the evening, an

> immense bonfire was lighted in the Bull Ring, onto which was hurled representations of His Majesty the Tsar n... Fireworks of ever kind flashed around, reminding us of the Great Siege so lately triumphantly ended.

The belligerent, Tory, Anglican *Wakefield Journal* provided the following description:

> A vast number of effigies ... in different parts of the borough ... Numerous Emperors of Russia, Prince Gortshakoffs, Menshikoffs, also a very fair sprinkling of Ludicrous Caricatures of John Bright in his Quaker Costume, laughably parodying the peace gentlemen.

Two soldiers, George Smith and John Johnson, became so inebriated, that they were handed over to the police on the Wednesday still drunk. Special services were held in many churches and chapels; at one Parish Church the Rev. E. Twells urged his congregation to 'love your enemies' and to pray for them whilst Rev. Madden at Holy Trinity ranted that,

> God has humbled the pride and crippled the resources ... the rapacity of Russia ... our cause is a righteous cause; oh! that Englishmen be animated with the spirit of the Royal Psalmist, then

251

we we might gain all the comfort which confidence and firm trust in our Christian God is so fitted to afford.

The Rev. Edward Higginson at the Unitarian Chapel on Westgate refused to hold a special service, but instead in his Sunday sermon quoted the Duke of Wellington: 'Next to a battle lost, the saddest thing is a battle won.' He reminded his congregation that 'God is on no man's side in war' and that it was immoral to hold a service of thanksgiving 'thanking God for the victory of our armies and the destruction of our fellow men.'

Rev. Higginson hoped that,

> God's Holy Spirit may support us in danger, control in victory, and raise us above our special template to evil; and that success may soon, very soon, issue the return of Holy peace and the restoration of Christian Brotherhood amongst all men and amongst all nations.

Monday, 30 September, was declared a national public holiday, with a renewed round of celebrations, with fireworks, bonfires and illuminations. The Parish Church in Wakefield was decorated with evergreens and on the tower the flags of the Allies were hung; the initials "V.A." and "N.E." (for Victoria and Albert, Napoléon and Eugénie) were placed either side of the chancel arch and the bells rung all day. By night the streets were illuminated and hung with bunting. The only members of the populace not to observer the holiday were the Quakers.

Despite all the rejoicings, Sevastopol had not fallen and nor was the war over. Sergeant James Wallis of the Rifles wrote home to family in Barnsley telling them to expect one more, final battle. A battle which never came:

> I think the Russians have nearly done with the north side; for as soon as our troops get round the other side they will cut off their supplies. They still keep firing at us across the water; but, thank God! they do not do us much harm. They will get another drubbing when we get behind them again; for, on the north side, there is no Malakoff to storm, but they have thrown up a great many batteries, which we can see very plainly from our side. I hope we shall have another go before winter sets in, for we can do nothing in the fighting line after.[1]

The Russians still controlled the north side of the harbour and were able to roam the Crimean Peninsula at will. An Allied expeditionary force under *général* d'Allonville was sent to Eupatoria, to seek out and destroy any Russian field army – colliding at Kanghill on 29 September. The French fleet also bombarded and stormed the fortress of Kinburn in an action with lasted about three hours on 17 October. Naval operations in the Sea of Azov also effectively cut the Russian supply lines to the Crimea.

The Imperial Guard and *maréchal* Pelissier had returned to France to a hero's welcome. The Imperial Guard had proved itself worthy of the title and had helped cement the traditionally republican army to the throne. It had also borne a heavy brunt of the fighting and the Guard paraded through Paris – led by its wounded veterans – on 29 December. Napoleon III trotted out to the outskirts of the city to meet his triumphantly returned warriors and to lead them through the city streets to the *Place Vendôme* where their Eagles were decorated with laurels, the Emperor shaking the hands of each of the walking-wounded to the adulation of massive crowds. But for the troops remaining in the Crimea, it was a different story: no laurels, no feasting and no pretty girls for them.

The bitter *capitaine* Menessier wrote:

> The Imperial Guard in its entirety has left, everything complete, to triumphantly return to Paris; the enormous gaps in its ranks were made up by men from the Line. The new clothing for the Guard has arrived, and the Guard returns in great completeness, to receive ovations, bouquets of flowers, the bravos and kisses of pretty girls at the windows. These are the vanquishers of Sebastopol ... The Line will remain here in the winter, under our old tents, or burrows in the ground covered with snow: for the Guard, joy and triumphal receptions: For the Line the cold, the mud, the snow, scurvy, typhus. Poor Line![2]

Peace was finally signed in Paris on 30 March 1856, bringing much-needed stability throughout the affected nations. Seventy-four miles (120 kilometres) of trenches had been dug; 100,000 French soldiers had died – making it the bloodiest French conflict of the nineteenth century – and 20,000 British. The final total of Russian losses is not known.

Turkey, aided by Britain and France, was able to modernise itself and deal with internal factions. For Russia, in the immediate post-war period was the reconstruction of its economy. Russian warships were banned from the Black Sea, which was re-opened for peaceful trading, and an international commission was established to guarantee the neutrality and commerce of the Danube.

The Åland Islands in the Baltic were to be demilitarised and the Principalities of Moldovia and Wallachia gained some degree of independence, but remaining in the Turkish Empire. Russia had been humbled militarily and the wobbly *status quo* of the 'Concert of Europe' (to which Turkey was now admitted) had been restored.

Whilst the siege of Sevastopol was the public, dramatic and often horrific face of the 'Great War with Russia', its human tragedy has obscured the far more successful Baltic Campaign and various naval operations. Furthermore, as Andrew Lambert and others have stated, the siege of Sevastopol did not bring the Tsar to seek peace in 1856. Whilst the siege had been an unfolding drama across French and British breakfast tables for nearly twelve months, it was the invisible, silent, economic war that had brought the Tsar to the peace table, his economy on its knees. Quite simply, Britain and France had economically out-competed Russia in a war of attrition: both had industrial economies and many thousands of miles of railway. Russia had 570 miles.

But what of the ordinary British and French soldier? The Crimean War – the Siege of Sevastopol in particular – was a watershed in how the common soldier was seen, thanks in large part to the burgeoning media. Letters home from the front, showing the plight of the men in the trenches, and the horrors of war, caused the 'heart of the nation to go out to soldiers as never before.' As the present author has argued, the ordinary soldier was no longer a drunkard or miscreant but a 'hero' to be honoured with medals and to be celebrated. No longer was the officer and the class they represented the hero of battles, but the men they commanded.

In Britain, the outcry generated by the reports of 'Special Correspondents' such as W. H. Russell of *The Times* or Lawrence Godkin (*Daily News*), led to the collapse of the British Government and a certain amount of navel gazing and limited Army reform based on the French Army which (thanks to the efforts of the British press) was believed to have a better working model. The establishment of the 'Land Transport Corps', 'Army Work Corps', 'Army Medical Corps' in 1855-1856 were all part of the response of the Army to the negative publicity the press had generated and harmful comparisons between British redcoats and French *piou-pious*.

The French Army was basking in the glow of victory, but, moreover, the praise of the British Press. W. H. Russell was the best 'P.R. Guru' the French army could not afford. His lavish praise of the French, and condemnation of the British Army, led to a skewed perception of the two armies: French soldiers were considered to be better fed, clothed, equipped and armed than their British counterpart, despite the very real complaints emanating from the French ranks. Complaints, which were ignored by the War Ministry in Paris and censored in the newspapers, revealed that the French army had succeeded in the Crimea despite the failings of its commissariat and the subsequent collapse of its medical services which were both in need of reform and modernisation.

These were reforms that never came – there was neither military or political will nor the money – and the French army marched off to war just three years later (1859) to face an even bigger crisis in the plains of North Italy when its medical services collapsed completely, leading to Hénri Dunant establishing the Red Cross. For the British army, the Indian Mutiny, and 'exaggerated comparisons' between the performance of British troops in India and the Crimea, led to any attempts at reform to peter-out.

The Crimean War is remembered as being a bloody mistake, and in Britain for the tragic heroism of the 'Charge of the Light Brigade' and the efforts of Florence Nightingale. There are countless 'Sebastopol Terraces', 'Alma Roads', 'Redoubt' and 'Lord Raglan' public houses across Britain. For a time, Alma became a popular girls name and Sebastopol for boys.

It had been the first war where the ordinary British soldier was awarded medals – Victoria Cross – and many returned veterans, especially those from the Light Brigade, became instant celebrities. The Siege of Sevastopol was a soldier's battle, and one from which the reputation of the ordinary soldier as a hero and sharer in the mystical quality of 'La Gloire' was cemented.

NOTES
[1] 'Letter from Sergeant Wallis', *Wakefield Express* (3 November 1855), p.8.
[2] 'Le 4e Bataillon des Chasseurs a Pied en Crimee', *Carnet de la Sabretache* (1903), p.281.

Bibliography

BRITISH SOURCES

Primary

ARCHIVAL
Anthony Dawson Collection
Letters, officer *Votigeurs de la Garde* to family AD001.
Letter, Patrick Robinson (4th King's Own) to family 7 March 1855 AD002.
Letters, French Cuirassier to M. Belley, April and August 1855 AD003.
Chester Archives and Local Studies Services, Chester.
Captain Hugh Robert Hibbert, Mss., Acc. Acc.2618 Ref. DHB.
Duke of Wellington's Regimental Museum, Halifax.
Transcript of Major Mundy Diary (original held at National Army Museum).
The Green Howard's Regimental Museum, Richmond.
Sergeant Charles Usherwood, Mss., service journal.
Herefordshire Record Office, Hereford.
General Richard Airey, Mss., Acc E47/G/IV/A.
The King's Own Royal Regiment Museum, Lancaster.
'Letters written home during the Crimean War 185 to 1856, to his sister Ellen'
    (typescript 1955).
'Recollections of the Crimean Campaign told by Major James Paton…October 1921'.
Lancashire Fusilier's Museum, Bury.
William Govett Romaine, Mss., diary Volume A, June 1854 to November 1854, Acc.
    LFA 0.1.
Lincolnshire Archives, Lincoln.
Lieutenant Robert Hunter, Mss., Acc. 1-Dixon 22/12/3.
The Manchester Regiment Archives, Ashton-Under-Lyne.
Ensign Clutterbuck, Mss., Acc. MR1/16/1.
Lieutenant Newenham, Mss., Acc. MR1/16/2.
National Archives, Kew, London
Land Transport Corps, Acc. WO 32/A.
National Army Museum, London
General R. Airey, Mss., Acc. 1962-10-94.
Lieutenant Thomas Bell, Mss., Acc. 2002-05-02.

Lieutenant H. Clark, Mss., Acc. 1964-02-33.
Charles Cocks, Mss., Acc. 1981-11-13.
General W. J. Codrington, Mss., Acc. 1968-07-380.
Lieutenant Frank Curtis, Mss., Acc. 1983-07-48.
Captain A. M. Earle, Mss., Acc. 1994-03-153.
General J. B. B. Estcourt, Mss, Acc.1962-10-95.
Lieutenant Arthur Godfrey, Mss., Acc. 2001-01-680.
Lieutenant Alexander Hood, Mss., Acc. 1978-05-47.
N. Kingscote, Mss., Acc. 1973-11-170.
Captain A. J. Layard, Mss., Acc. 1959-03-128.
Lieutenant E. P. Newman, Mss., Acc. 1996-07-70.
F. Newman, Mss., Acc. 2002-03-167.
Lieutenant Andrew Nugent, Mss., Acc. 1996-01-22.
Surgeon C. Pine, Mss., Acc. 1968-07-262.
Assistant-Surgeon J. J. Scott, Mss., Acc. 1993-07-39.
Captain Tower, Mss., Acc. 1982-02-18
Queens' Lancashire Regimental Museum, Fulwood Barracks, Preston.
Colonel J. B. Patullo, Mss., Letters to his wife, 1854-1856.
Lieutenant-Colonel Richard Thomas Farren, Mss., Acc. QLRH 963B
West Yorkshire Archive Service, Bradford.
J. Studholme-Brownrigg, Mss., Acc. WYAS SpSt.

NEWSPAPERS
British Library
Caledonian Mercury
Daily News
Derby Mercury
Glasgow Herald
Liverpool Mercury
Manchester Courier
Manchester Examiner and Times
Morning Chronicle
Morning Post
Reynolds's Newspaper
Spectator
Standard
Times
Huddersfield Central Library
Huddersfield Chronicle and West Yorkshire Advertiser
Leeds Central Library
Leeds Mercury
Leeds Intelligencer
Sheffield University Library
The Sheffield and Rotherham Independent
Drury Lane Library, Wakefield
Wakefield Journal and Examiner
Wakefield Express

PRINTED
Official Publications
'Army before Sebastopol. Third Report from the Select Committee on the Army before Sebastopol; with the Minutes of Evidence and Appendix', *House of Commons Papers, Reports from Committees: Army before Sebastopol* vol. IX, part II (December 1854-August 1855).

Report upon the State of the Hospitals of the British Army in the Crimea and Scutari (London: HMSO, 1855).

Reports from the Commissioners appointed to inquire into the system of purchase and sale of commissions in the army (London: HMSO, 1857).

Royal Warrant, dated 28 October 1858, and Report of the Committee Appointed to inquire into the Commissariat Department with Evidence and Appendix (London: Harrison and Sons, 1858).

Letters and diaries.
Anon, *Days of a Soldier's Life, being letters written by the late General Sir C. P. Beauchamp Walker* (London: Chapman and Hall, Ltd., 1894).

Anon, *Letters from India and the Crimea selected from the Correspondence of the late Deputy Surgeon-General Bostock* (London: George Bell and Sons, 1896).

Anon, *Letters from the Crimea. Captain Jasper Hall, of the 4th (King's Own) Regiment of Foot to his sister and father* (Lancaster: King's Own Royal Regiment Museum, 2000).

H. Addington, ed, 'The Crimean and Indian Mutiny Letters of the Hon. Charles John

Addington, 38th Regiment', *Journal for the Society of Army Historical Research*, vol. 46 (1968).

Countess of Airlie, Mabel, *With the Guards we shall go: A Guardsman's letters in the Crimea* (London: Hodder and Stoughton Ltd, 1933).

G. Brackenbury, *The Campaign in the Crimea* (London: Paul and Dominic Colnaghi and

Co, 1855).

S. Calthorpe, *Letters from Head-Quarters or the Realities of the War in the Crimea* (London: John Murray, 1856), 2 vols.

C. F. Campbell, *Letters from Camp to his relatives during the Siege of Sebastopol* (London: Richard Bentley and Son, 1894).

C. Douglas and G. D.Ramsey, ed., *The Panmure Papers* (London: Hodder and Stoughton, 1908), vol.1.

W. Douglas, *Soldiering in Sunshine and Storm* (Edinburgh: Adam and Charles Black, 1865).

C. Fitzherbert, ed, *Henry Clifford VC, his letters and sketches from the Crimea* (London: Michael Joseph, 1956).

K. Fenwick, ed, *Voice from the Ranks* (London: The Folio Society, 1954).

A. Griffiths, *Fifty Years of Public Service* (London: Cassell and Co., Ltd, 1905).

A. J. Guy and A. Massie, eds, *Captain L. E. Nolan, 15 Hussars. Expedition to the Crimea* (London: National Army Museum, 2010).

E. B. Hamley, *The story of the Campaigns of Sebastopol* (Edinburgh: William Blackwood and Sons, 1855).

General Sir George Higginson, *Seventy-one years of a Guardsman's Life* (London:

Smith, Elder and Co., 1916).

J. R. Hume, *Reminiscences of the Crimean Campaign with the 55th Regiment* (London: Unwin Brothers, 1894).

H. B. Jeffreys, *A month in the camp before Sebastopol* (London: Longman, Brown, Green and Longmans, 1855).

A.A. Lagden, ed, 'The Ainslie Letters', *Journal for the Society of Army Historical Research*, vol. 58 (1980).

C. Marsh, *The Life of Arthur Vandeleur, Major Royal Artillery* (New York: Robert Carter and Bros., 1862).

J. Martineau, *The Life of Henry Pelham, Fifth Duke of Newcastle 1811-1864* (London: John Murray and Co., 1908),

M. H. Mawson, ed, *Eyewitness in the Crimea: the Crimean Letters of Lieutenant Colonel George Frederick Dallas* (London: Greenhill Books, 2001).

T. Morris, W. Morris and W. Morris Jnr, *The Three Serjeants* (London: Effingham Wilson, 1858).

A. Money and G. H. Money, *Our Tent in the Crimea* (London: Richard Bentley, 1856).

R. Pack, *Sebastopol Trenches and five months in them* (London: Kerby, Endean and Co, 1878).

Lord Panmure, *Sidney Herbert, Lord of Lea. A memoire* (London: John Murray and Co, 1906).

G. S. Peard, *Campaign in the Crimea: Recollections of an Officer of the 20th Regiment.* (London: Richard Bentley, 1855).

A. Percy, *A Bearskin's Crimea: Colonel Henry Percy VC and his brother officers* (Barnsley: Leo Cooper, 2005).

W. Porter, *Life in the Trenches before Sebastopol* (London: Longman, Brown, Green and Longmans, 1856).

W. Bayne Ranken, *Six Months at Sebastopol: Being selections from the journal and correspondence of Major George Ranken RE* (London: Charles Westerton, 1857).

C. Robins, ed, *Murder of a Regiment – A Crimean War officer's journal* (Bowdon: Withycut House, 1994).

_____, *Romaine's Crimean War. The Letters and Journal of William Govett Romaine* (Stroud: Sutton Publishing Ltd., 2005).

F. Robinson, *Diary of the Crimean War* (London: Richard Bentley and Co, 1856).

N. Steevens, *The Crimean Campaign with the 'Connaught Rangers'* (London: Griffith and Farran, 1878).

A. C. Sterling, *The Highland Brigade in the Crimea*, (London: John Macqueen, 1897).

G. L. Smith, *A Victorian RSM* (Winchester: Royal Hussars' Museum, 1987).

M. Springman, *Sharpshooter in the Crimea: The letters of Captain Gerald Goodlake VC* (Barnsley: Pen and Sword, 2005).

B. Stuart, *Soldier's Glory, being 'Rough notes of an old soldier'* (Tunbridge Wells: Spellmount, 1991).

G. C. Taylor, *Journal of Adventures with the British Army* (London: Hurst and Blackett, 1856).

R. Thorold, ed, *Fifty years of my life* (London: Hurst and Blackett, 1894).

P. Warner, ed, *A Cavalryman in the Crimea: the Letters of Temple Godman, 5th Dragoon Guards* (Barnsley: Pen and Sword, 2009).

Lieutenant-Colonel G. Wrottesley, *The Life and Correspondence of Field Marshal Sir John Fox Burgoyne Bart* (London: Richard Bentley and Son, 1873), Vol. II.

M. Young, *Our camp in Turkey and the way to it* (London: Richard Bentley and Co., 1854).

Secondary

Books

Anon, *The War in Italy* (London: Day and Son, 1859).

O. Anderson, *A Liberal State at War: English Politics and Economy during the Crimean War* (New York: Macmillan, 1967).

D. Baguely, *Napoleon III and his regime: An Extravaganza* (Louisiana State University Press, 2000).

H. Barker, *Newspapers, Politics and English Society, 1695-1855* (London: Longman, 2000).

I. F. W. Beckett, *The Victorians at War* (London: Hambledon and London, 2003).

L. Brake and M. Demoor, eds, *Dictionary of Nineteenth Century journalism in Britain and Ireland* (London: The Academic Press, 2006).

F. Bresler, *Napoléon III: A life* (London: Harper Collins, 1999).

T. Brighton. *Hell Riders* (London: Penguin Books, 2004).

P. Burroughs, 'An Unreformed Army?' in D. Chandler and I. Beckett, eds, *The Oxford Illustrated History of the British Army* (Oxford: Oxford University Press, 1994).

D. Buttery *Messenger of Death. Captain Nolan and the Charge of the Light Brigade* (Barnsley: Pen and Sword, 2008).

Lieutenant-Colonel J. Campbell, *A British Army: As it was, – is, – and ought to be* (London: T. and W. Boone, 1843).

T. Coates, *Delane's War. How front-line reports from the Crimean War brought down the British Government* (London: Biteback, Publishing Ltd., 2009).

T. A. B. Corley, *Democratic Despot. A life of Napoleon III* (London: Barrie and Rockliffe, 1961).

A. L. Dawson, *French Infantry of the Crimean War* (Nottingham: Partizan Press, 2011).

_____, *Letters from the Light Brigade* (Barnsley: Pen and Sword, 2014).

R. Dutton, *Forgotten Heroes: Charge of the Light Brigade* (Prenton: InfoDial Ltd, 2007).

A. Ellegård, *The Readership of the Periodical Press in Mid-Victorian Britain* (Göteberg: Göteborgs Universitets Arsskrift, 1957).

O. Figes, *Crimea: The Last Crusade* (London: Allen Lane, 2010).

Sir W. A. Fraser, *Napoleon III (My recollections)* (London: Sampson, Low, Marston and Co. Ltd., 1896).

P. Gibbs *The Battle of the Alma* (London: Weidenfeld and Nicolson1963).

R. Glover *Peninsular Preparation: Reform of the British Army 1795-1809* (Cambridge: Cambridge University Pres, 1964).

L. Goldman, *Science, Reform and Politics in Victorian Britain: The Social Science Association, 1857-1886* (Cambridge: Cambridge University Press, 2002).

B. D. Gooch, *The New Bonapartist Generals* (The Hague: Martinus Nijhoff, 1959).

Sir C. A. Gordon, *Army Hygiene* (London: John Churchill and Son, 1866).

P. Griffiths, *Military thought in the French Army 1815-1851* (Manchester: University of Manchester Press, 1989).

P. Guedella, *The Second Empire* (London: Hodder and Stoughton, 1946).

A. Guérard, *Napoleon III* (Cambridge: Harvard University Press, 1943).

G. Harries-Jenkins, *The Army in Victorian Society* (London: Routledge and Kegan Paul, 1977).

S. Hazareesingh, *The Saint-Napoleon. Celebrations of Sovereignty in Nineteenth-Century France* (Harvard: Harvard University Press, 2004).

C. Hibbert, *The Destruction of Lord Raglan* (London: Longman, 1961).

M. Hudson and J. Stanier, *War and the Media* (Stroud: Sutton Publishing, 1999).

L. James, *Crimea 1854-1856. The War with Russia from Contemporary Photographs* (London: Hayes Kennedy, 1981).

A. W. Kinglake, *The Invasion of the Crimea: Its origin and an account of its progress down to the death of Lord Raglan* 8 vols. (London: William Blackwood and Sons, 1863-1888).

A. D. Lambert, *The Crimean War. British grand strategy against Russia 1853-1856* (Manchester: Manchester University Press, 2011).

Sir P. L. MacDougall, *The Theory of War* (London: Longman, Brown, Green, Longmans and Roberts, 1856).

S. Maccoby, *English Radicalism 1852-1886* (London: Routledge, 2002).

S. Markovits, *The Crimean War in the British Imagination* (Cambridge: Cambridge University Press, 2009).

D. Murphy, *Ireland and the Crimean War* (Dublin: Four Courts Press Ltd, 2002).

Lieutenant-General W. F. P. Napier, *Life and Opinions of General Sir Charles Napier* (London: John Murray, 1857).

C. Ponting, *The Crimean War* (London, 2005).

H. Rappaport, *No place for ladies* (London: Aurum Press, 2007).

T. Ropp, *War in the Modern World* (Baltimore: John Hopkins University Press, 2000).

S. Royce, *The Crimean War and its place in European Economic History* (London: University of London Press, 2001).

J. Selby, *The Thin Red Line* (London: History Book Club, 1970).

H. Small, *Florence Nightingale. Avenging Angel* (New York: St Martin's Press, 1998).

F. B. Smith, *Florence Nightingale. Reputation and Power* (London: Croom Helm Ltd., 1982).

E. M. Spiers, *The Army and Society 1815-1914* (London: Longman, 1980).

_____, *Radical General: Sir George de Lacy Evans 1787-1870* (Manchester: Manchester University Press, 1983).

_____, *The Scottish Soldier and Empire, 1854-1902* (Edinburgh: Edinburgh University Press, 2006).

J. Spilsbury, *The Thin Red Line: An eyewitness history of the Crimean War* (London: Weidenfeld and Nicolson, 2005).

I. Stewart and S. L. Carruthers, *War, Culture and the Media* (Trowbridge: Flicks Books, 1996).

H. F. A. Strachan, *Wellington's Legacy. Reform of the British Army 1830-1854* (Manchester: Manchester University Press, 1984).

H. Streets, *Martial Races: The Military, Race and Masculinity in British Imperial Culture* (Manchester: Manchester University Press, 2004).

J. Sweetman, *Raglan: From the Peninsula to the Crimea* (Barnsley: Pen and Sword, 2010).

Captain T. J. Thackeray, *The military organization and administration of France* (London: T. C. Newby, 1856).

Rev. W. Tuckwell, *A. W. Kinglake: A Biographical and Literary Study* (London: 1902).

V. Webb, *Florence Nightingale. The Making of a Radical Theologian* (Atlanta: Chalice Press, 2002).

V. Wellesley and R. Sencourt, *Conversations with Napoleon III* (London: Ernest Benn Ltd, 1934).

Journal Articles

A. L. Dawson, 'The French Army and British Army Crimean War Reforms' in *19: Interdisciplinary Studies in the Long Nineteenth Century* 2015(20).

S. Markovits, 'North and South, East and West: Elizabeth Gaskell, the Crimean War, and the Condition of England', *Nineteenth-Century Literature*, Vol. 59, no. 4 (2005).

J. Paynter, 'Report upon the Sanitary Condition of the French Troops serving in Algeria', *Army Medical Department. Statistical, Sanitary and Medical Reports for 1865*, vol. III (1865).

E. M. Spiers 'Military correspondence in the late nineteenth-century press', *Archives*, vol. 32 no. 116 (2007).

H. F. A. Strachen, 'Soldiers, Strategy and Sebastopol', *The Historical Journal*, vol. XXI. part 2 (1978).

Unpublished Papers and Conference Proceedings

A. L. Dawson, 'Wakefield and the Crimean War', *Wakefield Historical Society*, 27-6-2012.

_____, 'Manchester and the Crimean War', *Lancashire and Cheshire Antiquarian Society*, 13-7-2012.

_____, 'William Gaskell, Manchester Unitarians and the Crimean War' *The Gaskell Society*, 5-11-2013.

_____, 'The French Army and British Army Reform', Conference Proceedings *Charting the Crimean War: Contexts, Nationhood, Afterlives*, National Army Museum, 28-6-2013.

Unpublished academic thesis

A. L. Dawson, *British Army Perception of French Army Support Services during the Crimean War* Unpublished M. Res Thesis, University of Leeds, 2012.

FRENCH SOURCES

Primary

The Crimean War

Anon, *Collection des Ordres Genereux de l'armée d'Orient devant Sébastopol* (Paris: Imprimerie Impériale, 1855).

C. L. de Bazancourt, *Cinq mois au camp devant Sebastopol* (Paris: Amyot, 1855).

_____, *L'Éxpedition de Crimée jusqu'a la Prise de Sebastopol* (Paris: Amyot, 1856).

_____, *L'Éxpedition de Crimée: La Marine Française dans le Mer Noire et la Baltique* (Paris: Amyot, 1856).

_____, *L'Éxpedition de Crimée jusqu'a la Prise de Sebastopol. Revue, considérablement augmenté et suivie du'n Appendice sur les événements militaries devant Eupatoria et la prise de Kinburn* (Paris: Amyot, 1857).

Letters and memoires

Anon, *Campagnes de Crimée, d'Italie, d'Afrique, de Chine et de Syrie 1849*-1862 (Paris: E. Plon, Nourrit et Cie., 1898).

Anon, 'Le 1er Régiment de Chasseurs d'Afrique à Gallipoli Mai 1854', *Carnet de la Sabretache*, vol. 7 (1899).

Anon, 'Le 4e Bataillon de Chasseurs à Pied en Crimée: Lettres du Capitaine Mennessier', *Carnet de la Sabretache*, vol. 12 (1903).

Anon, 'Lettres du Général Vanson (extraits)' *Carnet de la Sabretache, v*ol. 14 (1905).

Anon, 'Lettres de Saint-Cyr et de Campagne: Lettres de Crimée du Capitaine A. Sauret', *Carnet de la Sabretache* vol. 20 (1911).

L. Baudens, *Souvenirs d'un Missions Medicale à l'Armée d'Orient* (Paris: J. Claye, 1857).

_____, *La Guerre de Crimée* (Paris: Michel Lévy Frères, 1858).

F. C. du Barail *Mes Souvenirs* (Paris: Plon, 1897).

M. de Baillehache, *Souvenirs intimes d'un Lancier de la Garde* (Paris: Paul Ollendorf, 1894).

G. Bapst, *Le Maréchal Canrobert, Souvenirs d'un Siecle* (Paris: Librairie Plon, 1912).

G. Bertin, 'Les 6eme Dragons en Crimée', *Carnet de la Sabretche*, vol. 10 (1902).

C. Bocher, *Lettres de Crimée: Souvenirs de Guerre* (Paris: Calman Lévy, 1877).

Commandant E. Boppe, *Crimée, Italie, Mexique: lettres de campagnes du General Vanson, 1854-1867* (Paris: Berger-Levrault, 1905).

Maréchal P. J. F. Bosquet, *Lettres* (Paris: Berger-Levrault and Co., 1894).

Dr Cabrol *Le Maréchal de Saint-Arnaud en Crimée* (Paris: Tresse and Stock, 1895).

General J. J. G. Cler, *Souvenirs d'un Officier du 2eme des Zouaves* (Paris: M. Levy Frères 1869).

General E-I Collineau *Un Soldat de Fortune. Notes et Souvenirs du General Collineau* (Paris: Guy Collineau, 1925).

Général Coste, 'Souvenirs de la Guerre de Crimee par le General de Division Coste' *Revue de Midi* Tome XXXXI (Decembre 1908).

M.O. Cullet, *Un Regiment de Ligne pendant la Guerre d'Orient: notes et souvenirs d'un officier d'infanterie* (Lyon: Librairie Generale Catholique et Classique, 1894).

Commandant Devanlay, 'Lettres de Crimée du General Breton', *Carnet de la Sabretache*, vol. 18 (1909).

Colonel C. Duban, *Souvenirs Militaires d'un Officier Française* (Paris: E.Plon, Nourrit and Co, 1896).

C. A. Fay, *Souvenirs de la guerre de Crimée*, 1854-1856 (Paris: J Dumaine, 1867).

J. de la Faye, ed., *Souvenirs du General Lacretelle* (Paris: Emile-Paul, 1907).

E. Févelat, 'Vieux papiers et Souvenirs d'un Combattant de Crimée', *Société Archeologique, Historique, et Artistique "Les Vieux Papiers": Conference 24 Mai 1910.*

G. Gilbert, ed., *Lettres écrites de Crimée par le Capitaine d'État-Major Henri Loizillon à sa Famille* (Paris: Ernest Flammarion, nd).

J-F J. Herbé, *Francaise and Russe en Crimée: Lettres d'un Officier Francaise à la Famille pendant la Campagne d'Orient* (Paris: Calman Lévy, 1892).

Commandant Joppé, 'La Campagne de Crimée d'après les lettres du Commandant Adrien' *Carnet de la Sabretache*, vol. 16 (1907).

Général B. L. J. Lebrun, *Souvenirs des Guerres de Crimée et d'Italie* (Paris: E Dentu, 1889).

L. Le Saint, *Les Récits d'un Capitaine* (Limoges: Eugene Ardant and Co., nd).

F. de Marcy, 'Lettres de Campagne du General de Division Henry de Bouillé', *Carnet de la Sabretache* vol.11, (1912).

Lieutenant A. E. A. E. Masquelez *Journal d'un Officier des Zouaves* (Paris: J Corréard, 1858).

F. Maynard, *Souvenirs d'un Zouave devant Sebastopol* (Paris: Librairie Nouvelle, 1856).

Capitaine Minart, 'Lettres écrites pendant la Campagne de Crimée par les frères Charles, Alfred et Édouard Minart', *Carnet de la Sabretache*, vol.8 (1909).

C. Mismer, *Souvenirs d'un dragon de l'armée de Crimée, avril 1854-juillet 1856* (Paris: Hachette, 1887).

_____, *Dix ans Soldat: Souvenirs et impressions de la vie militaire* (Paris: Hachette, 1889).

P. de Molènes, *Commentaires d'un Soldat* (Paris: Libraries des Bibliophiles, 1876).

Général J. B. A. Montaudon, *Souvenirs Militaires* (Paris: Librairie Charles Delagrave, 1898).

L. Noir, *Souvenirs d'un Zouave sous la tente* (Paris: Achille Faure and Co., 1868).

_____, *Souvenirs d'un Simple Zouave: Campagnes de Crimée de d'Italie* (Paris: Bureaux du Siècle, 1869).

Général Rébillot, 'Souvenirs de Crimee', *Revue de Cavalerie*, année 1912 (1912).

Maréchal de Saint-Arnaud, *Lettres* (Paris: Michel Levy et Frères, 1855), II vols.

W. Serman, ed, *Colonel Denfert Rocherau. Lettres d'un Officier Republicain (1842-1871)* (Vincennes: Service Historique de l'Armée du Terre, 1990).

C-A Thoumas, *Souvenirs de la Guerre de Crimée* (Paris: Berger-Levrault, 1892).

P. Verdun and A. Morin, *Sous Les Drapeaux: Turque, Crimée, Sébastopol* (Paris: Bibliothèque des Soirées en Famille, 1911).

Journals and Newspapers
Archives de Médécin Militaire.
Courrier de Marseilles.
Gazette Medicale de Paris.
Journal de Constantinople.
Journal Militiare Officiel.
Journal de Toulouse.
Le Spectateur Militaire.
Moniteur de l'Armée.
Revue Contemporaine.
Revue des deux mondes.

Secondary
1. The Crimean War

A. Goutman, *La Guerre de Crimée* (Paris: Perrin, 2006).

Goutman, 'Dossier Special: La Guerre de Crimée' *Napoleon III Magazine*, no. 1 (2008). (Paris: Dufour, Moulat et Boulanger, 1858), 2 vols.

C. F. M. Rousset, *Histoire de la Guerre de Crimée* (Paris: Librairie Hachette et Cie., 1877), II vols.

2. The French Army

P. Chalmin, *L'Officier français de 1815 à 1870* (Paris: Librairie Marcel Rivières, 1956)

L. Delpérier, *De la Crimée a la Grande Guerre: L'armée devant l'objectif, 1854-1914* (Paris: Charles-Lavauzelle, 1984).

L. Delpérier and B. Malvaux *La Garde Impériale du Napoleon III* (Nantes: Editions du

Cannonier, 2000).

G. Gossart, *Histoire de l'officier français* (Paris: H. Charles-Lavauzelle, 1907).

A. Joineau, *Grenadiers et Voltigeurs de la Garde Impériale* (Auzielle: LRT Editions, 2009).

H. Ortholan, *L'Armée du Second Empire* (Paris: Editions Napoleon III, 2010).

A. Pascal, M. Brahaut, and Capitaine Sicard, *Histoire de l'Armée et de tous Régiments* (Paris: Dutertre, Librairie-Editeur, 1864).

Lieutenant J. Spitz, *Histoire du 2eme Regiment de Zouaves* (Oran: Paul Perrier, 1901).

W. Serman, *Le corps des officiers français 1848-1870* (Paris: Publications de la Sorbonne, 1979).

Colonel P. Willing *L'Armée du Napoleon III* (Paris: Collections des Musée de l'Armée, 1982).

3. Biographies

P. Baud, *Général Cler* (Bourges: Cercle Généaloqique du Haut-Berry, 1995).

Dr. Cabrol, *Le Maréchal de Saint-Arnaud en Crimée* (Paris: Tresse and Stock, 1895).

A. Minc, *Louis Napoleon Revisité* (Paris: Éditions Gallimard 1997); T. Lentz, *Napoléon III* (Paris: Presses des Universitaires de France, 1995).

T. Lentz, *Napoléon III* (Paris: Presses des Universitaires de France, 1995).

J. Tulard, 'Napoléon III aujourd'hui?' *Napoleon III*, no. 1 (Janvier – Mars 2008).

P. Seguin, *Louis Napoléon le Grand* (Paris: Bernard Grasset, 1990).

Index

Index of Places

Index of Regiments